D1539676

TEACHER'S GUIDE

Great Source Education Group

a Houghton Mifflin Company

Wilmington, Massachusetts

www.greatsource.com

AUTHORS

Laura Robb
Author

Powhatan School, Boyce, Virginia

Laura Robb, author of *Reading Strategies That Work* and *Teaching Reading in Middle School*, has taught language arts at Powhatan School in Boyce, Virginia, for more than 30 years. She is a co-author of the *Reading and Writing Sourcebooks* for grades 3–5 and the *Summer Success: Reading* program. Robb also mentors and coaches teachers in Virginia public schools and speaks at conferences throughout the country on reading and writing.

Ron Klemp
Contributing Author

Los Angeles Unified School District, Los Angeles, California

Ron Klemp is the Coordinator of Reading for the Los Angeles Unified School District. He has taught Reading, English, and Social Studies and was a middle school Dean of Discipline. He is also a coordinator/facilitator at the Secondary Practitioner Center, a professional development program in the Los Angeles Unified School District. He has been teaching at California State University, Cal Lutheran University, and National University.

Wendell Schwartz
Contributing Author

Adlai Stevenson High School, Lincolnshire, Illinois

Wendell Schwartz has been a teacher of English for 36 years. For the last 24 years he also has served as the Director of Communication Arts at Adlai Stevenson High School. He has taught gifted middle school students for the last 12 years, as well as teaching graduate-level courses for National Louis University in Evanston, Illinois.

Editorial: Developed by Nieman, Inc.

Design: Ronan Design: Christine Ronan, Sean O'Neill, and Maria Mariottini

Illustrations: Mike McConnell

Printed in the United States of America
International Standard Book Number: 0-669-49085-7
1 2 3 4 5 6 7 8 9—DBH—09 08 07 06 05 04 03 02

READERS AND REVIEWERS

Jay Amberg
Glenbrook High School
Glenview, Illinois

Mary Baker
Beach Middle School
Chelsea, Michigan

Marlene Beirle
Westerville City Schools
Westerville, Ohio

Ann Bender
Guoin Creek Middle School
Speedway, Indiana

Martha Clarke
Roosevelt Center-Dayton
 Public Schools
Dayton, Ohio

Cindy Crandall
Suttons Bay Middle School
Suttons Bay, Michigan

Janet Crews
Wydown Middle School
Clayton, Missouri

Marilyn Crow
Wilmette Public Schools
Wilmette, Illinois

Deanna Day
Tucson, Arizona

Demetra Disotuar
Martin Luther King Lab School
Evanston, Illinois

Pam Embler
Allen Jay Middle School
High Point, North Carolina

Julie Engstrom
Hillside Junior High School
Boise, Idaho

Shelly Fabozzi
Holmes Middle School
Colorado Springs, Colorado

Aimee Freed
Perry Middle School
Worthington, Ohio

Patricia Fry
Templeton Middle School
Sussex, Wisconsin

Barb Furrer
Templeton Middle School
Sussex, Wisconsin

Lorraine Gerhart
Crivitz, Wisconsin

Laurie Goodman
Pioneer Middle School
Hanford, California

Jane Goodson
Brunswick, Georgia

Pam Grabman
Center Middle School
Youngstown, Ohio

Bianca Griffin
Audubon Middle School
Milwaukee, Wisconsin

Dorsey Hammond
Oakland University
Rochester, Michigan

Cheryl Harry
Southfield, Michigan

Jeff Hicks
Whitford Middle School
Beaverton, Oregon

Claire Hiller
Timber Ridge Magnet School
Skokie, Illinois

Terri Huck
John Bullen Accelerated
 Middle School
Kenosha, Wisconsin

Ralph Huhn, Jr.
Key West, Florida

Dana Humphrey
F. Zumwalt North Middle School
O'Fallon, Missouri

Dennis Jackson
Danvers Public Schools
Danvers, Massachusetts

Jean Lifford
Dedham High School
Dedham, Massachusetts

Linda Maloney
Ridgewood Junior High School
Arnold, Missouri

Nancy McEvoy
Anderson Middle School
Berkley, Michigan

Mary McHugh
Franklin School
Belleville, Illinois

Catherine McNary
Proviso West High School
Hillside, Illinois

Marsha Nadasky
Western Reserve Middle School
Berlin Center, Ohio

Cheryl Nuciforo
City School District of Troy
Troy, New York

Lucretia Pannozzo
John Jay Middle School
Katonah, New York

Brenda Peterson
Templeton Middle School
Sussex, Wisconsin

Evelyn Price
Grand Avenue Middle School
Milwaukee, Wisconsin

Richard Santeusanio
Danvers School District
Danvers, Massachusetts

Jennifer Sellenriek
Wydown Middle School
Clayton, Missouri

Jill Vavrek
Proviso West High School
Hillside, Illinois

Dave Wendelin
Educational Service Center
Golden, Colorado

Michel Wendell
Archdiocese of St. Louis
 Cathedral School
St. Louis, Missouri

Roberta Williams
Traverse City East Junior
 High School
Traverse City, Michigan

Sharon Williams
Bay Point Middle School
St. Petersburg, Florida

Table of Contents

Lessons

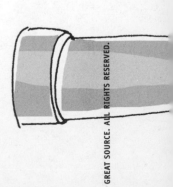

Guide to the Program

Teach with the *Reader's Handbook* program in three easy steps. First, use the *Teacher's Guide* to teach the lessons in the handbook. Then, use other teaching resources, such as the *Lesson Plan Books*, *Overhead Transparencies*, *Content Area Guides*, or the Website, to supplement the lesson. Then, practice with the *Student Applications Books* or through independent practice using your own texts.

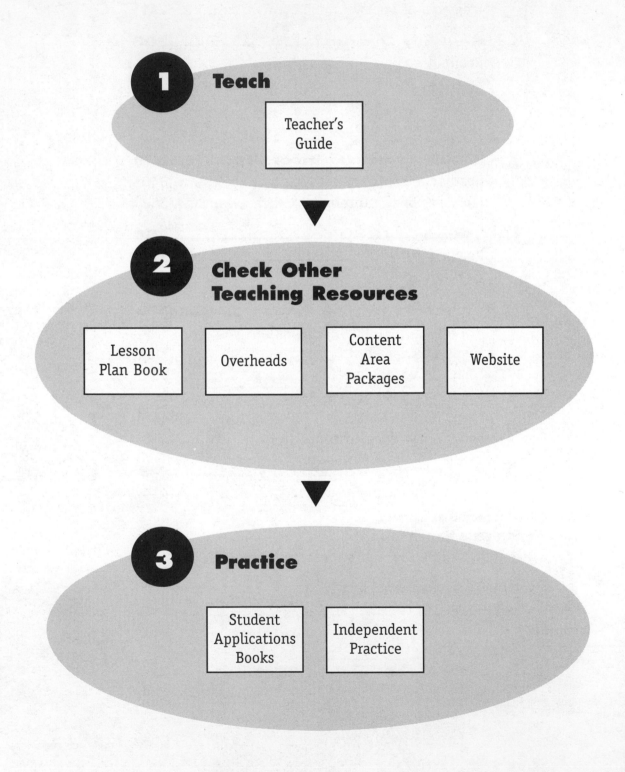

1 Teach

Teacher's Guide

2 Check Other Teaching Resources

Lesson Plan Book   Overheads   Content Area Packages   Website

3 Practice

Student Applications Books   Independent Practice

Program Components

The *Reader's Handbook* program includes the following materials in addition to the handbook:

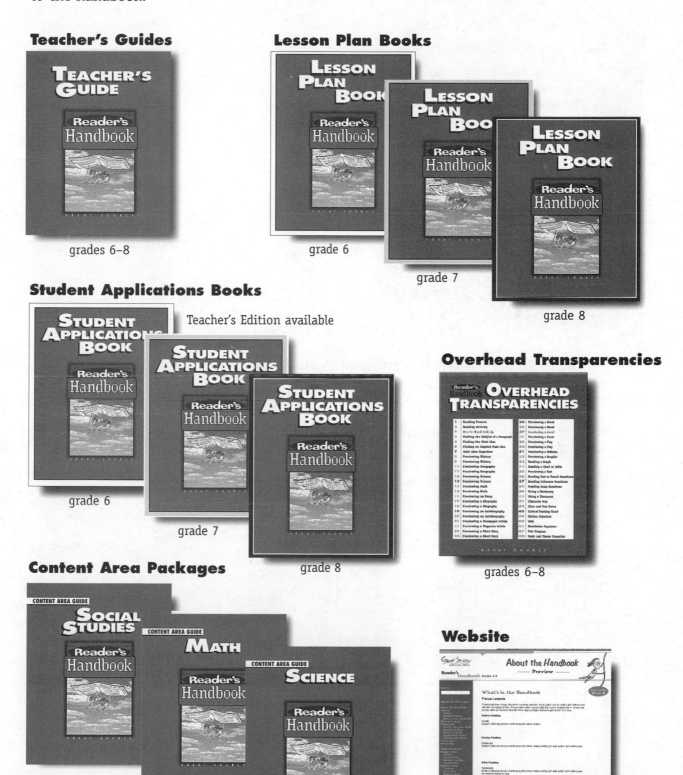

Teacher's Guides

grades 6–8

Lesson Plan Books

grade 6

grade 7

grade 8

Student Applications Books

Teacher's Edition available

grade 6

grade 7

grade 8

Overhead Transparencies

grades 6–8

Content Area Packages

CONTENT AREA GUIDE
SOCIAL STUDIES

CONTENT AREA GUIDE
MATH

CONTENT AREA GUIDE
SCIENCE

grades 6–8

Website

www.greatsource.com/rehand/

Teacher's Guide

The *Teacher's Guide* walks through each lesson in the *Reader's Handbook,* highlights what to teach, and suggests ways to extend lessons.

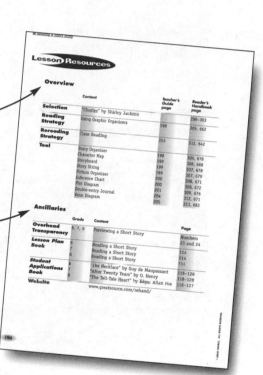

The **Overview** chart lists the literature, strategies, and tools taught in each lesson.

The **Ancillaries** chart shows where to find additional materials to supplement the lesson.

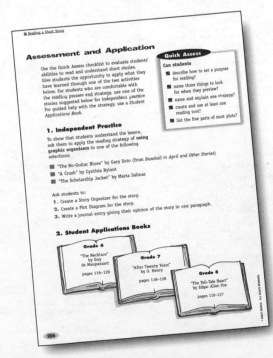

At the end of each lesson, you assess and then have students apply the strategies either a) independently or b) in guided practice in the *Student Application Books.*

Lesson Plan Book

The *Lesson Plan Book* (one per grade level) gives day-by-day and week-by-week lesson plans. These books show how to use the *Reader's Handbook* to set up a complete reading curriculum in middle school.

The curriculum plan suggests the year-long plan for teaching reading at each grade level.

Individual lesson plans outline weekly and daily lessons.

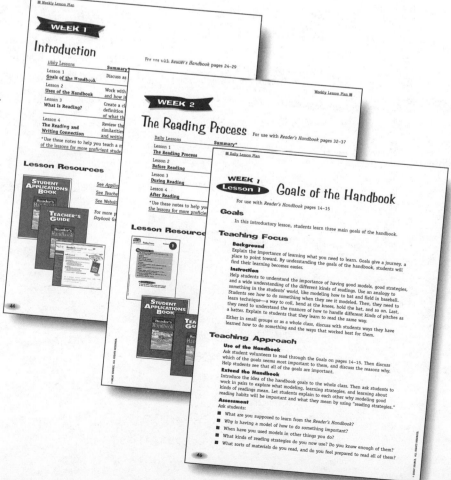

Student Applications Book

The *Student Applications Book* (one per grade level) extends the lessons with a new selection for students to work through.

Lessons let students apply the reading strategies and tools to a new selection, give them guided practice, and help you to assess their understanding.

The *Student Applications Book Teacher's Edition* includes suggested answers.

Overhead Transparencies

The *Overhead Transparencies* display key parts of the handbook to help in-class teaching of important concepts, such as the reading process and previewing different kinds of reading.

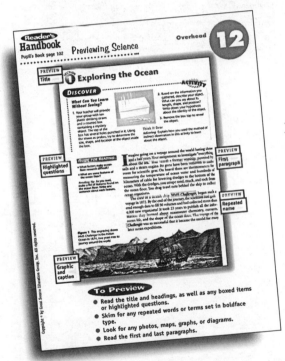

Included are overheads for key reading techniques, such as reading actively and finding the subject of a paragraph.

Transparencies for Using Reading Tools help students learn how to use graphic organizers.

Content Area Packages

Each package contains the following:
- A *Content Area Guide*
- Overhead Transparencies
- A *Reader's Handbook*

The *Content Area Guides* contain lesson plans and activities designed to build reading skills in social studies, science, and math.

Website

The *Reader's Handbook* Website contains a preview of the *Reader's Handbook* program as well as numerous resources both for teachers and students.

The *Teacher Center* has a lesson plan library, information on how to apply for grants, a reading bibliography, and web resources.

The *Test Center* has state-specific lessons to help prepare for standardized tests.

Reading Strategies Overview

Handbook Lesson	Selection	Reading Strategy	Rereading Strategies
Reading History	"Indian Wars"	Note-taking	Outlining
Reading Geography	"Population"	Using Graphic Organizers	Note-taking
Reading Science	"Exploring the Ocean"	Note-taking	Skimming
Reading Math	"Variables and Equations"	Visualizing and Thinking Aloud	Note-taking
Reading an Essay	"America the Not-so-Beautiful"	Outlining	Questioning the Author
Reading a Biography	*Harriet Tubman: Conductor on the Underground Railroad*	Looking for Cause and Effect	Outlining
Reading an Autobiography	*Up from Slavery*	Synthesizing	Looking for Cause and Effect
Reading a Newspaper Article	"Robots Get Ready to Rumble"	Reading Critically	Summarizing
Reading a Magazine Article	"A Killer Gets Some Respect"	Questioning the Author	Reading Critically
Reading a Short Story	"Charles"	Using Graphic Organizers	Close Reading
Reading a Novel	*Roll of Thunder, Hear My Cry*	Synthesizing	Using Graphic Organizers
Reading a Poem	"Winter Poem"	Close Reading	Paraphrasing
Reading a Play	*The Diary of Anne Frank*	Summarizing	Visualizing and Thinking Aloud
Reading a Website	"The International Dyslexia Association Website"	Reading Critically	Skimming
Reading a Graphic	"Gallup Poll Topics: A-Z Crime Issues"	Paraphrasing	Reading Critically
Reading a Test and Test Questions	*Geronimo: His Own Story*	Skimming	Visualizing and Thinking Aloud

14

Focus Lesson	Selection	Reading Strategy
Focus on Science Concepts	"Cell Growth and Division"	Using Graphic Organizers
Focus on Word Problems	Math Problems	Visualizing and Thinking Aloud
Focus on Persuasive Writing	"Parents, Not Cash, Can Enrich a School"	Reading Critically
Focus on Speeches	"The future doesn't belong to the fainthearted"	Reading Critically
Focus on Real-world Writing	Student Handbook Computer Game Instructions Train Schedule	Skimming
Focus on Characters	*The Cay*	Using Graphic Organizers
Focus on Setting	*Shiloh*	Close Reading
Focus on Dialogue	*Roll of Thunder, Hear My Cry*	Close Reading
Focus on Plot	"Last Cover"	Using Graphic Organizers
Focus on Theme	*Roll of Thunder, Hear My Cry*	
Focus on Comparing and Contrasting	King Midas and *A Christmas Carol*	Using Graphic Organizers
Focus on Language	"Words"	Close Reading
Focus on Meaning	"Those Winter Sundays"	Close Reading
Focus on Sound and Structure	"The Sloth"	Close Reading
Focus on Theme	*The Diary of Anne Frank*	
Focus on Language	*The Diary of Anne Frank*	
Focus on Essay Tests	Essay Test Directions	
Focus on Vocabulary Tests	Vocabulary Test Questions	
Focus on Social Studies Tests	Social Studies Test Questions	
Focus on Math Tests	Math Test Questions	
Focus on Science Tests	Science Test Questions	

How to Use a
Teacher's Guide Lesson

Begin by reading the **Goals** for the lesson to the class or by asking a student to read them.

A **Background** section helps you connect the lesson with students' own knowledge.

Introduce the lesson with an **Opening Activity**.

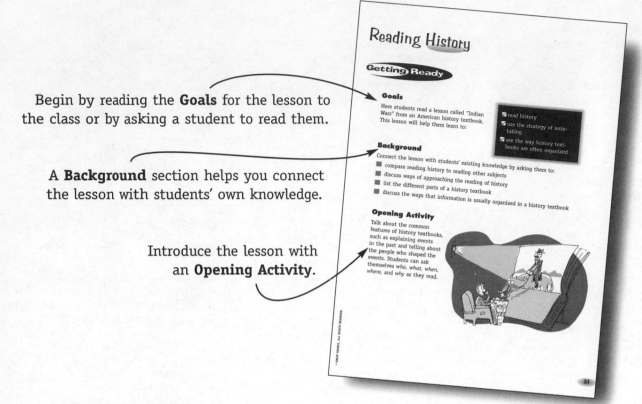

The **Overview** chart lists the content, strategies, and tools in the lesson.

The **Ancillaries** chart lists all supplementary materials available for the lesson.

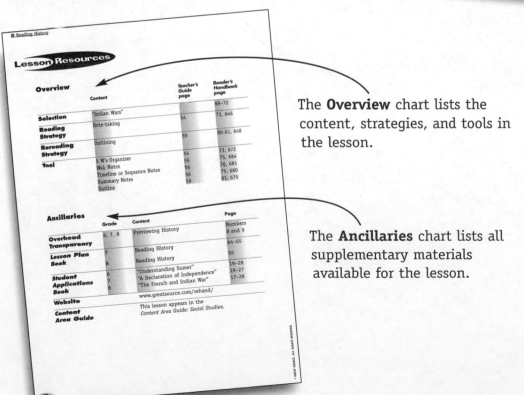

Before Reading

Use the questions in the **Setting a Purpose** section to give students a clear purpose for their reading.

Ask students to preview the text selection. Use the **Overhead Transparencies** to go over with the class what to preview.

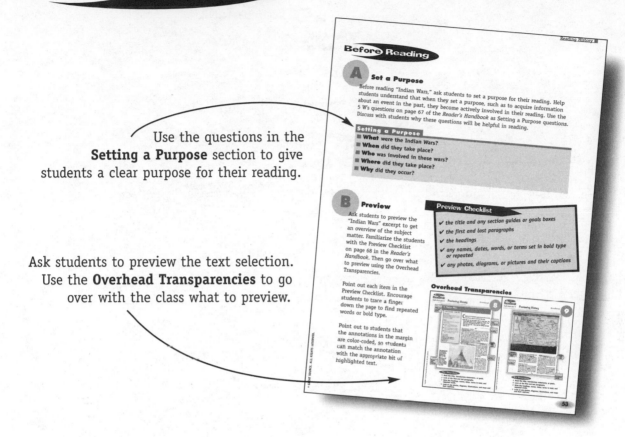

After previewing, help students **Plan** which Reading Tool to use. Point out how the reading purpose and type of reading affect which strategy to use.

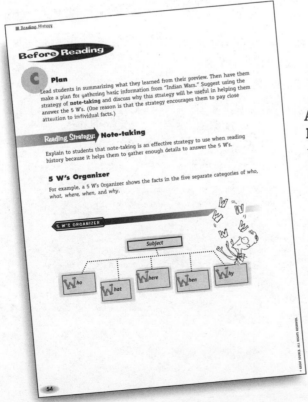

During Reading

Next, show students how to implement the reading strategy by using the Reading Tools suggested in the lesson.

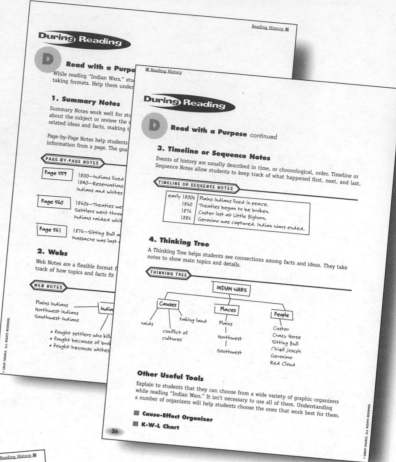

Use the **How Text Is Organized** section to teach students the ways in which different texts are organized.

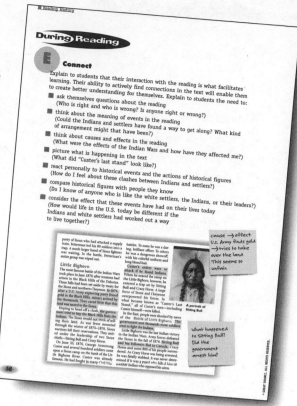

Use the questions in the **Connect** section to help students interact with the reading and see how it has meaning for them.

After Reading

After reading, ask students to reflect on whether they have met their reading purpose.

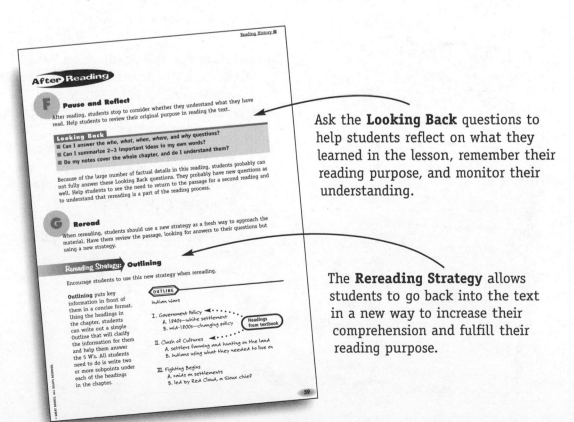

Ask the **Looking Back** questions to help students reflect on what they learned in the lesson, remember their reading purpose, and monitor their understanding.

The **Rereading Strategy** allows students to go back into the text in a new way to increase their comprehension and fulfill their reading purpose.

After Reading

Use the suggested activity in the **Remember** section to help students "make the material their own" and recall what they've learned.

Use the **Summing Up** feature to review the key points of the lesson with students.

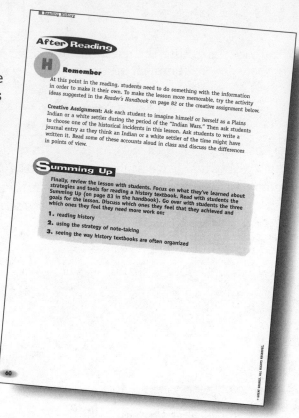

After Reading

H Remember

At this point in the reading, students need to do something with the information in order to make it their own. To make the lesson more memorable, try the activity ideas suggested in the *Reader's Handbook* on page 82 or the creative assignment below.

Creative Assignment: Ask each student to imagine himself or herself as a Plains Indian or a white settler during the period of the "Indian Wars." Then ask students to choose one of the historical incidents in this lesson. Ask students to write a journal entry as they think an Indian or a white settler of the time might have written it. Read some of these accounts aloud in class and discuss the differences in points of view.

Summing Up

Finally, review the lesson with students. Focus on what they've learned about strategies and tools for reading a history textbook. Read with students the *Summing Up* (on page 83 in the handbook). Go over with students the three goals for the lesson. Discuss which ones they feel that they achieved and which ones they feel they need more work on:

1. reading history
2. using the strategy of note-taking
3. seeing the way history textbooks are often organized

Assessment and Application includes a **Quick Assess** checklist and proposes two ways to extend the lesson.

1. Students able to work on their own are directed to apply the strategies to a suggested reading for independent practice.

2. Students who need more guided practice can use a new text selection in one of the *Student Application Books*.

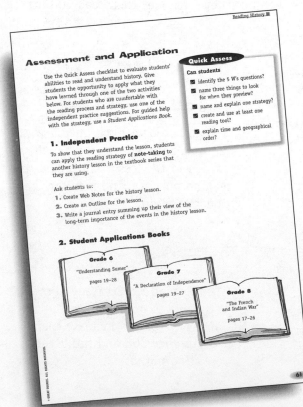

Assessment and Application

Use the Quick Assess checklist to evaluate students' abilities to read and understand history. Give students the opportunity to apply what they have learned through one of the two activities below. For students who are comfortable with the reading process and strategy, use one of the independent practice suggestions. For guided help with the strategy, use a *Student Applications Book*.

1. Independent Practice

To show that they understand the lesson, students can apply the reading strategy of **note-taking** to another history lesson in the textbook series that they are using.

Ask students to:

1. Create Web Notes for the history lesson.
2. Create an Outline for the lesson.
3. Write a journal entry summing up their view of the long-term importance of the events in the history lesson.

2. Student Applications Books

Quick Assess

Can students

- identify the 5 W's questions?
- name three things to look for when they preview?
- name and explain one strategy?
- create and use at least one reading tool?
- explain time and geographical order?

Grade 6
"Understanding Sumer"
pages 19–28

Grade 7
"A Declaration of Independence"
pages 19–27

Grade 8
"The French and Indian War"
pages 17–26

Getting Started Activities

Introduce the *Reader's Handbook* to students at the beginning of the year with one of the activities below. They afford a quick, fun way to start the year.

Self-Inventory, page 22

Use the Self-Inventory to prompt students to define reading and the way they read in their own words. Have students work individually with the inventory list. Then, encourage students to discuss and share their answers with a reading partner or the class. Supplement this activity with lessons in a *Student Applications Book* and a *Lesson Plan Book*.

Visualizing Reading, page 23

This activity will help students understand what happens when they read. Have them sketch their own reading process and share their drawings with a reading partner or the class.

Scavenger Hunt, page 24

Use this activity to help students become familiar with the handbook. Whether working in small groups or on their own, students can learn the various features in the handbook and become comfortable using it. Use the Scavenger Hunt activity to introduce the *Reader's Handbook* program to the class or use particular questions to introduce a specific lesson.

Preview of the *Reader's Handbook*, page 26

Introduce the idea of "previewing" by having students preview the handbook. Students can check off the items in the Preview Checklist as they find them in handbook. Then, they can fill in the statements to explain what the items showed them. Emphasize the importance of previewing when reading any kind of text. Supplement this activity with lessons in a *Student Applications Book* and a *Lesson Plan Book*.

Self-Inventory

Directions: Think about the way you read. Then, answer the questions below.

1. What does the reading process mean?

....

....

....

....

....

....

....

2. What reading strategies have you used while reading?

....

....

....

....

....

....

....

3. What kinds of literature do you read most often?

....

....

....

....

....

....

Visualizing Reading

Directions: Sketch what happens when you read. Draw a story in the boxes below to show the different things that happen when you read.

Scavenger Hunt

Directions: Work with a partner or small group to search the handbook to answer the following questions.

1. What are the three main stages of the reading process?

....

....

2. Where does the section "Word Parts" begin?

....

3. What is the reading strategy in "Reading a Short Story"?

....

....

4. What are all of the elements in "Elements of the Internet"?

....

....

5. What are the first and last entries in the "Skills and Terms Index"?

....

....

6. What are three ways of reading actively?

....

7. What are the names of four different kinds of paragraphs?

....

....

8. What are two types of note-taking techniques that can help you when you're reading a science textbook?

....

....

9. What are three key items to preview before reading a play?

....

....

10. What reading strategy can help you understand the Internet?

....

11. Where would you look to find the difference between an antagonist and a protagonist?

....

....

12. Your teacher assigns the short story lesson for homework. Under which tab in the handbook would you look?

....

....

13. A friend asks you for help defining *personification*. Where would you look for the answer?

....

....

14. You're on the Internet researching information for an essay. What reading tool can help you figure out if the website is reliable?

....

....

15. What are the three main parts of a graph?

....

16. Where would you look to find the difference between an inference test question and a recall question?

....

....

17. Where would you look when you're about to take a social studies test?

....

....

18. What are two types of context clues?

....

19. Where would you look to find what the words on the top of a dictionary page are called?

....

....

20. You are reading an analogy question on a vocabulary test. Where would you look to find what a single colon stands for? How about a double colon?

....

....

Preview of the *Reader's Handbook*

Directions: Preview the following items. Then complete the sentences below.

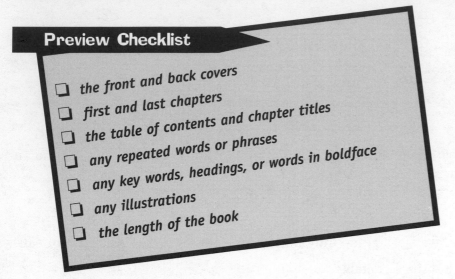

Preview Checklist

☐ the front and back covers
☐ first and last chapters
☐ the table of contents and chapter titles
☐ any repeated words or phrases
☐ any key words, headings, or words in boldface
☐ any illustrations
☐ the length of the book

1. The front and back covers show me

....

2. The table of contents and chapter titles tell me

....

3. The first and last chapters tell me

....

4. I noticed these repeated words:

....

5. Some key words, headings, and other words that stuck out were

....

6. The illustrations tell me

....

....

7. The length of the book is

....

ANSWER KEY

Self-Inventory

Some possible answers are as follows:

1. *I think it means how you read. When I pick up a book, I read the back cover to see what it's about and then I read from beginning to end. If I don't understand something, I ask my parents or my teacher for help.*

2. *Sometimes I reread parts that I didn't understand. I like to take notes to help me remember what I read. Sometimes I put a hard paragraph in my own words so I understand it better.*

3. *Mostly I read magazines, books, and comics.*

Scavenger Hunt

1. *Before Reading, During Reading, After Reading*
2. *page 685*
3. *Using Graphic Organizers*
4. *Bookmark, browser, email, link, search engine, World Wide Web*
5. *Active Reading* and *Writing*
6. Any three from the following list: *Mark or highlight, ask questions, react and connect, predict, visualize, clarify.*
7. *Narrative, persuasive, descriptive, expository*
8. Any two from the following list: *Class and Text Notes, Key Word Notes, Study Cards, Process Notes, Classification Notes*
9. Any three from the following list: *Title page, including the title and playwright (author); cast of characters; general setting; number of pages, acts, and scenes; any background information, photographs, or illustrations.*
10. *Reading Critically*
11. *Elements of Fiction*, or page 390
12. *Fiction*
13. *Elements of Poetry*, or page 459
14. *Website Profiler*
15. *Y-axis, X-axis,* and *legend*
16. *The Reading a Test Chapter*, or page 572
17. *Focus on Social Studies Tests*
18. Any two from the following list: *definitions or synonyms, concrete examples, contrast clues, description clues, words or phrases that modify, conjunctions showing relationships and connecting ideas, repeating words, unstated or implied meanings*
19. *Dictionary Dipping*, or *Learning to Use a Dictionary*
20. *Analogies*

Preview of the *Reader's Handbook*

Some possible answers are as follows: 1. *that the book is about learning to read better;* 2. *that I'm going to learn how to read a lot of different kinds of things;* 3. *the introduction to the book and some word parts;* 4. *reading process, tips, setting a purpose;* 5. *preview, reading strategy, graphic organizers, before reading, during reading, after reading;* 6. *that reading is fun, that I'll learn how to read graphics;* 7. *very long, 704 pages*

Lessons

Introduction

What Is Reading?

Why You Read

What Happens When You Read

Introduction

In this lesson, students will learn what reading is, why they read, and what happens when they read.

What Is Reading?

Begin by asking students what they think reading is. How would they describe it? After they've discussed their ideas, suggest to them that reading is like the following three things that are familiar to them.

A Tool

Read this section with students. Ask how they would describe what they can do with a hammer. They will probably offer more uses for a hammer than those mentioned in the paragraph. Then ask them what a *tool* is. In what sense is reading a tool? Let students consider the examples suggested in the paragraph and add some of their own. Drive home the idea that people use a variety of tools every day and that reading can be one of the most essential tools in the "box."

A Skill

Walk students through the main points made in this paragraph. In comparing reading to something else that requires practice, such as swimming, point out that swimmers learn to float before learning more advanced strokes. Explain that, like swimming, reading is a skill that needs work to achieve proficiency. Ask them for other examples of skills, such as learning to play a musical instrument, and how they acquire them. Remind them that they will read for the rest of their lives, so it is important to develop strong reading skills, which will give them the confidence and enthusiasm they need to enjoy a lifetime of reading.

An Ability

Go over this paragraph with students, and ask them how they think that good reading skills might help them pump up their "thinking power." Ask them what they think they could do if they developed really good "thinking power." Make a wish list of things that students say they want to accomplish. After this discussion, tell them that developing their ability to read can help them to achieve these things.

Why You Read

Ask students why they learned to read. List their responses on the board. Then ask students to imagine what it would be like if they couldn't read. What things would they miss? List these items for them, too. Stress to students that throughout their lives reading will be a vital skill in almost everything they do. Walk students through the six good reasons to read on page 25 and discuss their reactions to each one.

Six Good Reasons to Read

1. Enjoyment

Read this section with students and consider the examples given. Ask students to name the things that they like to read for fun.

2. Information

Point out that reading is a great source of information that can improve students' understanding and enjoyment of life. Read the examples and then ask students to brainstorm lists of things that they'd like to learn more about through reading.

3. Meaning

Go over the examples given on page 25. Explain that reading puts students in touch with whatever ideas and experiences others have had that could be meaningful to them.

4. Depth

Students may find it hard to understand the concept of reading for depth. Read the text and go over the examples given on page 25. Then ask students to name anything they've read, such as a novel or story, that taught them something important about other people, family life, life elsewhere in the world, ideas, or how to live better. Ask students what kinds of questions about life they'd like their reading to help them answer.

5. Beauty

Read this section and ask students whether they've ever simply enjoyed the sound of the way words are expressed. Point out that some writers can string together words in a beautiful, artful way. Their words can touch readers' hearts and expose them to a variety of new insights and emotions.

6. Fun and Ease

Read this section and ask students for their comments. What other types of things do they read, almost without thinking?

What Happens When You Read

Here students will look at what the reading process is like, first by visualizing what happens when they read and next by comparing it to a familiar process such as writing.

Visualizing Reading

Challenge students with the question "What happens when you read?" Students may find this hard to answer. Then read the section on pages 26 and 27 with students. Explain that the class will try the process that Jean Lifford and fellow teachers tried with their students.

Read with students the directions for visualizing reading. Stress that there is no right or wrong way to do this exercise and that the quality of their artwork isn't important. Then lead them through the five listed steps and let them draw what happens when they read. When all have finished, compare the results.

The Reading and Writing Process

Explain to students that the reading process is like the writing process.

Questions for Writers

Review the writing process, walking students through the list of questions and the five interactive steps of writing on page 28.

Questions for Readers

Now explain to students that the reading process also answers a list of important questions. Take time to read each of the questions on page 29. Then ask students whether they ask themselves these or other questions as they read.

- ■ What are you reading about?
- ■ Why are you reading?
- ■ What do you want to get out of your reading?
- ■ What kind of reading is it?
- ■ Should you read slowly or quickly?
- ■ How do you know if you've understood it?
- ■ What can you do if you don't understand something?
- ■ How can you remember what you read?
- ■ Should you reread?

> ### Quick Assess
>
> **Can students**
> - ☑ describe what they do when they read?
> - ☑ explain three different reasons to read?
> - ☑ identify several questions they should ask before starting to read?

Explain to students that this handbook suggests one reading process that will help them to read better and understand more. Their ultimate goal should be to develop the best reading process for their own particular needs.

The Reading
Process

Before Reading

During Reading

After Reading

The Reading Process

Tell students that they will use the reading process again and again in this handbook. Stress that it's important for them to get an overview of the steps of the process. They can use it with every kind of reading to help them learn and remember more.

Begin by asking students what they do when they have a reading assignment. Most of them will say that they just start reading and that they read through the assignment once. Ask them how this process works for them—do they understand everything and remember it afterward? Most will say that they don't.

Explain to students that the reading process has three main stages—Before Reading, During Reading, and After Reading. Tell them that there are some simple things they can do before and after reading that will greatly improve their understanding of what they read and their ability to remember it.

Before Reading

Tell students that the three steps of this first stage of the reading process should be done before they read. Stress that the Before Reading steps take only a few seconds to a few minutes, but they can make a big difference in reading results. As you introduce this material, take your time and make sure that students understand each step and why they should do it.

A. Set a Purpose
B. Preview
C. Plan

A   Set a Purpose

Read through this section with students, stressing the main points. Invite students to answer the question "Why do you read something?" Students' answers will vary. They read for assignments, for fun, for information, and so on. Emphasize that they read differently for each of these purposes. Ask: "Why do you think you need a reading purpose?" "What would happen if you read a bus schedule without a purpose?" Emphasize the importance of knowing why they are reading. Also give them examples of reading purposes, such as "What is this novel about, and what makes it interesting?" Explain that this handbook helps students by suggesting specific purposes for every main reading.

B   Preview

Read the Preview section on page 33 with students, emphasizing that previewing is looking over the material. Previews can give students an idea of what to expect— a reading's length, difficulty, vocabulary, organization, and content. Explain that it's like looking into the pool or sticking your toe in the water before diving in. This handbook will help students learn to preview by offering Preview Checklists that show them where to look for information they need.

C   Plan

Guide students through this section, underscoring what is meant by a "reading plan" and why they need one. Explain that the last step before reading involves choosing a reading strategy or plan, such as note-taking or using graphic organizers, that answers the question, "What's the best way for me to meet my reading purpose?"

To illustrate what a reading strategy is, turn to the Strategy Handbook, pages 641–665 in the Reader's Almanac. Point out the list of strategies on page 641 and tell students that learning which strategies work well with certain kinds of readings helps in planning. For example, they might want to use outlining or note-taking strategies to get information from a textbook chapter. If they are reading a novel, they'd choose a different strategy, such as using graphic organizers or synthesizing.

Explain to students that this handbook helps them learn about which reading strategies work well with different types of readings, from history textbooks to magazine articles to vocabulary tests.

During Reading

Explain that now that they've set a reading purpose, previewed the reading, and planned a reading strategy, students will read the selection in detail. Point out the two steps in the During Reading stage of the reading process.

D. Read with a Purpose
E. Connect

D Read with a Purpose

Read through this section with students, emphasizing the main points and relating them to students' experience. Ask students: "Have you ever felt lost when you were reading? Why did you feel lost?" (probably because of the amount of information and resources) Emphasize that knowing the reading purpose can help students to focus and make sense out of what's being presented. Challenge them to read actively and to assume the reading attitude of "I'm going to get something out of this." Explain that they should know why they're reading and expect to have learned something by the end of the reading. Tell them that this handbook will show them how to read with a purpose and will offer them information and tools that will help them achieve their purposes with many common types of readings.

E Connect

Direct students' attention to the material in the Connect section on page 35. Read through it together and discuss what it means. Emphasize that connecting with a reading is a very important habit to develop. It can make the material much more meaningful and memorable. Stress that almost everything that students read has some connection to their personal feelings or life.

Ask students to read the list of questions on page 35. Discuss each one and ask for examples of times when they've made connections like this while reading (for example, while reading a report of an accident injury in the news).

Tell students that asking questions helps them link the reading to something in their lives.

■ How does this touch you?

■ Where have you seen or heard something like this before?

■ What do you find surprising?

■ When did something like this happen to you?

■ What do you think about it? Is it believable or not?

After Reading

Explain to students that the last main stage of reading, After Reading, helps them understand and remember what they read. Point out the three steps in this phase.

F. Pause and Reflect
G. Reread
H. Remember

F Pause and Reflect

Read through this section with students. Tell them that pausing and reflecting involves assessing how well they've met their reading purpose. They ask themselves important questions, such as "Did I learn what I wanted to learn?" and "Does anything seem confusing?" Illustrate the value of pausing, looking back, and reflecting by asking students whether they've ever read a textbook chapter and wound up unsure or confused about the main points. What did they do next? If they just went on to something else, did they feel prepared when it was time to take the test? Point out that there are steps they can take right after reading something that will make their later pretest studying much easier. Emphasize that it's this step in which students should monitor how well they're understanding what they read.

G Reread

Ask students whether they ever reread anything and, if so, what and why. Tell students that good readers know rereading often is an essential step in getting all the facts straight. Ask students to offer examples of materials that probably won't require rereading (a comic strip) and materials that might require a second look (a science textbook). Stress that the rereading process should be done with a specific purpose in mind. Overall, rereading is a chance to go back and get what was missed, straighten out what was confusing, and finally get all the information the student set out to get.

H Remember

Ask students to name types of readings that they tend to remember easily and types of readings that they quickly forget. Suggest to them that using material in some creative way can help them remember it. This handbook will suggest ways to help them relate to the information.

Summing Up

To wrap up the lesson, point out the Summing Up section. Go back over all that students have learned about the reading process. Point out the steps listed under Summing Up and ask students to ask questions about each one.

The entire reading process can be boiled down to a few easy-to-follow steps.

Before
- Set a purpose.
- Preview the reading.
- Plan a reading strategy.

During
- Read with a purpose. Look for information that fits your purpose.
- Create some personal connection to the text.

After
- Pause, reflect, and look back to see if you found information that fits your purpose.
- Reread to find out things you might have missed the first time through.
- Remember what you learned.

One Last Word

Read the final paragraphs on page 37 with students. Review the major points. Ask students for their reactions, and let them know that the handbook offers a model for using the reading process so that it becomes an automatic and almost natural part of how they read.

Quick Assess

Can students

- ☑ name the three main stages of the reading process?
- ☑ explain what it means to preview a reading?
- ☑ describe how to connect to what they read?
- ☑ explain why they might need to reread?

Reading
Know-how

- **Essential Reading Skills**
- **Reading Actively**
- **Reading Paragraphs**
- **Kinds of Paragraphs**
- **Ways of Organizing Paragraphs**

Reading Know-how

Here students learn that they already have many reading skills. If they sharpen these skills, they can become even better readers. "Reading Know-how" will help students learn to:

- ☑ understand and use the essential reading skills of making inferences, drawing conclusions, comparing and contrasting, and evaluating
- ☑ understand how to find the subject and main idea in paragraphs
- ☑ recognize kinds of paragraphs and paragraph organization

Essential Reading Skills

Explain to students that they already have many of the core reading skills they need. The skills they use when they figure out a friend's mood, compare TV programs, or evaluate a purchase can be applied to reading. Explain that thinking skills can unlock their reading know-how and make them better readers. These thinking skills are used to implement the twelve reading strategies students learn in the *Reader's Handbook*.

Making Inferences

Direct students' attention to the text on page 40. Read it together and take them through its major points.

Emphasize the message in the graphic. "What I Learned" (what I'm reading) plus "What I Already Know" (my background knowledge) equals an inference. Use examples to clarify what making an inference is. Encourage students to explain in their own words and using examples from their own reading what "reading between the lines" means.

Drawing Conclusions

Read with students the material on page 41, underscoring the main points. Explain to students that just as they draw conclusions from personal experience, in the same way they draw conclusions while reading. They take bits of information and "put two and two together" to form conclusions. Illustrate the point with the Drawing Conclusions example on page 41.

Suggest other examples of drawing conclusions from reading and create a chart of facts and conclusions like the one in the text. Remind students to keep track of the bits of information they learn to "see how they add up."

Comparing and Contrasting

Guide students in reading this section, noting the examples of how they compare and contrast things in everyday life. Ask students for other examples of things they compare and contrast.

Take time to read each of the questions in the graphic on page 42, and point out the usefulness of looking at a reading selection from a number of different angles.

Use the illustration to expand on the idea of applying many points of view. Ask students to suggest a well-known story, website, or poem. Then ask the group to suggest contrasting points of view (such as that of a young child or an older adult).

COMPARING AND CONTRASTING

Who is "good," and who is "bad" in this story?

What sets apart the hero of this play from other characters?

How would someone from a different background view this essay?

How is this poem different from others written by the author?

How are these two websites alike?

Evaluating

Focus students' attention on the skill of evaluating by reading this text together and going over the examples. Emphasize that when reading, students should apply what they know to make judgments about what they read. Ask students to name examples of characters in literature that they evaluate in a positive or negative way because of the way they're described or the way they act. Point out that the author gives the characters traits and behaviors to create certain feelings and impressions. Advise students to be aware of such "signals" from the writer.

Sum up this section by recapping what students have learned. Ask them to list and explain each of the essential reading skills studied so far. Remind them that being good readers requires that they make inferences, draw conclusions, compare and contrast, and evaluate what they read. Tell them that they will use and build these reading skills over a lifetime.

Reading Actively

Make sure students understand the importance of staying focused, or concentrating, while reading. Compare being focused during reading to keeping their eyes on the ball when playing tennis or batting in a baseball game. Help them see what active reading is, why it is important, and how to read actively.

Being an Active Reader

Read through each paragraph with students, stopping to underscore and extend the important points.

Draw parallels between active participation in sports and active participation in reading. Prompt students to think about what being an active reader really means. (Thinking about what you are reading and making an effort to understand.) Tell them that this means focusing 100 percent on what they're reading. Help students to be aware of the things that can make their minds wander.

Direct students' attention to the graphic on page 43 in the *Reader's Handbook*. Go over each of these activities, giving examples and asking students to suggest some of their own.

Suggest that students can read more actively by writing things down as they read. Taking notes by writing on the material (if allowed) or taking side notes will help them stay focused and active. Sticky notes can act as note flags when students can't write in the book.

Look closely with students at the reading example on page 44 of the handbook. Read the text and relate each side note to an appropriate passage. Explain that marking up the text with questions, reactions, predictions, drawings, and clarifications will get students more fully involved in what they are reading.

Ways of Reading Actively

Read through the introductory text with students and spend time discussing each of the six common ways of reading actively shown in the chart on page 45.

Finding a Reading Place

Ask students whether they've ever tried to talk with a friend over loud music. When music is too loud, it's hard not to be distracted. Explain that reading is another form of communication that works best when the circumstances are right. That means finding a good, quiet spot. Direct students' attention to the checklist on page 46 in the handbook.

Finding Time for Reading

Ask students to evaluate their time management skills in doing homework. Do they allow enough time to finish their homework properly? Also discuss students' personal scheduling problems. What sorts of things make it difficult for them to find the time to read? Help students by suggesting ways to overcome these obstacles. Share your own success stories or tips for making reading a daily habit.

WAYS OF READING ACTIVELY

❶ Mark or Highlight *The most common way is to write a sticky note and put it in a text. Or, if you can, mark the text itself by highlighting with a marker or pen. You can also put highlighting tape over passages. This is another way of making some words, phrases, or sentences stand out as IMPORTANT. Highlighting parts of a text in this way helps you come back and find what's important when you reread.*

❷ Ask Questions *Active readers ask lots of questions. It's one of the best things a reader can do. "Why is the writer talking about this?" "Who says this is true?" "What does that mean?"*

❸ React and Connect *When you read, you need to listen to the author and to yourself. You need to think about what you are reading and relate it to your own life. Look for connections between you and the text, comparing and contrasting it to things you know.*

❹ Predict *As you read, you constantly wonder how things will turn out. Think ahead when you read. Share your ideas about what's going to happen with a friend. Write down your predictions. They will help you stay interested in what you're reading.*

❺ Visualize *Because your thoughts are mere flashes in the brain, you need to record them if you want to remember them. Making pictures in your mind can help you "see" what you were thinking and help you remember. A chart, a sketch, a diagram—any of these can help you "see."*

❻ Clarify *Because so much is happening as you read, you need to be sure of the things you do know. Pull together what you have learned. You can do this by writing notes to clarify things, whether it's a series of points in an argument or an important detail.*

Reading Paragraphs

Here students learn the two main steps to understanding every paragraph: finding the subject and finding the main idea. Skillful readers know what a *subject* and a *main idea* are and how to quickly locate both of them.

Introduce the idea of finding what a paragraph is about by directing students' attention to the graphic on page 47 in the handbook.

Finding the Subject

Introduce finding a paragraph's subject (topic) by directing students to read the three things to look for as readers that are listed on page 48. Then ask students to read the paragraph by Annie Dillard. Point out that the annotations are color-coded so that students can match them to the appropriate bits of text.

Now go over each of the steps on page 49, making sure that students can relate each point to the reading on page 48.

Finally, recap the three steps and give students practice in one of the *Student Applications Books* (Reading Paragraphs) or by applying the steps to a paragraph or two from one of their textbooks.

Finding the Main Idea

Introduce students to finding the main idea. Make sure that they understand that the main idea is what a writer says about the subject. Give them several examples of subjects and main ideas to illustrate this concept.

Point out to students that finding the main idea is a key reading skill. Sometimes they'll find it in the first sentence, other times in the last sentence, and often they'll need to figure it out for themselves.

Main Idea in the First Sentence

Read the first paragraph of this section with students. Show them the Web on page 50 in the handbook that diagrams the main idea and details from Dillard's paragraph from "Living Like Weasels." Model the use of this graphic organizer to diagram a paragraph.

Go through the details with students, pointing out that each one supports the main idea "Weasels are wild." Ask them to look through their textbooks to find paragraphs that give the main idea in the first sentence.

Main Idea in the Last Sentence

Introduce the sample reading on page 51. Show students how the paragraph is structured with a series of details followed by the main idea. Ask them to relate each of the notes to an appropriate bit of text. Direct students to read the Paragraph Notes on page 51, showing how the author builds up details about the main idea.

Invite students to compare the effects of the two paragraphs they've just read. How do they differ in terms of effect?

Implied Main Idea

Explain to students that sometimes the main idea isn't stated in the paragraph but is implied, or suggested. Direct their attention first to the introductory paragraph on page 52. Take time to read through the example, relating specific sentences to the notes on the side. Then lead students through the detailed steps on the following page.

Heading
Ask students to apply this information to the reading on page 52.

First Sentence
Students can use this information to analyze the first sentence in the reading.

Details
Have students read this section and then look carefully at the details in the paragraph on page 52. Model the use of the Main Idea Organizer on page 53, emphasizing that students must make a special effort to put together the various bits of information to determine the implied main idea.

Show students the graphic on page 54 and explain that it gives them a process for finding an implied main idea. After talking about each step, ask students to apply this method to other sample paragraphs with implied main ideas and to fill out a Main Idea Organizer for each paragraph.

Kinds of Paragraphs

Along with knowing how to find the subject and main idea, students should know how to recognize different kinds of paragraphs. Introduce this material to students, asking them to read the text on page 55 and to study the graphic.

Lead students through the points made in this graphic and then read through the final points at the bottom of page 55.

KINDS OF PARAGRAPHS

Narrative Paragraphs
- *tell a story*

Persuasive Paragraphs
- *express an opinion or try to convince the reader*

Descriptive Paragraphs
- *offer specific details and sensory images to give a picture*

Expository Paragraphs
- *present facts, opinions, definitions of terms, and examples to inform the reader about a specific topic*

Ways of Organizing Paragraphs

Introduce this section by telling students that there are several common ways of organizing paragraphs—in time order, location order, order of importance, cause-effect order, classification order, and comparison-contrast order. Learning to recognize paragraphs organized in these ways can help them to read more efficiently and effectively.

Spend time explaining the graphic on page 56. Ask students to give examples of writing that might use these different ways of organizing.

ORGANIZING PARAGRAPHS

Time Order
- *Chronological order*

Location Order
- *Geographic or spatial order*

Cause-Effect Order
- *Problem-solution*

Order of Importance
- *Most important to least important*
- *Least important to most important*

Comparison-Contrast Order
- *Similarities and differences*

Classification Order
- *Groups or categories*

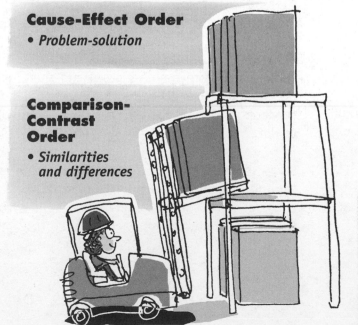

Time Order

Ask students to read the introductory sentences of this section, stressing that paragraphs written in time order list events in the order in which they happened. Explain that time (or chronological) order often is used in novels, stories, folktales, plays, biographies, autobiographies, news stories, and other types of readings.

Read with students the paragraph on page 57 from Jack London's *Call of the Wild*. Point out the numbers that are printed in this passage and direct students' attention to the graphic organizer.

SERIES OF EVENTS

1. Camp was reached.
2. Morning found Dave weak.
3. At harness-up time Dave was too weak to run.
4. Then he wormed his way forward.
5. The last his mates saw him he lay gasping in the snow.
6. They heard him howling as they passed out of sight.

Location Order

Read with students the introductory sentences of this section. Explain that writers use location (or geographic) order to help readers visualize a scene. The key to location order is that writers try to present details in organized ways, beginning in one place and moving around from place to place.

Guide students in reading the paragraph on page 58 from Theodore Taylor's *The Cay*. Show them how the sentences are mapped. Help them understand that the writer is describing things as if they were in a circle.

MAP OF LOCATION

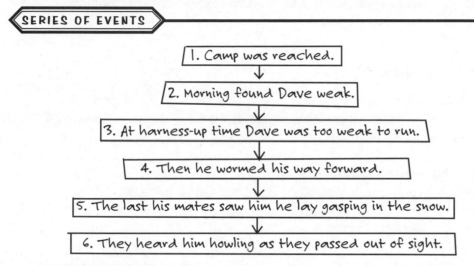

Aruba
② attacked big Lago oil refinery
③ blew up six tankers

Curaçao
① asleep in house on second floor in Willemstad
Willemstad
④ sighted submarine off Willemstad
coast of Venezuela

Cause-Effect Order

Read the introductory sentences with students, making sure that they understand that *cause* refers to what happens first and *effect* refers to something that happens as a result.

Then ask students to read the paragraph on page 59, noting the cause and various effects as shown in the highlighted text and annotations. Point out to students the cause and effects in the Cause-Effect Order chart on page 59 in the handbook.

Ask students to look through their history or science textbooks for examples of paragraphs that cite causes and effects.

Order of Importance

Ask students to read the introductory sentences of this section. Emphasize that in this type of paragraph organization, writers move either from the most important idea to the least important or vice versa.

Most Important to Least Important

Ask students to read the paragraph from *Creating America* on page 60. Tell them that it is from a history textbook and ask them to notice that the main idea comes first and then is followed by details.

Next, show students how the sentences in the reading are charted in the diagram on page 60.

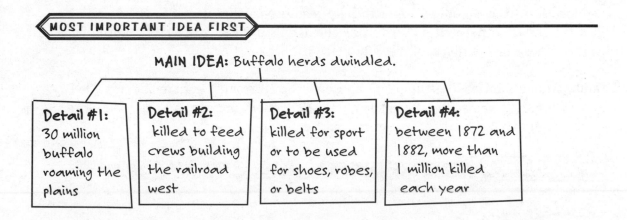

MOST IMPORTANT IDEA FIRST

MAIN IDEA: Buffalo herds dwindled.

Detail #1: 30 million buffalo roaming the plains

Detail #2: killed to feed crews building the railroad west

Detail #3: killed for sport or to be used for shoes, robes, or belts

Detail #4: between 1872 and 1882, more than 1 million killed each year

Least Important to Most Important

Show students the example in which the order of ideas goes from the details to the most important final sentence.

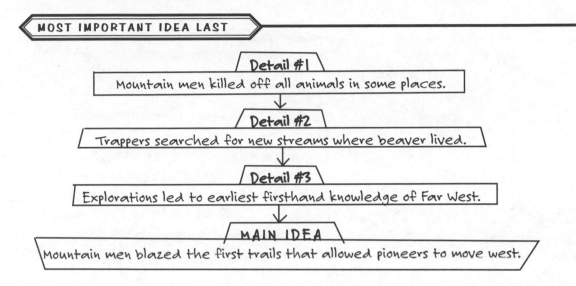

MOST IMPORTANT IDEA LAST

Detail #1
Mountain men killed off all animals in some places.

Detail #2
Trappers searched for new streams where beaver lived.

Detail #3
Explorations led to earliest firsthand knowledge of Far West.

MAIN IDEA
Mountain men blazed the first trails that allowed pioneers to move west.

Comparison-Contrast Order

Ask students to read the explanation of comparison-contrast order. Emphasize that a comparison-contrast order paragraph shows similarities or differences.

Read with students the paragraph comparing wolves and German shepherd dogs on page 62. Examine the Wolves vs. Dogs chart on that page and relate the information in it to the paragraph. Discuss with students how the same information could be presented in a Venn Diagram.

Classification Order

Guide students through the introductory text, underscoring the main points that classification means grouping similar things and that authors write paragraphs in classification order to show broad similarities and differences.

Read the paragraph from *Big Blue Ocean* on page 63 with students. Note the categories of living creatures in the ocean.

Now ask students to look at the chart at the bottom of the page. Explain that this organizer offers a clear way to note the groups mentioned in the paragraph.

Quick Assess

Can students

- ☑ explain what it means to make inferences?
- ☑ describe two ways to be an active reader?
- ☑ find the subject and main idea of a paragraph?
- ☑ name four types of paragraphs?
- ☑ list three ways paragraphs are organized?

Reading
Textbooks

Reading Different Subjects

Reading History
Reading Geography
Reading Science
Reading Math

Focus on School Reading

Focus on Science Concepts
Focus on Word Problems

Elements of Textbooks

Reading History

Getting Ready

Goals

Here students read a lesson called "Indian Wars" from an American history textbook. This lesson will help them learn to:

Background

Connect the lesson with students' existing knowledge by asking them to:

■ compare reading history to reading other subjects

■ discuss ways of approaching the reading of history

■ list the different parts of a history textbook

■ discuss the ways that information is usually organized in a history textbook

Opening Activity

Talk about the common features of history textbooks, such as explaining events in the past and telling about the people who shaped the events. Students can ask themselves *who, what, when, where,* and *why* as they read.

Lesson Resources

Overview

	Content	Teacher's Guide page	Reader's Handbook page
Selection	"Indian Wars"		69–72
Reading Strategy	Note-taking	54	73, 646
Rereading Strategy	Outlining	59	80-81, 648
Tool	5 W's Organizer	54	73, 672
	Summary Notes	55	75, 680
	Webs	55	75, 684
	Timeline or Sequence Notes	56	76, 681
	Thinking Tree	56	76, 680
	Outline	59	81, 675

Ancillaries

	Grade	Content	Page
Overhead Transparency	6, 7, 8	Previewing History	Numbers 8 and 9
Lesson Plan Book	7	Reading History	64–65
	8	Reading History	55
Student Applications Book	6	"Understanding Sumer"	19–28
	7	"A Declaration of Independence"	19–27
	8	"The French and Indian War"	17–26
Website		www.greatsource.com/rehand/	
Content Area Guide		This lesson appears in the *Content Area Guide: Social Studies.*	

Before Reading

A Set a Purpose

Before reading "Indian Wars," ask students to set a purpose for their reading. Help students understand that when they set a purpose, such as to acquire information about an event in the past, they become actively involved in their reading. Use the 5 W's questions on page 67 of the *Reader's Handbook* as Setting a Purpose questions. Discuss with students why these questions will be helpful in reading.

Setting a Purpose

■ **What** were the Indian Wars?

■ **When** did they take place?

■ **Who** was involved in these wars?

■ **Where** did they take place?

■ **Why** did they occur?

B Preview

Ask students to preview the "Indian Wars" excerpt to get an overview of the subject matter. Familiarize the students with the Preview Checklist on page 68 in the *Reader's Handbook*. Then go over what to preview using the Overhead Transparencies.

Point out each item in the Preview Checklist. Encourage students to trace a finger down the page to find repeated words or bold type.

Point out to students that the annotations in the margin are color-coded, so students can match the annotation with the appropriate bit of highlighted text.

Preview Checklist

✔ the title and any section guides or goals boxes

✔ the first and last paragraphs

✔ the headings

✔ any names, dates, words, or terms set in bold type or repeated

✔ any photos, diagrams, or pictures and their captions

Overhead Transparencies

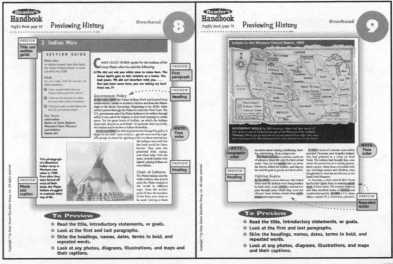

Before Reading

C Plan

Lead students in summarizing what they learned from their preview. Then have them make a plan for gathering basic information from "Indian Wars." Suggest using the strategy of **note-taking** and discuss why this strategy will be useful in helping them answer the 5 W's. (One reason is that the strategy encourages them to pay close attention to individual facts.)

Reading Strategy: Note-taking

Explain to students that note-taking is an effective strategy to use when reading history because it helps them to gather enough details to answer the 5 W's.

5 W's Organizer

For example, a 5 W's Organizer shows the facts in the five separate categories of *who, what, where, when,* and *why.*

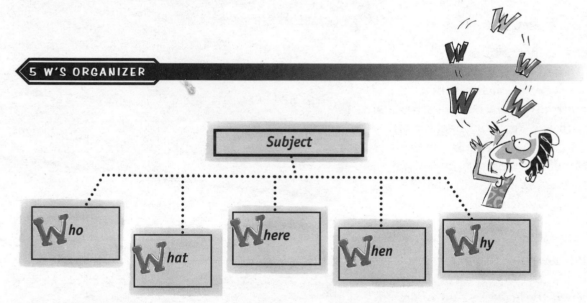

5 W'S ORGANIZER

Subject

Who   What   Where   When   Why

During Reading

D Read with a Purpose

While reading "Indian Wars," students record information in various types of note-taking formats. Help them understand when to use each format.

1. Summary Notes

Summary Notes work well for students who are well organized and need to write about the subject or review the material for a test. This kind of notes connects related ideas and facts, making them easier to remember.

Page-by-Page Notes help students by requiring them to pull out only the key information from a page. The goal is to learn at least one thing from each page.

PAGE-BY-PAGE NOTES

| Page 559 | 1800—Indians lived in peace.
1840—Reservations began.
Indians and whites clashed on Plains. |

| Page 560 | 1860s—Treaties were broken.
Settlers went through Indian lands and killed buffalo.
Indians raided white settlements. |

| Page 561 | 1876—Sitting Bull and Crazy Horse attacked Gen. Custer.
Massacre was last major Indian victory. |

2. Webs

Web Notes are a flexible format for recording notes. Web Notes help students keep track of how topics and facts fit together.

WEB NOTES

Plains Indians
Northwest Indians
Southwest Indians
— **Indian Wars** —
Cheyenne—Nebraska
Blackfoot—Washington
Apache—New Mexico
Sioux—Montana

- fought settlers who killed buffalo
- fought because of broken treaties
- fought because whites took their land

During Reading

D **Read with a Purpose** continued

3. Timeline or Sequence Notes

Events of history are usually described in time, or chronological, order. Timeline or Sequence Notes allow students to keep track of what happened first, next, and last.

◆ TIMELINE OR SEQUENCE NOTES ▷

early 1800s	Plains Indians lived in peace.
1860	Treaties began to be broken.
1876	Custer lost at Little Bighorn.
1886	Geronimo was captured. Indian Wars ended.

4. Thinking Tree

A Thinking Tree helps students see connections among facts and ideas. They take notes to show main topics and details.

◆ THINKING TREE ▷

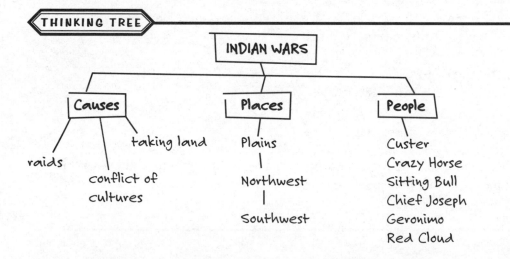

Other Useful Tools

Explain to students that they can choose from a wide variety of graphic organizers while reading "Indian Wars." It isn't necessary to use all of them. Understanding a number of organizers will help students choose the ones that work best for them.

■ **Cause-Effect Organizer**

■ **K-W-L Chart**

How History Textbooks Are Organized

As they use various note-taking techniques, students might begin to see a pattern in the way that history textbooks are written. History books are written purposely in a certain way and a certain order, making them easier to follow.

1. Time Order

Point out to students that in the excerpt below, the note-taker highlighted the dates and locations. This material, like most history material, is written in time order.

Dates
• 1877

Locations
• Oregon
• Idaho
• Montana

Chief Joseph, leader of the Nez Percé.

Chief Joseph

A few months after the death of Crazy Horse, another war began—this one with the Nez Percé people. The Nez Percé were Northwest Indians. They fished for salmon, hunted, and gathered food from eastern Oregon to Idaho. Their leader was Chief Joseph, who refused to sell the lands where his people had lived for centuries.

When the government ordered the Nez Percé to move to a reservation in 1877, Chief Joseph and his followers fled. Army troops followed them. Over the next four months, the Nez Percé traveled some 1,300 miles through Oregon, Idaho, and Montana, looking for safety.

The Nez Percé were about 40 miles from the Canadian border when the army caught up with them. Cold, hungry, weary, and outnumbered, the Nez Percé surrendered. Chief Joseph spoke eloquently for many western Indians when he said:

❝ Hear me, my chiefs. I am tired; my heart is sick and sad. From where the sun

Walk" east, away from their rugged lands to the edge of the Great Plains. Hundreds died during the trip from lack of food and warm clothing.

Arrival at the reservation did not end their problems. Guarded and watched, the Navajo were forced to dig irrigation ditches and plant crops. Insects killed the crops and the Pecos River overflowed, destroying the irrigation system. Finally, the government admitted that the reservation was a failure. The Navajo returned home.

In the mid 1870s the Chiricahua Apache were moved onto land away from their traditional territory in the Southwest. Geronimo, an Apache leader, led his followers off the reservation. His knowledge of southern Arizona allowed them to escape the U.S. Army time and time again.

Geronimo was finally captured just north of the Mexican border in 1886. He spent the rest of his life forced to live far from his people.

A Way of Life Destroyed

The Indians lost more than battles. Their

---

2. Geographic Order

The text in "Indian Wars" also follows geographic order from the Plains Indians to the Northwest Indians and then to the Southwest Indians. Explain to students that the writing is organized this way to make it easier for readers to understand. Once students recognize the order or pattern, the reading will be smoother.

During Reading

E Connect

Explain to students that their interaction with the reading is what facilitates learning. Their ability to actively find connections in the text will enable them to create better understanding for themselves. Explain to students the need to:

■ ask themselves questions about the reading
(Who is right and who is wrong? Is anyone right or wrong?)

■ think about the meaning of events in the reading
(Could the Indians and settlers have found a way to get along? What kind of arrangement might that have been?)

■ think about causes and effects in the reading
(What were the effects of the Indian Wars and how have they affected me?)

■ picture what is happening in the text
(What did "Custer's last stand" look like?)

■ react personally to historical events and the actions of historical figures
(How do I feel about these clashes between Indians and settlers?)

■ compare historical figures with people they know
(Do I know of anyone who is like the white settlers, the Indians, or their leaders?)

■ consider the effect that these events have had on their lives today
(How would life in the U.S. today be different if the Indians and white settlers had worked out a way to live together?)

> cause → effect
> U.S. Army finds gold → tries to take over the land This seems so unfair.

party of Sioux who had attacked a supply train. Fetterman led his 80 soldiers into a trap. A much larger band of Sioux fighters was waiting. In the battle, Fetterman's entire group was wiped out.

Little Bighorn

The most famous battle of the Indian Wars took place in June 1876 after tensions had arisen in the Black Hills of the Dakotas. These hills had been set aside by treaty for the Sioux and northern Cheyenne. In 1874, after a U.S. Army exploring party found gold in the Black Hills, miners arrived by the thousands. They cared little that this land was sacred to the Sioux.

Hoping to head off a clash, the government tried to buy the Black Hills from the Indians. The Sioux would not think of selling their land. As war fever mounted through the winter of 1875–1876, Sioux warriors left their reservations. They united under the leadership of two Sioux chiefs—Sitting Bull and Crazy Horse.

On June 25, 1876, George Armstrong Custer and several hundred soldiers came upon a Sioux camp on the bank of the Little Bighorn River. Custer was already famous. He had fought in many Civil War battles. To some he was a daring, brilliant officer. To others he was a dangerous showoff, with his colorful uniform and long blond hair.

Custer's orders were to attack if he found Indians. When he neared the camp on the Little Bighorn, however, he entered a trap set by Sitting Bull and Crazy Horse. A large force of Sioux and Cheyenne overpowered his forces. In what became known as "Custer's Last Stand," all of Custer's men—including Custer himself—were killed.

In the East, people were shocked by news of the **Battle of Little Bighorn.** The government sent thousands more soldiers west to fight the Indians.

Little Bighorn was the last Indian victory in the Indian Wars. Army forces defeated the Sioux in the fall of 1876. Sitting Bull and his followers fled to Canada. Crazy Horse and some 800 of his people surrendered. As Crazy Horse was being arrested, he was fatally stabbed. It was never determined if it was a guard who killed him or another Indian who opposed his aims.

A portrait of Sitting Bull

> What happened to Sitting Bull? Did the government arrest him?

After Reading

F Pause and Reflect

After reading, students stop to consider whether they understand what they have read. Help students to review their original purpose in reading the text.

Looking Back

■ Can I answer the *who*, *what*, *when*, *where*, and *why* questions?

■ Can I summarize 2–3 important ideas in my own words?

■ Do my notes cover the whole chapter, and do I understand them?

Because of the large number of factual details in this reading, students probably can not fully answer these Looking Back questions. They probably have new questions as well. Help students to see the need to return to the passage for a second reading and to understand that rereading is a part of the reading process.

G Reread

When rereading, students should use a new strategy as a fresh way to approach the material. Have them review the passage, looking for answers to their questions but using a new strategy.

Rereading Strategy: Outlining

Encourage students to use this new strategy when rereading.

Outlining puts key information in front of them in a concise format. Using the headings in the chapter, students can write out a simple Outline that will clarify the information for them and help them answer the 5 W's. All students need to do is write two or more subpoints under each of the headings in the chapter.

◆ OUTLINE ▷

Indian Wars

I. Government Policy ◀ • • • •
   A. 1840s—white settlement
   B. mid-1800s—changing policy
          (**Headings from textbook**)

II. Clash of Cultures ◀ • • • •
   A. settlers farming and hunting on the land
   B. Indians using what they needed to live on

III. Fighting Begins
   A. raids on settlements
   B. led by Red Cloud, a Sioux chief

After Reading

H Remember

At this point in the reading, students need to do something with the information in order to make it their own. To make the lesson more memorable, try the activity ideas suggested in the *Reader's Handbook* on page 82 or the creative assignment below.

Creative Assignment: Ask each student to imagine himself or herself as a Plains Indian or a white settler during the period of the "Indian Wars." Then ask students to choose one of the historical incidents in this lesson. Ask students to write a journal entry as they think an Indian or a white settler of the time might have written it. Read some of these accounts aloud in class and discuss the differences in points of view.

Summing Up

Finally, review the lesson with students. Focus on what they've learned about strategies and tools for reading a history textbook. Read with students the Summing Up (on page 83 in the handbook). Go over with students the three goals for the lesson. Discuss which ones they feel that they achieved and which ones they feel they need more work on:

1. reading history

2. using the strategy of note-taking

3. seeing the way history textbooks are often organized

Assessment and Application

Use the Quick Assess checklist to evaluate students' abilities to read and understand history. Give students the opportunity to apply what they have learned through one of the two activities below. For students who are comfortable with the reading process and strategy, use one of the independent practice suggestions. For guided help with the strategy, use a *Student Applications Book*.

1. Independent Practice

To show that they understand the lesson, students can apply the reading strategy of **note-taking** to another history lesson in the textbook series that they are using.

Ask students to:

1. Create Web Notes for the history lesson.

2. Create an Outline for the lesson.

3. Write a journal entry summing up their view of the long-term importance of the events in the history lesson.

Quick Assess

Can students

- ☑ identify the 5 W's questions?
- ☑ name three things to look for when they preview?
- ☑ name and explain one strategy?
- ☑ create and use at least one reading tool?
- ☑ explain time and geographical order?

2. Student Applications Books

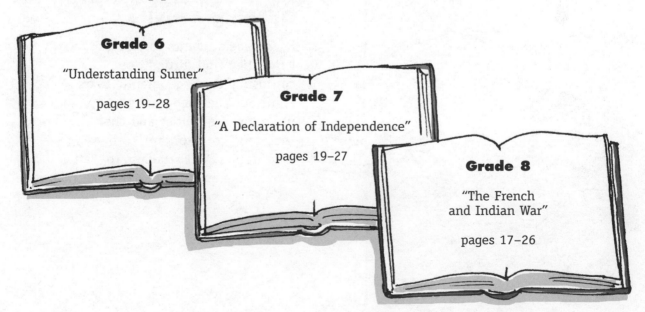

Grade 6

"Understanding Sumer"

pages 19–28

Grade 7

"A Declaration of Independence"

pages 19–27

Grade 8

"The French and Indian War"

pages 17–26

Reading Geography

Getting Ready

Goals

Here students read a lesson called "Population" in a geography textbook. This lesson will help them learn to:

- read informational writing like that found in geography books
- use the reading strategy of using graphic organizers
- understand the way geography textbooks are often organized

Background

Connect the lesson with the students' existing knowledge by asking them to:

- list the types of elements that are found in geography textbooks
- discuss the ways that information usually is organized in geography textbooks
- compare reading geography with reading other subjects
- discuss ways to approach reading geography

Opening Activity

Encourage students to discuss what they find difficult or confusing about geography texts. Point out that geography texts use a lot of graphics and that they tend to be organized by main topics. Tell students to watch for those elements as they read.

Lesson Resources

Overview

	Content	Teacher's Guide page	Reader's Handbook page
Selection	"Population"		87–90
Reading Strategy	Using Graphic Organizers	65	91, 662
Rereading Strategy	Note-taking	70	98, 646
Tool	K-W-L Chart	65, 66	91, 92, 673
	Concept Map	66	93, 670
	Main Idea Organizer	67	93, 674
	Study Cards	71	98, 679

Ancillaries

	Grade	Content	Page
Overhead Transparency	6, 7, 8	Previewing Geography	Numbers 10 and 11
Lesson Plan Book	6	Reading Geography	74–75
Student Applications Book	6	"Population Shift: Journey to Gold Mountain"	29-38
	7	"The Physical Geography of Southeast Asia"	28-36
	8	"The Mountains of Canada and the United States"	27-36
Website		www.greatsource.com/rehand/	
Content Area Guide		This lesson appears in the *Content Area Guide: Social Studies*.	

Before Reading

A Set a Purpose

Before reading "Population," ask students to set a purpose for reading. Direct students to the Setting a Purpose questions on page 85 in the handbook and discuss reasons why these are good questions to guide their reading.

Setting a Purpose

■ **What is population, and why is it important?**

■ **How is it changing?**

B Preview

Ask students to preview "Population," trying to get an idea of what to expect before they begin reading. Point out the Preview Checklist on page 86. Then walk through a preview using the Overhead Transparencies.

Discuss each item in the Preview Checklist. Suggest to students that they point to each item in the text.

Explain that some of the annotations have arrows to help students easily find the headings or other parts of the text. Other annotations are color-coded to help them match each annotation to the appropriate bit of highlighted text.

Preview Checklist

✔ *the title*

✔ *the headings*

✔ *any boxed items*

✔ *any repeated words or ones set in bold type*

✔ *any photos, maps, graphs, or diagrams and their captions*

✔ *the first and last paragraphs*

Overhead Transparencies

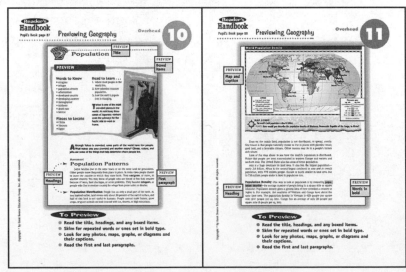

Before Reading

C Plan

Ask students to summarize what they learned in their preview. Now students should make a plan for getting information about population and its importance. Suggest the strategy of **using graphic organizers**. Explain why this strategy is useful in getting information from textbooks. (One reason is that graphic organizers already are formatted to assist students in focusing on the data that they need. The wide variety of graphic organizers allows students to be flexible, using the appropriate one for the specific reading.)

Reading Strategy: Using Graphic Organizers

One effective organizer is a K-W-L Chart. It is a valuable tool because it helps students to assess and organize their knowledge before, during, and after reading. A K-W-L Chart also helps students read with a purpose as they look for answers to their questions. They should consider and use several types of graphic organizers.

K-W-L Chart

With this graphic organizer, students list the things they *know* (K) about the topic, the things they *want* to know (W), and what they *learned* (L). Show students how to create a K-W-L Chart before they begin reading. In the first column, they write notes from their preview and whatever else they already know. During reading, they make notes in the middle column. They will return to the third column after they finish reading.

K-W-L CHART

(WHAT I KNOW)	(WHAT I WANT TO KNOW)	(WHAT I LEARNED)

During Reading

D Read with a Purpose

While reading the lesson on "Population," students write down information and ideas in graphic organizers.

1. K-W-L Chart

The K-W-L Chart gives students a format with which to focus their reading. It summarizes their prior knowledge, their reading purposes, and the main information that they gain from reading.

◀ K-W-L CHART ▶

WHAT I KNOW	WHAT I WANT TO KNOW	WHAT I LEARNED
Population means number of people.	What is population, and why is it an important idea?	This part of the chart is filled out after you've finished reading.
There are patterns of population.	Why is the world's population growing?	
The world's population is 6 billion.	What is the birthrate and death rate?	
Birthrate and death rate are important factors.	Where do most people in the world live?	
Our state has lost population recently.	What is population density?	

2. Concept Map

A Concept Map can help students understand a new term or concept. Students write the concept itself in the middle of the organizer and important details about the concept in boxes around it. Encourage students to list examples, definitions, key notes from the text, and descriptions around the concept.

◀ CONCEPT MAP ▶

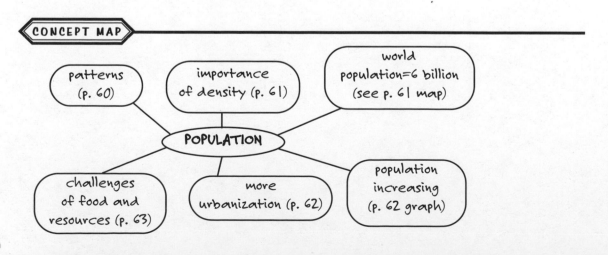

patterns (p. 60)

importance of density (p. 61)

world population=6 billion (see p. 61 map)

POPULATION

challenges of food and resources (p. 63)

more urbanization (p. 62)

population increasing (p. 62 graph)

 Read with a Purpose continued

3. Main Idea Organizer

A Main Idea Organizer lists important ideas and supporting details. Suggest that students create a Main Idea Organizer for each major chapter heading. It creates a mini-summary for each important idea.

◄ MAIN IDEA ORGANIZER ▶ ─────────────────────────

MAIN IDEA: There are patterns to the world's population.

DETAIL #1	DETAIL #2	DETAIL #3
Population distribution means that more people live in some areas than in others.	Population density increases and decreases, depending on food and resources.	Urbanization takes people to the cities.

Other Useful Tools

Point out to students that other reading tools also can be helpful with textbook material. If they're familiar with several reading tools, they can pull out a useful one when they need it.

■ **Thinking Tree**

■ **Cause-Effect Organizer**

■ **Outline**

■ **Classification Notes**

■ **Topic and Theme Organizer**

During Reading

How Geography Textbooks Are Organized

Explain to students that the best way to cope with a large amount of information is to find out how it's organized. Point out that geography textbooks have two main organizational features.

1. Topic Organization

Tell students that geography books often are organized around key concepts and topics. Walk students through the graphics on page 94 to show the topic organization of the "Population" chapter.

TOPIC ORGANIZATION: POPULATION

    I. Population Patterns
        A. population distribution
        B. population density
        C. urbanization
    II. Population Growth
        A. measuring growth
        B. population challenges

2. Use of Graphics

Students may have noticed that geography textbooks use many graphics. Emphasize to them that graphics and text work together to communicate facts. They should pay close attention to the graphics in geography books because the visuals are often trying to make points similar to points made in the text. Encourage students to read the graphics and put them into their own words. A one-sentence summary is often all they need.

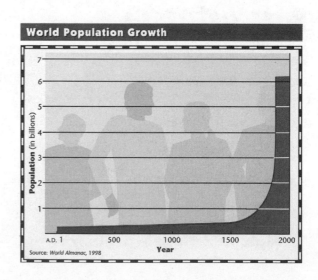

World Population Growth

Population (in billions)

A.D. 1   500   1000   1500   2000
Year

Source: *World Almanac*, 1998

ONE-SENTENCE SUMMARY

Our world's population is exploding!

During Reading

E Connect

Point out to students that when they read, they should react to and connect with what they are learning. Remind students to ask questions and to add their personal thoughts to their note-taking. Help students by telling them to:

■ ask themselves questions
(Why did the population double between 1800 and 1900?)

■ personalize the information they are reading
(What will my life be like in 2010 when the earth's population reaches 7 billion?)

■ think about the meaning of the facts they are reading
(Where will the food come from for 7 billion people?)

■ react emotionally to what they learn
(It must be terrible to live in a place with high population density.)

■ apply the information they read to their own experience
(Why did my school's population jump this year?
Why do people want to move to this area?)

> I dislike getting shots. I hate it, but it prevents disease.

A Visit to the Doctor's Office

> I know people are living longer in the U.S. than ever before.

As more children receive medical care in this South African clinic, the country's death rate will drop.
PLACE: What other factor can reduce a country's death rate?

Growth rates tend to be high in developing countries. Better health care and living conditions have cut the death rate, and people are living longer. Birthrates also may remain high because some cultures favor large families.

Population Challenges Rapid population growth presents many challenges. A growing population requires more food. Since 1950 food production fortunately has increased faster than population on all continents except Africa. Millions of people, however, still suffer **famine**, or lack of food. Another challenge is that expanding populations use up resources more rapidly than stable populations. Some developing countries face shortages of water, housing, and jobs. Others face the threat of AIDS, a worldwide disease that has claimed hundreds of thousands of lives.

> This summer's benefit concert is for famine relief.

After Reading

F Pause and Reflect

After reading, students stop to reflect and consider whether they have met their original reading purposes. The questions under Looking Back can provide a quick, helpful assessment for students to monitor their own reading. Review the list with students.

Looking Back

■ **Can I answer my reading purpose questions?**

■ **Can I identify several key topics and main ideas?**

■ **Do the graphs and maps make sense?**

■ **If there are study questions, can I answer them?**

With the great amount of detail in the lesson, students probably cannot answer all of these questions well. Explain the importance of rereading to pin down key information. Point out that rereading is a natural part of the reading process.

G Reread

Tell students to incorporate rereading into their usual routine when reading a textbook. Emphasize the fact that textbooks have so much information that they will almost always need to go over a reading again for different reasons and in different ways.

Rereading Strategy: ▶ Note-taking

Encourage students to use the strategy of **note-taking** when rereading. Taking notes helps them remember important points in the text, in part because the act of writing something down clarifies the meaning.

Study Cards help students keep track of small chunks of material. Finished Study Cards provide concise information for later review and study. Remind students that they do not need to write complete sentences when they take notes.

After Reading

 G **Reread** continued

STUDY CARDS

Question:
What is population density?

Question:
Where do most people in the world live?

Answer:
the average number of people living in a square mile or square kilometer (page 61)

Answer:
western Europe, eastern and southern Asia, and areas of the United States (page 61)

H Remember

At this point in the reading process, students should make the material in the lesson their own. They will remember the information more readily by using one of the assignments on page 99 in the *Reader's Handbook* or the assignment below.

Creative Assignment: Divide students into groups and invite them to try making up a song or a rhyming poem that uses the most important information from the text. This can be a homework assignment. After writing down the key facts, students can make up the text that ties the facts together. If they choose to write a song, they should use a familiar tune that is "catchy" enough to be memorable. Have the groups memorize their songs or poems and perform them for the class.

Summing Up

Finally, review the lesson with students. Review what they've learned about strategies and tools for reading a geography textbook. Read with students the Summing Up on page 99. Review with them the three goals for this lesson. Discuss which ones they feel they achieved and which ones they need more work on:

1. reading informational writing like that found in geography books

2. using the reading strategy of using graphic organizers

3. understanding how geography textbooks are often organized

Assessment and Application

Use the Quick Assess checklist to evaluate students' abilities to read and understand geography textbooks. Give students the opportunity to apply what they have learned through one of the two activities below. For students who are able to work independently, use one of the suggestions below for independent practice. For guided help with the strategy, use a *Student Applications Book*.

1. Independent Practice

To show that students understand the lesson, ask them to apply the reading strategy of **using graphic organizers** to a chapter of the geography textbook series that the class is using.

Ask students to:

1. Create a Concept Map for the lesson.
2. Create a K-W-L Chart for the lesson.
3. Write a paragraph on the importance of what they learned in the lesson to their daily lives.

2. Student Applications Books

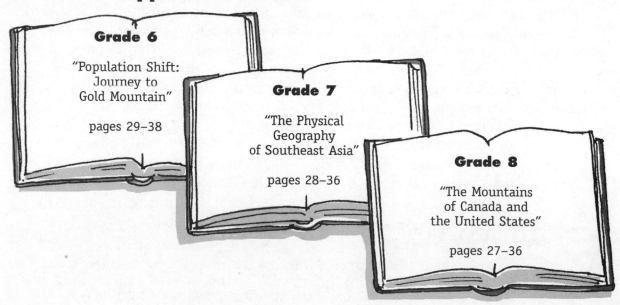

Grade 6

"Population Shift: Journey to Gold Mountain"

pages 29–38

Grade 7

"The Physical Geography of Southeast Asia"

pages 28–36

Grade 8

"The Mountains of Canada and the United States"

pages 27–36

Reading Science

Getting Ready

Goals

Here students read "Exploring the Ocean" from a middle school science book. This lesson will help them learn to:

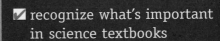

- ☑ recognize what's important in science textbooks
- ☑ apply the strategy of note-taking
- ☑ understand the organization of science textbooks and science writing

Background

Connect the lesson with students' existing knowledge by asking them to:

- ◾ compare reading science with reading other subjects
- ◾ discuss ways of approaching the reading of science
- ◾ describe what they usually find in a science textbook
- ◾ discuss the ways that information is usually organized in a science textbook

Opening Activity

Have students work in partners and use their science textbook to make a list of the features in a chapter, such as titles and headings, boxed information, repeated or boldface words, and graphics. Have students watch for these as they read.

Overview

	Content	Teacher's Guide page	Reader's Handbook page
Selection	"Exploring the Ocean"		102–105
Reading Strategy	Note-taking	76	106, 646
Rereading Strategy	Skimming	82	656
Tool	Thinking Tree	76	107, 115, 680
	Class and Text Notes	77	108, 669
	Key Word Notes	77	109, 673
	Study Cards	78	109, 679
	Process Notes	78	110, 677
	Classification Notes	79	110, 669

Ancillaries

	Grade	Content	Page
Overhead Transparency	6, 7, 8	Previewing Science	Numbers 12 and 13
Lesson Plan Book	8	Reading Science	64–65
Student Applications Book	6	"Earthquakes"	39–47
	7	"Insects of the World"	37–47
	8	"Understanding Light"	37–45
Website		www.greatsource.com/rehand/	
Content Area Guide		This lesson appears in the *Content Area Guide: Science*.	

Before Reading

A Set a Purpose

Ask students to set a purpose before reading "Exploring the Ocean." Focus students on the Setting a Purpose questions on page 101 in the *Reader's Handbook,* and discuss why these are good questions to guide their reading.

Setting a Purpose
- ▪ **What is the subject?**
- ▪ **What is the author saying about it?**

B Preview

The subject of a science chapter often is clearly described in its title and section heads. Ask students to do a quick preview to get a general idea of what they'll be reading. Use the Preview Checklist on page 101 of the *Reader's Handbook* with students. Then walk through what to preview using the Overhead Transparencies.

Preview Checklist

- ✔ the title and headings
- ✔ any boxed items
- ✔ any repeated words or terms set in boldface
- ✔ any photos, maps, graphs, or diagrams
- ✔ the first and last paragraphs

Remind students that a preview should only take a few minutes. They can skip over words to find each item in the Preview Checklist. Explain that using these elements is a way to get a feel for the reading. Once they know the structure, they'll feel more at home when they return to read the chapter in detail.

Point out to students that the annotations in the margin are color-coded, so students can match the annotation with the appropriate bit of highlighted text.

Overhead Transparencies

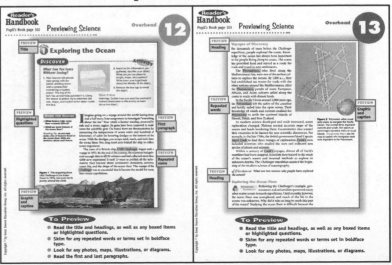

Before Reading

C Plan

At this point in the reading process, have students make a plan for getting information they need from "Exploring the Ocean." Suggest using the strategy of **note-taking**. Talk about some of the reasons this might be the best strategy to use. (One reason is that when students take notes, they have to process the information mentally before writing. This initial, active processing will help them understand and remember the information.)

Reading Strategy: Note-taking

There are many note-taking strategies for writing and organizing important information. As students read, suggest they also use other kinds of note-taking to help them get the information they need from the selection. Students need to be familiar with several kinds of note-taking.

Thinking Tree

For example, a Thinking Tree helps students make notes using the headings from the chapter. The main headings for this chapter would be "Voyages of Discovery" and "Exploring the Ocean Floor." Discuss the general organizer below. Then be sure students know how to begin to make it more specific, as shown in the handbook on page 107.

◀ THINKING TREE

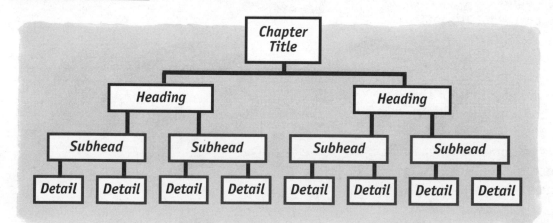

During Reading

D Read with a Purpose

While they are reading "Exploring the Ocean," remind students that going slowly and taking notes is a great way to learn the material. The following note-taking methods suggest a few different approaches.

1. Class and Text Notes

Class and Text Notes are a great way to combine what's said in class with what the student reads in the text. This organizer helps students fuse class and text information by placing them side by side in a clear, two-column format.

CLASS AND TEXT NOTES

EXPLORING THE OCEAN

Class	Notes from the Text
importance of Sonar	Stands for sound navigation and ranging uses sound waves to figure distances invented during World War I
Jacques Cousteau	Invented SCUBA in 1943

2. Key Word Notes

Key Word Notes help students to organize what they read around key concepts. Students list key words or concepts in the left column and write related information in the right column.

KEY WORD NOTES

EXPLORING THE OCEAN

Key Words	Text Notes
exploration methods	Challenger and weighted lines Polynesians and stick charts
important explorers	U.S. Challenger James Cook's 3 voyages

 Read with a Purpose continued

3. Study Cards

Study Cards help students learn key concepts and terms. Students use index cards, writing the term on one side and the note or definition on the other. Study Cards can be used when studying alone or with friends. For those students who don't like using cards, the same style can be easily adapted to a notebook.

STUDY CARDS

CONTINENTAL SHELF

a gently sloping, shallow area of the ocean floor that extends outward from the edge of the continent

4. Process Notes

Process Notes are an excellent way to organize science reading material because science includes many processes and steps. Students can use Process Notes to chart the key developments in ocean exploration.

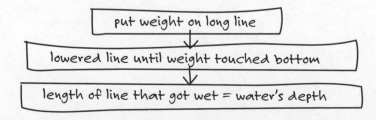

PROCESS NOTES

EARLY MAPPING OF OCEAN FLOOR

put weight on long line

↓

lowered line until weight touched bottom

↓

length of line that got wet = water's depth

Read with a Purpose continued

5. Classification Notes

Classification Notes are a way to classify scientific terms and list their characteristics. This style of note-taking helps to pull together a variety of information into groups and explain the characteristics of each group.

◀ CLASSIFICATION NOTES ▶

EXPLORING	METHOD	FINDING
Phoenicians	wooden boats?	sea routes
Polynesians	?	islands
James Cook	3 voyages	new species
Challenger	sailing ship	50 volumes of Information 4,000 organisms

Other Useful Tools

Point out to students the wide variety of note-taking tools used in the lesson on "Exploring the Ocean." Be sure students understand that they do not have to use all of them. However, it's a good idea to know about all of the tools that are available so that they can pull out the right one when they need it. Here are a few other possibilities to consider.

■ **Timeline or Sequence Notes**

■ **K-W-L Chart**

■ **Web**

■ **Main Idea Organizer**

How Science Textbooks Are **Organized**

Explain to students that reading science textbooks requires that they think like scientists, using three important thought patterns that underlie much of science.

1. Cause-Effect Order

Cause-effect order explains how and why things happen. By charting the initial cause and its related effects, students will get a firmer grasp of concepts from a scientific mindset.

◀ **CAUSE AND EFFECT** ▶

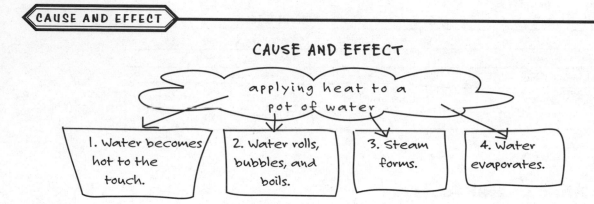

CAUSE AND EFFECT

applying heat to a pot of water

1. Water becomes hot to the touch.

2. Water rolls, bubbles, and boils.

3. Steam forms.

4. Water evaporates.

2. Classification Order

Scientists often group things by related characteristics. Students can create classification lists to keep track of the various groups or types they discover as they read.

◀ **CLASSIFICATION** ▶

GROUP 1	GROUP 2	GROUP 3
jawless fishes	cartilaginous fishes	bony fishes
lampreys	sharks	perch

During Reading

3. Problem-Solution Order

Problem-solution order works on the premise that nature and humans often correct the problems they face. Students can use this approach to understand how and why such scientific patterns develop.

PROBLEM-SOLUTION ORDER

PROBLEM	SOLUTION
Darkness, cold temperatures, and extreme pressure make exploring the ocean floor difficult.	Use sound waves—not humans—to explore the bottom of the ocean.

E Connect

Explain to students that while reading, it's important to interact and make connections with the reading. Relating the reading to their own lives and interests will help them understand and remember what they read. Help students by telling them to:

■ ask themselves questions
(How does this fit with what I already know about the ocean?)

■ think about the meaning of what they learn
(What could scientists do with an accurate map of the ocean floor?)

■ think about someone who would share their interest
(Who might be interested in what I learned about oceanography?)

■ compare what they learn to their own experience
(What could've been "down there" the last time I went fishing?)

Remind students that science is all around them and that, like the reader here, they will learn more by making the effort to connect to what they're reading.

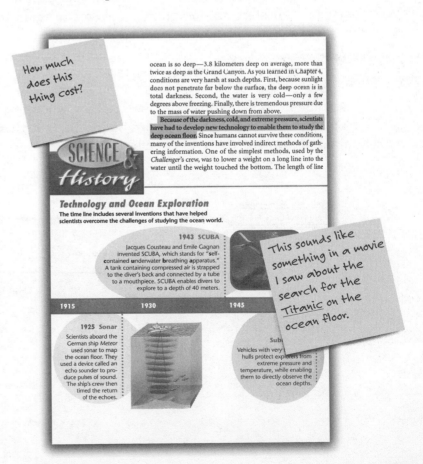

After Reading

F Pause and Reflect

After reading, students stop to consider whether they understand the selection's meaning. Ask students to review their original purpose of identifying the subject and what the author is saying about it.

Looking Back

■ **Do I understand what are the main topics?**

■ **Can I explain the key terms?**

■ **Do the graphics, pictures, and captions make sense?**

Though students probably can answer many of these questions, they also may have new and unanswered questions that came up during their first reading. Encourage them to reread "Exploring the Ocean" to fill in any gaps in their understanding. Tell them that rereading is an important part of the reading process.

G Reread

At this point students need a fresh way to go back into the reading. Have them review the selection, looking for answers to their questions but using a new strategy.

Rereading Strategy: Skimming

Encourage students to try a new strategy when rereading. **Skimming** offers students a way to focus on the key terms and ideas that they'd like to clarify. While students skim, encourage them to complete a Thinking Tree to keep track of the main ideas and relationships in the selection.

THINKING TREE

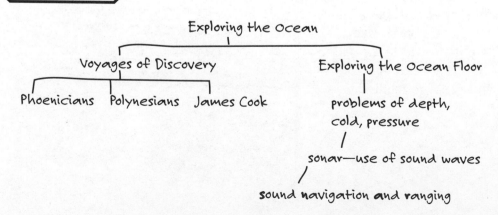

After Reading

H Remember

At this point, students need to do something that will help them to remember what they've learned. Walk students through the activities shown on pages 115–116 of the *Reader's Handbook* or use the assignment below.

Creative Assignment: Encourage students to learn more about the subject of this lesson through Internet research. After the class creates a list of appropriate search words and phrases, divide them into small groups. Ask each group to try two or three different search engines to see which ones provide the most promising links and site listings. (To find a list of search engines, search for "search engines" or consult http://www.mediametrix.com for a list of those that are most popular.) Tell students to look for two or three websites with good information that are sponsored by scientific organizations, institutions, or museums across the world. Ask students to print out site pages to show the class.

Summing Up

Finally, review the lesson with students. Focus on everything they've learned about strategies and tools for reading a science textbook. Read with students the Summing Up (on page 116 in the handbook). Go over with students the three goals for this lesson. Discuss which ones they feel they achieved and which ones they feel they need more work on:

1. recognizing what's important in science textbooks

2. applying the strategy of note-taking

3. understanding the organization of science textbooks and science writing

Assessment and Application

Use the Quick Assess checklist to evaluate students' abilities to read and understand science. Give students the opportunity to apply what they have learned through one of the two activities below. For students who are comfortable with the reading process and strategy, use one of the independent practice suggestions below. For guided help with the strategy, use a *Student Applications Book*.

1. Independent Practice

To show that students understand the lesson, ask them to apply the reading strategy of **note-taking** to another chapter of the science textbook series that the class is using.

Ask students to:

1. Create a Thinking Tree for the chapter.

2. Write Key Word Notes or Study Cards for the material.

3. Write a paragraph about the importance of what they learned in the lesson to their daily lives.

2. Student Applications Books

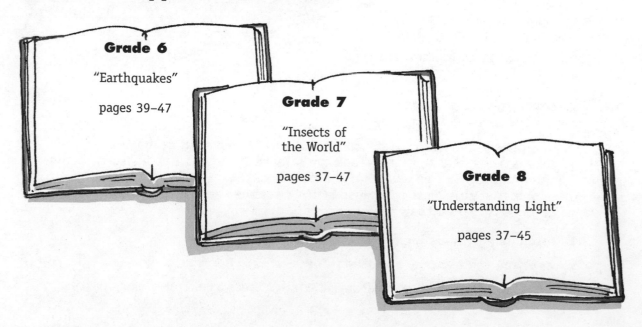

Grade 6

"Earthquakes"

pages 39–47

Grade 7

"Insects of the World"

pages 37–47

Grade 8

"Understanding Light"

pages 37–45

Reading Math

Getting Ready

Goals

Here students read a mathematics lesson called "Variables and Equations." This lesson will help them learn to:

- ☑ read about math and math concepts
- ☑ use the strategy of visualizing and thinking aloud
- ☑ understand the organization of math textbooks

Background

Connect the lesson with students' existing knowledge by asking them to:

- ■ compare reading math with reading other subjects
- ■ discuss ways of approaching the reading of math
- ■ describe what they usually find in a math textbook
- ■ discuss the ways that information usually is organized in a math textbook

Opening Activity

Talk about the common features of most math textbooks, such as titles and headings, boxed information, repeated or boldface words, and graphics. Students should watch for these as they read.

Lesson Resources

Overview

	Content	Teacher's Guide page	Reader's Handbook page
Selection	"Variables and Equations"		120–121
Reading Strategy	Visualizing and Thinking Aloud	88	125–126, 664–665
Rereading Strategy	Note-taking	92	129–130, 646
Tool	Key Word Notes	92	130, 673

Ancillaries

	Grade	Content	Page
Overhead Transparency	6, 7, 8	Previewing Math	Numbers 14 and 15
Lesson Plan Book	7 8	Reading Math Reading Math	74 74
Student Applications Book	6 7 8	"Estimation and Mental Math" "Order of Operations" "Percents, Fractions, and Decimals"	49–57 48–56 46–53
Website		www.greatsource.com/rehand/	
Content Area Guide		This lesson appears in the *Content Area Guide: Math.*	

Before Reading

A Set a Purpose

Before reading the lesson, ask students to set a purpose for reading "Variables and Equations." Focus students on the Setting a Purpose question on page 118 in the *Reader's Handbook,* and discuss why this is a good question to guide their reading.

Setting a Purpose

■ **What's important about variables and equations?**

B Preview

Ask students to preview "Variables and Equations" to get a general idea of what they'll be reading. Use the Preview Checklist on page 119 in the *Reader's Handbook* with students. Then walk through what to preview using the Overhead Visuals.

Point out each item in the Preview Checklist. Suggest to students that they touch items on the page as they scan for information.

Preview Checklist

✓ any headings and highlighted terms

✓ any boxed items

✓ any words in boldface

✓ any models, diagrams, or examples

✓ the introductory paragraph

Overhead Visuals

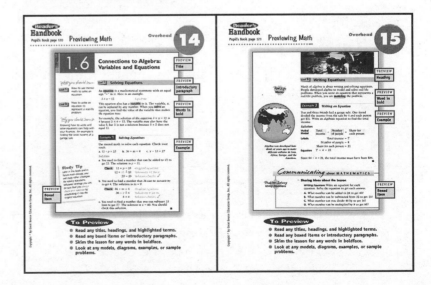

Before Reading

C Plan

Review what students found during their preview of the lesson. Go over the Tips for Working with a Partner described on page 122 in the *Reader's Handbook*. Now students should make a plan for getting information about "Variables and Equations." Suggest the strategy of **visualizing and thinking aloud** as a great approach to learning math. Talk about some of the reasons this might be the best strategy to use. (One reason is that it is easier to work with abstract objects when they are pictured as real objects.)

Reading Strategy: Visualizing and Thinking Aloud

Visualizing can help students "see" an abstract problem, while thinking aloud can help them keep track of how they work through it.

Visualizing

Visualizing a math problem helps to translate abstract numbers and concepts into a format that makes sense.

◄ VISUALIZING ►

$$T \div 4 = 21$$

Thinking Aloud

When thinking aloud, students quietly "talk themselves through" a problem in a logical manner.

◄ THINK ALOUD ►

$\underline{T}$ is the variable. I need to figure out what that is.

The next part is the sign for division ($\div$).

So, I divide $\underline{T}$ by 4 to get the answer 21.

If something ($\underline{T}$) divided by 4 equals 21, then 4 times 21 equals $\underline{T}$.

Imagine $\underline{T}$ has 4 parts. Each is 21.

When you add them up, you get 84. That means $\underline{T}$ = 84.

During Reading

D Read with a Purpose

While reading "Variables and Equations," students should use the four-step problem-solving plan outlined on page 124 in the handbook and record their ideas by drawing a sketch or thinking aloud.

Make a Sketch

Students can visualize math problems by drawing familiar objects like the hamburgers or the triangle below. By doing so, they make a strange, vague thing more familiar and easier to understand. Explain to students how some of us learn better by seeing, others of us by touching or feeling, and still others by hearing.

VISUALIZING

$12 \div 3 = x$

$x = 4$

An equilateral triangle is a triangle whose sides are all the same length.

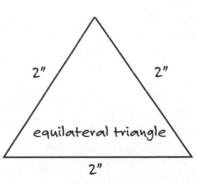

2"   2"

equilateral triangle

2"

Talk Through a Problem

Tell students that thinking aloud gives them the ability to hear themselves think and put problems into their own words. Students will feel more confident when they work through a problem in their own logical manner. Emphasize that there are different ways to talk through a problem.

THINK ALOUD

$36 \div \underline{m} = 4$

This means that 36 divided by some number equals 4. I know that I need to put the variable, $\underline{m}$, alone on one side of the equation. What if I divided 36 by 4? That would be 9.

Now, will 9 work as the answer for $\underline{m}$?

Yes, $36 \div 9$ does equal 4.

During Reading

How Math Textbooks Are Organized

As students read, understanding how math textbooks are organized can help them to comprehend what they're reading and know what to expect.

Introduce students to the organizational patterns of a math chapter, which often (but not always) has four different elements. Remind students not to skip over the sample problems and drawings, graphs, or diagrams.

1. **Opening Explanation**
2. **Sample Problems**
3. **Drawings, Graphs, or Diagrams**
4. **Exercises**

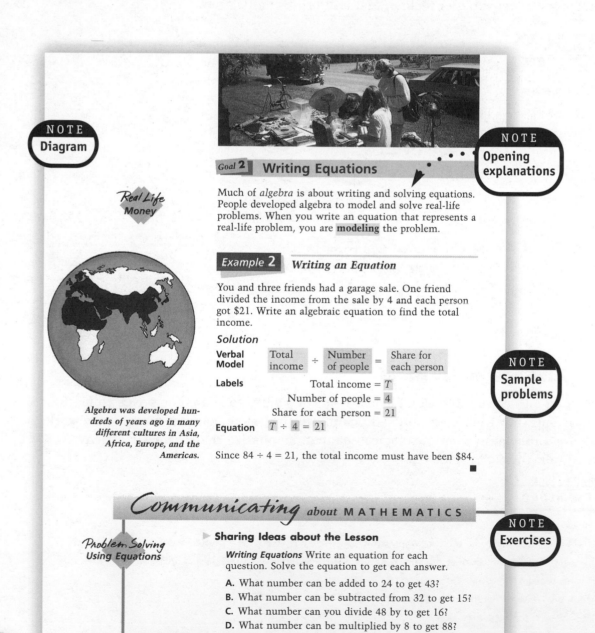

NOTE
Diagram

Real Life **Money**

Algebra was developed hundreds of years ago in many different cultures in Asia, Africa, Europe, and the Americas.

Problem Solving Using Equations

NOTE
Opening explanations

Goal **2** **Writing Equations**

Much of *algebra* is about writing and solving equations. People developed algebra to model and solve real-life problems. When you write an equation that represents a real-life problem, you are **modeling** the problem.

Example **2** **Writing an Equation**

You and three friends had a garage sale. One friend divided the income from the sale by 4 and each person got $21. Write an algebraic equation to find the total income.

Solution

NOTE
Sample problems

Verbal Model	Total income	÷	Number of people	=	Share for each person

Labels
Total income = T
Number of people = 4
Share for each person = 21

Equation $T \div 4 = 21$

Since $84 \div 4 = 21$, the total income must have been $84. ■

Communicating *about* MATHEMATICS

▶ **Sharing Ideas about the Lesson**

NOTE
Exercises

Writing Equations Write an equation for each question. Solve the equation to get each answer.

A. What number can be added to 24 to get 43?
B. What number can be subtracted from 32 to get 15?
C. What number can you divide 48 by to get 16?
D. What number can be multiplied by 8 to get 88?

Connect

Explain to students that, while reading, it's important to interact and make connections with a math lesson. Understanding the importance of math in their lives can help motivate students. Remind them of how often they use math to schedule their day, handle their money, or predict their overall grades.

THINK ALOUD

PROBLEM	CONNECTION
What number can be subtracted from 32 to get 15?	The score in the basketball game was something like that—about 32 to 15. How much did the other team win by?

Help students by telling them to:

■ ask themselves questions
(Why should math be important to me?)

■ think about the meaning of what they learn
(How could I use this lesson in my life?)

■ think about someone who would share this interest
(Who would be a good math study partner?)

■ compare what they learn to their own experience
(How do I use math, and how can I get better at it?)

Remind students that math has many everyday uses and that they will learn more if they take the time to connect the concept to something in their own lives.

After Reading

F Pause and Reflect

After reading, help students go back and review their original purpose-setting question, "What's important about variables and equations?"

> **Looking Back**
> ■ Do I understand the key vocabulary?
> ■ Can I explain what each term means?
> ■ Do I understand the sample problems?
> ■ Can I take what I learned and use it to solve problems that appear on sample exercises or tests?

Because of the complexity of math textbooks, students will probably reread a chapter more than once. Help students understand that rereading is a good way to learn terms and how to solve problems.

G Reread

Have students review the selection, looking for key vocabulary and examples but using a new strategy.

Rereading Strategy: Note-taking

Encourage students to use note-taking when they return to reread the material. **Note-taking** gives students a way to record information that they aren't particularly clear on. It also provides a format for jotting down any new questions that might arise during rereading. Suggest students follow the note-taking style below. Have students suggest other key terms or concepts they might add.

KEY WORD NOTES

VARIABLES AND EQUATIONS

KEY TERMS	EXAMPLES
Equation—mathematical statement that has an equal sign in it	$8 \times 3 = 24$
Variable—symbol or letter that can stand for a quantity that changes	$3 \times \underline{N} = 12$ (N is the variable)
Modeling—writing an equation that shows a real-life problem	(number of lunches) $\times$ ($2.00 per lunch) = total amount due to cafeteria Equation: $18 \times \$2.00 = \$36.00$

Remember

At this point in the reading, students need to do something that will help them to remember what they've learned. Encourage them to try the activities described on page 130 in the *Reader's Handbook* or the creative assignment suggested below.

Creative Assignment: Invite students to teach one problem from this lesson to a friend or family member, using the reading strategies and tools suggested. Have students report back to the class on their results, including any especially successful techniques they discovered.

Summing Up

Finally, review the lesson with students. Focus on everything they have learned about strategies and tools for reading. Read with students the Summing Up (on page 131 in the handbook). Go over with students the three goals for this lesson. Discuss which ones they feel they achieved and which ones they feel they need more work on:

1. understanding abstract concepts and operations

2. using the strategy of visualizing and thinking aloud

3. understanding the organization of math textbooks

Assessment and Application

Use the Quick Assess checklist to evaluate students' abilities to read and understand math. Give students the opportunity to apply what they have learned through one of the two activities below. For students who are comfortable with the reading process and strategy, use one of the independent practice suggestions. For guided help with the strategy, use a *Student Applications Book*.

1. Independent Practice

Ask students to apply the reading strategy of **visualizing and thinking aloud** to another lesson from the math textbook series that the class is using.

Ask students to:

1. Create a complete sketch or drawing of how they visualize one problem.

2. Write down their "thinking aloud" in three to five steps about how to solve one problem.

3. Write a paragraph about how concepts in this math lesson can be used in everyday life.

Quick Assess

Can students

- ☑ describe the four-step plan for solving math problems?
- ☑ name three things to look for when they preview?
- ☑ name and explain one strategy?
- ☑ make a sketch that clarifies a math problem?
- ☑ identify two common features of most math chapters?

2. Student Applications Books

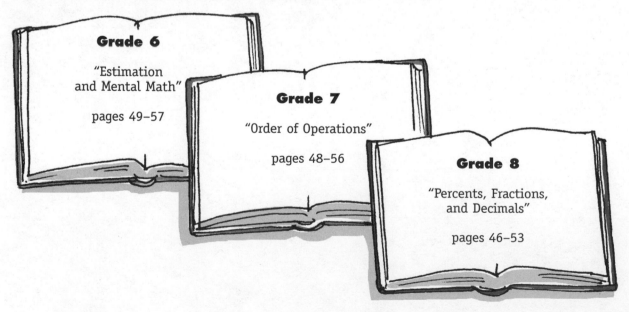

Grade 6

"Estimation and Mental Math"

pages 49–57

Grade 7

"Order of Operations"

pages 48–56

Grade 8

"Percents, Fractions, and Decimals"

pages 46–53

Focus on Science Concepts

Goals

Here students focus on science concepts—the "big ideas" they read about in science—by reading the excerpt "Cell Growth and Division" from a textbook. This lesson will help students learn to:

☑ use tools that can help them read about and understand science concepts

☑ remember and keep track of science terms

Background

Connect this lesson with students' existing knowledge by asking them to:

■ define the terms *concept* and *process*

■ list examples of scientific concepts and processes with which they're familiar

■ give reasons why it's important to understand science concepts and processes

Overview

	Content	Teacher's Guide page	Reader's Handbook page
Selection	"Cell Growth and Division"		133-136
Reading Strategy	Using Graphic Organizers	97	139-140, 662
Tool	Concept Map	97	137, 138, 670
	Thinking Tree	97	139, 680
	Process Notes	97	140, 677
	Study Cards	97	140, 679

Ancillaries

	Grade	Content	Page
Lesson Plan Book	8	Reading Science	65
Student Applications Book	6	Photosynthesis	58–59
	7	Nitrogen Cycle	57–58
	8	Oxygen Cycle	54–55
Website		www.greatsource.com/rehand/	
Content Area Guide		This lesson appears in the *Content Area Guide: Science*.	

Before Reading

Point out that scientific concepts often involve two things: a process or series of steps and a number of terms that students will need to remember. Ask them to preview the reading to get a basic overview. Direct students to the Preview Checklist and then to the reading itself. When you read about science, look for key information in the following areas:

Preview Checklist

■ **the title and headings**

■ **the steps in the process**

■ **any diagrams, photos, or graphics and their captions**

■ **any key words in boldface or that are repeated**

■ **the first and last paragraphs**

Help students skim through the reading, looking for basic information about processes and key terms involved in cell division. Because the subject matter is complex, stress that students need to keep track of information they are learning. Help them create a Concept Map like the one on page 137.

Concept Map

Since students will be dealing with scientific concepts, this useful tool will help them "pull together" key terms, stages, and characteristics relating to a concept, as indicated on page 137. Stress that a Concept Map is easy to use and will help them to remember more. Encourage students to put examples, definitions, and descriptions in the Concept Map.

During Reading

As students read, they can see how graphic organizers help them to understand science concepts and processes.

Concept Map

Point out the completed Concept Map shown on page 138. Read through it with students. Ask them what the specific stages are and what is some other important related information. Though this tool helps to pull together terms and ideas, explain that it is often not enough to gather all the information they need from a science reading.

During Reading

CONCEPT MAP

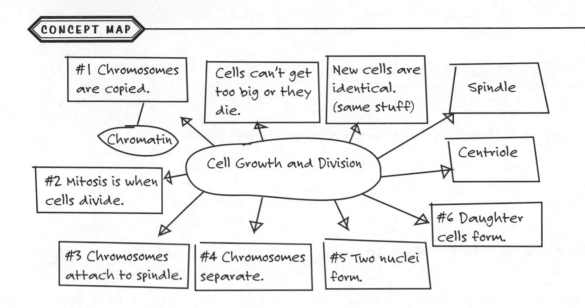

#1 Chromosomes are copied.

Cells can't get too big or they die.

New cells are identical. (same stuff)

Spindle

Chromatin

Cell Growth and Division

Centriole

#2 Mitosis is when cells divide.

#6 Daughter cells form.

#3 Chromosomes attach to spindle.

#4 Chromosomes separate.

#5 Two nuclei form.

Reading Strategy: Using Graphic Organizers

Graphic organizers are "word pictures" that help students to "see" ideas. Go over the details about this key strategy with students. Emphasize that there are many graphic organizers they can use and that it's important to be familiar with as many of them as possible, since different ones are useful for different types of readings.

1. Thinking Tree

Explain the value of a Thinking Tree when students are not able to predict what a concept is or where it will lead. Discuss the completed Thinking Tree on page 139. It branches off as necessary to describe the ideas in the chapter.

2. Process Notes

Show students the Process Notes on page 140 and explain how this organizer helps in keeping track of the steps and their order in a process like cell division. Encourage students to use this organizer any time they read about a process.

3. Study Cards

Direct students to the finished Study Cards shown on page 140. Explain their usefulness in helping students to memorize key words. Tell students these are especially useful when they study in groups because it makes it easy to share notes and test one another.

After Reading

After reading, students need to think about what they have learned. Because of the complexity of science terms, processes, and science writing in general, point out to students that a second, careful reading usually is necessary.

Here are three ways for students to deepen their grasp of science concepts and processes they encounter in their reading.

1. Look at Your Notes and Organizers

Have students go back over the reading to make sure their notes and organizers accurately reflect the terms, processes, and other key information in the chapter. Suggest that students revise or add to their notes when rereading.

2. Create a Study Guide

Ask students to come up with information from the chapter on which they think they will be tested. Being able to predict and answer questions based on headings and key terms will help them remember more and be better prepared for assignments and tests.

STUDY GUIDE

1. How would you describe the concept of cell division?

2. What are the key stages?

3. What does the term <u>mitosis</u> mean?

4. What does the term <u>daughter cell</u> mean?

3. Redraw or Retell Information

Help students demonstrate their understanding by having them explain the process of cell division in their own words in a paragraph or redraw the process graphically, as shown on page 142. Ask students what other things they could draw. They may suggest things such as a flower, a happy face, or a football.

Summing Up

Finally, point out and discuss the Summing Up section. Review all that students have learned about how to read science concepts and processes. Then have students tell what they learned in their own words.

Assessment and Application

Use the Quick Assess checklist to evaluate students' abilities to read and understand science concepts. Give students the opportunity to apply what they have learned through one of the two activities below. For students who are able to work independently, use the suggestion below. For guided help with the strategy, use a *Student Applications Book.*

1. Independent Practice

Ask students to apply the reading strategy and tools they just learned to the terms and process of another concept in their science text.

2. Student Applications Books

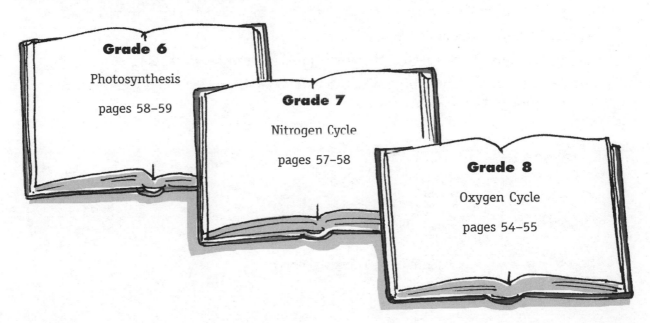

Grade 6

Photosynthesis

pages 58–59

Grade 7

Nitrogen Cycle

pages 57–58

Grade 8

Oxygen Cycle

pages 54–55

Quick Assess

Can students

☑ name three things to look for when they preview?

☑ name and explain one strategy?

☑ create and use a reading tool to keep track of steps in a process?

☑ create and use a reading tool to help remember key terms?

Focus on Word Problems

Goals

Here students focus on word problems—the often tricky and troubling mathematical problems that are written out in words. As they read and analyze a number of sample word problems, this lesson will help students learn to:

- ☑ follow a four-step plan when solving word problems
- ☑ visualize what the problem is asking
- ☑ recognize the basic organization of word problems

Background

Introduce the topic of word problems by either asking students what they know about them or writing one on the board. Students will know them as interesting, yet challenging, mathematical puzzles that are often tricky to answer. Continue to explore students' existing knowledge of word problems by asking them to:

- ▓ create short and simple word problems as examples
- ▓ discuss some of the reasons that word problems can be difficult to solve
- ▓ talk about how they approach the solving of word problems and whether these techniques work or don't work

Overview

	Content	Teacher's Guide page	Reader's Handbook page
Selection	Word Problems		145, 147–149, 151–153
Reading Strategy	Visualizing and Thinking Aloud	101-102	145, 664

Ancillaries

	Grade	Content	Page
Lesson Plan Book	7	Focus on Word Problems	75
Student Applications Book	6	Water Park Problem	60-61
	7	School Dance Problem	59–60
	8	Donut Sale Problem	56–57
Website		www.greatsource.com/rehand/	
Content Area Guide		This lesson appears in the *Content Area Guide: Math*	

100

Before Reading

Help students to see the importance of reading word problems slowly and carefully. Explain that they are about to learn the Four-Step Plan for Word Problems that can help them solve problems more effectively.

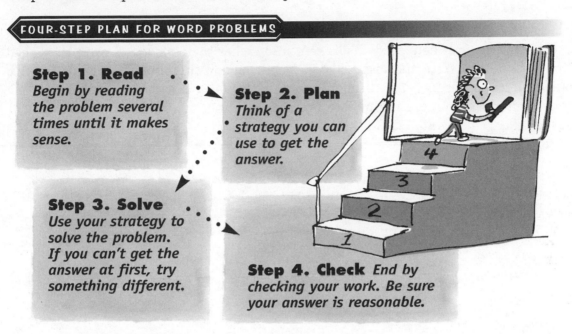

FOUR-STEP PLAN FOR WORD PROBLEMS

Step 1. Read
Begin by reading the problem several times until it makes sense.

Step 2. Plan
Think of a strategy you can use to get the answer.

Step 3. Solve
Use your strategy to solve the problem. If you can't get the answer at first, try something different.

Step 4. Check *End by checking your work. Be sure your answer is reasonable.*

Walk students through the steps of this plan, as shown on page 144. Ask students to read the sample problem on page 145. Point out that noting the topic, the given, and the unknown will increase their chances of answering the problem correctly.

EXAMPLE

■ Ticket sales for this year's annual concert at Riverside Stadium were $1,050,000. The sponsor predicts next year's ticket sales will be 40% more than they were this year. How much does the sponsor think ticket sales will be next year?

NOTES

TOPIC: ticket sales
GIVEN: last year's total:
$1,050,000
Prediction: 40% more
TO FIND: next year's
ticket sales

Help students recognize the importance of choosing a strategy for solving word problems, such as **visualizing and thinking aloud**.

Reading Strategy: Visualizing and Thinking Aloud

This strategy involves sketching a picture to clarify the problem and then talking through a process to solve it.

During Reading

As students read, they continue using the Four-Step Plan to solve word problems.

Thinking Aloud

Point out the value of thinking aloud when trying to solve a puzzling problem. Explain that this strategy can help students to zero in on what they know and what they need to find out. Demonstrate and discuss how visualizing and thinking aloud helps to solve the problem on pages 145–146. Students may think that a drawing or think aloud wastes time. Help them see the importance of taking time to find the right answer.

◀ **THINK ALOUD** ▶────────────────────────

The sponsor thinks sales will be 40% higher. So, take the sales and put 40% more with it. That would be 100% of sales in Year 1 plus 40%, or 100% + 40% = 140%. That's the same as 1.4, if you write 140% as a decimal.

So,

$1,050,000 × 1.40 = Z
Z = next year's sales

Checking Your Work

Finding another way to solve the problem will help confirm students' answers. Go over the Checking Your Work graphic on page 146.

◀ **CHECKING YOUR WORK** ▶──────────────────

$1,050,000 × 1.40 = $1,470,000

or

$1,050,000 + 420,000 = $1,470,000
Year 1 sales + 40% more = Year 2 sales

How Word Problems Are Organized

Being able to see the two word problem characteristics shown on page 147 can help students understand and solve problems more easily.

Discuss the points under Order of Numbers, Use of Words, Making Sense of Sentences, and Making Sense of Diagrams. Point out that part of what makes word problems tricky is that the numbers are often presented in a mixed-up order.

Encourage students to construct equations that suit the problem. Highlight the fact that the word *is* in word problems means "is equal to" and that *of* means "multiplied by."

Introduce and discuss each of the Problem-Solving Tips presented on page 150 and then work with students on applying them to word problems.

1. Guess, Check, and Revise

Walk students through the sample problem and solution on page 151. Be sure that students can explain this process in their own words. To make a guess, students should think about a range of reasonable answers.

2. Work Backward

Discuss this useful technique, using the example and process shown on page 152. The key is to solve the big problem first and then work backward to find the answer to one of its pieces, in this case, a slice of pizza.

3. Use Simpler Numbers

Introduce this tip as explained on page 153. With students, round some difficult numbers into easy numbers. Point out that this technique can help to predict the approximate answer for the problem.

4. Work with a Partner

Encourage students to work with partners to check and reinforce their word problem answers, approaches, and equations. Explain the brief guidelines for this approach on page 154.

Summing Up

To conclude the lesson, go over the Summing Up section. Discuss what students have learned about reading word problems and the different steps and techniques involved in solving them. Then ask students to tell what they learned in their own words.

Assessment and Application

Use the Quick Assess checklist to evaluate students' abilities to read and understand word problems. Give students the opportunity to apply what they have learned through one of the two activities below. For students who are able to work on their own, use the suggestion for independent practice. For guided help with the strategy, use a *Student Applications Book*.

1. Independent Practice

Photocopy a number of word problems from a level-appropriate mathematics textbook, preferably enough problems for each member of the class to have one. Cut up the sheets into separate problems and put these in a hat. Ask students to apply the reading strategies and tips they learned to the word problem they pull from the hat. Check, collect, and repeat. To make the activity more fun, group students in teams and time how long it takes for teams to solve their problems.

2. Student Applications Books

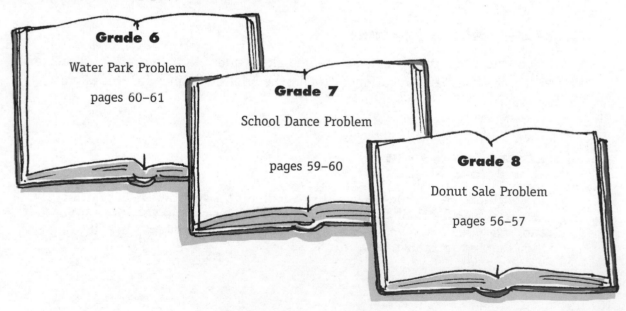

Grade 6

Water Park Problem

pages 60–61

Grade 7

School Dance Problem

pages 59–60

Grade 8

Donut Sale Problem

pages 56–57

Elements of Textbooks

The terms or elements in this section are commonly found in textbooks. Each one is shown in an example, described, and defined.

Use this section to introduce these terms to students so that they will learn what they are, how to find them, and what their overall purposes are in a textbook.

Element	Teacher's Guide page	Reader's Handbook page
Boldface Terms	106	156
Charts	106–107	157
Glossary	107–108	158
Graphs	108–109	159
Headings and Titles	109	160
Index	110	162
Maps	110–111	163
Photos and Illustrations	111–112	165
Preview	112	166
Table of Contents	113	168

Also see *Lesson Plan Book 6* (page 84),
Lesson Plan Book 7 (page 84),
and *Lesson Plan Book 8* (page 75).

Boldface Terms

Set Goal

Help students recognize **boldface terms** and understand that boldface type draws attention to what is important in a text.

Teach and Discuss

Read the **Example** on page 156 of the handbook with students. Emphasize that this example has boldface type to identify key names, events, and terms in the passage. Ask students to point out what they notice about the example. Responses will most likely be similar to these:

■ Boldface type is a guide to what's important in the section.

■ Boldface helps students know what to study for tests.

■ Grouping of boldface terms helps them to remember the material.

Now go through the key points in the **Description** with students. **Emphasize that students should pay attention to and take notes on terms, names, and events that are in boldface because they represent the most important information in the section.**

Check Understanding

Have students review the **Definition** on page 156. Check their comprehension by having students turn to a page in a textbook and find the use of boldface. Have them address questions like these:

■ What elements are in boldface type?

■ Why do you think these particular elements are in boldface?

■ How would reading and studying this page be different if key terms were not in boldface in this text?

Charts

Set Goal

Help students recognize charts and understand that charts are resources intended to present information, often with pictures and symbols.

Teach and Discuss

Look over the charts in the **Example** on page 157 with students. Point out that the first chart lists data and the second chart compares two things. Explain that the main point of the first chart is to show information about the slave era while the second makes comparisons between Jeffersonian and Jacksonian democracy. Encourage students to describe what they notice about the two charts. They are likely to observe the following:

■ Charts list information in rows and columns.

■ Charts present a lot of facts.

■ Seeing information presented in this way makes analyzing the information easier.

■ Charts are colorful and can be fun to read.

Now read through the major points in the **Description** with students. **Emphasize that students should figure out the point of a chart and then use it as a resource for specific information.**

Check Understanding

Ask students to review the **Definition** on page 157. Broaden students' understanding by having them point out charts in textbooks or magazines that give information, show processes, or make comparisons. Have them answer questions like these:

■ What elements do most charts have?

■ How do you figure out the main point of a chart?

■ What specific information is of particular interest to you in these charts? Why?

Glossary

Set Goal

Guide students in finding glossaries in their books and understanding that a glossary is a handy textbook tool that can help them understand the specialized vocabulary of a subject.

Teach and Discuss

Go over the glossary **Example** on page 158 with students. Explain that this example lists key terms in boldface type and in alphabetical order. It provides definitions or descriptions for students to study. Have students point out what they notice about the sample glossary, such as the following:

■ This glossary looks like a dictionary.

■ A glossary is convenient for looking up terms, learning their meanings, and taking notes.

■ Page numbers in the entries tell where in the book the terms are used.

Now take students through the major points in the **Description. Stress that the glossary helps students master the specialized language of the subject they are studying.**

Check Understanding

Review the **Definition** on page 158 with students. Check their comprehension by having students look through the glossary of one of their textbooks. To make the task more fun, you might turn the activity into a scavenger hunt. Have them answer questions like these:

■ What are the parts of a glossary entry?

■ When would you use a glossary instead of a dictionary?

■ How does this tool help you in your study?

■ Where else in your book might you find a particular term?

Graphs

Set Goal

Help students to recognize graphs and understand that they present information with lines, pictures, and symbols instead of words.

Teach and Discuss

Look over with students the sample graphs on page 159. Point out how the **Example** makes specific points about the U.S. economy during the New Deal era. Students will likely notice the following:

■ It is important to read the title and the vertical and horizontal axes to understand what the graphs are about.

■ The graphs make comparisons based on time. The labels on the horizontal axes are all years.

■ It's not always easy to decide what point is being made.

Now go over the major points in the **Description** with students. **Stress to students that they need to be able not only to read graphs but also to summarize the "idea" in the graph.**

Check Understanding

Ask students to review the **Definition** on page 159. Gauge their comprehension by having students look over another graph from one of their textbooks. Have them answer questions like these:

■ What is this graph about?

■ What is the main point being expressed in the graph?

■ Could you explain what this graph is saying in a single sentence?

Headings and Titles

Set Goal

Help students recognize the headings in a textbook and understand that headings point to which topics will be covered.

Teach and Discuss

Read and discuss with students the **Example** on page 160. Point out that this example shows a series of headings within a unit, from the broadest unit heading for the topic ("Three Worlds Meet") to the narrowest heading ("The First People in America"). Students will probably observe the following:

■ Headings are a good, general guide to the subject matter.

■ Heading size goes from large to small depending on the heading's importance.

■ Headings help organize information.

Now go over the key points and inverted triangular charts in the **Description** with students. **Students should understand that headings display the main points or ideas in a topic area and go from the most important information (largest type) to the least important (smallest type).**

Check Understanding

Read the **Definition** on page 161 with students. To check their comprehension, have students create their own inverted triangular charts based on a unit in one of their textbooks. Encourage them to answer questions like these:

■ In what ways do the headings relate to each other?

■ How might understanding this heading format help you to study better?

Index

Set Goal

Help students to find indexes and understand that they are alphabetical listings of where important ideas, terms, definitions, and names can be found in a book.

Teach and Discuss

Look over the **Example** on page 162 with students. Explain that indexes like this one present entries in alphabetical order for easy referencing. Point out that they group related terms (subentries) under major topics (main entries), as in "abolition of slavery." Call upon students to point out what they notice in the example. Be sure students understand that an *i* before the page number (as in the Bella Abzug entry) stands for illustration. Students might notice the following:

■ Indexes are like glossaries, but with less information.

■ People are listed by their last names.

Now read and discuss the key points made in the **Description** with students. **Stress that the index is a quick and easy search tool intended to help them find important terms, people, places, and events in a textbook.**

Check Understanding

Review the **Definition** on page 162 with students. Tap their understanding of this textbook element by having them use the index of one of their textbooks to look up specific information. To make this activity more interesting, put students in teams and time how long it takes them to find five to ten items. Have them answer questions like these:

■ On what page is _____? On what other pages can it be found? Why?

■ What are the subentries under _____? Why are they grouped this way?

Maps

Set Goal

Guide students in recognizing maps and understanding that maps present and summarize information in terms of *where* something is located.

Teach and Discuss

Closely read with students the **Example** map, "The War of 1812," on page 163. Emphasize that this map has symbols, labels, a map legend, a map scale, and so on to show important locations during the War of 1812. Have students point out what they notice about the example. Likely responses include these:

■ Reading maps can be interesting and even fun.

■ Seeing where battles happened on a map helps in understanding the war.

■ The map legend and scale are guides to understanding the map.

Now walk students through the major points made in the **Description**. **Emphasize that students should read map titles, labels, keys, legends, and scales to fully understand what the map is showing.**

Check Understanding

Have students review the **Definition** on page 164. To check their understanding, have students read another map from their history textbooks, looking for answers to these questions:

■ What are the main parts of this map? Point out each one.

■ What is the purpose of this map?

■ What information can you find on this map? Give examples.

Photos and Illustrations

Set Goal

Help students identify photos and illustrations and understand that they serve as an interesting preview of a topic and make important points about what is in a chapter.

Teach and Discuss

Look over and discuss with students the sample photo on page 165. Explain that the **Example** provides a visual way to help make a point. Ask students what they notice about the example. Students probably will report the following:

■ The photo has a caption that explains what it is about.

■ The students in the photo look lifeless and unhappy.

Now read and discuss with students the key points made in the **Description**. Encourage students to ask themselves why that photo or illustration was selected to be used on that particular page. **Because captions explain why a picture or illustration is being used in the text, it is important to read them as guides to the visuals.**

Check Understanding

Read with students the **Definition** on page 165. To demonstrate their understanding, ask students to look through their books for photos and illustrations with captions. Choose some as examples and ask students to answer questions like these:

■ What point is this photo or illustration trying to make?

■ How does the caption contribute to that point?

■ How does the photo or illustration itself contribute to that point?

■ In what ways does this visual add to the learning experience?

Preview

Set Goal

Help students to recognize a chapter preview and understand that it summarizes the most important information in the chapter.

Teach and Discuss

Read and discuss with students the **Example** chapter previews on pages 166–167. Point out the different types of previews that are possible. Go through each of these in detail and explain why the preview format is used. Explain that previews are brief yet include very important basic information. Have students comment on what they notice about the examples. They may respond with the following:

■ The information gives a "big picture" of the chapter.

■ The illustrations and timeline provide an interesting orientation to the material.

■ Previews seem to indicate what key information students will be responsible for.

Now go over and discuss with students the major points in the **Description**. **Help students see that the "warm-up" a preview provides can be an indispensable tool in their study and understanding of a textbook.**

Check Understanding

Review with students the **Definition** on page 167. Gauge understanding by having students examine one of their textbooks for previews. Have them trace the key ideas, titles, or terms in the preview. Have students answer questions like these:

■ Which elements are part of the preview?

■ What does this preview tell you about the contents of the chapter?

Table of Contents

Set Goal

Help students recognize a table of contents in a textbook and understand that it can serve as a very useful overview or study outline for key topics in the book.

Teach and Discuss

Look over and discuss with students the **Example** table of contents on page 168. Point out the structure—the units, chapter titles, features, and part titles. Have students match the annotations with specific information in the table of contents. Also show how the table of contents gives an overview of content. Ask students what they notice about the example. Responses may be similar to these:

■ It seems that each title or feature summarizes the content it represents.

■ The table of contents is very clear and easy to read.

■ Page numbers make it easy to find an assignment or look up major topics.

Now discuss with students the major points made in the **Description. Besides telling students that the table of contents serves as a search tool for a textbook, stress that it is a useful study outline of the book's content.**

Check Understanding

Review with students the **Definition** on page 169. Check students' comprehension by having them review the table of contents from another textbook. Have them answer questions like these:

■ Which of these headings is a unit title, chapter title, feature title, or part title?

■ In what chapter and on what page can you find _____?

■ Does this table of contents look like a good outline to take notes or study from? Why or why not?

Reading
Nonfiction

Reading Kinds of Nonfiction

Reading an Essay
Reading a Biography
Reading an Autobiography
Reading a Newspaper Article
Reading a Magazine Article

Ways of Reading Nonfiction

Focus on Persuasive Writing
Focus on Speeches
Focus on Real-world Writing

Elements of Nonfiction

Reading an Essay

Getting Ready

Goals

Here students read an expository essay called "America the Not-so-Beautiful" by Andy Rooney. This lesson will help them learn to:

- ☑ recognize the purposes of various essays
- ☑ use the reading strategy of outlining
- ☑ look closely at the organization of different kinds of essays

Background

Explain to students that an essay is a short work of nonfiction that deals with a single subject. Connect the lesson with students' existing knowledge by asking them to:

- name or describe essays that they have read and tell who the authors were
- list types of publications where essays might be found
- discuss why they think authors might write essays
- discuss reasons that they might read essays

Opening Activity

Talk about the way that essays usually are organized into three parts: an introduction, a body, and a conclusion. Students can look for these structural parts as they read.

Overview

	Content	Teacher's Guide page	Reader's Handbook page
Selection	"America the Not-so-Beautiful" by Andy Rooney	119	174–176
Reading Strategy	Outlining	118	177, 648
Rereading Strategy	Questioning the Author	124	185, 652
Tool	Outline	118, 120	178, 180, 675
	Main Idea Organizer	122	182, 674
	Double-entry Journal	124	185, 671

Ancillaries

	Grade	Content	Page
Overhead Transparency	6, 7, 8	Previewing an Essay	Number 16
Lesson Plan Book	7	Reading an Essay	94-95
	8	Reading an Essay	84
Student Applications Book	6	"How to Eat a Guava" by Esmeralda Santiago	62–71
	7	"How Can America Be My Home?" by Lee Chew	61–70
	8	"Vesuvius" by Pliny the Younger	58–67
Website		www.greatsource.com/rehand/	

Before Reading

A   Set a Purpose

Before reading "America the Not-so-Beautiful," ask students to set a purpose for reading the essay. The Setting a Purpose questions on page 173 in the *Reader's Handbook* are a good guide for their reading.

Setting a Purpose

- What is the subject of the writing?
- What is the author saying about the subject?
- How do I feel about the author's message?

B   Preview

Ask students to look over the essay, trying to learn a little bit about it before they begin. Use the Preview Checklist on page 173 in the handbook with students. Then walk through what to preview using the Overhead Transparency.

Point out each item in the Preview Checklist. Suggest that students trace a line down the page in a zigzag fashion looking for repeated words.

Point out to students that the annotations in the margin are color-coded, so students can match the annotation with the appropriate bit of highlighted text.

Preview Checklist

- ✔ the title and author
- ✔ the first and last paragraphs
- ✔ any key words, headings, or words in boldface
- ✔ any repeated words or phrases

Overhead Transparency

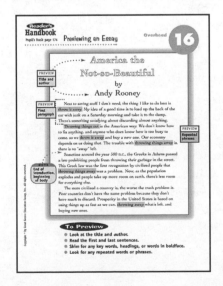

Before Reading

C Plan

Ask students to summarize what they learned in the preview. Now have them make a plan for getting more information about the subject and the author's message. Suggest using the strategy of **outlining**. Explain some of the reasons that this strategy might be useful. (It helps them to identify the three main parts of an essay, and it will show how an author develops and supports his or her main points.)

Reading Strategy: Outlining

An Outline provides an easy way for students to organize an essay's most important facts and details. As students read, suggest that they consider other ways of getting the information they need from the essay, such as looking for the main idea and supporting details.

After reading about the strategy of outlining, direct students to the Outline model on page 178 in the *Reader's Handbook*.

OUTLINE

I. Introduction
    A. introductory detail
    B. introductory detail
    C. thesis statement (if it appears here)
II. Body
    A. support for thesis
        1. example
        2. example
    B. support for thesis
        1. example
        2. example
    C. support for thesis
        1. example
        2. example
III. Conclusion
    A. concluding detail
    B. concluding detail
    C. thesis statement (if it appears here)

During Reading

D Read with a Purpose

While reading "America the Not-so-Beautiful," students try to discover what the author is saying and how they feel about what is being said. Discuss the material on main point and supporting details. Guide students in finding the main idea.

1. Finding the Main Idea

Walk students through the steps of finding the main idea. Refer to pages 47–54 in the *Reader's Handbook* for a description of the steps in finding the main idea.

1. Find the subject.

2. Decide what the author is saying about the subject.

3. Then find details that support the main idea.

Help students know where to begin looking for the main idea:

■ the first sentence or paragraph

■ the last sentence or paragraph

In Andy Rooney's essay, the main idea comes in the last sentence of the second paragraph.

> **from "America the Not-so-Beautiful"**
>
> Next to saving stuff I don't need, the thing I like to do best is throw it away. My idea of a good time is to load up the back of the car with junk on a Saturday morning and take it to the dump. There's something satisfying about discarding almost anything.
>
> Throwing things out is the American way. We don't know how to fix anything, and anyone who does know how is too busy to come, so we throw it away and buy a new one. Our economy depends on us doing that. The trouble with throwing things away is, there is no "away" left.

NOTE
Main idea

2. Finding Supporting Details

Review what supporting details are and what students need to look for: personal experiences, facts or statistics, examples, and comments from experts.

During Reading

D Read with a Purpose continued

The completed Sentence Outline divides the essay into an Introduction, Body, and Conclusion. An Outline works well with essays and other nonfiction. Point out that this Outline has an introductory detail and main point in the introduction, support and examples in the Body, and concluding details in the Conclusion.

SENTENCE OUTLINE

I. Introduction
   A. Rooney describes his trash "habits."
   B. Main point: Throwing things out is the American way.
      This is a problem.

II. Body
   A. Our economy depends on using things up as fast as we can.
      This is wasteful.
      1. People don't fix things.
      2. Our economy depends on us buying new things.
   B. What we're throwing away can poison us. Big companies
      carelessly dump poisonous waste.
      1. People don't know how to dispose of dangerous products.
      2. Poison seeps into the ground.
   C. There's nowhere to put all the stuff we're throwing away.
      1. People of New York City throw out nine times their
         weight in trash.
      2. Wasteful packaging is used.
      3. Landfills are filled.

III. Conclusion
   A. If people don't change their habits, the planet will be filled
      with trash.
   B. The best solution may be for all of us to move to Mars
      and trash it.

Other Useful Tools

Introduce graphic organizers appropriate for reading essays. Students do not have to use all of them, but they need to be able to pull out the right one when they need it.

■ **Viewpoint and Evidence Organizer**
■ **Argument Chart**

During Reading

How Essays Are Organized

Explain to students that knowing how essays are organized will help them find
the most important information: the author's main point and supporting details.
Explain that essays usually follow one of the patterns below.

1. Narrative Essay Organization

Walk students through the structure of the Narrative Essay Organization diagram
on page 181 in the handbook. Point out that this organization usually follows
a chronological order.

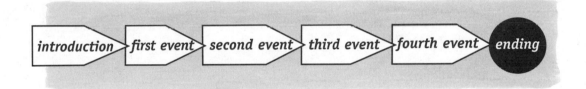

NARRATIVE ESSAY ORGANIZATION

introduction › first event › second event › third event › fourth event › ending

2. Expository Essay Organization

Remind students that "America the Not-so-Beautiful" is an expository essay following
the structure of the Expository Essay Organization diagram on the left on page 181
in the handbook. In this particular essay, it is difficult to find where the body starts
and stops. Alert students that the introduction may be more than one paragraph long.

EXPOSITORY ESSAY ORGANIZATION

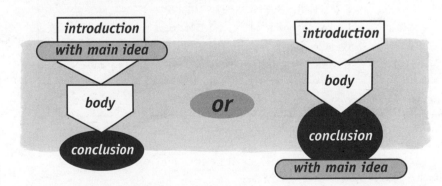

introduction
with main idea
body
conclusion

or

introduction
body
conclusion
with main idea

3. Essay Openings

Point out the Funnel Pattern diagram on page 182 in the handbook and encourage students to discuss why Rooney uses this pattern. Like many writers, he wants to first hook a reader by grabbing his or her interest before stating the subject and main idea of the essay.

FUNNEL PATTERN

opening sentence or paragraph

next sentence or paragraph

main idea

Main Idea Organizer

Students may also adapt their Sentence Outlines of Rooney's essay into a Main Idea Organizer. This organizer makes it easy to distinguish between the main idea and important supporting details.

MAIN IDEA ORGANIZER

TITLE:	"America the Not-so-Beautiful"	
MAIN IDEA: Throwing things out is the American way. This is a problem.		
DETAIL Our economy depends on using things up as fast as we can. This is wasteful.	**DETAIL** What we're throwing away can poison us.	**DETAIL** There's nowhere to put all the stuff we're throwing away.
CONCLUSION: The way Americans get rid of trash creates big problems.		

During Reading

E Connect

Explain to students that, while reading, it's important to interact and make personal connections with the essay. Recording their reactions to the essay and relating it to their own lives will help them to evaluate it. Help students react to and evaluate the essay in these ways:

■ ask themselves questions
(How do I feel about throwing away trash?)

■ think about the meaning of the essay's main point
(Why do I think Rooney is writing this essay?)

■ evaluate the essay by comparing it to their own experience
(How do I feel about throwing away trash? recycling?)

■ share what sticky note reactions they might have written
(What kind of trash do I have and how can I get rid of it?)

from "America the Not-so-Beautiful"

I have two pint bottles of insecticide with 5 percent DDT in them in my own garage that I don't know what to do with. I bought them years ago when I didn't realize how bad they were. Now I'm stuck with them.

> We have stuff like this in our garage, too. There's a special pick-up once a year.

After Reading

F Pause and Reflect

After reading, students stop to consider whether they understand the essay's main point and meaning. Help students go back and review their original purpose in reading the essay.

Looking Back
■ **What is the subject?**
■ **What is the author saying about the subject?**
■ **How do I feel about the author's message?**

Because "America the Not-so-Beautiful" has a number of key examples and broad details, these questions probably weren't fully answered on the first reading of the essay. Help students see the need to return to the essay for a second reading and to understand that rereading is a natural part of the reading process.

G Reread

Have students review the essay again, looking for answers to their questions. To give them a fresh approach, use a new reading strategy, questioning the author. This strategy can be helpful in reading an expository essay.

Rereading Strategy: Questioning the Author

Questioning the author helps students to better understand the author's purpose. It also helps them understand why certain words or details were used. A graphic organizer called the Double-entry Journal can help students to focus on specific statements from the text.

DOUBLE-ENTRY JOURNAL

WHAT WRITER SAYS	WHAT I THINK WHEN I READ
"Throwing things out is the American way. We don't know how to fix anything, and anyone who does know how is too busy to come, so we throw it away and buy a new one."	Why does he say people don't fix anything? Some people obviously do fix things—service people, mechanics, etc. That's just a fact. He must be exaggerating, probably trying to be funny. At the end when he mentions Mars, he's also trying to exaggerate.

After Reading

Remember

At this point in the process, it's important for students to do something with the essay in order to remember it. Discuss the essay, use one of the activities on page 186 in the *Reader's Handbook*, or suggest doing the creative assignment.

Creative Assignment: Divide students into small teams and ask them to come up with big and small solutions to the kinds of waste issues and problems posed by Rooney. What does America and the rest of the world need to do to avoid being buried in its own trash? What can individuals do on a daily basis to minimize the trash they create? Share the results and discuss.

Summing Up

Finally, review the lesson with students. Focus on everything they have learned about strategies and tools for reading an essay. Read with students the Summing Up (on page 187 in the handbook). Go over with students the three goals for this lesson. Discuss which ones they feel that they achieved and which ones they feel they need more work on:

1. recognizing the purposes of various essays

2. using the reading strategy of outlining

3. understanding the organization of different kinds of essays

Assessment and Application

Use the Quick Assess checklist to evaluate students' abilities to read and understand essays. Give students the opportunity to apply what they have learned through one of the two activities below. For students who are comfortable with the reading process and strategy, use one of the essays suggested below or another one in your curriculum. For guided help with the strategy, use a *Student Applications Book.*

Quick Assess

Can students

☑ identify two common kinds of essays?

☑ name three things to look for when they preview?

☑ name and explain one strategy?

☑ create and use at least one reading tool?

☑ explain a funnel pattern opening?

1. Independent Practice

To show that students understand the lesson, ask them to apply the reading strategy of **outlining** to one of the following selections:

■ "The Bike" by Gary Soto (from *Growing Up Chicana/o,* edited by Tiffany Ana Lopez)

■ "Jackie's Debut: A Unique Day" by Mike Royko (from *One More Time: The Best of Mike Royko*)

■ "The Civil Rights Movement: What Good Was It?" by Alice Walker

Ask students to:

1. Create an Outline of the essay.

2. Explain whether the essay follows a narrative or expository organization.

3. Write a journal entry giving their opinion of the essay in one paragraph.

2. Student Applications Books

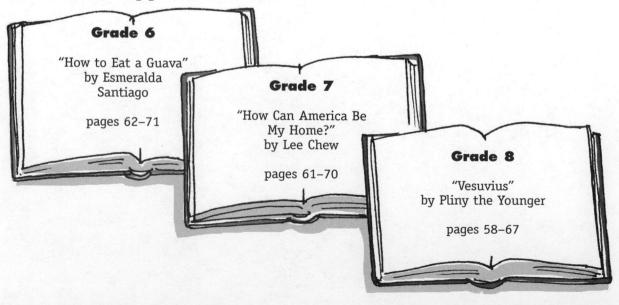

Grade 6

"How to Eat a Guava" by Esmeralda Santiago

pages 62–71

Grade 7

"How Can America Be My Home?" by Lee Chew

pages 61–70

Grade 8

"Vesuvius" by Pliny the Younger

pages 58–67

Reading a Biography

Goals

Here students read parts of a biography, *Harriet Tubman: Conductor on the Underground Railroad*, written by Ann Petry. This lesson will help them learn to:

- ☑ appreciate two major elements of a biography
- ☑ use the strategy of looking for cause and effect
- ☑ understand the organization biographers use in telling the story

Background

Connect the lesson with students' existing knowledge by asking them to:

- ▇ define the term *biography*
- ▇ name some of the general features of biographies
- ▇ talk about why people read biographies
- ▇ list people they would like to read biographies about

Opening Activity

Talk about the common elements that biographies include, such as real facts and details about the time, place, key events, and accomplishments of the subject. Students should watch for these as they read.

Overview

	Content	Teacher's Guide page	Reader's Handbook page
Selection	*Harriet Tubman: Conductor on the Underground Railroad* by Ann Petry		190–191, 193–195
Reading Strategy	Looking for Cause and Effect	130	192, 644
Rereading Strategy	Outlining	135	202, 648
Tool	Cause-Effect Organizer	130, 131	192, 196, 667
	Timeline	132	198, 681
	Character Map	133	199, 668
	Topic Outline	135	202, 675

Ancillaries

	Grade	Content	Page
Overhead Transparency	6, 7, 8	Previewing a Biography	Numbers 17 and 18
Lesson Plan Book	6	Reading Biographies and Autobiographies	94–95
	8	Reading Biographies and Autobiographies	85
Student Applications Book	6	*One Thousand Paper Cranes: The Story of Sadako* by Takayuki Ishii	72–79
	7	*Isabella of Spain: Her Life* by Cristina Maria Bernal	71–79
	8	*The Boys' Life of Abraham Lincoln* by Helen Nicolay	68–77
Website		www.greatsource.com/rehand/	

Before Reading

A Set a Purpose

Before beginning, ask students to set a purpose for reading a biography of Harriet Tubman. Direct students' attention to the Setting a Purpose questions on page 189 in the *Reader's Handbook*. Discuss with students how these questions follow up the goals most biographers have when writing.

Setting a Purpose

■ **What kind of life did this person have?**

■ **What was he or she really like?**

B Preview

Ask students to preview the reading to get an overview. Introduce the Preview Checklist on page 189 in the handbook to students. Go over these items one by one, using the Overhead Transparencies.

Have students point out and talk about each item in the reading on Harriet Tubman, from the title and author to any repeated words.

Preview Checklist

✓ the title and author

✓ the front, back, and inside covers

✓ the table of contents or chapter titles

✓ any photographs or illustrations

✓ any dedication, preface, introduction, or note to the reader

✓ the first paragraph or two of the text

✓ any repeated words

Overhead Transparencies

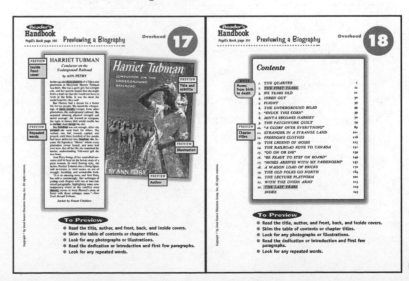

Before Reading

C Plan

Ask students what they learned about Harriet Tubman from their preview. Now have them make a plan for getting information about Harriet Tubman's life and personality. Suggest using the strategy of **looking for cause and effect**. Offer reasons as to why this might be a good strategy to use. (One reason is that it can help students discover what this person was like by evaluating the important, "life-shaping" events of her life.)

Reading Strategy: Looking for Cause and Effect

A Cause-Effect Organizer helps to keep track of the "life-shaping" events in a person's life and shows what effects the key events had on that person's development.

Cause-Effect Organizer

Being able to sort out the events (causes) and the effects in a person's life will make students better readers and help them get to know the person in depth.

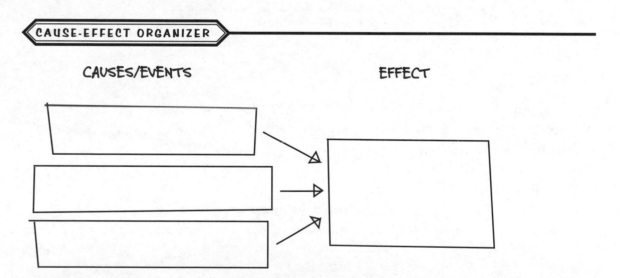

CAUSE-EFFECT ORGANIZER

CAUSES/EVENTS   EFFECT

Students can make notes on the Causes/Events side as they are reading and fill in the Effect part after they are finished. The model has four boxes, but remind students that they may need fewer or more boxes to show the cause and the effects. Point out to students that any number of causes may trigger an event, or even two or more events.

Read with a Purpose

Discuss the important questions that students need to keep in mind as they read a biography. These are noted on page 193 in the *Reader's Handbook*.

Cause-Effect Organizer

Direct students' attention to the completed Cause-Effect Organizer on page 196. Cause-Effect Organizers pinpoint important events and show how they influence a person's character and behavior. These organizers also are useful for nonfiction, fiction, and textbooks.

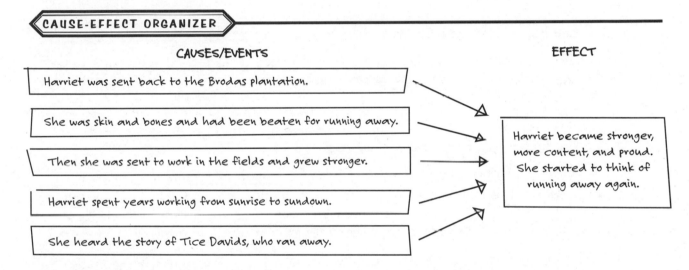

CAUSE-EFFECT ORGANIZER

CAUSES/EVENTS

EFFECT

Harriet was sent back to the Brodas plantation.

She was skin and bones and had been beaten for running away.

Then she was sent to work in the fields and grew stronger.

Harriet spent years working from sunrise to sundown.

She heard the story of Tice Davids, who ran away.

Harriet became stronger, more content, and proud. She started to think of running away again.

Other Useful Tools

Encourage students to use other reading tools as they read the biography of Harriet Tubman. Remind them they do not have to use all of them, but it's good to know they're helpful and available. As with any type of tool, students need to be able to apply the right one when needed. If not familiar with the tools below, they can find them in the Reader's Almanac and briefly discuss their applications. These are especially useful reading tools for biographies:

■ **Character Map**

■ **Paraphrase or Retelling Chart**

■ **Inference Chart**

■ **Summary Notes**

■ **Timeline**

How Biographies Are Organized

Biographies are usually organized in chronological order, based on the stages and events of the subject's life. Chapters or sections often separate these key life periods. Point out the importance of looking for details about the changes in a person's life.

1. Details about Time

Introduce students to the list of words and phrases on page 197. Explain that these allow the reader to track the sequence of events in the subject's life. Encourage them to highlight or take notes on these time indicators.

2. Details about Place

Explain the importance of place in the life of a subject, as indicated on page 198. Tell students that keeping track of *where* events take place will help them understand the subject better.

3. Details about Key Events

Encourage students to take detailed notes about important events in chronological order. Review the Timeline on page 198 in the handbook with students. Point out that not every event is listed under a specific year. A Timeline can be used to keep track of the order of events even if the dates are not given.

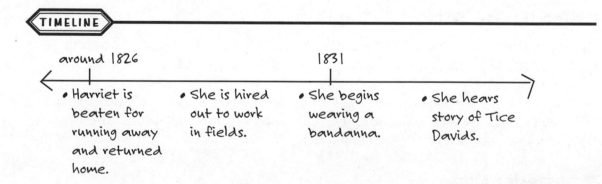

TIMELINE

around 1826

1831

- Harriet is beaten for running away and returned home.

- She is hired out to work in fields.

- She begins wearing a bandanna.

- She hears story of Tice Davids.

During Reading

4. Details about the Subject

Tell students that when reading a biography, they also should focus on what the person was like. Explain why a Character Map is a good tool for this kind of reading. (One reason is that it provides a format for looking at a person from many angles.)

< CHARACTER MAP >────────────────

HOW SHE ACTS AND FEELS
- shy
- sings
- feels content outdoors and appreciates nature
- interested in story of Tice Davids

HOW OTHERS FEEL ABOUT HER
- Miss Susan thinks she's worthless.
- Old Rit cares about her and watches over her.
- Brodas and new master know she's strong and beat her if she doesn't work hard enough.
- She's no longer seen as a child.

(HARRIET TUBMAN)

HOW I FEEL ABOUT HER
I admire her. I could never do that kind of hard work every day without getting angry or giving up.

HOW SHE LOOKS AND TALKS
- is skinny and covered with scars
- gets stronger, more muscles
- has calloused hands
- wears long dress and bandanna
- has husky voice and sullen eyes

During Reading

E Connect

Explain to students that when they read it's important to make connections with what they're reading. With biographies, students should think about how they feel about the subject of the biography. Help students evaluate and react to the biography by telling them to:

- ■ ask themselves questions
  (What do I think of Harriet Tubman? Would I want to be like her?)

- ■ think about the importance of Tubman's life events
  (Why did the biographer Ann Petry choose to write about her?)

- ■ compare figures in Tubman's life to people they know
  (Who do I know like Old Rit?)

- ■ evaluate Tubman's story by comparing it to their own experience
  (How does it compare to my life? What can I learn from her life?)

---

from Harriet Tubman

That night, in the slave cabins in the quarter, they talked about Harriet. If she lived, she would be sold South; the overseer and the master would not keep an intractable, defiant slave, a slave who refused to help the overseer tie up a runaway, blocking the door like Harriet did. She would be sold. It was a dangerous thing that she had done. Dangerous, yes, but a brave thing, too. Why wasn't she afraid? What had made her so bold?

I admire her for taking such a big risk.

I predict she won't be sold. Maybe she'll escape.

Help students understand the importance of recording their own thoughts as they read a biography. Their predictions and comments are a means of connecting to the writing.

After Reading

F Pause and Reflect

After reading, students stop to think about what they have read. Help students to review their original purposes in reading the biography.

Looking Back
■ **What are several important events in the subject's life?**
■ **How did these events affect the subject?**
■ **What was the person really like?**
■ **How do I feel about the subject?**
■ **Can I support how I feel with evidence from the reading?**

These Looking Back questions probably weren't fully answered on the first reading of the biography.

G Reread

Help students see the need to return to the biography for a second reading and to understand that rereading is an opportunity to learn more and a natural and important part of the reading process.

Rereading Strategy: Outlining

Outlining is a good rereading strategy to record the key events that make up the "big picture" of the person's life. Outlines provide an easy way for students to process and organize the most important facts and details. They also help students see how an author develops and supports an argument or portrait.

TOPIC OUTLINE

Title or Subject
  I. *Early Years*
    A. *important event*
    B. *important event*
  II. *School-age Years*
    A. *important event*
    B. *important event*
  III. *Young Adulthood*
    A. *important event*
    B. *important event*
  IV. *Adulthood*
    A. *important event*
    B. *important event*

HARRIET TUBMAN
I. Early Years
  A. born a slave in Maryland in 1820
  B. sent to work as a maid at age six
  C. hated the work and was beaten severely
  D. sent back to the Brodas plantation
II. School-age Years
  A. worked from sunrise to sundown in the fields
  B. listened to other slaves talk and began to understand the injustice of slavery

After Reading

H Remember

Remind students that, at this point, they need to do something with the biography in order to remember it. The activities mentioned on page 203 in the *Reader's Handbook* can help them to do that. So can the creative assignment that follows.

Creative Assignment: Divide the classroom into two teams, with one side representing the "events" of Tubman's life and the other half representing the "life-shaping" effects these had on her character. As one side recalls an event in Tubman's life, the other side describes the various ways that the event could have affected her character. Encourage discussion of the slave era, plantation life, the people in Tubman's life, and her specific hardships. You also may want to explain and highlight the legendary role she played in the Underground Railroad. This biography may relate to lessons in students' history or geography textbooks.

Summing Up

Finally, review the lesson with students. Focus on everything they've learned about strategies and tools for reading a biography. Read with students the Summing Up (on page 203 in the handbook). Go over with students the three goals for this lesson. Discuss which ones they feel that they achieved and which ones they feel they need more work on:

1. knowing the two major elements of a biography

2. using the reading strategy of looking for cause and effect

3. understanding the organization biographers use in telling a person's life story

Assessment and Application

Use the Quick Assess checklist to evaluate students' abilities to read and understand biographies. Give students the opportunity to apply what they have learned through one of the two activities below. For students who are comfortable with the reading process and strategy, use one of the biographies suggested below or another one in your curriculum. For guided help with the strategy, use a *Student Applications Book*.

Quick Assess

Can students

- ☑ identify the two goals of most biographers?
- ☑ name three things to look for when they preview?
- ☑ name and explain one strategy?
- ☑ create and use at least one reading tool?
- ☑ explain how biographies use chronological order?

1. Independent Practice

To show that they understand the lesson, students can apply the reading strategy of **looking for cause and effect** to an excerpt from one of the following selections:

- ■ *Christopher Columbus: Voyager to the Unknown* by Nancy Smiler Levinson
- ■ *Let It Shine: Stories of Black Women Freedom Fighters* by Andrea Davis Pinkney
- ■ *First Woman in Congress: Jeannette Rankin* by Florence Meiman White

Ask students to:

1. Create a Timeline for the biography.

2. Create a Cause-Effect Organizer for the biography.

3. Write a paragraph giving their final impression of the life and character of the biography's subject.

2. Student Applications Books

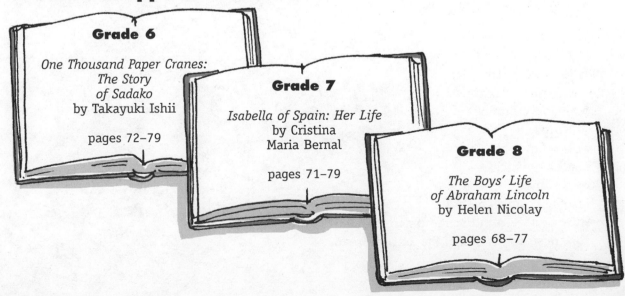

Grade 6

One Thousand Paper Cranes: The Story of Sadako by Takayuki Ishii

pages 72–79

Grade 7

Isabella of Spain: Her Life by Cristina Maria Bernal

pages 71–79

Grade 8

The Boys' Life of Abraham Lincoln by Helen Nicolay

pages 68–77

Reading an Autobiography

Getting Ready

Goals

Here students read a section from *Up from Slavery*, the autobiography of Booker T. Washington. This lesson will help them to learn to:

- ☑ recognize the major elements of an autobiography
- ☑ use the reading strategy of synthesizing, or pulling together key topics
- ☑ understand the organization of autobiographies

Background

Connect the lesson with students' existing knowledge by asking them to:

- ■ describe or define the term *autobiography*
- ■ list characteristics that they think autobiographies have
- ■ name reasons that a person might want to write an autobiography
- ■ list reasons that they would read an autobiography
- ■ name people whose autobiographies they would like to read or have read

Opening Activity

Talk with students about what they would need to cover if they were to write their own life stories. Mention common features in autobiographies, such as critical experiences, life lessons, and personal interests. Remind students to watch for these kinds of things as they read.

Overview

	Content	Teacher's Guide page	Reader's Handbook page
Selection	*Up from Slavery* by Booker T. Washington		206–207, 210–211
Reading Strategy	Synthesizing	141	208, 660
Rereading Strategy	Looking for Cause and Effect	145	216, 644
Tool	Key Topic Notes	141, 142	209, 212, 673
	Character Trait Web	142	212, 684
	Timeline	143	213, 681
	Inference Chart	144	214, 672
	Cause-Effect Organizer	146	216, 667

Ancillaries

	Grade	Content	Page
Overhead Transparency	6, 7, 8	Previewing an Autobiography	Numbers 19 and 20
Lesson Plan Book	6	Reading Biographies and Autobiographies	94–95
	8	Reading Biographies and Autobiographies	85
Student Applications Book	6	*The Autobiography of Benjamin Franklin*	80–89
	7	*Theodore Roosevelt: An Autobiography*	80–90
	8	*Twenty Years at Hull House* by Jane Addams	78–87
Website		www.greatsource.com/rehand/	

Before Reading

A Set a Purpose

Before reading the excerpt, ask students to set a purpose for reading *Up from Slavery*. Focus students on the "Setting a Purpose" questions on page 205 in the *Reader's Handbook*, and discuss why they are good questions to guide their reading.

Setting a Purpose

■ **What kind of life did this person have?**

■ **How do I feel about him or her?**

B Preview

Ask students to look over the reading to try to get a general idea about the person who wrote the autobiography before they begin. Use the Preview Checklist on page 205 in the handbook.

Talk about each item in the Preview Checklist. Have students point out and discuss each of the items as they find it in Booker T. Washington's autobiography, from the title and front cover to the summary on the back cover of the book.

Preview Checklist

✔ *the title and author*

✔ *the front, back, and inside covers*

✔ *any dedication, preface, introduction, or note to the reader*

✔ *any summaries or reviews*

✔ *the table of contents or any chapter titles*

✔ *any photographs or illustrations*

✔ *the first paragraph or two*

Overhead Transparencies

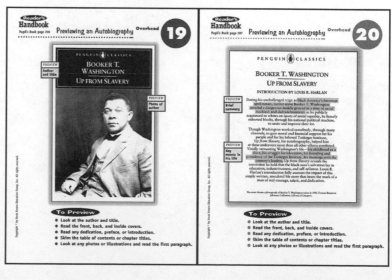

Before Reading

C Plan

Briefly discuss students' findings from their previews, as on page 208 in the *Reader's Handbook*.

At this stage, students need to come up with a plan for getting information about the life of Booker T. Washington. Suggest using the strategy of **synthesizing**. Talk about some of the reasons this might be the best strategy to use. (One reason is that it helps students to unify the key parts or elements of an autobiography.)

Reading Strategy: Synthesizing

Explain to students that synthesizing can help them to pull together the childhood experiences, major achievements and problems, and character traits of the subject into one clear picture. It also allows them to keep track of key topics that are found in any autobiography (page 208 in the handbook) and details from the beginning to the end of the reading. As students read, suggest that they use Key Topic Notes to help them get the information they need from the autobiography.

Key Topic Notes

This tool offers an easy way to break down and synthesize the main areas of the person's life, as shown on page 209.

KEY TOPIC NOTES

KEY TOPICS	NOTES FROM READING
childhood	(Facts and details about the author's childhood go here.)
family	(Facts and details about the author's family go here.)
school	(Facts and details about the author's education go here.)
work	(Facts and details about the author's jobs go here.)
major achievements	(Facts and details about achievements go here.)
major problems	(Facts and details about big problems go here.)
character traits	(Facts and details about the author's personality go here.)

During Reading

D Read with a Purpose

While reading the selection from *Up from Slavery*, students record their ideas on graphic organizers. Remind students to use the tools that will clarify what confuses them.

1. Key Topic Notes

This tool helps students unify their information about various areas of the subject's life. The reading focuses on Booker T. Washington's early years, so the key topics cover three main areas: school, work, and character traits, as displayed on page 212 in the handbook.

KEY TOPIC NOTES

KEY TOPICS	NOTES FROM READING
school	• school in his town not very good • hears about Hampton Institute in Virginia • thinks it sounds like heaven
work	• works in a coal mine • takes job with Mrs. Ruffner
character traits	• wants to get a good education • not afraid of a challenge

2. Character Trait Web

The Character Trait Web is a great tool for exploring a character's personality. It also is useful because it requires students to supply proof from the reading for every character trait that they suggest.

CHARACTER TRAIT WEB

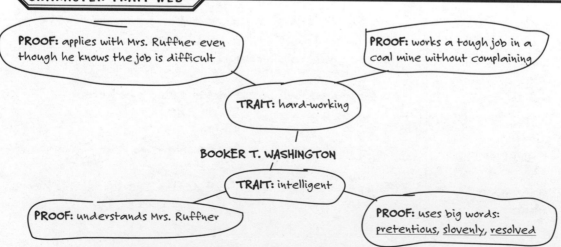

PROOF: applies with Mrs. Ruffner even though he knows the job is difficult

PROOF: works a tough job in a coal mine without complaining

TRAIT: hard-working

BOOKER T. WASHINGTON

TRAIT: intelligent

PROOF: understands Mrs. Ruffner

PROOF: uses big words: pretentious, slovenly, resolved

During Reading

D **Read with a Purpose** continued

Other Useful Tools

Discuss with students other possible reading tools that might be useful with reading an autobiography. A few possibilities are given below.

■ **Inference Chart**

■ **Double-entry Journal**

■ **Viewpoint and Evidence Organizer**

■ **Venn Diagram**

How Autobiographies Are Organized

Explain to students that knowing the common features of autobiographies will help them to know what to expect from the reading. As noted on page 213, autobiographies are usually written in the first person, slanted in favor of the author, and organized in the chronological order of events in the person's life.

A Timeline is a very good tool to use when trying to keep track of the key events or experiences of the subject. Point out the date-based Timeline of Booker T. Washington's life, as shown on page 213 in the handbook.

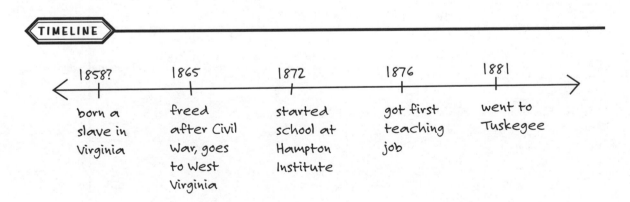

TIMELINE

1858?	1865	1872	1876	1881
born a slave in Virginia	freed after Civil War, goes to West Virginia	started school at Hampton Institute	got first teaching job	went to Tuskegee

During Reading

E Connect

A key part of the reading process is to respond to or make connections with the reading. With autobiographies, students should develop an impression of the subject and relate it to their own lives and experiences. Help students to evaluate and react to the autobiography by encouraging them to:

■ ask themselves questions
(What do I think of Booker T. Washington? Would I want to be like him?)

■ think about the importance of Washington's life experiences
(In what ways do his experiences affect me and our times?)

■ compare figures in Washington's life to people they know
(Do I know anyone who is like Mrs. Ruffner?)

■ evaluate Washington's life by comparing it to their own experience
(How does his life compare to mine? What can I learn from him?)

■ evaluate the quality of Washington's autobiographical account
(Does Washington's portrayal of himself seem fair, well written, and reliable? Why or why not?)

An Inference Chart can be a good tool for recording students' reactions to and questions about various facts or events in the reading. Review the model of how to make an inference on page 214 in the *Reader's Handbook*. Ask whether students agree with these interpretations. Would they add other events or reactions to the chart?

◁ INFERENCE CHART ▷

WHAT CHARACTER SAID OR DID	MY IMPRESSION OF HIM . . .
He worked hard jobs (like mining).	I really admire that he was willing to do anything possible to realize his dream.
He used long, formal words like <u>resolved</u>, <u>secured</u>, <u>sympathized</u>, and <u>pretentious</u>.	He sounds very educated.
He made a "library" out of a box.	He seems very creative and hopeful.

Pause and Reflect

After reading, have students stop to consider what they have learned about the person. Have students go back and review their original purposes in reading Booker T. Washington's autobiography.

Looking Back

■ **What are several important events in this person's life?**

■ **What kind of life did this person have?**

■ **How do I feel about him or her?**

Because *Up from Slavery* is a brief excerpt from a longer work, students probably can't fully answer these Looking Back questions with the first reading. Students may have new questions, and they will need to consider specific events to decide how they feel about this person. Reading the selection a second time is a good idea and a natural part of the reading process. Explain to students that they do not have to read the whole selection again word for word. Encourage them to skim and reread selected portions of the text and to focus on parts that can help answer their remaining questions.

G Reread

To help students pick up key details and evidence, introduce a new reading strategy before students begin rereading.

Rereading Strategy: Looking for Cause and Effect

Looking for cause and effect is a good strategy for students to use when rereading a person's life story. It can help them to pinpoint the pivotal events that influenced the subject's character and behavior. Remind students that there are often a string of causes leading to the effect. Readers can look for causes within a single chapter or the entire autobiography.

Cause-Effect Organizer

A Cause-Effect Organizer provides a format for listing the key events in a person's life with the effects these had on that person's development. Understanding the connections between causes and effects in a person's life will make students better readers by helping them describe the character's motivations.

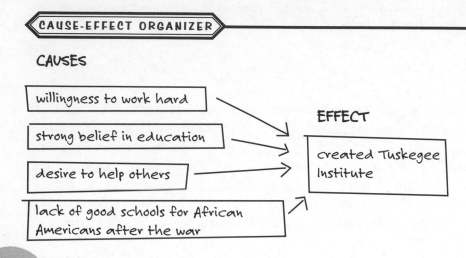

CAUSE-EFFECT ORGANIZER

CAUSES

willingness to work hard

strong belief in education

desire to help others

lack of good schools for African Americans after the war

EFFECT

created Tuskegee Institute

H Remember

At this stage in the reading, it is time for students to make the reading their own. They need to do something with the subject matter in order to remember it. Discuss the activities highlighted on page 217 in the *Reader's Handbook* and suggest doing the creative assignment.

Creative Assignment: Divide students into small groups and ask them to create bookstore advertising posters about *Up from Slavery*. Share the results. Which posters best portray the events and importance of Washington's life? Which would be most likely to sell the book to readers? Which posters best suggest the book?

Summing Up

As a final task, review the lesson with students. Focus on everything they've learned about strategies and tasks for reading an autobiography. Read with students the Summing Up (on page 217 in the handbook). Go over with students the three goals for their lesson. Discuss which ones they feel that they achieved and which ones that they need more work on:

1. recognizing the major elements of an autobiography

2. using the reading strategy of synthesizing, or pulling together key topics

3. understanding the organization of autobiographies

Assessment and Application

Use the Quick Assess checklist to evaluate students' abilities to read and understand autobiographies. Give students the opportunity to apply what they have learned through one of the two activities below. For students who are comfortable with the reading process and strategy, use one of the autobiographies suggested below or another one in your curriculum. For guided help with the strategy, use a *Student Applications Book*.

1. Independent Practice

To show that students understand the lesson, ask them to apply the reading strategy of **synthesizing** to one of the following selections:

■ *Homecoming* by Jean Fritz

■ *Leon's Story* by Leon Walter Tillage

■ *Boy: Tales of Childhood* by Roald Dahl

Ask students to:

1. Create a Character Trait Web for the autobiographer.

2. Create Key Topic Notes for a selection from the autobiography.

3. Write a one-paragraph journal entry giving their opinion of the person's life, as portrayed in the autobiography.

Quick Assess

Can students

☑ explain the main difference between a biography and an autobiography?

☑ name three things to look for when they preview?

☑ name and explain one strategy?

☑ create and use at least one reading tool?

☑ list three key topics that appear in many autobiographies?

2. Student Applications Books

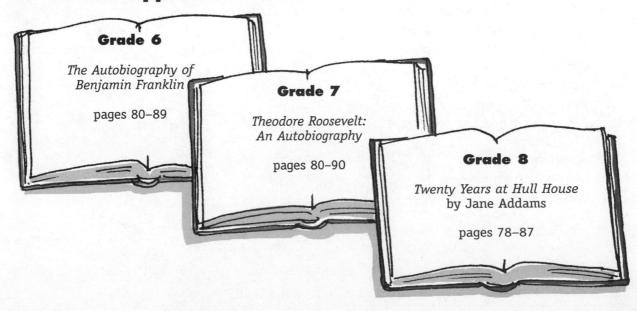

Grade 6

The Autobiography of Benjamin Franklin

pages 80–89

Grade 7

Theodore Roosevelt: An Autobiography

pages 80–90

Grade 8

Twenty Years at Hull House by Jane Addams

pages 78–87

Reading a Newspaper Article

Getting Ready

Goals

Here students read a newspaper article called "Robots Get Ready to Rumble" by David Colker. This lesson will help them learn to:

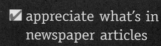

- ☑ appreciate what's in newspaper articles
- ☑ use the strategy of reading critically
- ☑ understand the organization of many news stories

Background

Connect the lesson with students' existing knowledge by asking them to:

- ■ talk about newspapers that they read or are familiar with
- ■ discuss some of the reasons that people read newspapers
- ■ list some of the general characteristics of newspaper articles
- ■ explain what they think the goals of newspaper writers are
- ■ compare newspapers with other types of media

Opening Activity

Pick up a newspaper published the day of your lesson. Talk about the common parts and features of most newspaper articles. Discuss the lead or opening paragraphs, any accompanying graphics, and the focus on providing complete information quickly. Ask students to watch for these parts and features as they read.

Lesson Resources

Overview

	Content	Teacher's Guide page	Reader's Handbook page
Selection	"Robots Get Ready to Rumble" by David Colker		221, 224–227
Reading Strategy	Reading Critically	151	222, 654
Rereading Strategy	Summarizing	156	232, 658
Tool	5 W's Organizer	151	220, 222, 672
	Critical Reading Chart	151, 152	228, 670
	Viewpoint and Evidence Organizer	153	228, 683
	Summary Notes	157	232, 680

Ancillaries

	Grade	Content	Page
Overhead Transparency	6, 7, 8	Previewing a Newspaper Article	Number 21
Lesson Plan Book	6	Reading a Newspaper Article	104
Student Applications Book	6	"Fire at a New York Shirtwaist Factory" by W. G. Shepherd	90–99
	7	"San Francisco Assessor Tells Story of the Wreck of the *Titanic*"	91–100
	8	"Earthquake and Fire: San Francisco in Ruins"	88–96
Website		www.greatsource.com/rehand/	

Before Reading

A Set a Purpose

Before beginning, ask students to set a purpose for reading "Robots Get Ready to Rumble." Direct students' attention to the Setting a Purpose question on page 219 in the *Reader's Handbook* and ask why it is a good question to guide their reading. Can students think of any other good questions for "Robots Get Ready to Rumble"?

Setting a Purpose

■ **What do robots do when they rumble, and what's the point of it?**

B Preview

News articles are written for people in a hurry, so previewing is a key process. Ask students to look over the article and try to learn something about the topic before they begin. Use the Preview Checklist on page 220 in the handbook with students.

Explain and discuss each item in the Preview Checklist. Using the article, have students point out each item in the pages, from the headline and attention-getting lead to any repeated words they might find.

Emphasize that the lead usually answers the most important questions of the article—or the 5 W's—as explained on page 220 in the handbook. Have students try to answer the 5 W's as they preview.

Preview Checklist

✔ the headline and author

✔ any words that are repeated or in bold or larger type

✔ the opening paragraphs (the lead)

✔ any photographs and captions

✔ any maps, diagrams, charts, or other graphics

Overhead Transparency

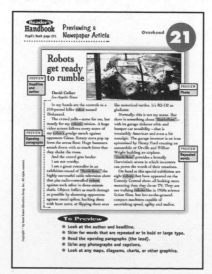

Before Reading

C Plan

Discuss students' findings from their preview while referring to the completed 5 W's Organizer on page 222 in the handbook.

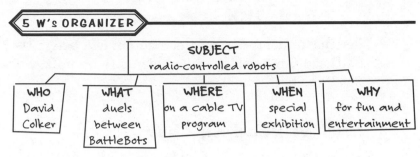

5 W's ORGANIZER

SUBJECT
radio-controlled robots

| WHO | WHAT | WHERE | WHEN | WHY |
| David Colker | duels between BattleBots | on a cable TV program | special exhibition | for fun and entertainment |

At this stage in the reading process, have students come up with a plan for getting information from the newspaper article. Introduce the strategy of **reading critically**. Talk about some of the reasons this might be the best strategy to use for newspaper articles. (One reason is that it helps students to go beyond the facts and details to see the point the writer is trying to make.)

Reading Strategy: Reading Critically

Reading critically is a natural part of the reading process. It involves encouraging readers to go beyond the facts to think about what they really mean, separating fact from opinion, evaluating the quality of the evidence, and identifying possible supporting views.

Critical Reading Chart

Examine the Critical Reading Chart on page 223 in the handbook. Highlight how it helps to differentiate fact from opinion and to evaluate the quality of the reporting.

CRITICAL READING CHART

QUESTIONS	MY THOUGHTS
1. Is the main idea or viewpoint clear?	(Look for the author's central point or opinion on a topic.)
2. What evidence is presented?	(Evidence can include facts and statistics, quotations from experts, statements by eyewitnesses, and personal experiences.)
3. Are the sources authoritative and reliable?	(An authoritative source is one with a great deal of experience or expertise. A reliable source is one that is not biased.)
4. Is the evidence convincing?	(Evaluate how much evidence is presented.)
5. Is there another side of the story?	(Often a newspaper article only gives one side of a story. You may need to identify a possible opposing viewpoint.)

During Reading

D Read with a Purpose

Remind students of their reading purpose before they begin. While reading "Robots Get Ready to Rumble," ask students to record key details and ideas on a Critical Reading Chart.

Critical Reading Chart

A Critical Reading Chart allows students to note their own thoughts, ideas, and reactions to what they are reading. Encourage students to create such a chart before reading an article for a report or class assignment. Then, as they read, they can record their thoughts and reactions.

CRITICAL READING CHART

QUESTIONS	MY THOUGHTS
1. Is the main idea or viewpoint clear?	Yes—Colker thinks the fights are fun.
2. What evidence is presented?	Colker uses facts, expert sources, eyewitness accounts, and personal experience.
3. Are the sources authoritative and reliable?	Yes, he talks with Christian Carlberg and other makers of BattleBots.
4. Is the evidence convincing?	By taking part in a duel, Colker got a firsthand look at BattleBots and what it's like to run them. He also draws on many other people's experiences.
5. Is there another side of the story?	The match was held to help promote a line of toys. The article doesn't really look critically at the violence issue. The question is, "Is watching these violent battles really a good idea, especially for kids?"

Read with a Purpose continued

Other Useful Tools

Point out to students the large number of graphic organizers in the lesson. Reinforce that students do not have to use all of them, but it is good to know that they are available. Students need to be familiar with the tools that are available so they can call upon the right one when they need it. Suggest to students that they could also use some of the reading tools shown in the lesson "Reading a Magazine Article," such as a Viewpoint and Evidence Organizer and a Main Idea Organizer.

■ **Viewpoint and Evidence Organizer**

■ **Main Idea Organizer**

■ **Argument Chart**

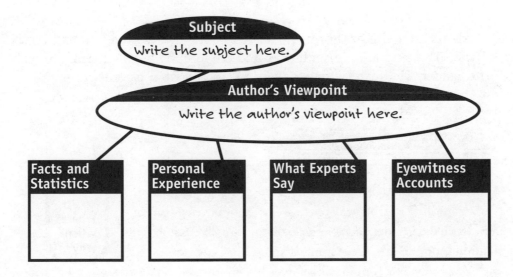

During Reading

How Newspaper Articles Are Organized

As students read, an inverted pyramid can help them to understand an article's typical structure and know what to expect. Newspaper articles tend to follow the standard pattern shown in the inverted pyramid below.

Inverted Pyramid

Walk students through the features listed in the inverted pyramid organization for a newspaper article. Explain how the lead, which gives information to answer the 5 W's, is followed by most important, less important, and least important details.

INVERTED PYRAMID

Lead

Most important details

Less important details

Least important details

Explain to students that the author of this article uses an inverted pyramid structure in a general way. The first couple sentences and paragraphs of the article are designed to "hook" the reader. The lead, which is "buried" in the fifth paragraph, gives information about the 5 W's.

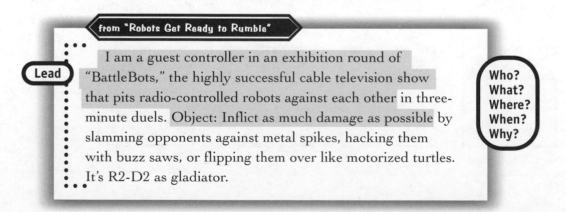

from "Robots Get Ready to Rumble"

Lead

I am a guest controller in an exhibition round of "BattleBots," the highly successful cable television show that pits radio-controlled robots against each other in three-minute duels. Object: Inflict as much damage as possible by slamming opponents against metal spikes, hacking them with buzz saws, or flipping them over like motorized turtles. It's R2-D2 as gladiator.

Who?
What?
Where?
When?
Why?

Tell the students they will know they have found the lead when they find one or more sentences that answer *who, what, where, when,* and *why*.

During Reading

E Connect

Remind students that it's important to interact and make connections with the article as they read. Relating the subject matter to their own lives will help them learn more, remember it better, and have more thought-provoking reactions. Help students to evaluate and react to the article by telling them to:

- ask themselves questions
  (Do I know the 5 W's of this article?)

- think about the meaning of the article's main point as it relates to them
  (Why did Colker choose to write about the BattleBots? Why is this newsworthy?)

- compare what they learn with what they already know about the topic
  (Didn't I see part of this television show last week? Isn't it really destructive?)

- evaluate the article by comparing it to their own experience
  (Is this something I would care to watch? Why or why not?)

- evaluate the quality of Colker's reporting, evidence, and sources
  (Does Colker's reporting and view of the BattleBots seem to me reliable and sound?)

Asking questions like the ones above will help students go beyond the facts and details and answer bigger and more fundamental questions that the author may not have addressed. This process will help them evaluate the other side of the story. Invite students to share what reactions they would write on sticky notes.

from "Robots Get Ready to Rumble"

In the first match of the evening, Carlberg's Toe Crusher is pitted against Jonathan Ridder's Ziggo. Although this is an exhibition, the two go at each other fiercely, with Ziggo almost flying across the floor and using its whirling blades to inflict early harm. Carlberg, who remains so calm he could almost be described as serene, strikes back with Toe Crusher's metal scoop and hammering spike.

This sounds very violent.

Is violent entertainment a good idea?

After Reading

F Pause and Reflect

After reading, students stop to consider whether they understand the article's main facts and general message. Help students go back and review their original purpose in reading the article about the robots. (What do robots do when they rumble, and what's the point of it?)

Looking Back

- ■ Can I state the author's main idea or viewpoint in my own words?
- ■ Do I understand how the article is organized?
- ■ Can I answer the *who, what, where, when,* and *why* questions?
- ■ Have I examined the author's evidence and judged how reliable it is?

Because Colker uses a "buried lead" and offers a lot of facts and personal opinions, chances are that students may not be able to answer all of the Looking Back questions when first reading the article.

Help students to see the reasons to return to the article for a second reading. Because most people read articles in a hurry, rereading for key details and evidence evaluation is a very common and important part of the reading process.

G Reread

At this point students need a fresh way to go back into the reading. Have them review the article, looking for answers to their questions but using a new strategy.

Rereading Strategy: Summarizing

Encourage students to use this new strategy when rereading. Summarizing is a good strategy when you are going back into an article to find and pull together critical points and details.

Summarizing is a strategy that works well for any type of reading. It calls on students to retell the main events or ideas in a selection using their own words. Discuss with students the process and the Summary Notes, as on page 232 in the *Reader's Handbook.* Caution students not to use the exact wording of the original article when they summarize.

SUBJECT: robots that fight

AUTHOR'S VIEWPOINT: It's fun to watch robots battle.

1. "BattleBots," cable television show
2. unique names like Overkill or Diesector
3. cost from $1,000 to $70,000
4. robots with saws, hammers, and axes on them trying to destroy the other robots
5. popular—matches, toys, websites

H Remember

At this stage, students need to do something with the article in order to learn from it and remember it. Try the assignments described on pages 232–233 in the *Reader's Handbook* and the creative assignment listed below.

Creative Assignment: Pose a question to the class: "Do you think the new 'BattleBots' show is a positive or negative development in American society?" Divide the class into two sides—one that is in favor of the show and the other that opposes it. Debate issues concerning violence, science, entertainment, futurism, effect on young viewers, and other related issues. If you prefer, have students answer this question in a short essay.

Summing Up

Review the lesson with students. Focus on everything they've learned about strategies and tools for reading a newspaper article. Read with students the Summing Up (on page 233 in the handbook). Go over with students the three goals for this lesson. Discuss which ones they feel that they achieved and which ones they feel they need more work on:

1. appreciating what's in newspaper articles

2. using the strategy of reading critically

3. understanding the organization of many news stories

Assessment and Application

Use the Quick Assess checklist to evaluate students' abilities to read and understand newspaper articles. Give students the opportunity to apply what they have learned through one of the two activities below. For students who are comfortable with the reading process and strategy, use one of the newspaper suggestions below for independent practice. For guided help with the strategy, use a *Student Applications Book*.

Quick Assess

Can students

- ☑ explain the purpose of a lead?
- ☑ name three things to look for when they preview?
- ☑ name and explain one strategy?
- ☑ create and use at least one reading tool?
- ☑ describe inverted pyramid organization?

1. Independent Practice

To show that students understand the lesson, ask them to apply the reading strategy of **reading critically** to a recent article in one of these:

- ■ a school or small local newspaper (*Charleston Elementary Gazette*, *Riverfront Times*, one in your school or local area)
- ■ a city or regional newspaper (*Chicago Tribune*, *St. Louis Post Dispatch*, one in your region)
- ■ a nationally recognized newspaper (*USA Today*, *New York Times*)

Ask students to:

1. Create a 5 W's Organizer for the article.

2. Create a Critical Reading Chart for the article.

3. Write a one-paragraph journal entry summarizing their reaction to the article they chose.

2. Student Applications Books

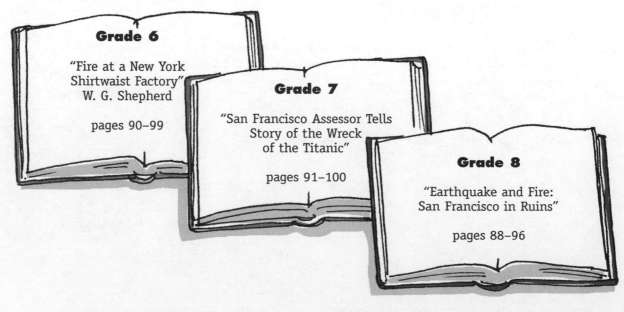

Grade 6

"Fire at a New York Shirtwaist Factory" W. G. Shepherd

pages 90–99

Grade 7

"San Francisco Assessor Tells Story of the Wreck of the Titanic"

pages 91–100

Grade 8

"Earthquake and Fire: San Francisco in Ruins"

pages 88–96

Reading a Magazine Article

Getting Ready

Goals

Here students read a magazine article about sharks called "A Killer Gets Some Respect" by Michael Tennesen. This lesson will help them learn to:

- ☑ appreciate different kinds of magazine articles
- ☑ use the reading strategy of questioning the author
- ☑ understand the organization of many magazine articles

Background

Connect the lesson with students' existing knowledge by asking them to:

- ▪ name their favorite magazines and explain why they read them
- ▪ describe kinds of magazine articles
- ▪ discuss the goals of magazine writers
- ▪ describe some of the general characteristics of magazine articles
- ▪ compare magazine articles with other media

Opening Activity

Show the class different kinds of magazines covering various subjects. Describe features that articles in these magazines have in common, such as titles, photos and other graphics, captions, headings, and the first paragraph. Ask students to look for these features as they read.

Overview

	Content	Teacher's Guide page	Reader's Handbook page
Selection	"A Killer Gets Some Respect" by Michael Tennesen		236–239
Reading Strategy	Questioning the Author	162	240, 652
Rereading Strategy	Reading Critically	167	245, 654
Tool	Main Idea Organizer	162	240, 674
	Viewpoint and Evidence Organizer	164	243, 683
	Critical Reading Chart	167	245, 670

Ancillaries

	Grade	Content	Page
Overhead Transparency	6, 7, 8	Previewing a Magazine Article	Number 22
Lesson Plan Book	7	Reading a Magazine Article	104
	8	Reading a Magazine Article	94
Student Applications Book	6	"Middle School Formula: High Stress = High Burnout"	100–108
	7	"Journey to a Secret City"	101–110
	8	"Sweet Victory: The Return of the Bald Eagle"	97–106
Website		www.greatsource.com/rehand/	

Before Reading

A   Set a Purpose

Before reading, ask students to set a purpose for reading "A Killer Gets Some Respect." Focus students on the Setting a Purpose questions in the *Reader's Handbook*, page 235, and discuss how these questions relate to a topic.

Setting a Purpose

■ **What do I need to know about sharks?**

■ **Are sharks really killers?**

B   Preview

Have students look over the article and try to learn something about it before they begin. Use the Preview Checklist on page 235 in the handbook with students. Then go through what to preview, using the Overhead Transparency.

Discuss each item in the Preview Checklist. Have students look for each item during their preview, from the title and author to the article's general length.

Preview Checklist

✔ the title and author

✔ any photographs, illustrations, and captions

✔ any headings or any larger type

✔ the first paragraph

✔ the general length or number of pages

Overhead Transparency

Before Reading

C Plan

Ask students to summarize what they learned during the preview. Then have them make a plan for getting information about the shark article. Suggest using the strategy of **questioning the author**. Discuss some of the reasons why this might be the best strategy to use. (One reason is that the strategy enables readers to examine and gain a greater understanding of the author's ideas or message.)

Reading Strategy: Questioning the Author

This strategy involves asking and answering questions that students would ask the author directly in order to better understand the author's message. Introduce the questions listed on page 240 in the *Reader's Handbook*. Encourage students to use graphic organizers to help them get the information they need to answer their questions.

A Main Idea Organizer helps students clarify how the separate ideas, examples, or paragraphs of the article fit together.

◆ **MAIN IDEA ORGANIZER** ◆ ─────────────────────

SUBJECT
MAIN IDEA

DETAIL 1	DETAIL 2	DETAIL 3	DETAIL 4

CONCLUSION

This organizer will help students identify the subject and the most important idea. Once students know the main idea, they can begin to see how the examples, details, and other information support it.

During Reading

D Read with a Purpose

While reading "A Killer Gets Some Respect," students consider what they already know about sharks to write questions for the author.

Questions and Answers

By writing questions and possible answers, students will better understand and piece together what the author is trying to say.

◀ QUESTIONS AND ANSWERS ▶ ─────────────────

PAGE 1
Why does the writer begin with two stories about shark attacks?
(He probably wants to grab the reader's interest.)

PAGE 2
Why include such a scary picture of a shark?
(He wants to scare us and get our attention.)

PAGE 3
Why does he include all of the information about tiger sharks?
(He wants to help readers understand what their lives are like.)

PAGE 4
Why does he end with the story of a shark attack?
(The victim makes it sound like the shark was defending itself.)

Other Useful Tools

Encourage students to consider the wide variety of graphic organizers in the lesson on "A Killer Gets Some Respect." Of course, students do not have to use all of them, but it's important to know the organizers are available. If students are familiar with several tools, they'll be able to pull out the right one when they need it.

■ **Outline**

■ **Thinking Tree**

■ **Inference Chart**

■ **Viewpoint and Evidence Organizer**

■ **Cause-Effect Organizer**

During Reading

How Magazine Articles Are Organized

The article "A Killer Gets Some Respect" has some narrative elements, but it mainly follows an organization built around its main idea: Sharks need to be understood, not destroyed.

Viewpoint and Evidence Organizer

Walk students through the completed Viewpoint and Evidence Organizer on page 243 in the handbook. This tool helps to break down and evaluate the writer's point of view, as well as the evidence that supports it. It also helps to illustrate the article's overall structure.

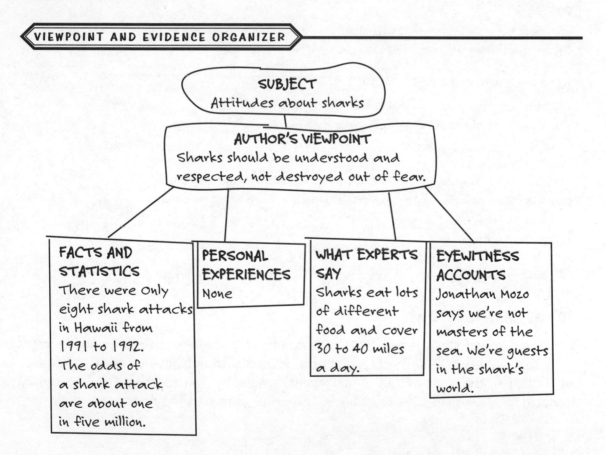

VIEWPOINT AND EVIDENCE ORGANIZER

SUBJECT
Attitudes about sharks

AUTHOR'S VIEWPOINT
Sharks should be understood and respected, not destroyed out of fear.

FACTS AND STATISTICS
There were only eight shark attacks in Hawaii from 1991 to 1992. The odds of a shark attack are about one in five million.

PERSONAL EXPERIENCES
None

WHAT EXPERTS SAY
Sharks eat lots of different food and cover 30 to 40 miles a day.

EYEWITNESS ACCOUNTS
Jonathan Mozo says we're not masters of the sea. We're guests in the shark's world.

The Viewpoint and Evidence Organizer helps students see the various kinds of support writers use to make the main idea convincing. Showing how an article is organized helps students know how to support a main idea when they write.

During Reading

E Connect

Explain to students that as they read, they should interact and make connections with the article. Responding emotionally and relating the content of the article to their own lives will help them learn more about the subject and remember it better. Help students by telling them to:

■ ask themselves questions
(Which of the facts, ideas, or personal examples best support the main point?)

■ think about the significance of the article's main points to them
(What myths do I know about people's views and actions toward tiger sharks?)

■ consider the educational information they know about tiger sharks
(How does knowing about tiger sharks' biology and behavior affect my view of them?)

■ evaluate the article by comparing it to their own opinions
(How do I feel about sharks? Do I think they deserve respect?)

■ evaluate the quality of Tennesen's ideas, evidence, and sources
(Do I feel that Tennesen's views and facts are fair, sound, and reliable?)

Note one reader's reactions to a passage in the article, as displayed on page 243 in the handbook.

from "A Killer Gets Some Respect"

Mozo expresses the feelings of many Hawaiians who have now come to accept the tiger shark as part of the marine environment. "I have no feelings of hatred against the shark," he says. "I don't want revenge. I don't think they should be eliminated. We are not the masters of sea. If it were our territory we'd have been born with gills and fins. I was out there a guest in his world. I just feel lucky he let me live."

Michael Tennesen, a freq___ ___ributor to National Wildlife, sw___ ___ Southe___ ___bout aut___ ___rks in t___

He makes a strong point. It's the shark's world, not ours.

Did the shark really make that decision? I doubt it.

After Reading

F Pause and Reflect

After reading, students need to consider whether they understand the article's primary message. Have students go back and review their original purposes in reading the article about tiger sharks. (What do I need to know about sharks? Are sharks really killers?)

Looking Back

■ **What have I learned about the topic?**

■ **What is the author's main idea?**

■ **Are there parts that I don't understand?**

■ **Do I agree with the author's viewpoint?**

Because "A Killer Gets Some Respect" offers many facts, details, and personal experiences, students probably won't be able to answer fully these Looking Back questions after their first reading. They also will have new questions of their own. Emphasize the need to return to the article for a second reading to grasp better all the facts about shark attacks, the research findings, and ultimately determine whether they agree with Tennesen's argument.

G Reread

Introduce a new strategy to help students look for answers to their questions in their second reading. The strategy of reading critically will help them consider both sides of the story and evaluate the quality of the supporting evidence and sources.

After Reading

Rereading Strategy: Reading Critically

Encourage students to use the strategy of reading critically when rereading. It will help them to go beyond the facts and details to see the point the writer is trying to make, and perhaps see some things the writer hasn't covered as well.

Reading critically involves looking for and evaluating the main message of the article, thinking about what the facts mean, separating fact from opinion, and judging the quality of the evidence.

A Critical Reading Chart is a useful tool when reading critically because it allows students to separate facts from opinions in the article and asks them to judge the evidence. It also allows students to see whether the other side of the story has been adequately addressed.

◄ CRITICAL READING CHART ►

1. VIEWPOINT?	• Sharks should be understood and respected. • They shouldn't be killed out of fear.
2. KINDS OF EVIDENCE?	• facts about sharks and attacks • expert source, Kim Holland • eyewitness account of victim
3. RELIABILITY OF SOURCES?	• knowledgeable scientists • Hawaii Institute of Marine Biology
4. QUALITY OF EVIDENCE?	• good quotations and lots of data • Where do attack statistics come from?
5. ANOTHER SIDE OF THE STORY?	• What about quotes from people who favored the bill to kill sharks?

After Reading

H Remember

At this point in the reading, students need to do something with the article in order to remember it and learn from it. Suggest one of the activities on page 246 in the *Reader's Handbook* or the creative assignment below.

Creative Assignment: "If Tiger Sharks Could Talk—The *Other, Other* Side of the Story." Ask students to discuss what they think tiger sharks would say about the issues, myths, and viewpoints expressed in the article as well as their past and present relationships with human beings. If you'd like, set up a forum-like discussion with individuals or groups arguing from three points of view: that of the biologists and pro-shark people, that of the anti-shark people, and that of the tiger sharks. You also can assign this as a short essay, a journal topic, or a small group discussion.

Summing Up

As a last step, review the lesson with students. Focus on everything they've learned about strategies and tools for reading a magazine article. Read with students the Summing Up (on page 246 in the handbook). Go over with students the three goals for this lesson. Discuss which ones they feel that they achieved and which ones they feel they need more work on:

1. appreciating different kinds of magazine articles

2. using the strategy of questioning the author

3. understanding the organization of many magazine articles

Assessment and Application

Use the Quick Assess checklist to evaluate students' abilities to read and understand magazine articles. Give students the opportunity to apply what they have learned through one of the two activities below. For students who are comfortable with the reading process and strategy, use one of the magazines suggested below for independent practice. For guided help with the strategy, use a *Student Applications Book*.

1. Independent Practice

To show that they understand the lesson, students can apply the reading strategy of **questioning the author** to an article in one of these magazines:

■ *Teen People*

■ *Boys' Life*

■ *Odyssey* (science)

■ *National Geographic for Kids*

Ask students to:

1. Write questions for the author of the magazine article.

2. Create a Main Idea Organizer for the article.

3. Write a one-paragraph critique of the article, giving their opinions about the author's perspective and the quality of the reporting and evidence.

2. Student Applications Books

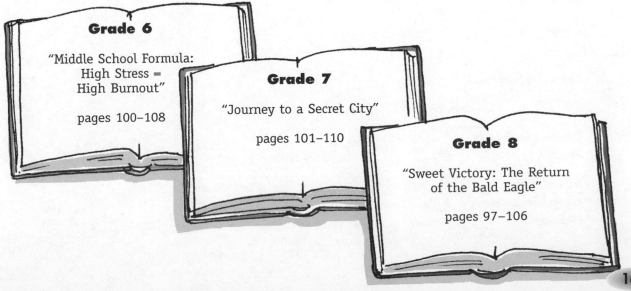

Grade 6

"Middle School Formula: High Stress = High Burnout"

pages 100–108

Grade 7

"Journey to a Secret City"

pages 101–110

Grade 8

"Sweet Victory: The Return of the Bald Eagle"

pages 97–106

Focus on Persuasive Writing

Goals

Here students focus on persuasive writing–ɑ type of writing that seeks to change readers' actions and views. Students will read "Parents, Not Cash, Can Enrich a School" by Mike Royko. This lesson will help students learn to:

> ☑ recognize the topic and the author's viewpoint
>
> ☑ identify the three parts of an argument
>
> ☑ use the strategy of critical reading to evaluate the argument

Background

Students are like most people in that they seldom think of advertisements, speeches, or emails from friends as being forms of "persuasive writing." Help students to see that these and other kinds of writing often set out to make an argument and change readers' opinions or actions. Connect this lesson with students' existing knowledge by asking them to:

■ define terms like *persuasive writing* and *viewpoint*

■ discuss the various places and media in which persuasive writing can be found

■ explore the different kinds of subjects and purposes of persuasive writing

Overview

	Content	Teacher's Guide page	Reader's Handbook page
Selection	"Parents, Not Cash, Can Enrich a School" by Mike Royko		248, 250–252
Reading Strategy	Reading Critically	171	249, 654
Tool	Argument Chart	172	249, 253, 667

Ancillaries

	Grade	Content	Page
Lesson Plan Book	6	Focus on Persuasive Writing	105
	8	Focus on Persuasive Writing	95
Student Applications Book	6	"Zoo Fire: A Community Disgrace"	109–111
	7	"Helmets Save Lives"	111–112
	8	"Dairy Farm Proposal a Terrible Mistake"	107–109
Website		www.greatsource.com/rehand/	

Before Reading

Ask students to preview the reading, looking for the topic and the author's viewpoint about it. Go over the Preview Checklist on page 248, and ask students to identify each item in the example editorial just below it.

Review the graphics for the organization of persuasive writing. Discuss with students how authors do not always state their opinions so plainly. Often an opinion is embedded in the first few paragraphs or the last few. Tell students that these are the best places to look for it.

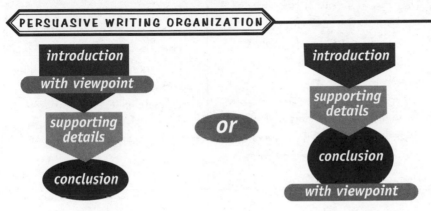

PERSUASIVE WRITING ORGANIZATION

introduction
with viewpoint
→
supporting details
→
conclusion

or

introduction
supporting details
conclusion
with viewpoint

Ask students to summarize what they learned in their preview. Then explain that they need a plan for reading persuasive writing more closely. Introduce the strategy of reading critically.

Reading Strategy: Reading Critically

Point out that the strategy of **reading critically** is useful with persuasive writing because it helps students see beyond facts and details to the main argument the writer is making.

During Reading

As students read, encourage them to keep their minds open. Their first job is to find the author's subject and decide on his viewpoint about it. Then ask them to examine Royko's argument and evidence.

Argument Chart

Explain and discuss the terms *viewpoint, support,* and *opposing viewpoint.* Point out that these key elements may appear in any order in a piece of writing. Model the use of an Argument Chart and refer students to the example on page 249.

During Reading

Discuss one reader's Argument Chart for Royko's editorial on page 253.

ARGUMENT CHART

VIEWPOINT	SUPPORT	OPPOSING VIEWPOINT
• Parents, not cash, make a school succeed. • Families need to be involved.	#1 The Roykos were poor, but kids did well in school because of family. #2 Des Plaines school has involved parents and high scores. #3 School in southwest suburbs has parents involved in reading contests. #4 School in western suburbs has no money, but it has packed open houses, and the parents spend time at the school.	• Royko admits that some will say more money means better test scores. • Royko argues against those who say money is the reason: ". . . crying out for more money for Chicago's schools isn't the answer, unless the money is spent in a way that will get results."

After Reading

After reading, have students think about what they learned about the topic and Royko's main argument. Quite often one reading of a complex editorial will not be enough to assure good comprehension. Students also will need to reread the editorial to decide what their own opinion of Royko's argument is. Even relatively short texts may need to be reread.

Below are three ways for students to learn from the persuasive writing they read.

1. Connect with the Writing

A critical part of the reading process is noting one's personal reactions to the material. Help students to make the topic their own by relating to it personally.

2. Evaluate the Argument

Students need to judge whether the argument made was "clear, convincing, and well supported." What are their feelings about the quality of evidence?

3. Decide How You Feel

Last, students need to consider how they feel about the author's viewpoint. One way to express their view is to write out their own argument about it.

Summing Up

To conclude the lesson, read with students the Summing Up on page 255. Remind students of all that they have learned about persuasive writing. Then have students talk about what they have learned in their own words.

Assessment and Application

Use the Quick Assess checklist to evaluate students' abilities to read and understand persuasive writing. Give students the opportunity to apply what they have learned through one of the two activities below. For students who are able to work independently, use one of the suggestions for independent practice. For guided help with the strategy, use a *Student Applications Book*.

Quick Assess

Can students

- ☑ give examples of different kinds of persuasive writing?
- ☑ identify the three parts of an argument?
- ☑ explain two common ways persuasive writing is organized?
- ☑ summarize what to look for in evaluating an argument?

1. Independent Practice

Ask students to apply the reading strategies and tools they just learned to an editorial, commentary, or column in their favorite magazine or their local newspaper.

2. Student Applications Books

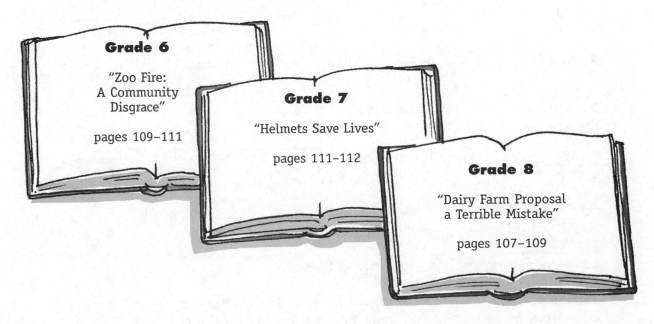

Grade 6

"Zoo Fire: A Community Disgrace"

pages 109–111

Grade 7

"Helmets Save Lives"

pages 111–112

Grade 8

"Dairy Farm Proposal a Terrible Mistake"

pages 107–109

173

Focus on Speeches

Goals

Here students focus on reading the kind of historical or political speeches found in textbooks. In this lesson, they read Ronald Reagan's famous speech, "The future doesn't belong to the fainthearted," made after the *Challenger* disaster in 1986. This lesson will help students learn to:

☑ sharpen their critical reading skills

☑ understand how speeches are organized

☑ recognize common propaganda techniques

Background

Ask students whether they know anything about NASA, the *Challenger*, or space exploration. Since students are more accustomed to listening to speeches than reading them, help them see the value of using a reading process, and explain that their main reading purpose is to find out the speaker's viewpoint, or message. Continue to connect this lesson with students' prior knowledge by asking them to:

■ explain what a speech is and tell its various purposes (including eulogies)

■ talk about speeches they've found memorable and why

■ explore ways in which speeches could influence an audience

Overview

	Content	Teacher's Guide page	Reader's Handbook page
Selection	"The future doesn't belong to the fainthearted" by Ronald Reagan		258-259
Reading Strategy	Reading Critically	175	260, 654
Tool	Main Idea Organizer	176	262, 674

Ancillaries

	Grade	Content	Page
Lesson Plan Book	7	Focus on Speeches	105
Student Applications Book	6	"My Heart Feels Like Bursting" by Satanta	112–113
	7	John Brown's Final Address to the Court	113–115
	8	"Ain't I a Woman" by Sojourner Truth	110–112
Website		www.greatsource.com/rehand/	

Before Reading

A brief preview will help students learn quite a bit about a speech. Looking for "the basics"—the subject, speaker, and occasion—will help them find and follow the speaker's main viewpoint (persuasive) or message (informative). Direct students to the Preview Checklist on page 257 and then the speech itself.

Preview Checklist

- ■ the title
- ■ any background information
- ■ the opening and closing paragraphs
- ■ any repeated words or phrases
- ■ overall length of the speech

As students skim through the speech, help them look for the critical background information that often appears before a speech, giving them basic information and a clue about the speaker's purpose. Point out to students that the annotations in the margin are color-coded, so they can match each annotation to the appropriate bit of highlighted text. After this preview, discuss what students have learned.

Once students have a good understanding, introduce the strategy of reading critically. Explain why this is a good strategy to use when reading speeches.

Reading Strategy: Reading Critically

Reading critically involves going beyond the facts and details to find the author's main purpose. With speeches, critical readers will want to identify the subject, decide on the speaker's viewpoint, and then evaluate how well the speaker supports the viewpoint. As noted on page 260, speakers can support their purposes with many different kinds of "evidence," including logical reasoning and emotional appeals.

During Reading

As students read Reagan's speech, encourage them to go slowly, keep an open mind, and imagine the real circumstances surrounding the occasion.

1. Find the Three Main Parts of a Speech

Introduce the three main parts of a speech as explained on page 261. Discuss the value of knowing a speech's basic structure. Model the use of a Nonfiction Organizer, as shown on page 261. Walk through the content in this organizer and stress that it can help students learn the author's viewpoint or main idea because it helps them to break a speech into its parts. Then they can look first at the introduction, where speakers often state their viewpoint.

During Reading

2. Identify the Main Idea and the Support

Using the Main Idea Organizer on page 262, ask students about Reagan's main idea and the details he includes to support it. Help them find the main idea in the body of the speech.

◄ MAIN IDEA ORGANIZER ►

TITLE: "The future doesn't belong to the fainthearted"			
MAIN IDEA: Explorers like the astronauts are brave.			
DETAIL 1 Three earlier astronauts died.	DETAIL 2 Astronauts are pioneers.	DETAIL 3 Expanding the frontiers is risky. The risks are part of the discovery process.	DETAIL 4 Challenger astronauts are like Sir Francis Drake, who also died while exploring.
CONCLUSION: The Challenger astronauts lived with honor and won't be forgotten.			

After Reading

After reading, ask students to pause and think about what they have read. Have them consider Reagan's viewpoint and the support that he used. Tell students that a second careful reading can help them to understand and evaluate this speech. Walk students through the Common Propaganda Techniques listed on page 263. Ask students to offer examples of their own. Point out that propaganda techniques are used in advertisements, magazine articles, and many other types of reading.

Summing Up

To complete the lesson, point out the Summing Up section. Go over what students have learned about the organization of a speech and the process of analyzing a speech. Then ask students to tell what they learned in their own words.

Assessment and Application

Use the Quick Assess checklist to evaluate students' abilities to read and understand speeches. Give students the opportunity to apply what they have learned through one of the two activities below. For students who are comfortable with the reading process and strategy, use the one of the speeches suggested below or another in your curriculum. For guided help with the strategy, use a *Student Applications Book*.

Quick Assess

Can students

- ☑ identify two general types of speeches?
- ☑ name three things to look for when they preview?
- ☑ list the three main parts of a speech?
- ☑ name and explain two common propaganda techniques?

1. Independent Practice

Ask students to apply the reading strategy and tools they just learned to all or part of one of the following speeches or another of your choice.

- ■ "I Have a Dream" by Martin Luther King, Jr.
- ■ "The Gettysburg Address" by Abraham Lincoln
- ■ "On Women's Right to Vote" by Susan B. Anthony
- ■ "Give Me Liberty or Give Me Death" by Patrick Henry

2. Student Applications Books

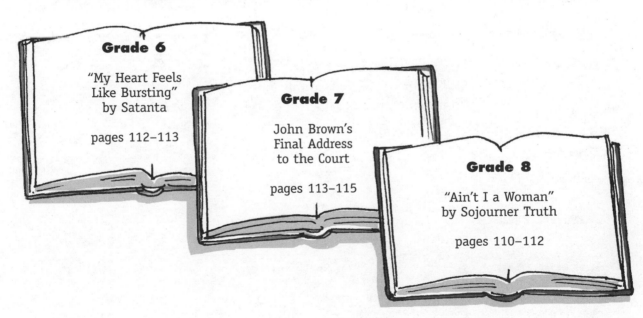

Grade 6

"My Heart Feels Like Bursting" by Satanta

pages 112–113

Grade 7

John Brown's Final Address to the Court

pages 113–115

Grade 8

"Ain't I a Woman" by Sojourner Truth

pages 110–112

Focus on Real-world Writing

Goals

Here students focus on "real-world" or "informational" writing. They read a school handbook, computer game instructions, and a train schedule. This lesson will help students learn to:

- ☑ identify a purpose when reading real-world writing
- ☑ understand the organization of the writing
- ☑ skim to find the information they need

Background

Ask students about the kinds of things they read in the course of a day other than books, magazines, or newspapers. On the board, write down all the real-world items they may need to read, such as bus schedules, menus, or instructions. Continue to connect this lesson with students' existing knowledge by asking them to:

- ■ discuss the reasons why real-world writing is necessary
- ■ note the kinds of real-world writing they usually read and why they are important
- ■ consider the ways in which real-world writing is written

Overview

	Content	Teacher's Guide page	Reader's Handbook page
Selection	Student Handbook Computer Game Instructions Train Schedule		267–268
Reading Strategy	Skimming	180	269, 656

Ancillaries

	Grade	Content	Page
Lesson Plan Book	8	Focus on Real-world Writing	104
Student Applications Book	6 7 8	School Dance Flier Field Trip Flier Graduation Announcement	114–115 116-117 113-115
Website		www.greatsource.com/rehand/	

Before Reading

Remind students that a quick preview of any reading is always helpful and worthwhile. With real-world writing, the extent of the preview will depend on the type of reading and the situation. Discuss the two types of real-world writing identified on page 265.

1. Free-reading

Ask students to suggest examples other than those provided in the text. Emphasize that this type of reading is important because it improves their speed in reading and their vocabularies.

2. Informational Reading

Point out to students that informational reading is often done quickly and informally. Stress that ability to read such materials as manuals, instructions, and calendars effectively can make their lives easier.

Real-world Reading Plan

Though students will not be tested on comic books, email messages, or software manuals, reading these kinds of materials is easier with a reading plan. Discuss the process shown in the plan on page 266 and stress that having a plan prior to reading will help students to spend less time looking for the information that they want.

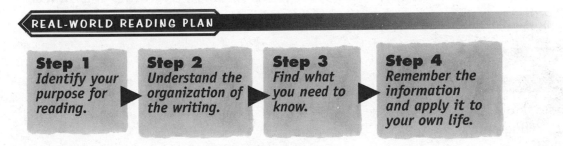

REAL-WORLD READING PLAN

Step 1 Identify your purpose for reading.

Step 2 Understand the organization of the writing.

Step 3 Find what you need to know.

Step 4 Remember the information and apply it to your own life.

Identifying a Reading Purpose

Read the section on page 266 with students. Emphasize the differences in reading purposes for real-world writing. Review the "Reading Purpose" chart on page 266.

READING PURPOSE

REAL-WORLD EXAMPLE	READING PURPOSE
1. Student Handbook	to find if religious holidays are excused absences or not
2. Computer Game Instructions	to learn how to load software and begin playing
3. Train Schedule	to find out which train will arrive in Hubbard Woods closest to 6:00 p.m. on a Friday

Before Reading

Understanding the Organization

Write the items that students should look for on the board. Emphasize that the key to finding information is figuring out how a source is organized. Provide several examples of real-world writing and guide students through the process of finding information in them.

Reading Strategy: Skimming

The strategy of **skimming** involves scanning or glancing at the writing to find specific information. Stress that when skimming, students follow clues in a reading's organization—its headings, boldfaced words, labels, and so forth—to zero in on the information that they need. Establishing their purpose is key to knowing what to look for.

During Reading

To help students find information, discuss the three tips on page 270. Students can use a highlighter to mark information that has to do with their purpose for reading. They should skim for headings and skip information they don't need. Students need to know that they don't have to look up all of the technical terms they find in real-world writing. Point out the *jargon* can often be understood from the context.

After Reading

If students didn't at first find the information they needed, they can try again using the following steps.

1. Reread

Sometimes students look up something in a hurry and get the wrong information. Students can go back to the chart, manual, or schedule and check carefully for the information they need.

2. Ask a Friend for Help

Remind students that "two heads are better than one," particularly if one is in a hurry to catch a train, join a program, or assemble a bookcase.

After Reading

3. Remember and Use the Information

Explain to students that the last step of the Real-world Reading Plan, remembering and using the information they've found, is critical. Discuss the circumstances in which students may want to remember real-world information, as found on page 272.

Summing Up

To conclude, point out the Summing Up section. Go over what students have learned about skimming, knowing one's reading purpose, and figuring out a reading's organization. Ask students to tell what they learned in their own words.

Assessment and Application

Use the Quick Assess Checklist to evaluate students' abilities to read and understand real-world writing. Give students the opportunity to apply what they have learned through one of the two activities below. For students who are able to work independently, use one of the real-world writings. For guided help with the strategy, use a *Student Applications Book*.

Quick Assess

Can students

- ☑ identify two types of real-world writing?
- ☑ explain the first step in the real-world reading plan?
- ☑ name and explain one strategy?
- ☑ define *jargon*?

1. Independent Practice

Ask students to apply the reading strategy and tips they just learned to baseball schedules, lunch menus, recipes, game instructions, newspaper indexes, or handbooks.

2. Student Applications Books

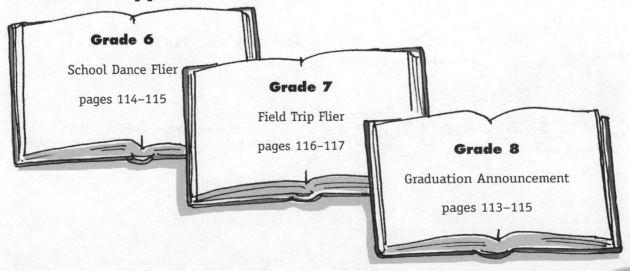

Grade 6

School Dance Flier

pages 114–115

Grade 7

Field Trip Flier

pages 116–117

Grade 8

Graduation Announcement

pages 113–115

Elements of Nonfiction

The following elements are commonly used in works of nonfiction, such as biographies, autobiographies, essays, and newspaper articles. In this section, each of these terms is presented with a teaching goal, an example, and a definition.

Use this section to introduce these terms to students so that they will learn to recognize them and use them when reading and analyzing nonfiction.

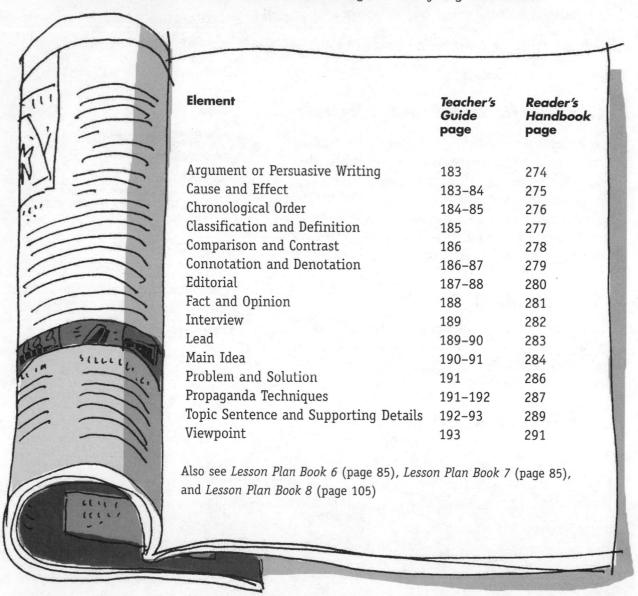

Argument or Persuasive Writing

Set Goal

Help students to recognize argument or persuasive writing, to understand that its general purpose is to advance an opinion, and to locate the support for that opinion.

Teach and Discuss

Read with students the **Example** quotation on page 274 in the handbook. Explain that this example shows Forbes taking a clear and strong stand on a particular issue. Ask students what they notice about the example and chart in the **Description**. Students probably will report the following:

■ Forbes's viewpoint represents one side of the issue.

■ Seeing the supporting details makes the argument look better, more persuasive.

Now discuss and emphasize the major points made in the chart. Highlight for students the need to have three or more supporting details for any persuasive writing. **Make it clear that argument or persuasive writing is aimed at convincing readers to share the same viewpoint as the author.**

Check Understanding

Ask students to review the **Definition** on page 274. To show comprehension, students can find magazine and newspaper features and columns that are examples of persuasive writing. Ask them to look for answers to these questions:

■ What is the viewpoint?

■ What details support it?

■ Do you agree with the opinion of the author? Why or why not?

Cause and Effect

Set Goal

Help students recognize the use of cause-effect writing and understand its purpose, which is to answer the question, "Why did this happen?"

Teach and Discuss

Read with students the **Example** on page 275. Diagram the cause and effect in this sample. Ask students what they notice about the example. They are likely to say the following:

■ The grandmother's death was the *cause* of the man's return.

■ His decision to return and be at his grandmother's grave appears to be an *effect*.

■ Looking for connections between causes and effects is interesting.

Now read with students the major points made in the **Description. Emphasize that analyzing a situation in terms of cause and effect helps to shed light on what happens and why it happens. Also, seeing the connections between events is part of what makes reading interesting.**

Check Understanding

Review with students the **Definition** on page 275. To test their comprehension, present them with another example of a cause-effect pattern. Students need to be able to answer questions like these:

■ What is the cause (or causes) of the event?

■ What are the effects?

■ What diagram can you draw for this sample?

Chronological Order

Set Goal

Help students recognize and understand chronological order in nonfiction writing.

Teach and Discuss

Read with students the **Example** on page 276. Explain that it describes events in the life of Galileo over a nine-year period. Ask students to react to the example. They will likely respond with the following:

■ Putting things in chronological order makes the example easy to understand.

■ The time periods and various ages of Galileo give information for putting the events on a Timeline.

Now go over the key points made in the **Description** with students. **Make sure students understand that times, dates, and transition words in a reading can help them keep track of the order of details.**

Check Understanding

To gauge students' understanding of the **Definition** on page 276, have them explain events in their own lives using chronological order. Encourage other students to answer questions about when certain events happened in the person's life and what occurred at the same time.

Classification and Definition

Set Goal

Help students identify classification and definition in nonfiction writing. Explain that textbooks and other nonfiction writing often define terms by grouping or classifying things.

Teach and Discuss

Read through the **Example** on page 277 with students. Explain that it tells about objects from space that are related yet have their own distinct characteristics. Encourage students to describe what they notice about the example. They will likely mention these things:

■ They didn't realize there are different kinds of space objects.

■ It makes sense to present and define objects in groups of similar items.

■ The objects are very much alike, yet different.

Now read over the major points made in the **Description** with students. **Reinforce that classification or definition is used in textbooks and nonfiction writing to explain something by putting it in a group while showing how it differs from other members of the group.**

Check Understanding

Have students review the **Definition** on page 277. As a way to gauge their understanding, have students assess this unit, "Elements of Nonfiction," and answer questions such as these:

■ Why are the items in the index classified as "elements"?

■ In what ways are the "elements" alike?

■ What is the same and what is unique about each of these elements?

Comparison and Contrast

Set Goal

Help students recognize examples of comparison and contrast in nonfiction and understand that writers use comparison and contrast to broaden understanding about a subject.

Teach and Discuss

Read the **Example** on page 278 with students. Ask students to volunteer what they notice about the comparison and contrast of crows and ravens. Likely responses include these:

■ Crows apparently do not live in the deserts, as ravens do.

■ To understand one of the birds, you should discuss the other.

Now go over the major points in the **Description. Stress that comparison and contrast in writing is only effective when the two things being compared are two types of the same thing.**

Check Understanding

Review with students the **Definition** on page 278. To test their comprehension, have them come up with detailed comparisons and contrasts of their own, such as two books, two opinions, or two biographies. They can write their comparisons in lists or in sentences. Have them also answer questions like these:

■ How does learning the similarities and differences between the two improve your understanding of them?

■ Why might nonfiction writers want to compare things like these?

Connotation and Denotation

Set Goal

Guide students in understanding that words can have both connotative (emotional) and denotative (literal) meanings.

Teach and Discuss

Read with students the **Example** on page 279. Point out that in this example Bailey White chose to describe the plight of turkeys using words not for their literal meanings but for their strong emotional suggestions. Ask students to describe what they notice about the example. Responses might include the following:

■ White is making this issue sound much more serious than it is.

■ The connotations she's using would be more appropriate for issues of world peace or human disasters.

■ White is using words with connotations to make a point.

Now go over the major points made in the **Description. Stress that students should watch for writing heavy with connotative words rather than hard evidence.**

Check Understanding

Have students review the **Definition** on page 279. To gauge their comprehension, have students look at the connotative and denotative uses of words such as *unhappy* and *miserable* and answer questions like these:

■ What is the literal meaning of each word?

■ In what ways can authors use the words to suggest meaning? Offer examples.

■ Look at an example of persuasive writing and identify the words with connotations. Explain why the author may have used them.

Editorial

Set Goal

Help students recognize editorials and understand that people write them to express their concerns or opinions about important current topics or issues.

Teach and Discuss

Read with students the **Example** on page 280. Point out that this editorial from a newspaper states the author's opinion about the school and supports it with numerous facts. Encourage students to say what they notice about the example. They are likely to respond with these ideas:

■ Use of concrete examples before the opinion makes the editorial more interesting.

■ The opinion is clearly stated.

■ The author's opinion is well supported.

Now read over the major points in the **Description** with students. **Emphasize that people write editorials in an attempt to persuade readers to share their opinions about timely or important topics.**

Check Understanding

Ask students to review the **Definition** on page 280. To show their comprehension, have students read another short editorial. Have them address questions like these:

■ What is the viewpoint of the writer?

■ What details does he or she use to support this viewpoint?

■ What do you think about this opinion? Why?

Fact and Opinion

Set Goal

Help students identify fact and opinion in writing and understand the difference between them.

Teach and Discuss

Go over the **Example** on page 281 with students. Point out each statement that is a fact and each that is an opinion and explain why. Have students discuss what they notice about the excerpt. They will probably report the following:

■ It's easy to identify numbers as facts.

■ The opinion about why officers were elected may be supported by research, but no research is mentioned here.

■ Sometimes it is hard to tell the difference between fact and opinion.

Now discuss the major points in the **Description** with students. **Emphasize that it is important to separate facts from opinions and be able to evaluate whether the opinions are well supported and the facts based on reliable sources.**

Check Understanding

Review with students the **Definition** on page 281. For practice, have students use newspapers or magazines that have persuasive writing to find examples of fact and opinion. Have them answer questions like these:

■ Do the facts seem to be from reliable sources? Why or why not?

■ How well does the author support his or her opinion?

■ Are the details sound and is the opinion well founded?

Interview

Set Goal

Guide students in understanding that interviews are planned, recorded conversations intended to give insights into people's personal lives or offer valuable information about particular areas of expertise.

Teach and Discuss

Read over the Dave Barry **Example** on page 282 with students. Explain that this excerpt from an interview allows readers to get to know and learn from this famous columnist. Ask students what they notice about the example. They are likely to report the following:

■ Barry seems like an easygoing, casual guy.

■ The questions seem to be on different topics.

■ Barry believes that the practice of writing improves one's literacy.

Now go over the major points in the **Description** with students. **Make it clear that an interview is usually conducted to explore the personal life of a significant person or topics related to the person's profession.** Discuss the importance of asking good questions in an interview. Talk with students about what some good and not-so-good questions might be.

Check Understanding

Have students review the **Definition** on page 282. To check their understanding, have students read a different interview and answer questions like these:

■ What is the purpose of this interview?

■ What do you learn about this person or a topic this person knows well?

Lead

Set Goal

Help students to identify the lead paragraph in an article and to understand its value in establishing what the article is about.

Teach and Discuss

Read the **Example** on page 283 with students. Point out that the set goal of the lead is to give readers an overview of the article and establish what it is about. Ask students what they notice about the lead. They will probably comment as follows:

■ The lead contains a lot of information.

■ The information appears to address the most important points of the article.

■ "Who" represents the "new Hispanic residents," "where" is Chicago, and so on.

Now go over the major points in the **Description** with students. **Emphasize that the lead is the opening paragraph or paragraphs and it answers basic journalistic questions about** *who, what, where, when,* **and** *why* **(and often also** *how***).**

Check Understanding

Have students review the **Definition** on page 283. To gauge their understanding, have them find the lead in several newspaper articles and answer questions like these:

■ What are the 5 W's of the article?

■ What, if anything, has been left out of the lead?

■ Where in the article is the lead located?

■ Would you like to continue reading the article? Why or why not?

Main Idea

Set Goal

Help students to recognize the main idea in a paragraph and to understand that the main idea is the "big idea" an author wants to convey.

Teach and Discuss

Read and discuss with students the **Example** on page 284. Identify the subject of the paragraph (volcano) and the main idea (before the volcano erupted, the place was beautiful and peaceful). Discuss with students the process of inferring the main idea. Ask students for their ideas on the example. They will most likely reply as follows:

■ The author uses a lot of examples to support the statement about the volcano.

■ Distinguishing between subject and main idea can be confusing.

Now walk students through the major points in the **Description**, including the charts on finding and inferring the main idea in a selection. **Make sure that students understand the difference between the subject and the main idea and how to find both.**

Check Understanding

Review with students the **Definition** on page 285. Choose several example paragraphs and have students follow the formula given for finding the main idea. Ask students questions like these:

∎ What is the subject, and what is the main idea?

∎ Is the main idea clearly stated, or does it have to be inferred?

∎ What details does the author use to support the main idea?

Problem and Solution

Set Goal

Guide students in recognizing a problem-solution pattern and in understanding that it is a method of organization that explains a problem and how it was solved.

Teach and Discuss

Go over the **Example** on page 286 with students. Explain that this example first describes the problem of the runaway Civil War and then goes on to explain how Lincoln sought to contain and ultimately end the national conflict. Have students indicate what they notice about the example. They will probably report the following:

∎ It's logical to describe the problem first and then the solution.

∎ The problem-solution approach adds to the tension in the Lincoln example.

Now walk students through the major points made in the **Description. Stress that taking notes or using an organizer can help make clear the problem-solution pattern in a piece of writing.**

Check Understanding

Have students review the **Definition** on page 286. Gauge their understanding by having them read problem-solution examples in magazine articles, biographies, or other nonfiction. Ask them to answer questions like these:

∎ What is the problem? What is the solution?

∎ Why do nonfiction writers often use problem-solution organization?

Propaganda Techniques

Set Goal

Help students to recognize propaganda techniques (often called *fallacies*) and to understand that they are appeals to emotions rather than logic.

Teach and Discuss

Read with students the **Example** on page 287. Explain that the author uses the bandwagon technique as a way of justifying cheating on tests. Have students point out what they notice about the example. Some probably will comment as follows:

■ The author first argues for cheating and then argues against it.

■ People use the bandwagon technique a lot.

■ Sometimes it's hard to identify techniques like this one.

Now walk students through the key points in the **Description**. Spend time discussing each of the propaganda techniques on page 288, giving additional examples as necessary. **Stress that propaganda techniques are not based on fact and can be used intentionally or by accident. They are very common and critical readers need to be able to spot them.**

Check Understanding

Ask students to review the **Definition** on page 288. To demonstrate understanding, students, either individually or as a group, can come up with two to three examples of each type of propaganda technique. They can choose from persuasive writing, TV or other commercials, speeches, editorials, or essays. Ads are a rich source and fun to analyze. Have students answer questions like these:

■ What argument is being made here?

■ What kind of propaganda technique is this? How do you know?

■ What kind of real evidence is needed to make this a valid argument?

Topic Sentence and Supporting Details

Set Goal

Help students to identify and differentiate between the topic sentence (focus of the writing) and the supporting details (sentences that relate to the topic sentence).

Teach and Discuss

Read with students the **Example** on page 289. Point out that the highlighted text and numbers will help them find the topic sentence and then the supporting details. Have students talk about what they notice in the example. Many will likely make the following observations:

■ A topic sentence makes reading easier.

■ Each of the details supports the author's point about the British military.

Now walk students through the major points made in the **Description. Stress that this kind of structure can help them spot what's important in a paragraph.**

Check Understanding

Review with students the **Definition** on page 290. To show understanding, students can look through their textbooks and other types of nonfiction to find examples of paragraphs with the topic sentence–supporting details pattern. Have students fill out organizers like the one on page 290 and answer questions like these:

■ What is the topic sentence in this paragraph?

■ What are the supporting details?

Viewpoint

Set Goal

Help students to recognize an author's viewpoint in persuasive writing and to understand that it is the author's perspective, or opinion, on an issue or topic.

Teach and Discuss

Read with students the **Example** on page 291. Point out the authors' stated viewpoint and the details that support this view. Ask students what they notice about the example. Students probably will report the following:

■ The authors are straightforward about their view.

■ This paragraph appeals to emotions because of word choice, as in the phrase "armed gangs of white ruffians."

Now go over the key points made in the **Description**. **Stress that it's important to identify an author's viewpoint and that viewpoints are not always clearly stated but often need to be inferred.**

Check Understanding

Ask students to review the **Definition** on page 291. To demonstrate their understanding, ask students to review examples of persuasive writing from speeches, newspaper editorials, magazine columns, and other nonfiction in which a viewpoint is expressed either directly or indirectly. Have them answer questions like these:

■ What is the author's viewpoint?

■ How do you know what the viewpoint is?

■ What evidence is used to support it?

■ Is the opposing side of the argument presented?

Reading
Fiction

Reading Kinds of Fiction

Reading a Short Story
Reading a Novel

Ways of Reading Fiction

Focus on Characters
Focus on Setting
Focus on Dialogue
Focus on Plot
Focus on Theme
Focus on Comparing and Contrasting

Elements of Fiction

Reading a Short Story

Goals

Here students read a short story called "Charles" by Shirley Jackson. This lesson will help them learn to:

- ☑ appreciate the genre of short story
- ☑ use the strategy of using graphic organizers
- ☑ understand the way short stories are often organized

Background

Connect the lesson with students' existing knowledge by asking them to:

- ■ define *short story*
- ■ name different kinds of short stories
- ■ list favorite stories and authors
- ■ discuss reasons that people read short stories

Opening Activity

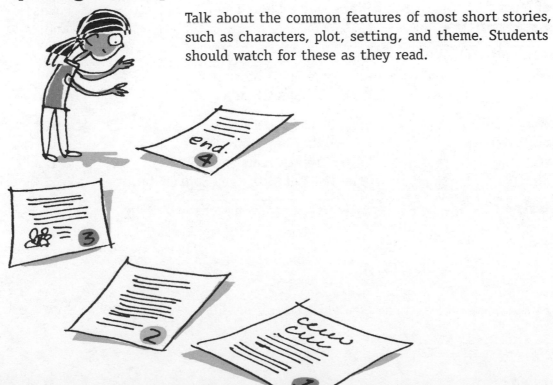

Talk about the common features of most short stories, such as characters, plot, setting, and theme. Students should watch for these as they read.

Lesson Resources

Overview

	Content	Teacher's Guide page	Reader's Handbook page
Selection	"Charles" by Shirley Jackson		296–303
Reading Strategy	Using Graphic Organizers	198	305, 662
Rereading Strategy	Close Reading	203	312, 642
Tool	Story Organizer	198	305, 678
	Character Map	199	306, 668
	Storyboard	199	307, 678
	Story String	199	307, 679
	Fiction Organizer	200	308, 671
	Inference Chart	200	308, 672
	Plot Diagram	201	309, 676
	Double-entry Journal	204	312, 671
	Venn Diagram	205	313, 683

Ancillaries

	Grade	Content	Page
Overhead Transparency	6, 7, 8	Previewing a Short Story	Numbers 23 and 24
Lesson Plan Book	6	Reading a Short Story	114
	7	Reading a Short Story	114
	8	Reading a Short Story	114
Student Applications Book	6	"The Diamond Necklace" by Guy de Maupassant	116–128
	7	"After Twenty Years" by O. Henry	118–128
	8	"The Tell-Tale Heart" by Edgar Allan Poe	116–127
Website		www.greatsource.com/rehand/	

Before Reading

A Set a Purpose

Before beginning the story, ask students to set a purpose for reading "Charles."
Focus students on the Setting a Purpose question on page 295 in the *Reader's Handbook* and discuss why it is a good question to guide their reading.

Setting a Purpose

■ **Who is Charles, and what is he like?**

B Preview

Ask students to look over the story, trying to learn a little bit about it before they begin. Use the Preview Checklist on page 295 in the handbook with students. Then walk through what to preview using the Overhead Transparencies.

Point out each item in the Preview Checklist. Suggest that students trace a finger down the page looking for characters' names and repeated words.

Point out to students that the annotations in the margin are color-coded, so students can match the annotation with the appropriate bit of highlighted text.

Preview Checklist

✔ any background or biographical material
✔ the title and author
✔ the first paragraph or two
✔ any names of characters or places
✔ anything repeated or set off in larger or bolder type
✔ any questions printed at the end

Overhead Transparencies

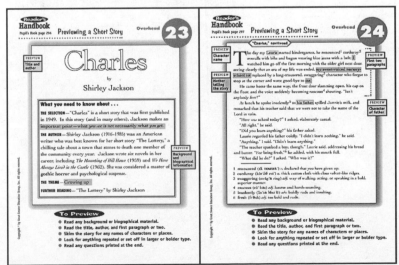

Before Reading

C Plan

Ask students to summarize what they learned in the preview. At this point in the reading process, have students make a plan for getting information about the character Charles. Suggest the strategy of **using graphic organizers**. Talk about some of the reasons this might be the best strategy to use. (One reason is that it offers a large number of reading tools for students to use, depending what the story is.)

Reading Strategy: Using Graphic Organizers

A Story Organizer presents information visually and helps put the major events of a story in order. As students read, suggest that they use other graphic organizers that will help them get the information they need from the story. Students need to be familiar with several kinds of graphic organizers. See the examples shown later in this lesson.

For example, a Story Organizer helps to clarify the plot by charting what happens at the beginning, middle, and end of a story.

◇ STORY ORGANIZER ▷

BEGINNING	MIDDLE	END

During Reading

D Read with a Purpose

While reading "Charles," students record their ideas on graphic organizers.
They do not use all of the organizers but choose the ones most useful to them.

1. Character Map

A Character Map works best with a story that focuses strongly on one or more characters. In "Charles," which has only a few characters, a Character Map works especially well.

CHARACTER MAP

WHAT HE SAYS
He is fresh and rude.

"CHARLES"

WHAT OTHERS THINK ABOUT HIM
Laurie says Charles gets into trouble and tells all of the bad things Charles did.
The teacher says she's never heard of Charles.

HOW HE LOOKS AND ACTS
He hit the teacher.
He bounces a see-saw on to a girl's head.
He throws chalk.
He kicks the teacher's friend.

HOW I FEEL ABOUT HIM
He is a bad kid, but who is he?

2. Storyboard

A Storyboard works best with a simple, straight forward story. It is a tool that gives students a clear, easy way to keep track of the major events in a story. This is an especially good tool for students who struggle as readers because it's so simple.

STORYBOARD

BEGINNING	MIDDLE	END
Laurie tells about a boy named Charles in his kindergarten class.	Charles does lots of bad things.	Laurie's mother learns that the teacher has never heard of Charles.

3. Story String

A Story String works best with a long story in which the plot has a lot of twists and turns. Here is an example from page 307 in the handbook.

STORY STRING

1. Laurie goes off to kindergarten. He tells about Charles.
2. Charles hits the teacher.
3. Charles bounces a see-saw on to a girl's head.
4. Charles throws chalk.
5. Charles kicks the teacher's friend.
6. The mother learns that no one named Charles is in the class.

During Reading

 Read with a Purpose continued

4. Fiction Organizer

A Fiction Organizer summarizes all of the key information about a story: its title, characters, point of view, setting, plot, theme, and style. It comes in handy when students need to prepare book reports.

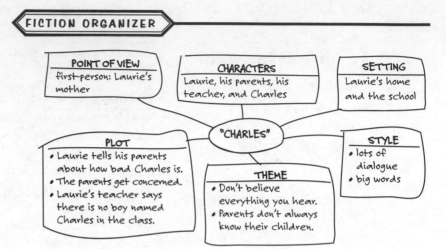

FICTION ORGANIZER

POINT OF VIEW
first-person: Laurie's mother

CHARACTERS
Laurie, his parents, his teacher, and Charles

SETTING
Laurie's home and the school

"CHARLES"

PLOT
• Laurie tells his parents about how bad Charles is.
• The parents get concerned.
• Laurie's teacher says there is no boy named Charles in the class.

THEME
• Don't believe everything you hear.
• Parents don't always know their children.

STYLE
• lots of dialogue
• big words

5. Inference Chart

An Inference Chart helps the reader pull together conclusions about a character. This chart can be useful when characters are hard to understand.

INFERENCE CHART

WHAT THE CHARACTER SAID OR DID:	WHAT I CAN CONCLUDE ABOUT THE CHARACTER:
1. hit a teacher	• has no respect for authority
2. bounced a see-saw on to girl's head	• is reckless
3. threw chalk	• does not listen and has little control

Other Useful Tools

Point out to students the wide variety of graphic organizers in the lesson on "Charles." Be sure students know that they *do not* have to use all of them, but it's good to know about them. As with any type of tool, students need to be able to pull out the right one when they need it. Other useful tools for short stories include the following:

■ **Viewpoint and Evidence Organizer**

■ **Paraphrase or Retelling Chart**

■ **K-W-L Chart**

■ **Webs**

During Reading

How Stories Are Organized

As students read, a Plot Diagram can help them to understand the plot and know what to expect.

Walk students through the Plot Diagram.

1. the exposition (background on setting and situation)

2. the rising action (where the tension or suspense increases)

3. the climax (where the tension or suspense reaches a critical point or peak)

4. the falling action (where tension lessens as the conflict starts to be settled)

5. the resolution (where the problem or conflict is solved)

PLOT DIAGRAM

3. Climax
The situation reaches a critical point. The tension that has been building reaches a peak.

2. Rising Action
Characters try to solve a problem or conflict, but the situation usually grows worse before the problem gets solved.

4. Falling Action
Tension decreases as the conflict begins to be settled.

1. Exposition
Background is given about the setting and situation the main characters find themselves in.

5. Resolution
The solution to the problem occurs at the story's end.

During Reading

E Connect

Explain to students that while reading, it's important to interact and make connections with the story. Relating a story to their own lives will help them remember it better and get more from it. Help students by telling them to:

- ask themselves questions
  (What would I say to Laurie?)

- think about the meaning of the story's events
  (What is the theme?)

- compare characters to people they know
  (Do I know anyone like Charles?)

- evaluate the story by comparing it to their own experience
  (What do I really think about the story?)

Show students the responses of one reader to this passage from "Charles."

> **from "Charles"**
>
> *Laurie's a brat like my neighbor.*
>
> "How *was* school today?" I asked, elaborately casual.
> "All right," he said.
> "Did you learn anything?" his father asked.
> Laurie regarded his father coldly. "I didn't learn nothing," he said.
> "Anything," I said. "Didn't learn anything."
> "The teacher spanked a boy, though," Laurie said, addressing his bread and butter. "For being fresh," he added, with his mouth full.
> "What did he do?" I asked. "Who was it?"
> Laurie thought. "It was Charles," he said. "He was fresh. The teacher spanked him and made him stand in a corner. He was awfully fresh."
> "What did he do?" I asked again, but Laurie slid off his chair, took a cookie, and left, while his father was still saying, "See here, young man."
>
> *My parents wouldn't let me act that way.*

Then ask students to make some inferences of their own about "Charles."

After Reading

F Pause and Reflect

After reading, students stop to consider whether they understand the story's meaning. Help students go back and review their original purpose in reading the story.

Looking Back

■ **Do I follow what happened?**

■ **Can I describe what the main characters are like?**

■ **Did the ending come as a surprise? Why or why not?**

■ **Does anything in the story confuse me?**

■ **What is the story's theme?**

Because "Charles" has a surprise ending, the Looking Back questions probably weren't fully answered on the first reading of the story. Help students see the need to return to the story for a second reading and understand that rereading is a natural part of the reading process.

G Reread

At this point students need a fresh way to go back into the reading. Have them review the story, looking for answers to their questions but using a new strategy.

Rereading Strategy: Close Reading

Encourage students to use this new strategy when rereading. Close reading is a good strategy when you are going back into a story to find details and interpret them.

Close reading provides a way for students to note facts carefully and think about why they're included in the story. With close reading, students select a part of the story for closer inspection, such as the beginning or ending. Then they interpret what it means, one sentence at a time.

Reread continued

Help students to see that in taking a closer look, they can use graphic organizers as well. Two organizers in the lesson help students interpret the text and compare characters in the story.

A Double-entry Journal helps students to analyze the meaning of text passages. They write key passages in the first column and their thoughts about the passages in the second column.

DOUBLE-ENTRY JOURNAL

TEXT OF "CHARLES"	WHAT I THINK ABOUT IT
"The day my Laurie started kindergarten, he renounced corduroy overalls with bibs and began wearing blue jeans with a belt . . . "	He "gave up" overalls, because he wanted to seem grown-up.
"I watched him go off the first morning with the older girl next door, seeing clearly that an era of my life was ended, my sweet-voiced nursery-school tot replaced by a long-trousered, swaggering character who forgot to stop at the corner and wave good-bye to me."	"I watched" suggests the mother is telling the story because he's her "tot." Era was ended—the one of her "sweet-voiced nursery-school tot." What's starting? Now Laurie is trying to act "cool."

A Double-entry Journal is one of the best ways to do a close reading. Students choose sentences that seem important or ones they don't quite understand. Then, with the Double-entry Journal, they try to gain a better understanding of the text. Help students understand why a reader may have chosen these passages as key. (The first one shows Laurie wanting to seem grown-up. The second shows that the story is told from the point of view of Laurie's mother.)

After Reading

G Reread continued

A Venn Diagram shows how characters are alike and different from each other. Point out to students that it's a tool for comparing and contrasting. The overlapping part of the two circles shows ways that the two characters are alike. The outer parts show ways in which they are different.

VENN DIAGRAM

LAURIE
- not a "sweet-voiced tot" anymore
- swaggering
- talks to parents a lot

BOTH
- rude
- disrespectful of adults (teachers and parents)
- kind of mean
- like to slam or bang things
- loud and kind of noisy
- in Kindergarten
- Kept after school

CHARLES
- likes to hit and kick
- punished by teacher
- gets others in trouble

H Remember

At this point in the reading, students need to make the story their own. They need to do something with the story in order to remember it. Encourage them to try the activities on page 314 in the *Reader's Handbook* or suggest this creative assignment.

Creative Assignment: Divide students into small groups and ask them to create movie posters about "Charles." Share the results. Which would be most likely to attract movie audiences?

Summing Up

Finally, review the lesson with students. Focus on everything they've learned about strategies and tools for reading a short story. Read with students the Summing Up (on page 314 in the handbook). Go over with students the three goals for this lesson. Discuss which ones they feel that they achieved and which ones they feel they need more work on:

1. recognizing the major parts of a story

2. using the strategy of using graphic organizers

3. understanding the way short stories are often organized

Assessment and Application

Use the Quick Assess checklist to evaluate students' abilities to read and understand short stories. Give students the opportunity to apply what they have learned through one of the two activities below. For students who are comfortable with the reading process and strategy, use one of the stories suggested below for independent practice. For guided help with the strategy, use a *Student Applications Book.*

Quick Assess

Can students

- ☑ describe how to set a purpose for reading?
- ☑ name three things to look for when they preview?
- ☑ name and explain one strategy?
- ☑ create and use at least one reading tool?
- ☑ list the five parts of most plots?

1. Independent Practice

To show that students understand the lesson, ask them to apply the reading strategy of **using graphic organizers** to one of the following selections:

- ■ "The No-Guitar Blues" by Gary Soto (from *Baseball in April and Other Stories*)
- ■ "A Crush" by Cynthia Rylant
- ■ "The Scholarship Jacket" by Marta Salinas

Ask students to:

1. Create a Story Organizer for the story.

2. Create a Plot Diagram for the story.

3. Write a journal entry giving their opinion of the story in one paragraph.

2. Student Applications Books

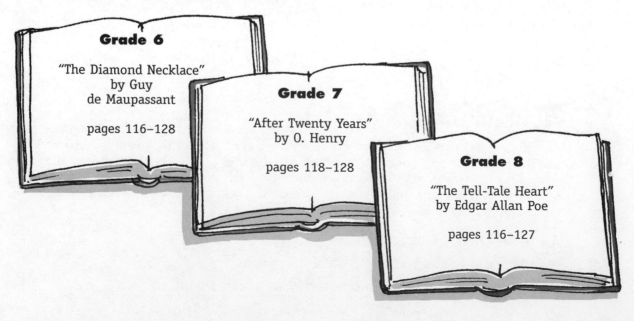

Grade 6

"The Diamond Necklace" by Guy de Maupassant

pages 116–128

Grade 7

"After Twenty Years" by O. Henry

pages 118–128

Grade 8

"The Tell-Tale Heart" by Edgar Allan Poe

pages 116–127

Reading a Novel

Goals

Here students read parts of the novel *Roll of Thunder, Hear My Cry* by Mildred D. Taylor. This lesson will help them learn to:

☑ examine the basic elements of a novel

☑ use the reading strategy of synthesizing

☑ recognize the plot organization of a novel

Background

Connect the lesson with students' existing knowledge by asking them to:

- define *novel* in their own words
- name some elements—such as character, theme, and so on—that are found in novels
- discuss the differences between a novel and a short story
- name novels that they have read or heard about
- discuss novels that they have enjoyed or not enjoyed

Opening Activity

Talk about the basic elements of a novel: characters, setting, plot, theme, point of view, and style. Remind students to watch for these as they read.

Overview

	Content	Teacher's Guide page	Reader's Handbook page
Selection	*Roll of Thunder, Hear My Cry* by Mildred D. Taylor		318–320, 323–324, 327–330, 335
Reading Strategy	Synthesizing	210	321, 660
Rereading Strategy	Using Graphic Organizers	217	336–338, 662
Tool	Fiction Organizer	210, 217	321, 337, 671
	Character Map	211	326, 338, 668
	Setting Chart	212	329, 677
	Summary Notes	212	331, 680
	Plot Diagram	213	332, 676
	Topic and Theme Organizer	214	333, 681
	Double-entry Journal	214	334, 671
	Venn Diagram	215	683
	Story String	215	679

Ancillaries

	Grade	Content	Page
Overhead Transparency	6, 7, 8	Previewing a Novel	Numbers 25–27
Lesson Plan Book	6	Reading a Novel	134–135
	7	Reading a Novel	115
	8	Reading a Novel	115
Student Applications Book	6	*The Secret Garden* by Frances Hodgson Burnett	129–140
	7	*Don Quixote de la Mancha* by Miguel de Cervantes	129–140
	8	*The Adventures of Tom Sawyer* by Mark Twain	128–139
Website		www.greatsource.com/rehand/	

Before Reading

A Set a Purpose

Before they read the excerpt from *Roll of Thunder, Hear My Cry*, students need to set a purpose for their reading. Ask students to read the Setting a Purpose questions on page 316 in the handbook and explain that these are good questions to guide their reading because they cover the important elements in reading fiction.

Setting a Purpose

- **Who is telling the story?** *(point of view)*
- **Who are the main characters, and what are they like?** *(characters)*
- **Where and when does the story take place? What is this place, culture, or historical period like?** *(setting)*
- **What happens?** *(plot)*
- **What is the author's central idea or message?** *(theme)*
- **How does the author express his or her ideas?** *(style)*

B Preview

Ask students to preview the novel to get some advance information before reading. Point out the Preview Checklist on page 317. Then walk students through what to preview using the Overhead Transparencies.

Read each item on the Preview Checklist with students. Ask them to point to and name as many of the items in the checklist as possible.

Point out to students that the annotations are color-coded, so they can match each annotation to the appropriate bit of highlighted text.

Preview Checklist

✓ the title and author

✓ the front and back covers

✓ any summaries or excerpts from book reviews

✓ any information about the author

✓ any introductory material, such as a preface

✓ any chapter names or illustrations

Overhead Transparencies

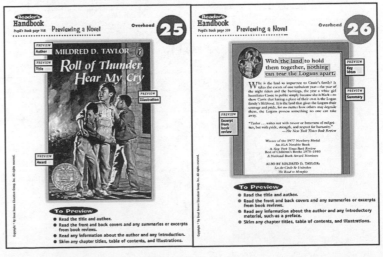

Before Reading

C Plan

Help students to summarize the information they gathered in their preview. Now have them make a plan for putting this information together. Suggest using the strategy of synthesizing.

Reading Strategy: Synthesizing

The strategy of **synthesizing** will help students read the novel because it enables them to gather information about many separate elements and pull the information together. You might compare readers of a novel to jugglers, because readers also need to keep their eyes on a number of things at once.

A Fiction Organizer is a good basic tool for reading a novel or any other fictional work. It offers a framework for keeping track of the novel's main elements—point of view, characters, setting, plot, theme, and author's style. Students should also use other graphic organizers as they read. Explain that they should be familiar with several types of graphic organizers.

Fiction Organizer

A Fiction Organizer gathers students' ideas about all the major elements of the novel in one place.

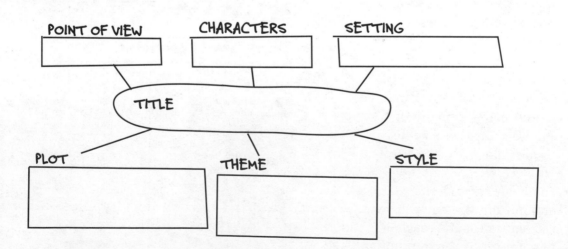

During Reading

D Read with a Purpose

While reading the selections from *Roll of Thunder, Hear My Cry,* students think about the elements of fiction and record information and ideas on organizers.

1. Point of View

Explain to students that understanding the **point of view**, or perspective from which the author tells the story, is important to understanding the information you learn as a reader. Walk students through the text excerpt and notes on page 323.

2. Characters

Discuss the element of **characters** in a novel and explain the notes on one character shown on page 326. A Character Map is helpful in organizing observations about each character's behavior, feelings, and interactions.

◁ CHARACTER MAP ▷

WHAT SHE SAYS AND DOES	WHAT SHE THINKS AND FEELS
• bosses Little Man	• hates dresses and shoes
• talks back to Stacey	• prefers woods and pond to school

CASSIE

HOW OTHERS REACT TO HER	WHAT I THINK ABOUT HER
• Stacey tells her to leave Little Man alone.	• understand why she likes to be outdoors
	• glad she's outspoken

Point out that the Family Tree Web organizer on page 325 gives students a way to keep track of all the characters and their relationships to each other.

3. Setting

Explain to students what **setting** means. Discuss the two types of settings, "general" and "immediate," giving the students an overview and examples of each one. If students are confused about the difference between a general and an immediate setting, compare the overall time period and place with the scenes in particular places. Review the excerpts and notes relating to setting on pages 327–330.

During Reading

D **Read with a Purpose** continued

A Setting Chart provides a format for recording the time and place of a fictional work, along with other details about setting. Talk with students about the kind of details they should look for and record.

> ◆**SETTING CHART**〉

ROLL OF THUNDER, HEAR MY CRY	
TIME: 1933 Few blacks own land. Most blacks are sharecroppers, always in debt to white landlords.	PLACE: rural Mississippi Settings are farms and plantations on which cotton is grown. Logans have 400-acre farm next to Granger plantation.

4. Plot

Discuss the element of **plot** with students. One way to keep track of the plot of a novel is to write brief Summary Notes for each chapter.

Chapter-by-chapter Summary Notes give students a way to remember plot details. Explain how this is a quick, easy tool to help students remember what happens in a novel.

> ◆**SUMMARY NOTES**〉

CHAPTER 1
Cassie and Little Man get whipped at school for refusing to accept books that whites hand down to blacks. Mama stands by them.

CHAPTER 2
Papa brings Mr. Morrison home to protect the family after the Berrys are burned by some white men.

A Timeline can also help students keep track of plot events in chronological order. See page 331 for an example.

How Novels Are Organized

As students read, a knowledge of the five stages in a traditional plot structure can help them understand the plot and what to expect.

TRADITIONAL PLOT STRUCTURE

3. Climax
Conflict and tension reach a peak.

2. Rising Action
Conflict and suspense build.

4. Falling Action
Conflict gets worked out, and tensions lessen.

1. Exposition
Characters, setting, and conflict are introduced.

5. Resolution
Conflict is resolved.

After reviewing the description of a plot's five stages, point out that fictional plots can be easily organized on a Plot Diagram. Show students the Plot Diagram on page 332, which applies these five stages to *Roll of Thunder, Hear My Cry*.

PLOT DIAGRAM

CLIMAX
Papa starts a fire to prevent hanging of T. J.

RISING ACTION
Mama loses job, Papa gets shot, and violence increases.

FALLING ACTION
Men work together to fight fire.

EXPOSITION
Logans are trying to hold on to their land in tough times.

RESOLUTION
T. J. goes to jail, but Logans are unhurt.

213

During Reading

D **Read with a Purpose** continued

5. Theme

Discuss the element of **theme** with students, as introduced on page 333. A Topic and Theme Organizer gives students a step-by-step plan for figuring out what a novel's theme is.

▷ **TOPIC AND THEME ORGANIZER**

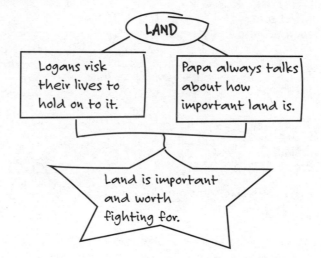

1. Big idea or topic:

2. What characters say or do:

3. What is important to learn:

LAND

Logans risk their lives to hold on to it.

Papa always talks about how important land is.

Land is important and worth fighting for.

6. Style

Explain the element of **style** to students as discussed on page 334. A Double-entry Journal provides a good format for commenting on an author's style.

▷ **DOUBLE-ENTRY JOURNAL**

QUOTES	MY THOUGHTS AND REACTIONS
• Uncle Hammer speaking to T. J.: "Then if you want something and it's a good thing and you got it in the right way, you better hang on to it and don't let nobody talk you out of it. You care what a lot of useless people say 'bout you you'll never get anywhere, 'cause there's a lotta folks don't want you to make it. . . . "	• I love all the dialect and slang the characters use. • I can hear how Uncle Hammer speaks. • The long sentences make me take time reading it. • It's a very informal feeling.

During Reading

D **Read with a Purpose** continued

Other Useful Tools

Point out to students the wide variety of organizers offered in this lesson. It's a good idea for students to be familiar with many organizers, so they can pull out the right one when they need it. Here are a few more possibilities for organizers that work well with novels.

■ **Venn Diagram**

■ **Character Development Chart**

■ **Inference Chart**

■ **Paraphrase or Retelling Chart**

■ **Story String**

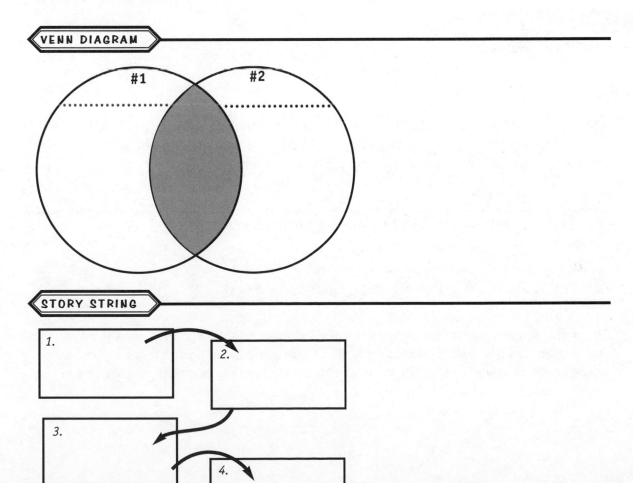

During Reading

E Connect

Remind students to read actively. Have them record their personal reactions to characters and events and connect what they read to their own lives and experiences. Help students by asking them the questions on page 335.

> *How did you feel about each character? Which did you like and which did you dislike? Why?*

> *What was your reaction to major events in the novel?*

> *How can you relate what happened in the novel to your own feelings and experiences?*

> *What else have you read that's like this novel?*

After Reading

F Pause and Reflect

Ask students to pause and think about whether they have grasped the novel's meaning when they've finished reading. Help them to go back and think about the basic elements and how well they understand them.

Looking Back

■ Can I describe the main characters and setting?

■ What is the theme?

■ What's the central conflict of the novel?

■ Are there parts of the novel that I don't understand?

Given the length and complexity of a novel, students probably can't answer all of these questions. Ask students what parts still are confusing for them and what new questions they have. Help them to see that rereading is a natural part of the reading process.

After Reading

G Reread

When they reread, students will benefit from taking a fresh approach to the material. Encourage them to use a new reading strategy.

Rereading Strategy: **Using Graphic Organizers**

Encourage students to use this new strategy when rereading.

Using graphic organizers can help students get a sense of any single aspect of a novel or of the novel as a whole.

Looking at the Whole Novel

Help students to pull together their information about all the elements of the novel. The Fiction Organizer helps them to build this kind of summary.

◀ FICTION ORGANIZER ▶

POINT OF VIEW
Cassie, a first-person narrator

CHARACTERS
Logan family
Mr. Morrison
the Wallaces
the Simms family
the Averys

SETTING
1933–34
rural Mississippi
farmland near forests

ROLL OF THUNDER, HEAR MY CRY

PLOT
Conflict: Logans trying to keep land and fight racism
Rising Action: Mama losing job, Papa getting shot, T. J. almost hanged
Climax: Papa setting the fire

THEME
Big Ideas:
land, racism, family, friendship
Theme Statements:
Land is worth fighting for.
Stand up to injustice.
Family support makes people stronger.
Friends should help each other, no matter what.

STYLE
casual style
lots of dialect
lots of slang words like "ain't" and "gotta"
vivid descriptions

Looking at One Part

A Character Map provides an example of a graphic organizer that addresses one aspect of a novel. See page 338 for what this looks like.

After Reading

 Remember

As a final step, students can try one of the activities suggested in the handbook on pages 338–339 or the Creative Assignment below.

Creative Assignment: Ask students to write about how their friends would react to T. J. or Cassie. Ask students to consider how their friends would feel about what T. J. or Cassie says and does. When students are finished, let volunteers read what they have written to the class.

Summing Up

Finally, review the lesson with students. Remind them of everything they've learned about strategies and tools for reading a novel. Read with students the Summing Up on page 339. Go over with students the three goals for this lesson. Ask them to discuss which of these they feel that they achieved and which they feel they need more work on:

1. examining the basic elements of a novel

2. using the reading strategy of synthesizing

3. recognizing the plot organization of a novel

Assessment and Application

Use the Quick Assess checklist to evaluate students' abilities to read and understand novels. Give students the opportunity to apply what they have learned through one of the two activities below. For students who are comfortable with the reading process and strategy, use one of the novels suggested below for independent practice or another novel in your curriculum. For guided help with the strategy, use a *Student Applications Book*.

1. Independent Practice

To show that students understand the lesson, ask them to apply the reading strategy of **synthesizing** to one of the following selections:

■ *Freak the Mighty* by Rodman Philbrick

■ *Jade Green: A Ghost Story* by Phyllis Reynolds Naylor

■ *Taking Sides* by Gary Soto

Ask students to:

1. Create a Character Map or Setting Chart for the novel.

2. Create a Fiction Organizer for the novel.

3. Write a journal entry about what the novel meant to them.

Quick Assess

Can students

☑ list the six basic elements of a novel?

☑ name three things to look for when they preview?

☑ name and explain one strategy?

☑ create and use at least one reading tool?

☑ explain traditional plot structure?

2. Student Applications Books

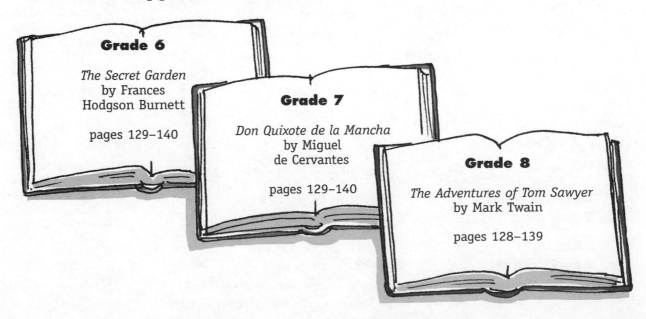

Grade 6

The Secret Garden by Frances Hodgson Burnett

pages 129–140

Grade 7

Don Quixote de la Mancha by Miguel de Cervantes

pages 129–140

Grade 8

The Adventures of Tom Sawyer by Mark Twain

pages 128–139

Focus on Characters

Goals

Here students focus on characters—who the events happen to—by reading an excerpt from the novel *The Cay* by Theodore Taylor. This lesson will help students learn to:

Background

Explain to students that their knowledge about characters will help them understand the plot, give them insight into other characters, and help them find the theme. Ask students to:

■ define what a *character* is

■ discuss memorable characters they've encountered in fiction or the movies

Overview

	Content	Teacher's Guide page	Reader's Handbook page
Selection	from *The Cay* by Theodore Taylor		342, 346, 347, 348
Reading Strategy	Using Graphic Organizers	222	344, 662
Tool	Character Map	221, 222	341, 343, 668
	Character Web	222	344, 684
	Inference Chart	223	347, 672
	Character Development Chart	225	350, 668

Ancillaries

	Grade	Content	Page
Lesson Plan Book	6	Focus on Characters	124
Student Applications Book	6	"The Reluctant Dragon" by Kenneth Grahame	141–143
	7	*Onion John* by Joseph Krumgold	141–143
	8	*I Am the Cheese* by Robert Cormier	140–141
Website		www.greatsource.com/rehand/	

Before Reading

Point out to students several ways to categorize characters.

Major and Minor Characters

Explain that the main character is the person that the main conflict in the plot revolves around. Point out that *protagonist* is another name for the main character and that minor characters are not as important as the main character but they interact with the main character and each other. Show students how to use the title, chapter titles, picture captions, and skimming to identify the main character, as explained on page 340 in the *Reader's Handbook*.

Clues about Characters

Point out to students that authors are careful to place clues about their characters throughout the story or novel. Direct students' attention to the list of things they should pay attention to on page 341.

■ physical appearance and personality

■ speech, thoughts, feelings, and actions

■ interactions with other characters

■ direct comments by the author

Encourage students to use a Character Map to sort out the details that they find about each character. Explain this tool's usefulness in pulling many different kinds of details together to enable them to draw conclusions.

◄ CHARACTER MAP

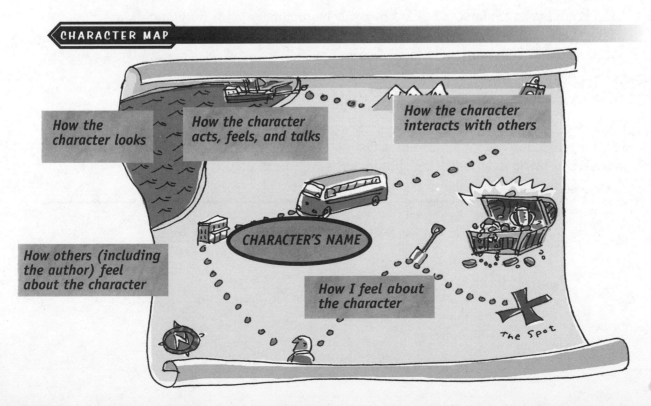

How the character looks

How the character acts, feels, and talks

How the character interacts with others

How others (including the author) feel about the character

CHARACTER'S NAME

How I feel about the character

The Spot

During Reading

Point out to students that they need to focus on what the characters are saying and doing, how they are described, and how they interact with other characters. Have students read the excerpt from *The Cay*. Work through the text with them, making sure that they understand the notes about how different aspects of characters have been "read."

Analyzing Characters

Show students how they can get a lot of information from that brief passage. Go over the sample Character Map with them. Ask them to comment on this reader's notes on Timothy and point to the text that supports these points.

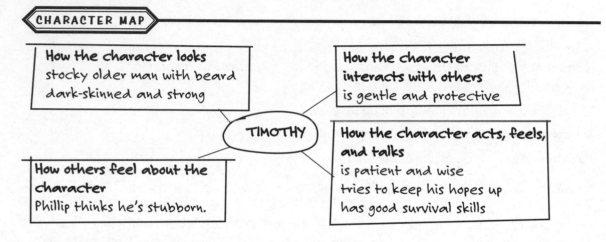

CHARACTER MAP

How the character looks
stocky older man with beard
dark-skinned and strong

How the character interacts with others
is gentle and protective

TIMOTHY

How others feel about the character
Phillip thinks he's stubborn.

How the character acts, feels, and talks
is patient and wise
tries to keep his hopes up
has good survival skills

Creating a Portrait

Help students to understand that they will be gradually learning more about characters as they read through the novel and that they should adjust their notes accordingly. Encourage students to discuss the characters with other students.

Reading Strategy: Using Graphic Organizers

Character clues can be hard to keep organized, which is why using graphic organizers is a helpful strategy. Model use of a Character Web for students and explain the benefits of using this tool. (It's simple and easy to make.)

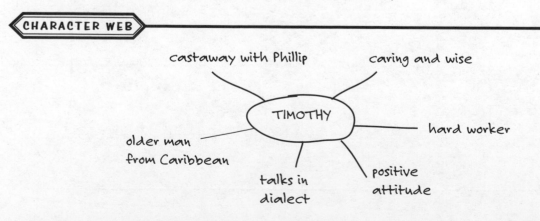

CHARACTER WEB

castaway with Phillip   caring and wise

TIMOTHY

older man from Caribbean   hard worker

talks in dialect   positive attitude

Character and Plot

Read with students the information about character and plot on page 345. Help students to understand that, most of the time, a character has a role in the plot, and their job as readers is to figure out what the character is intended to reveal.

What is this character's role in the plot?

How would the plot be different without this particular character?

How do the events in the plot affect this character?

Remind students that the plot is often built on the conflict that is facing the main character. Remembering to keep track of the character's problems will help them to understand what is keeping the plot going.

Character and Other Characters

Emphasize that students should pay attention to characters' interactions with each other, since even the most minor characters' reactions can give clues about the main character. Go over the excerpt to illustrate these points.

Model use of the Inference Chart to organize thoughts on characters' interactions. Make sure that students understand the importance of making these kinds of inferences as readers.

▸ INFERENCE CHART ▸

WHAT CHARACTERS SAID OR DID	WHAT I CAN CONCLUDE ABOUT THEM
Phillip and Timothy exchange names.	Timothy is nice to Phillip, but Phillip shows little patience with or respect for Timothy.

Character and Theme

Explain to students that theme is the author's statement about life. Prepare students for study of character and theme by telling them to watch for two types of clues.

1. A Character's Statements or Thoughts about Life

Sometimes a character states the theme or drops clues about it. Alert students to the fact that they should watch for important statements on life and other "big ideas" from characters. As an example, read with students the excerpt on page 347.

2. A Change in a Character

Direct students' attention to the material about changes in character on page 348. Stress that changes in character can reveal theme. Go over the definitions of *static character* (doesn't change) and *dynamic character* (does change). Read and discuss with students the four questions below.

> **Does the character learn anything?**

> **Does the character feel different about himself or herself?**

> **Does the character's physical appearance change?**

> **Do other characters notice differences in him or her?**

Tell students to keep these questions in mind as they read. Remind them when they see a change to ask themselves what the author was trying to say. Be sure that students understand how the highlighted text relates to the note about changes in Phillip. Remind them that often the text will not directly state that a change has occurred as the highlighted passage from *The Cay* does.

After Reading

Ask students to take some time to reflect on what they've learned about characters. Read through each of the questions below with students. Tell students to ask themselves these questions after reading a story or novel.

Can I identify the main and minor characters?

Why do they act the way they do?

Do I know what they are like?

Do any of the characters change from the beginning to the end?

How does my view of characters affect my understanding of plot, other characters, and theme?

Encourage students to reread as a final step in the reading process. Suggest going back to the very first description of a character and the very last to see the contrast. Ask students to keep notes. Model the use of the Character Development Chart as a way to organize information on characters. Read through this chart with students and make sure they understand the meaning of changes in Phillip.

CHARACTER DEVELOPMENT CHART

PHILLIP ENRIGHT

BEGINNING	MIDDLE	END
Phillip is adventurous and immature. He doesn't like Timothy because he's different from him.	Phillip begins to grow up. He grows physically stronger and mentally tougher. He becomes friendly with Timothy.	Phillip has learned many new things. He gets to go back home, and he understands life better.

POSSIBLE THEMES: Accept people for who they are, not what they look like.
Don't take life for granted.

Summing Up

To finish the lesson, point out the Summing Up section. Review all that students have learned about character types; how characters influence plot, other characters, and theme; and how to use tools when studying characters. Ask students to tell what they have learned in their own words.

Assessment and Application

Use the Quick Assess checklist to evaluate students' abilities to read and understand characters. Give students the opportunity to apply what they have learned through one of the two activities below. For students who are comfortable with the reading process and strategy, use the suggestion below for independent practice. For guided help with the strategy, use a *Student Applications Book*.

1. Independent Practice

Ask students to create a Character Map or Character Development Chart for the protagonist in a novel they are currently reading.

2. Student Applications Books

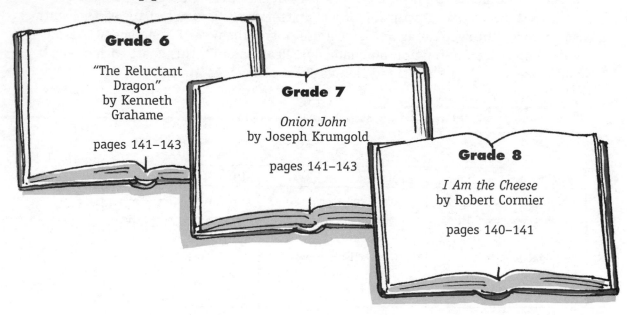

Grade 6

"The Reluctant Dragon" by Kenneth Grahame

pages 141–143

Grade 7

Onion John by Joseph Krumgold

pages 141–143

Grade 8

I Am the Cheese by Robert Cormier

pages 140–141

Focus on Setting

Goals

Here students focus on the setting—the time and place—of a fictional work. In this lesson, students will learn to:

☑ spot clues about setting

☑ relate the setting to the mood, characters, and plot

☑ analyze the setting

Background

Students often see setting as "description" that is just a lot of "extra words." Help students see what these words mean and how setting can help them learn about a story's mood, characters, and plot. Connect this lesson with students' existing knowledge by asking them to:

■ define *setting*

■ discuss fiction they've read in which setting is important

■ explore ways that setting could influence other elements of a story

Overview

	Content	Teacher's Guide page	Reader's Handbook page
Selection	*Shiloh* by Phyllis Reynolds Naylor		352, 354–357
Reading Strategy	Close Reading	228	353, 642
Tool	Setting Chart	228	353, 677
	Double-entry Journal	229	355, 671
	Inference Chart	229	356, 672
	Summary Notes	230	358, 680

Ancillaries

	Grade	Content	Page
Lesson Plan Book	6	Focus on Setting	125
Student Applications Book	6	*The Wonderful Wizard of Oz* by L. Frank Baum	144–145
	7	*M.C. Higgins, the Great* by Virginia Hamilton	144–145
	8	"To Build a Fire" by Jack London	142–143
Website		www.greatsource.com/rehand/	

Before Reading

Help students see how much they can learn from a quick look through a reading. By looking for specific clues about the setting, they can quickly learn a lot about the story. Direct students to the Preview Checklist on page 352 and then the reading itself.

Preview Checklist

■ **the time of day, the day of the week, month, season, or year**
■ **any specific dates or historical details**
■ **any feelings about particular places**
■ **any place names (such as city, state, and country names)**
■ **the physical environment, including weather conditions and landscape**

When students focus on setting, they need a strategy that helps them to find details.

Reading Strategy: Close Reading

Close reading helps students analyze the parts of a text that give clues about setting. Help students look through the excerpt for information about time and place. Work with students to create a Setting Chart like the one below to help them summarize their findings.

SETTING CHART

NOVEL NAME: <u>Shiloh</u>

CLUES ABOUT TIME	CLUES ABOUT PLACE
time of day afternoon	place names Friendly, Sistersville, Wheeling, and Parkersburg
season summer	physical environment high in the hills

During Reading

As students read, they can see how the setting helps them understand the mood, characters, and the plot.

Setting and Mood

Point out the passage on page 354. Read through it with students. Then ask them what feeling the passage gives them. Point out the connection between their "feeling" as a reader and **mood**. Writers convey things through the mood created by a setting. Model the use of a Double-entry Journal as a way to delve into a setting and see the mood a writer is creating. Explain to students that they need to infer what this information about the setting is telling them.

◄ DOUBLE-ENTRY JOURNAL ►

QUOTE	MY THOUGHTS
"River to one side, trees the other—sometimes a house or two."	Sounds like a pretty place. I can see why Marty would like it.
". . . slinking along with his head down, watching me, tail between his legs like he's hardly got the right to breathe."	Poor dog. Sounds like he's scared. Maybe he's been beaten. Marty's probably worried.

Setting and Characters

With the Inference Chart on page 356, show students how readers use inferences. Walk students through the steps of first seeing what a **character** says or does and then making inferences. It may help to tell students that an inference takes something you find as a reader and puts it with something you bring to the reading.

◄ INFERENCE CHART ►

WHAT CHARACTER SAYS OR DOES	MY INFERENCES ABOUT THE CHARACTER
enjoys walking in hills	finds beauty in nature
notices different animals too	knows a lot about nature and animals
likes living where he does	enjoys the country life, not a city boy

Setting and Plot

A change in the setting often signals that something will happen. For example, in the passage, Marty walks from the woods, where he is thinking about Shiloh's needs, to his home, where he begins to worry about what his parents will think. Go through the passage with students. Help them see how the change in the setting signals a change in the **plot** and the conflict with Marty's parents over Shiloh.

After Reading

After reading, have students pause and ask themselves what they learned about the setting and its effect on the story. Help them also to see what else they might learn by looking at a reading a little more closely.

1. List Key Settings

Suggest to students that, after reading, they take a moment to jot down what the settings are. All too often students let the information pass by without taking note of what it can tell them about the overall mood, characters, and plot of the work. They can record what they learn in Summary Notes like those in the text on page 358.

◀ SUMMARY NOTES ▶

SETTING	WHAT HAPPENED
woods near Marty's house	Marty finds Shiloh.
Judd Travers's yard	Shiloh's scared when he's taken back.
hills nearby	Marty hides Shiloh to protect him.

2. Make Sketches

Ask students to draw a simple sketch of the setting. Sketching will help visual learners especially. The quality of the sketch is less important than the image it creates for students because the image will help them remember the story.

Here is another way for students to probe the settings of the fiction they read.

Try a Creative Assignment

Ask students to create a movie poster showing the setting of the story. Encourage students to add details that will help them picture one scene of the story.

Summing Up

To wrap up the lesson, point out the Summing Up on page 359. Go back over all that students have learned about how setting relates to characters, mood, and plot. Then ask students to tell what they learned in their own words.

Assessment and Application

Use the Quick Assess checklist to evaluate students' abilities to read and understand setting. Give students the opportunity to apply what they have learned through one of the two activities below. For students who are ready to work independently, use one of the books suggested below or another one in your curriculum. For guided help with the strategy, use a *Student Applications Book*.

Quick Assess

Can students

- ☑ explain two kinds of setting clues?
- ☑ name and explain one strategy?
- ☑ create and use at least one reading tool?
- ☑ explain how setting relates to mood, characters, and plot?

1. Independent Practice

Ask students to apply the reading strategies and tools they just learned to the descriptions of setting in one of the following novels.

- ■ *The Call of the Wild* by Jack London
- ■ *Cookcamp* by Gary Paulsen
- ■ *On the Far Side of the Mountain* by Jean Craighead George

2. Student Applications Books

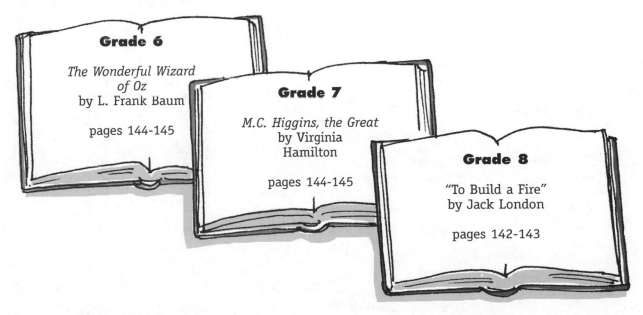

Grade 6

The Wonderful Wizard of Oz by L. Frank Baum

pages 144-145

Grade 7

M.C. Higgins, the Great by Virginia Hamilton

pages 144-145

Grade 8

"To Build a Fire" by Jack London

pages 142-143

Focus on Dialogue

Goals

Here students will focus on dialogue by reading excerpts from *Roll of Thunder, Hear My Cry*. This lesson will help students learn to:

- ☑ recognize the form of dialogue
- ☑ appreciate how dialogue affects the plot, characters, and mood
- ☑ use close reading to understand dialogue

Background

Help students to understand how important dialogue can be in a story or novel. Point out the three key roles that dialogue can play in a work, as listed on page 360 in the handbook. Connect this lesson with students' existing knowledge by asking them to:

- define *dialogue* and point it out in a fictional work
- name works they've read in which dialogue seemed to be important
- analyze the effect that dialogue can have in a piece of writing

Overview

	Content	Teacher's Guide page	Reader's Handbook page
Selection	*Roll of Thunder, Hear My Cry* by Mildred D. Taylor		361, 362, 364, 365, 366
Reading Strategy	Close Reading	233	363, 642
Tool	Double-entry Journal	234	364, 671
	Thinking Tree	235	367, 680

Ancillaries

	Grade	Content	Page
Lesson Plan Book	7	Focus on Dialogue	124
Student Applications Book	6	*Alice in Wonderland* by Lewis Carroll	146–147
	7	"The Adventure of the Dying Detective" by Sir Arthur Conan Doyle	146–147
	8	*Dicey's Song* by Cynthia Voigt	144–145
Website		www.greatsource.com/rehand/	

Before Reading

Point out to students that they need to recognize the way dialogue is written and used in a piece of literature.

Quotation Marks and Speech Tags

Show students that dialogue is always set off with quotation marks. Explain that speech tags give readers information about the tone and who is speaking. To illustrate these points, review the excerpt on page 361.

New Paragraph for New Speaker

Students will easily be able to identify a new speaker during their reading because a new paragraph is used each time. Ask students to go back to the previous reading and point out when the speaker changes. Tell them to explain how they spot the change (new paragraphs and speech tag changes).

Continued Dialogue

Explain to students that sometimes a quote will continue on for another paragraph or two until the person is finished speaking. Quotation marks will show when the speaker is finished. Walk students through the excerpt on page 362 as an example. Have students point out the clues that the dialogue continues.

Quote within a Quote

Show students that if a character quotes someone else, the author will use single quotation marks. Gauge their understanding of this convention by working through the excerpt on page 362. If necessary, model it for students by quoting one of them and then writing out what you said on the board.

During Reading

As students read with a focus on dialogue, remind them to stay focused on who's talking, what is being said, and how it is said.

 **Close Reading**

Explain to students that close reading is a useful strategy when studying dialogue, since it involves close, word-by-word and line-by-line examination of text. Stress that careful reading of dialogue will help them to understand more about the characters, the plot, and the mood of a work.

During Reading

Clues about Character

Direct students' attention to the section on clues about character on page 363. Help students to realize that they can learn about people or characters (in real life and fiction) by what they say and do. Point out to students that this is how they decide who their friends are—by listening to what they say. Read with students the excerpt on page 364. Ask students what hints about character they find based on what the characters say and their tones of voice.

Model for students the use of a Double-entry Journal to keep a record of their reactions to the dialogue and characters. Make sure that students understand how this tool is used. It can help them "translate" the dialogue into words they understand.

◆ DOUBLE-ENTRY JOURNAL ◆

QUOTE	MY THOUGHTS
"Big Ma," I said, "what Mr. Granger need more land for?" "Don't need it," Big Ma said flatly. "Got more land now than he know what to do with."	Cassie's grandmother knows that Mr. Granger is just greedy. She's trying not to lose her temper.

Clues about Plot

Let students know that the characters' interactions in a story are much like their own with their friends. Show them that by observing these interactions carefully, students can learn about plot, including earlier events and events to come. Read the excerpt on page 365 with students. Make sure that students understand how the highlighted parts of the text reveal plot events.

Clues about Mood

Ask students to explain what is meant by *mood* (feeling in a piece of writing). Have them cite examples of conversations they've had or could have in which someone reveals his or her feelings by words or by the manner in which the words are said. Point out to them that conversations in a story or novel also can convey sadness, anger, happiness, and other moods.

Ask students to look over the reading log on page 366 and consider whether they agree with this interpretation.

After Reading

Tell students that, after they read a fictional work, a Thinking Tree provides one way for pulling together their clues about plot, character, and mood. Model use of a Thinking Tree such as the one on page 367. Spend time reading and discussing the material recorded in this Thinking Tree. It affords a clean, easy way for students to examine dialogue and infer what it's telling them as readers. Suggest that they note page numbers of any examples they include.

THINKING TREE: DIALOGUE

PLOT

what will happen next

Example:
"I'll show y'all how we're gonna stop that bus from splashing us."

what has come before

Example:
Finally T. J. said, "Okay. See, them Berry's burnin' wasn't no accident. . . ."

CHARACTER CLUES

what the character says

Example:
"You were born blessed, boy, with land of your own."

how the character says it

Example:
"Ah, man, don't look so down," T. J. said cheerfully.

MOOD

adds humor

Example:
"You wanna be bald, girl?"

adds tension

Example:
"Stacey, they're coming after us!"
"What!" squeaked Christopher-John.

Summing Up

To conclude the lesson, ask students to review the Summing Up section. Go over all that they've learned about the forms and importance of dialogue and how it affects plot, characters, and mood. Then ask students to tell what they learned in their own words.

Assessment and Application

Use the Quick Assess checklist to evaluate students' abilities to read and understand dialogue. Give students the opportunity to apply what they have learned through one of the two activities below. For students who are comfortable with the reading process and strategy, use one of the books suggested below, or another one in your curriculum, for independent practice. For guided help with the strategy, use a *Student Applications Book*.

1. Independent Practicep

Ask students to apply the reading strategy and tools they just learned to the dialogue in one of these books:

■ *Dragonwings* by Laurence Yep

■ *Black Beauty* by Anna Sewell

2. Student Applications Books

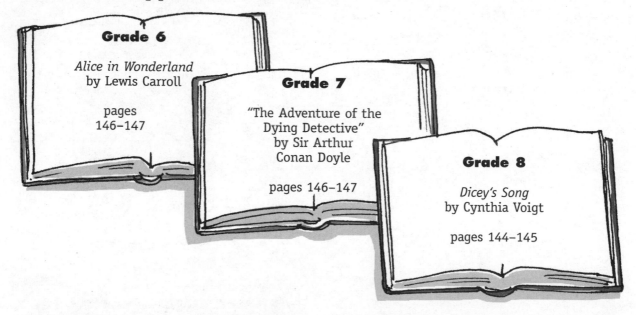

Grade 6

Alice in Wonderland
by Lewis Carroll

pages
146–147

Grade 7

"The Adventure of the Dying Detective"
by Sir Arthur Conan Doyle

pages 146–147

Grade 8

Dicey's Song
by Cynthia Voigt

pages 144–145

Focus on Plot

Goals

Here students focus on the plot—the events that occur throughout a story, from beginning to end, with one event usually leading to another. Students will read from the short story "Last Cover" by Paul Annixter. This lesson will help students learn to:

- ☑ track the events of a plot
- ☑ identify the story's subplots and think about subplot's relationship to a main plot
- ☑ consider how the plot contributes to a story's theme

Background

Make sure students understand that plot refers to what happens in a story or other fictional work. Connect with students' knowledge by asking them to:

- ▪ give examples of plot events from fiction they've read
- ▪ discuss the differences between plot and other elements of a story
- ▪ identify the different elements that affect the plot

Overview

	Content	Teacher's Guide page	Reader's Handbook page
Selection	from "Last Cover" by Paul Annixter		370, 372
Reading Strategy	Using Graphic Organizers	238	371, 662
Tool	Plot Diagram	238, 240	369, 375, 676
	Storyboard	238	371, 678
	Story Organizer	239	373, 678

Ancillaries

	Grade	Content	Page
Lesson Plan Book	6	Focus on Plot	115
	8	Focus on Plot and Theme	124
Student Applications Book	6	"The Ugly Duckling" by Hans Christian Andersen	148–149
	7	"Little Red Cap"	148–149
	8	"King Midas"	146–148
Website		www.greatsource.com/rehand/	

Before Reading

Explain to students that they need to understand the parts of a plot in order to follow the action in fiction. Read with them the five parts of a plot as listed on page 369 in the handbook. Discuss each part separately and relate it to the Plot Diagram on that page. Make sure that students are aware of the words that signal a change in plot, including *next, later*, and *then*.

◄ PLOT DIAGRAM

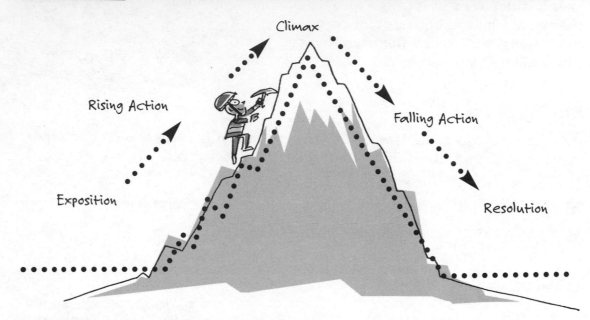

Getting Background Information

As you read this part with students, emphasize the three types of information students should watch for when skimming the opening paragraphs of a novel or story. Remind students to take brief notes as they go along. Call attention to the highlighted clues and sticky notes with the excerpt on page 370.

During Reading

As students read, make sure that they watch for plot changes and for clues about how plot events fit together.

Reading Strategy: Using Graphic Organizers

Explain that using graphic organizers can help students identify and keep track of plot events. A Storyboard can be a fun way for students to record the events of a plot. Model the use of the Storyboard with the example on page 371.

During Reading

Understanding Flashbacks

Make sure that students understand what a flashback is (a jump back in time). Explain to them that some stories are written with flashbacks and that students need to learn to expect them. Authors often will start at an important point in a story to pull readers in and then double back to provide background needed for telling the story. Walk students through the excerpt from "Last Cover" on page 372 as an example of a flashback. Model the use of a Story String (page 679 in the Almanac) or a Timeline (page 681 in the Almanac) to keep track of plot events and note interruptions such as flashbacks.

Understanding Subplots

Explain to students what a subplot is (a less important, subordinate plot). Stress to students that they need to differentiate between the main plot and subplots in a story. Model the use of a Story Organizer to record details about a subplot, as shown on page 373. Be sure, too, that students know not all stories have a subplot.

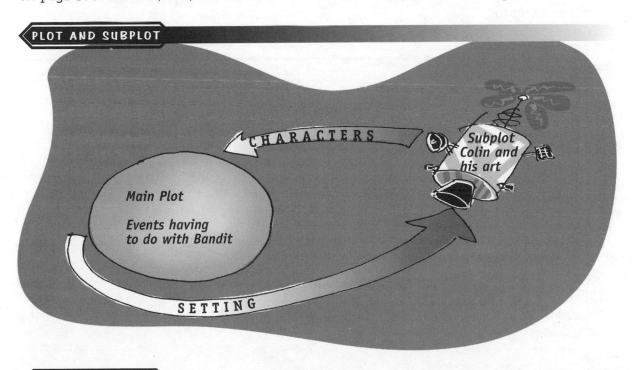

PLOT AND SUBPLOT

CHARACTERS

Main Plot

Events having to do with Bandit

Subplot Colin and his art

SETTING

STORY ORGANIZER

"LAST COVER" SUBPLOT

BEGINNING	MIDDLE	END
Father criticizes Colin for making picture frame.	Colin doesn't draw anything.	Father appreciates picture of Bandit hiding.

After Reading

After reading, students need to focus on summarizing the plot. To help them do this, review the five parts of a plot as explained earlier. Suggest these additional methods that will help them understand the plot.

1. Ask Questions

Ask students if there is anything about what they've read in the plot that sparks their interest or curiosity. Ask them to pursue that and other questions about why the author wrote the plot that particular way or used devices such as flashbacks. Discuss the two questions on page 374 and follow up with the journal entry on that page.

2. Consider the Climax

For meaning, students should think about the story's climax, or turning point. They can review this part of the plot for clarification on theme and for better understanding of the story. Use the Plot Diagram on page 375 as a model to show the detailed breakdown of a fictional plot. Discuss the finished Plot Diagram with students.

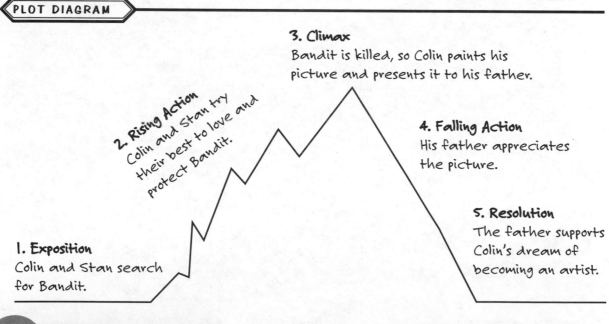

PLOT DIAGRAM

3. Climax
Bandit is killed, so Colin paints his picture and presents it to his father.

2. Rising Action
Colin and Stan try their best to love and protect Bandit.

4. Falling Action
His father appreciates the picture.

5. Resolution
The father supports Colin's dream of becoming an artist.

1. Exposition
Colin and Stan search for Bandit.

Summing Up

To conclude the lesson, go over the Summing Up section. Review what the students have learned about the five parts of a plot and the various tips on understanding plot, subplots, and theme and how they are all related. Then ask students to tell what they learned in their own words.

Assessment and Application

Use the Quick Assess checklist to evaluate students' abilities to read and understand a story's plot. Give students the opportunity to apply what they have learned through one of the two activities below. For students who are comfortable with the reading process and strategy, use one of the books suggested, or another one in your curriculum, for independent practice. For guided help with the strategy, use a *Student Applications Book*.

Quick Assess

Can students

☑ summarize the five parts of a plot?

☑ define a flashback?

☑ define a subplot?

☑ create and use at least one reading tool?

1. Independent Practice

Ask students to apply the reading strategies and tools they just learned to the plot in one of the following books:

■ *Walk Two Moons* by Sharon Creech

■ *A Girl Named Disaster* by Nancy Farmer

■ *Johnny Tremain* by Esther Forbes

2. Student Applications Books

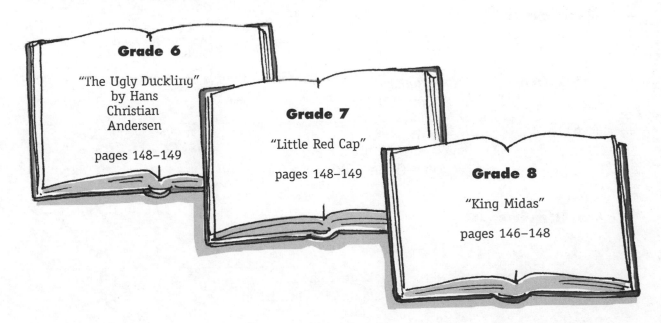

Grade 6

"The Ugly Duckling" by Hans Christian Andersen

pages 148–149

Grade 7

"Little Red Cap"

pages 148–149

Grade 8

"King Midas"

pages 146–148

Focus on Theme

Goals

Here students focus on theme—the author's main point or message—by looking back at Mildred D. Taylor's novel *Roll of Thunder, Hear My Cry*. This lesson will help them learn to:

Background

Theme can be a difficult concept for students to understand. Authors' messages can be hard to find in fiction. Prepare students by helping them to see that they find the theme through the other elements of a story. Explain that they will learn a three-step plan for finding a theme. Ask students to:

■ define *theme* in their own words

■ give examples of statements that they think might be themes of works

Overview

	Content	Teacher's Guide page	Reader's Handbook page
Selection	*Roll of Thunder, Hear My Cry* by Mildred D. Taylor		
Tool	Summary Notes	244	378, 680
	Double-entry Journal	244	379, 671
	Topic and Theme Organizer	245	381, 681

Ancillaries

	Grade	Content	Page
Lesson Plan Book	7	Focus on Theme	125
	8	Focus on Plot and Theme	124
Student Applications Book	6	*The Secret Garden* by Frances Hodgson Burnett	150–151
	7	*Don Quixote de la Mancha* by Miguel de Cervantes	150–151
	8	*The Adventures of Tom Sawyer* by Mark Twain	149–151
Website		www.greatsource.com/rehand/	

Before Reading

Read with students the three-step plan they can use to find the theme of a story, as listed on page 377. Explain that they can use this plan for understanding the theme in any story, novel, or play.

Plan for Understanding Theme

Step 1 Find the "big ideas" or general topics in the work.

Step 2 Find out what the characters do and say that relates to the general topics.

Step 3 Come up with a statement of the author's point or message about the topic.

Step 1: Find the "big ideas" or general topics in the work.

Explain to students that a general topic is the "big idea" or subject. Direct their attention to the list at the bottom of page 377. Read it aloud. Ask students whether they've read fiction or seen movies that use any of these topics for themes. Carefully go over how they should begin looking for topics the minute they begin previewing. Use Mildred Taylor's *Roll of Thunder, Hear My Cry* as an example of a novel with a number of possible themes.

COMMON TOPICS FOR THEMES

childhood	growing up	loyalty	self-reliance
courage	hate	nature	success
death	hope	patience	trust
faith	Identity	patriotism	truth
family	independence	prejudice	unhappiness
freedom	justice	race relations	violence
friendship	love	self-improvement	war

During Reading

As students read, urge them to watch for information on the topic or "big idea" of the work. Encourage them to write this information down as they go.

Step 2: Find out what the characters do and say that relates to the general topics.

Emphasize to students that theme is revealed through character and plot. Ask them to look for specific information on general topics that they've identified. Go over the different forms that these clues can sometimes take, as listed on page 378 (repeated words or ideas, symbols, important plot events or dialogue, and changes in characters).

During Reading

Model the use of Summary Notes and a Double-entry Journal as two ways of keeping track of details as they relate to the theme. Ask students to notice that the actions and quotes are used as supporting material around the topic of racism.

Summary Notes

Show students how to write chapter-by-chapter or page-by-page Summary Notes for a fictional work. Explain that this type of note-taking will help them to keep track of the events of a fictional work and that it is particularly useful for a long novel.

SUMMARY NOTES

Racism in <u>Roll of Thunder, Hear My Cry</u>

Chapter 1	African-American students get worst books.
Chapter 4	Wallaces make Logans go in back door of store.
Chapter 6	Mama explains that some white people think they're better.

Double-entry Journal

Show students how to fill in a Double-entry Journal. Note that they write important quotes or pieces of pertinent information in column one and their ideas about these quotes in column two. Review the completed Double-entry Journal on page 379 with students. Make sure students know that this tool will help them to clarify their thoughts and make inferences.

DOUBLE-ENTRY JOURNAL

Quotes	What I Think about It
about Mr. Simms: ". . . he's one of those people who has to believe that white people are better than black people to make himself feel big."	Mama feels bad that Cassie has to learn about prejudice. What she says about slavery and how people don't believe blacks and whites are equal really upsets Cassie. I would feel bad, too.
"White people may demand our respect, but what we give them is not respect but fear. What we give to our own people is far more important because it's given freely."	Mama is very realistic. She wants Cassie to understand that racism can lead to danger. Maybe something bad will happen.

Go over with students the list of other themes in Taylor's novel. Suggest to students that they fill out separate organizers for each theme.

After Reading

Tell students that after reading, it's time to collect their clues about theme and figure out what they mean.

Step 3: Come up with a statement of the author's point or message about the topic.

Remind students not to get confused about the terms *topic* and *theme*. Review the definitions to clarify your point. Use the example in paragraph one of Step 3 on page 380 in the handbook to illustrate the point.

Explain to students that people's ideas about the theme of a work might vary and that it's important to have notes, examples, and details that support the theme they decide on. Model the use of a Topic and Theme Organizer as a format for pulling together the main topic of the work, the actions and words of the characters, and students' conclusions about theme. Review the Topic and Theme Organizer based on *Roll of Thunder, Hear My Cry*, pointing out that this organizer includes four examples from the novel to support the theme statement. Also walk students through the Tips for Making Theme Statements on page 382. Practice coming up with different possible theme statements for the same topic.

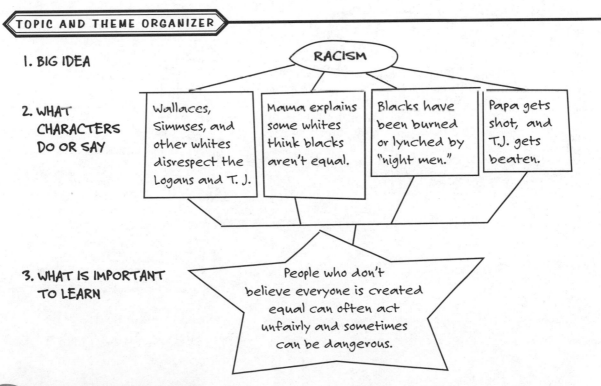

TOPIC AND THEME ORGANIZER

1. BIG IDEA — RACISM

2. WHAT CHARACTERS DO OR SAY

- Wallaces, Simmses, and other whites disrespect the Logans and T. J.
- Mama explains some whites think blacks aren't equal.
- Blacks have been burned or lynched by "night men."
- Papa gets shot, and T.J. gets beaten.

3. WHAT IS IMPORTANT TO LEARN

People who don't believe everyone is created equal can often act unfairly and sometimes can be dangerous.

Summing Up

To wrap up the lesson, point out the Summing Up section. Go back over all that students have learned about the three-step plan for finding the theme in fiction. Then ask students to tell what they learned in their own words.

Assessment and Application

Use the Quick Assess checklist to evaluate students' abilities to read and understand story themes. Give students the opportunity to apply what they have learned through one of the two activities below. For students who can work independently, use one of the books suggested below or another one in your curriculum. For guided help with the strategy, use a *Student Applications Book*.

1. Independent Practice

Ask students to apply the reading tools they just learned to the theme of one of these books:

■ *Belle Prater's Boy* by Ruth White

■ *Holes* by Louis Sachar

■ *Kidnapped* by Robert Louis Stevenson

Quick Assess

Can students

■ explain the three-step plan for understanding theme?

■ explain the difference between topic and theme?

■ give three examples of common topics?

■ write a theme statement?

2. Student Applications Books

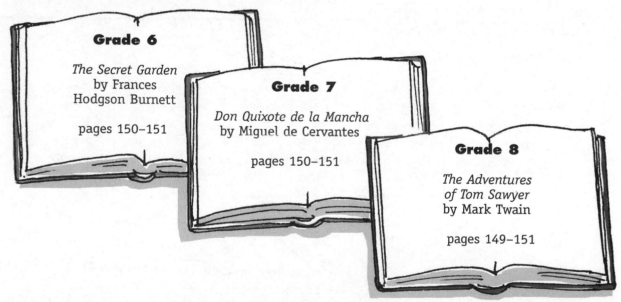

Grade 6

The Secret Garden by Frances Hodgson Burnett

pages 150–151

Grade 7

Don Quixote de la Mancha by Miguel de Cervantes

pages 150–151

Grade 8

The Adventures of Tom Sawyer by Mark Twain

pages 149–151

Focus on Comparing and Contrasting

Goals

Here students focus on comparing and contrasting two pieces of literature. This lesson will help students learn to:

☑ use the reading process to make strong comparisons

☑ find and organize details from the literary works to back up the points made in their comparisons

Background

Start by explaining to students that there are two types of comparisons: general (comparing two entire works) and specific (comparing a specific element of two works). Connect this lesson with students' existing knowledge by asking them to:

■ explain what is meant by *comparison* and *contrast*

■ think of examples of general or specific comparisons they've made for assignments

Overview

	Content	Teacher's Guide page	Reader's Handbook page
Selection	King Midas *A Christmas Carol* by Charles Dickens		
Reading Strategy	Using Graphic Organizers	248	385-387, 662
Tool	Fiction Organizer Two-story Map Venn Diagram	248 249 249	385, 671 386, 682 387, 683

Ancillaries

	Grade	Content	Page
Lesson Plan Book	8	Focus on Comparing and Contrasting	125
Student Applications Book	6	*The Phantom Tollbooth* by Norton Juster and *Johnny Tremain* by Esther Forbes	152–153
	7	*Crash* by Jerry Spinelli and *The Root Cellar* by Janet Lunn	152–153
	8	*Summer of the Monkeys* by Wilson Rawls and *The Pearl* by John Steinbeck	152–153
Website		www.greatsource.com/rehand/	

Before Reading

Explain to students that, if possible, they should think about comparing two works before they begin reading. Remind them to set a purpose for reading. Direct their attention to the list of questions on page 384 of the handbook as examples of possible reading purposes.

If students' goal is comparing works, they should watch for similarities and differences as they preview the works and during their reading.

Read with students each item on the Preview Checklist on page 384. These questions help them focus on key aspects of a fictional work as they read.

Explain that students need to read for the information necessary for making a comparison or contrast.

During Reading

Ask students to remember their purpose and to determine whether they will be comparing generally or specifically, so they know what type of notes to take.

Reading Strategy: Using Graphic Organizers

Explain to students that graphic organizers can help them to take parallel notes on two works in a focused way.

1. General Comparisons

Model the use of a Fiction Organizer to summarize the main aspects of a single work, using the example on page 385.

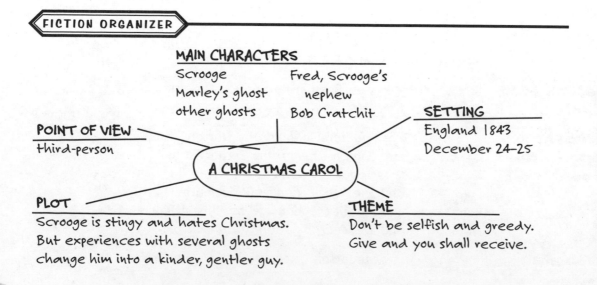

FICTION ORGANIZER

MAIN CHARACTERS
Scrooge
Marley's ghost
other ghosts
Fred, Scrooge's
nephew
Bob Cratchit

SETTING
England 1843
December 24–25

POINT OF VIEW
third-person

A CHRISTMAS CAROL

PLOT
Scrooge is stingy and hates Christmas.
But experiences with several ghosts
change him into a kinder, gentler guy.

THEME
Don't be selfish and greedy.
Give and you shall receive.

During Reading

Also show students how to create a Two-story Map. Point out that this is a concise way to summarize important aspects of two works.

◁ **TWO-STORY MAP** ▷ ─────────────────────

	A CHRISTMAS CAROL	KING MIDAS
MAIN CHARACTER	Scrooge: older businessman rich and powerful	Midas: King rich and powerful
MAIN SETTING	19th-century England Scrooge's home and business	ancient Greece Midas's kingdom
PLOT EVENTS	supernatural— visits from ghosts goes places	supernatural— gets magic powers stays at home
THEME	Being greedy and caring about being rich can lead to unhappiness.	Being greedy and caring about being rich can lead to unhappiness.
ENDING	Scrooge learns lesson and changes. Ghosts leave.	Midas sees his wish was foolish. Spell is undone.

2. Specific Comparisons

Point out to students that if they're allowed to choose which aspect to compare, they should choose one that offers a number of interesting points of comparison. Point out the Venn Diagram on page 387. Explain to students that the outer parts of the two circles contain unique traits of the two characters and the circles' intersection contains traits shared by both characters. Ask for volunteers to create a Venn Diagram of a different element—perhaps the setting or plot in the two works.

After Reading

Point out that an initial reading of both works gives students a good overview, but rereading will probably be necessary to complete and check the comparisons.

Drawing Conclusions

Explain that the best conclusions are specific, come from details, and are not obvious in each work. Rereading at least some parts of the works will be important in order to clarify details of the comparisons.

Organizing a Comparison or Contrast

Read the Model of Comparison or Contrast. Explain that this is an outline for writing a comparison or contrast paper. Work with students on how to write a sample opening, body, and conclusion of a paper on some aspect of the King Midas–Scrooge comparison on page 387.

MODEL OF COMPARISON OR CONTRAST

Opening
- *Topic Sentence*
  Sentence that names what's being compared or contrasted and whether the works are similar or different for at least two reasons

Body
- *Reason One*
  supporting detail or quote from work #1
  supporting detail or quote from work #2
- *Reason Two*
  supporting detail or quote from work #1
  supporting detail or quote from work #2

Conclusion
- *Concluding Sentence*
  Sentence that restates how the works are alike or different or explanation of why the similarities or differences are important

Summing Up

To wrap up the lesson, point out the Summing Up section. Go back over all that students have learned about comparing and contrasting general and specific aspects of two literary works. Then ask students to tell what they learned in their own words.

Assessment and Application

Use the Quick Assess checklist to evaluate students' abilities to read and understand comparing and contrasting. Give students the opportunity to apply what they have learned through one of the two activities below. For students who are comfortable with the reading process and strategy, use one of the suggestions below for independent practice. For guided help with the strategy, use a *Student Applications Book*.

1. Independent Practice

Ask students to apply the reading strategy and tools they just learned to make a general or specific comparison of two short stories or characters. If students have difficulty in coming up with what to compare, suggest they compare two movies they've recently seen.

2. Student Applications Books

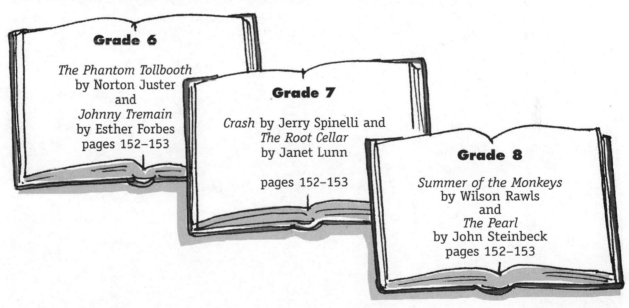

Grade 6

The Phantom Tollbooth by Norton Juster and *Johnny Tremain* by Esther Forbes pages 152–153

Grade 7

Crash by Jerry Spinelli and *The Root Cellar* by Janet Lunn

pages 152–153

Grade 8

Summer of the Monkeys by Wilson Rawls and *The Pearl* by John Steinbeck pages 152–153

Elements of Fiction

The literary terms or elements in this section are commonly used to analyze and discuss fiction. In the text, each of these terms is shown in an example, described, and defined.

Use this section to introduce these literary terms to students so that they will learn what they are, how to recognize them, and what their overall purposes are in describing fiction.

Also see *Lesson Plan Book 6* (pages 144–145), *Lesson Plan Book 7* (page 134), and *Lesson Plan Book 8* (page 134).

Antagonist and Protagonist

Set Goal

Help students recognize and understand the differences between the protagonist (main character) and the antagonist (person or force working against the protagonist).

Teach and Discuss

Read with students the excerpt from *Rumble Fish* **Example** on page 390 in the handbook. Have students identify the antagonist (Biff Wilcox) and the protagonist (the narrator, Rusty-James). For those familiar with the novel, explain how the conflict between Biff and Rusty-James affects, forms, and fuels the plot of the novel. Encourage students to describe what they notice about the nature of the relationship between the protagonist and antagonist in this passage. They may offer responses like the following:

■ Biff's threat against Rusty-James seems very serious.

■ Rusty-James seems fearful of Biff.

■ Waiting for their encounter adds to the suspense.

Now read through the major points in the **Description** with students. **Emphasize that the protagonist is often the hero or central figure of a story while the antagonist might be a person, a group, a force of nature, or a force within a character.**

Check Understanding

Have students review the **Definition** on page 390. To demonstrate their understanding, students can name and discuss protagonists and antagonists in popular novels, stories, or movies. Have them answer questions like these:

■ Who are the protagonist and antagonist?

■ What is the conflict between these two figures or forces?

■ How does the conflict form and affect the overall plot of the work?

Author's Purpose

Set Goal

Guide students in recognizing the author's purpose in writing—whether it is to inform, entertain, persuade, or reveal an important truth.

Teach and Discuss

Read with students the title and first sentence from the **Example** on page 391. Have students describe what they notice about the myth about Shiva. They are likely to report the following:

■ The author's purpose is very clearly stated.

■ Authors don't usually state their purposes quite this obviously.

■ The purpose of the story seems to be to explain and to entertain.

As you go over the major points in the **Description**, make it clear that the author's purpose is the reason that he or she is writing. **Read through and emphasize the four possible reasons that an author might write—to inform, to entertain, to persuade, or to reveal a truth. Point out that an author may have more than one purpose in writing.**

Check Understanding

Have students review the **Definition** on page 391. To show their understanding, ask students to point out the authors' purposes in fictional works that they know, and encourage them to answer questions like these:

■ What is the author's purpose in writing?

■ Is the author's purpose clearly stated, or do you have to dig to find it?

■ How does identifying the author's purpose help you get more out of the reading?

Character

Set Goal

Help students to understand character and how authors use characterization to develop fictional characters. Also help students to recognize different types of characters and understand the differences between them.

Teach and Discuss

Closely read the **Example** on page 392 with students. Point out that readers learn a lot about Calpurnia from Scout's descriptions of her appearance, personality, and actions. Encourage students to describe what they learn from the passage, pointing out lines that give specific information. They are likely to report the following:

■ Calpurnia seems to be tough, mean, cold, and unfair.

■ Calpurnia appears to dislike Scout and favor Jem.

■ Scout has always been in conflict with Calpurnia.

Now read through the major points in the **Description** with students. Begin with the description of what a character is.

Next, spend time reading and discussing the points under Characterization. Go over the list of aspects of a character that authors might use to describe a character. Tell students they need to watch for clues about character as they read fiction. Ask students which of those character aspects they see revealed in the passage about Calpurnia.

Read with students the part on Character Types on page 393. Help students to learn the distinctions between a *main character* (*protagonist*) and *minor characters* and between *static characters* (characters that stay the same) and *dynamic characters* (characters that change). Point out that the main character in most fiction is a dynamic character, whose development may help point to the theme.

Emphasize that students need to watch for various clues about the characters. They should be able to distinguish between main and minor characters and static and dynamic characters.

Check Understanding

Ask students to review the **Definition** on page 393. To assess students' understanding, ask them to discuss characters in a novel or story with which the whole class is familiar, such as *The Pinballs* by Betsy Byars or *The View from Saturday* by E. L. Konigsburg. Have them answer questions like these:

■ Who are the main and minor characters in this work? How do you know?

■ What characterization techniques does the author use to describe this character?

■ Is this character static or dynamic? How do you know?

Dialogue and Dialect

Set Goal

Help students to identify the characteristics of written dialogue and understand that dialect is often used to add color, humor, and authenticity to a fictional work.

Teach and Discuss

With students, closely read the **Example** from *Tom Sawyer* on page 394. Ask students to point out the dialogue in this passage and explain how they can identify it (quotation marks and speech tags). Then see whether they can point out examples of dialogue. Explain that the purpose of dialogue is to move the plot along while revealing information and insights about the characters' personalities. Have students describe what they notice about the excerpt. They are likely to report these observations:

■ Dialogue is easy to follow because new paragraphs start when a new character speaks.

■ Dialogue can give life to writing.

■ Tom's dialect shows a lot about his personality, regional background, and point of view.

Now read the **Description** with students. Make sure that students understand what dialogue and dialect are and how to recognize them. **Stress that dialogue moves the plot forward and provides information about characters. Point out that dialect can make writing more realistic by portraying the unique sound of a particular people and place.**

Check Understanding

Have students review the **Definition** on page 395. Broaden students' understanding by having them read a passage from another dialogue-and-dialect-rich novel, such as *Where the Red Fern Grows* (Wilson Rawls), *Remembering the Good Times* (Richard Peck), or *The Keeping Room* (Anne Myers). Encourage students to answer questions like these:

■ How do you know which character is talking here? Why?

■ In what ways does this dialogue advance the plot of the story?

■ How would you describe the dialect and personality of the speaker?

Genre

Set Goal

Help students to understand what genre is as well as the names and distinctive features of common literary genres.

Teach and Discuss

Read with students the **Description** of genre and the Genre chart on page 396. Ask students to name examples of other works in each genre. Encourage students to describe what they notice about the three charted genres. Responses are likely to include the following:

■ Characters in fantasy works can be complicated while folktale characters are often simple.

■ Folktales take place long ago while works of realistic fiction take place in the present or the recent past.

Stress that knowing the names and characteristics of the most important literary genres will be helpful in studying and analyzing literature.

Check Understanding

Have students review the **Definition** on page 396. To gauge their understanding, ask them to name as many examples as possible of works that fit into each of the genres shown in the Genre chart. Have them answer questions like these:

■ What is an example of another fantasy?

■ What realistic fictional characters can you think of?

■ What is your favorite folktale or fairy tale?

Mood

Set Goal

Help students to understand what mood is and to recognize ways in which authors create mood in fiction.

Teach and Discuss

With students, read the **Example** from *The Giver* on page 397. Ask students to point out the sights, smells, and sounds reported in this passage. Show students how these descriptions and the writer's choice of words help to bring the reader into the scene. What mood do students think is created? Ask students to point to specific wording that makes them respond, such as "firelight glowing," "yellow, twinkling," and "golden-haired dog lay sleeping." Encourage students to point out what they notice about the reading. Responses may include the following:

■ The scene feels like a holiday gathering.

■ Reading the passage makes me feel relaxed.

■ The author uses sights, smells, and words that suggest warmth to create the mood.

Now read through and discuss the major points in the **Description** with students. Make sure that they understand what mood is and how it is used in fiction. **Emphasize that authors use words, phrases, and images to create mood.**

Check Understanding

Have students review the **Definition** on page 397. To demonstrate understanding, they can read an excerpt from another novel or short story. Have them answer questions like these:

■ How does reading this excerpt make you feel? Why?

■ What key words, phrases, or images help to establish the mood of the piece?

■ What is the author's purpose in describing the scene this way?

Point of View

Set Goal

Guide students in understanding that point of view is the perspective from which a story is told and in distinguishing between the first-person point of view and the third-person point of view.

Teach and Discuss

Read with students the **Example** on page 398. Have students try to determine from whose perspective the story is being told (Roy's perspective). Ask students to tell whether the story is in the first person (told by one of the characters) or in the third person (told by a narrator who is outside the story). Point out that the pronouns *he* and *their* signal third-person point of view. Further explain that although this story is told by an outside narrator, that narrator seems to see into the mind of Roy and tell the story from his point of view. Encourage students to describe what they pick up from the reading. Responses will likely include the following:

■ *He*, *their*, and *them* are third-person pronouns.

■ Having the narrator describe Roy's reaction helps to show how Roy feels.

■ Telling the story from Roy's point of view is more interesting because he is the most troubled person at the scene.

Talk about an omniscient narrator and a limited omniscient narrator. Be sure students know they are different. Then read with students the **Description**, including the parts about first-person and third-person points of view. **Alert students to the basic differences between these two common points of view.**

Check Understanding

Ask students to review the **Definition** on page 399. To gauge their understanding, ask students how they think the example would read if it were told from the first-person point of view rather than the third-person point of view. Then ask them to name stories or novels they've read that were told from these two points of view. Ask them questions like these:

■ From whose point of view is the story being told? How can you tell?

■ What would the story be like if it were told from _____ (another character's) perspective? Why?

■ In the case of a third-person perspective, is the story being told by an omniscient or limited omniscient narrator?

Plot

Set Goal

Help students recognize that plot is the action or sequence of events in a story that typically has five main parts—exposition, rising action, climax, falling action, and resolution.

Teach and Discuss

Look over and discuss the **Example** on page 400 with students. Ask students to point out various events and developments in the story, as listed in the summary. Point out how keeping track of the chronological events in a story makes it possible to document the plot of a story from the beginning to the end. Have students describe what they notice about the plot summary. They are likely to report the following:

■ The phrase "In the beginning" is a good way to identify the first part of the plot.

■ Sara's crying after finding Charlie is the high point (climax) of the story.

■ Sara seems able to reflect on her feelings after the conflict is over.

Read the **Description**, and take time to define and give examples of the five parts of a plot. Make sure that students understand these stages by asking them to identify them in the plot of a simple fictional work that they all know well (for example, "The Three Little Pigs"). Go on to discuss the Plot Diagram on page 401, which shows the events of *The Summer of the Swans* in a graphic format. Students should understand that fictional works vary a great deal in the way they follow these stages.

Continue by reading with students the part called "Understanding Conflict" on page 401. Point out that every plot revolves around some kind of conflict. **Emphasize that identifying the main stages of a plot and understanding the problem or struggle can help students to analyze the characters and theme of the story.**

Check Understanding

Ask students to review the **Definition** on page 401. To gauge their understanding, hand out a brief story or folktale, and have students identify and discuss the different parts of the plot using a plot diagram. Have them answer questions like these:

■ How can you tell the difference between the *rising action* and *climax* of the story? Explain.

■ How does seeing the plot's different parts help you better understand what is happening?

■ What is the conflict?

Setting

Set Goal

Help students understand setting—the time and place in a fictional work—and recognize clues about setting.

Teach and Discuss

Have students read the **Example** from *Journey to Topaz* on page 402. Ask students to point out the details of time and place. Help them see how the author's descriptions of the characters, surroundings, and mood help to establish the fact that the setting is bleak and remote. Encourage students to describe what they notice about the excerpt. They are likely to report the following:

■ The characters are Japanese and seem to be held against their will.

■ The passage describes a group of tar-papered barracks in a pool of white dust in a bleak desert and mountainous area.

■ This description of setting probably is important to the story.

Now read with students the key points in the **Description**. Make sure that students understand the variety of times and places that setting can encompass. **Stress that the setting—when and where a story takes place—usually is described in the opening paragraphs and can play an important part in plot and mood.**

Check Understanding

Have students review the **Definition** on page 402. To allow them to demonstrate their comprehension, provide students with paragraphs of a story or novel that offer clues to the setting, such as *Catherine Called Birdy* (Karen Cushman) or *The True Confessions of Charlotte Doyle* (Avi). Have them answer questions like these:

■ Where and when do you think this story takes place? How do you know?

■ What clues help you determine the time and place of the story?

■ What do the descriptions of the physical setting tell you about the conflict or mood of the story?

Style

Set Goal

Help students understand that style is the way a writer expresses ideas and that it can be recognized by the writer's word choice, sentence structure and length, and use of literary devices.

Teach and Discuss

Closely read with students the **Example** on page 403. Ask them to point out what is unusual about the way this passage is written. Possibilities include the writer's talking directly to the reader, the short sentences and frequent paragraph breaks, and the humor, as pointed out in the notes. Encourage students to express what they notice about the example. They are likely to report these observations:

■ The author's words are simple, but his attitude is very strong and definite.

■ The use of short sentences helps to convey the narrator's critical attitude.

■ The word choices of "bad boy" and "good boy" show his disapproval of the attitude behind those labels.

Now read the three elements of style in the **Description**. Guide students in looking for these things in the excerpt from *Holes*. **Emphasize that style is *how* the writer says something, not *what* is said, and that students should watch for the three elements of word choice, sentence structure, and use of literary devices.**

Check Understanding

Have students review the **Definition** on page 403. To allow students to demonstrate their comprehension, provide them with another reading from *Holes* that illustrates the writer's style. Have them answer questions like these:

■ How would you describe the author's writing style? Why?

■ What is unique about the author's choice of words or use of sentence structure?

■ How does the author's writing style help to express his or her ideas?

Symbol

Set Goal

Help students understand that a symbol is a person, place, thing, or event used to represent an abstract concept or idea and that authors use symbols to bring greater meaning or emphasis to their writing.

Teach and Discuss

Read with students the **Example** from *The Fragile Flag* on page 404. Ask them to enumerate the various things that the flag represents to this character. Encourage students to explain what they notice in this example. Responses are likely to include these observations:

■ For this character, the flag represents patriotic strength and bravery.

■ The symbolism of the flag adds a strong mood.

■ The flag is often associated with America, the Marines, and the Statue of Liberty.

Now read with students the major points in the **Description**. Talk about the familiar symbols given on page 404, and ask students to suggest symbols and meanings of their own. **Emphasize that symbols help bring meaning and emphasis to writing.**

Check Understanding

Ask students to review the **Definition** on page 404. To gauge students' comprehension, provide them with selections that have other symbols, such as a friendship ring, an eagle, or a flashy sports car. Have them answer questions like these:

■ What is the symbol and what does it represent?

■ What context clues help you determine what the symbol means?

■ How does the symbol broaden the author's writing or purpose?

Theme

Set Goal

Help students to learn what a theme is—the main idea or statement about life that the author wishes to express in a work—and that themes can be directly stated or located through clues in the work.

Teach and Discuss

Read with students the **Example** from "Eleven" on page 405. Ask them what they learn about Rachel in this reading. What are her thoughts on her birthday? Point out that Rachel's words in this passage may be clues to the theme, the main point about life that the writer is making. Encourage students to tell what they notice about the example. They are likely to report the following:

■ Ironically, Rachel is unhappy about her birthday.

■ She wants to be very far away.

■ The theme may be that growing up isn't easy.

Now read with students the key points in the **Description. Emphasize that finding a theme can be challenging, but that writers' ideas about life are important and worth the search.** Refer students also to the lesson "Focus on Theme" for more help.

Check Understanding

Have students review the **Definition** on page 405. To demonstrate their understanding, they can discuss the theme of a simple work that they all know, such as a folktale. Have them answer questions like these:

■ What do you think the theme of this story is?

■ What clues in the story tell you what the theme is?

■ How does identifying the theme add to your overall understanding of the story?

Reading
Poetry

Reading a Poem

Ways of Reading Poetry

Focus on Language
Focus on Meaning
Focus on Sound and Structure

Elements of Poetry

But he
signed
upon
sill, He
gave the
sash a shake
As witness
all within

Reading a Poem

Getting Ready

Goals

Here students read "Winter Poem" by Nikki Giovanni. This lesson will help them learn to:

- ☑ get more from the poems they read
- ☑ use the strategy of close reading on a poem
- ☑ understand how poems are organized

Background

Connect the lesson with the students' existing knowledge by asking them to:

- define *poem*
- name some of the poems they have read
- talk about their favorite poems and poets
- discuss reasons that people read poetry

Opening Activity

Explain to students that most poems include common features. These include meaning, structure, language, and feeling. Students should watch for these as they read.

265

Lesson Resources

Overview

	Content	Teacher's Guide page	Reader's Handbook page
Selection	"Winter Poem" by Nikki Giovanni		410, 418
Reading Strategy	Close Reading	268	412, 642
Rereading Strategy	Paraphrasing	273	420, 650
Tool	Double-entry Journal	268, 269, 271	412, 415, 671
	Paraphrase Chart	273	420, 676

Ancillaries

	Grade	Content	Page
Overhead Transparency	6, 7, 8	Previewing a Poem	Number 28
Lesson Plan Book	6	Reading a Poem	154
	7	Reading a Poem	144
	8	Reading a Poem	144
Student Applications Book	6	"Paul Revere's Ride" by Henry Wadsworth Longfellow	154–164
	7	"Hiawatha's Childhood" by Henry Wadsworth Longfellow	154–163
	8	"O Captain! My Captain!" by Walt Whitman	154–161
Website		www.greatsource.com/rehand/	

poem about snow ✱

5 miles ahead

Before Reading

A Set a Purpose

Before reading, remind students to set a purpose for reading "Winter Poem." Direct students' attention to the Setting a Purpose questions on page 409 in the handbook. Talk about why these are good questions to guide their reading. Point out that the questions are general because poems are very different in their forms, subjects, and meanings.

Setting a Purpose

■ **What is the poem saying?**
■ **What meaning do I find in the poem?**

B Preview

Ask students to preview the poem in order to get an overview of it before they read it in detail. Direct their attention to the Preview Checklist on page 410. Then walk through what to preview.

Preview using the Overhead Transparency. Go over the items on the Preview Checklist one at a time. Suggest to students that they trace their fingers down the page as they look for repeated or otherwise emphasized words.

Point out to students that the annotations in the margin are color-coded so they can match each annotation to the appropriate bit of highlighted text.

Preview Checklist

✔ *the title and name of the poet*
✔ *the structure and overall shape of the poem on the page*
✔ *any rhymes and where they occur*
✔ *any words or names that are repeated or that stand out*
✔ *the first and last several lines*

Overhead Transparency

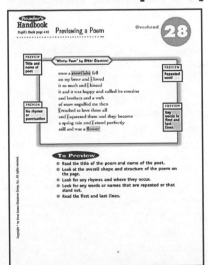

Before Reading

C Plan

Now have students make a plan for finding the meaning in "Winter Poem." Suggest that they use the strategy of **close reading**. Explain to students why this strategy is useful when reading poetry. (One reason is that it focuses on careful examination of the text and gives students a format for interpretation and personal responses.)

Reading Strategy: Close Reading

Close reading involves word-by-word, phrase-by-phrase examination of the text of a poem. As students read, suggest that they use organizers to get the information they need from the poem. Students need to be familiar with several kinds of organizers. A Double-entry Journal helps students choose quotes from the poem and write down their thoughts about the quotes.

During Reading

D Read with a Purpose

Explain to students that reading a poem a number of times helps them understand it better because they don't have to look for everything at one time. While reading "Winter Poem," students can write their ideas in a notebook or organizers.

First Reading

On their first reading of a poem, students read for enjoyment and to record their personal responses to the poem. With this reading, students can use the Double-entry Journal to concentrate on lines that are difficult or surprising, or that they especially like.

DOUBLE-ENTRY JOURNAL—ENJOYMENT

QUOTE	MY THOUGHTS ABOUT IT
"once a snowflake fell on my brow and i loved it so much and i kissed it and it was happy . . ."	The first lines set the tone of a fairy tale. Everything seems so happy. It makes me feel good. The words are simple—like a child telling a story.

During Reading

D Read with a Purpose continued

Second Reading

On the second reading, students use their imaginations and the Double-entry Journal to try to find meaning in the poem. This time students write their interpretations and even make sketches. Students may have different ideas about which words are the most important when they choose two per line to circle.

DOUBLE-ENTRY JOURNAL—MEANING

QUOTE	MY THOUGHTS ABOUT IT
"i reached to love them all and i squeezed them and they became a spring rain and i stood perfectly still and was a flower"	The speaker loves the snow. When she squeezes the snowflakes, they melt. She feels like she's a flower coming up in the spring. The poem is saying how beautiful nature is.

Third Reading

On a third reading, students can analyze structure and language.

DOUBLE-ENTRY JOURNAL—STRUCTURE AND LANGUAGE

QUOTE	MY THOUGHTS ABOUT IT
"once a snowflake fell on my brow and i loved it so much and i kissed it and it was happy and called its cousins and brothers and a web of snow engulfed me then i reached to love them all and i squeezed them and they became a spring rain and i stood perfectly still and was a flower"	There are no capital letters or punctuation or fancy rhymes. It's all one stanza, and there's no regular rhythm. I like the image of a "web" of snowflakes. The snow has human qualities. It's a family.

During Reading

How Poems Are Organized

As students read, they should realize that poems come in all sizes and shapes. Though poems often are written in stanzas and have structure, rhyme, imagery, and rhythm, there is no one formula. Poets have a choice of structures and features. Bring in a variety of poems to share with students the range in poetry.

Variety of Poetry

Encourage students to keep an open mind when they read poetry. Not all poems have the same elements. For instance, some have many stanzas, but others do not. Some, but not all, poems have strong rhythm and rhyme. In many poems, it's the imagery or figurative language that's most important. As they read each new poem, students should ask themselves why the poet chose this structure and these particular features.

Understanding a Poet's Choices

With students, review the text on page 416. Explain each of the features of "Winter Poem" and discuss why the poet may have chosen it. Help students understand that the free verse form of the poem matches the lack of order in falling snow. Writing in one stanza emphasizes that snow is a simple thing.

During Reading

D Read with a Purpose continued

Fourth Reading

On a fourth reading, students can record their feelings about the poem. This step is different from the first reading in which students write their personal responses.

◁ DOUBLE-ENTRY JOURNAL—FEELING ▷────────────────

QUOTE	MY THOUGHTS ABOUT IT
"i reached to love them all and i squeezed them and they became a spring rain and i stood perfectly still and was a flower"	This gives me a sense of peace. It's a quiet, beautiful scene. The speaker's love of being out in nature comes through. It makes me feel happy.

Other Useful Tools

Other reading tools also can be useful in analyzing poetry. Be sure students know that they do not have to use all of them. However, it's a good idea to know what's available so that students can pull out a useful tool when they need it.

■ **Concept Map**

■ **Inference Chart**

■ **Web**

■ **Magnet Summary**

During Reading

E Connect

As students read, encourage them to interact and make connections with the poem. Reacting to the poem and relating it to their own experience will help them to remember it. Help students by telling them to:

■ think about what they like or enjoy most about the poem
  (Do you enjoy quiet poems about how nature makes people feel?)

■ connect again with the meaning of the poem
  (What is Giovanni trying to say in her poem?)

■ restate why the poet chose the structure and language she used
  (Why did Giovanni use all lower-case letters?)

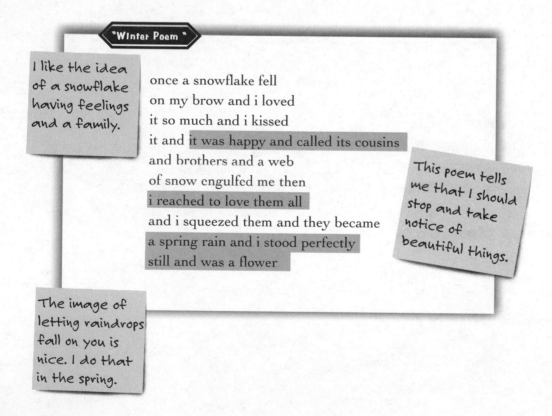

"Winter Poem"

I like the idea of a snowflake having feelings and a family.

once a snowflake fell
on my brow and i loved
it so much and i kissed
it and it was happy and called its cousins
and brothers and a web
of snow engulfed me then
i reached to love them all
and i squeezed them and they became
a spring rain and i stood perfectly
still and was a flower

This poem tells me that I should stop and take notice of beautiful things.

The image of letting raindrops fall on you is nice. I do that in the spring.

After Reading

F Pause and Reflect

After reading, students need to pause to think about whether they understand the poem's meaning. Help students to go back and review their original purpose in reading the poem.

Looking Back

- ■ Do I feel comfortable explaining what the poem is about?
- ■ Do I have a clear picture of the poem in my head?
- ■ What particular words or images come to mind?
- ■ What is the "big idea" of the poem?

Even though the students have read "Winter Poem" several times, they may not be able to fully answer these questions. Have students return to the poem once again and encourage them to view rereading as a natural part of the reading process.

G Reread

At this point students need a new way to approach the reading. They can go back to the poem to choose a line or two to paraphrase. Help them see that a line worth paraphrasing might be a line key to the poem or one especially meaningful to them.

Rereading Strategy: Paraphrasing

Encourage students to use this new strategy when rereading. **Paraphrasing** is a good strategy for rereading a poem because it asks students to articulate in their own words what the poem is saying to them.

Paraphrasing can help students grasp the meaning of passages that they didn't understand on previous readings. They can paraphrase by talking to a classmate, writing in a journal, or writing a summary.

PARAPHRASE CHART

LINES	MY PARAPHRASE
"...i stood perfectly still and was a flower"	I didn't move and felt like something alive and beautiful.

MY THOUGHTS
It's not like the speaker is somehow becoming a flower in a magic spell. The speaker is just comparing herself to a flower. She liked feeling the raindrops like a flower might.

After Reading

H Remember

At this stage in reading, students may need an activity that helps them make the poem memorable on a personal level. Discuss the poem in class and ask students to try the assignments on pages 420 and 421 in the *Reader's Handbook* or the one listed below.

Creative Assignment: In addition to writing in a journal or making a sketch, suggest that students write poems of their own. The poems can be about anything in nature, an experience, a dream, or a friend or family member. Ask students to model their poems on the Giovanni poem. When students finish, invite any who are interested to read their poems aloud to their classmates.

Summing Up

Finally, review the lesson as a class. Focus on everything students have learned about strategies and tools for reading a poem. Read with students the Summing Up on page 421. Review with students the three goals for this lesson. Discuss which ones they feel that they have mastered and which ones they feel they need more work on:

1. getting more from the poems they read

2. using the strategy of close reading with a poem

3. understanding how poems are organized

Assessment and Application

Use the Quick Assess checklist to evaluate students' abilities to read and understand poetry. Give students the opportunity to apply what they have learned through one of the two activities below. For students who are comfortable with the reading process and strategy, use one of the poems suggested below for independent practice or another one in your curriculum. For guided help with the strategy, use a *Student Applications Book*.

1. Independent Practice

To show that students understand the lesson, they can apply the strategy of close reading to one of the following selections:

- ◼ "I, Too, Sing America" by Langston Hughes

- ◼ "The Basket Counts: Three" by Arnold Adoff, illustrated by Michael Weaver

- ◼ "Crossing Ohio When Poppies Bloom in Ashtabula" by Carl Sandburg

Ask students to:

1. Create a Double-entry Journal to find the meaning of the poem.

2. Create a Double-entry Journal for other aspects of the poem.

3. Make a sketch to accompany the poem.

2. Student Applications Books

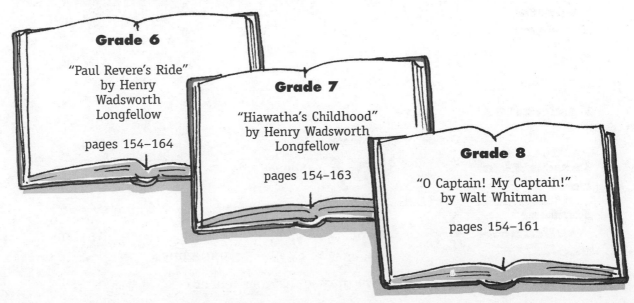

Grade 6

"Paul Revere's Ride" by Henry Wadsworth Longfellow

pages 154–164

Grade 7

"Hiawatha's Childhood" by Henry Wadsworth Longfellow

pages 154–163

Grade 8

"O Captain! My Captain!" by Walt Whitman

pages 154–161

Focus on Language

Goals

Here students focus on the language of poetry by reading "Words" by Pauli Murray. This lesson will help students learn to:

- ☑ recognize word connotations, figurative language, and imagery
- ☑ use the strategy of close reading
- ☑ understand how a poem's language affects their reading

Background

Students do not usually read poetry just for its language. Help them see the importance of language. Point out that poets use only a few words but choose each word very carefully. Connect this lesson with students' existing knowledge by asking them to:

- ■ define what makes the language of poetry special—figurative language, imagery, and word connotations
- ■ discuss poetry they've read and ways in which the language was special
- ■ explore ways the sounds of the words make poetry special

Overview

	Content	Teacher's Guide page	Reader's Handbook page
Selection	"Words" by Pauli Murray		423, 424, 427, 428
Reading Strategy	Close Reading	277	423, 642
Tool	Two Per Line	277	424, 682

Ancillaries

	Grade	Content	Page
Lesson Plan Book	7	Focus on Language	145
Student Applications Book	6	"Annabel Lee" by Edgar Allan Poe	165–166
	7	"Jabberwocky" by Lewis Carroll	164–165
	8	"The Eagle" by Alfred, Lord Tennyson	162–163
Website		www.greatsource.com/rehand/	

Before Reading

Help students see how useful a preview of a poem can be. Focus their attention on the list of things to watch for on page 422. Ask students what they might add to the list, such as rhythm or rhyme. Explain that by focusing on difficult words or phrases, words that trigger a strong emotional response, striking imagery, and figurative language, they can learn a lot about the language of the poem.

Help students skim through the poem, looking for special language. Encourage them to discuss what they learn. Also help them see how carefully the words have been chosen. At this point, ask students to jot down their initial responses.

Next, they need a plan for reading a poem for language.

Reading Strategy: Close Reading

With close reading, students examine the lines of a poem word by word and phrase by phrase. Then they note their interpretations and responses to the text. Its emphasis on detail makes this strategy very useful for considering a poem's language. Suggest that students read slowly and pronounce each word.

During Reading

As students read, help them see that they need to think about finding key words, connotations, figurative language, and a poem's images.

Finding Key Words

Point out the passage and the Two Per Line tool on page 424. Read through it with students. Ask them to note the two words per line that have been selected. Encourage them to see how those words become important. Then ask them to discuss what the two words in each line might mean or how the words make them feel.

> **TWO PER LINE**
>
> Comradely words,
> Shy words tiptoeing from mouth to ear.
>
> But the slowly wrought words of love
> And the thunderous words of heartbreak—
> These we hoard.

During Reading

Using a Dictionary and Thinking about Connotations

With Using a Dictionary on page 425 and Thinking about Connotations on pages 425–426, help students understand the difference between the meaning of a word found in a dictionary (denotation) and the emotional response or suggestions the same word triggers (connotations). Use the example of the word *squander* to illustrate this difference.

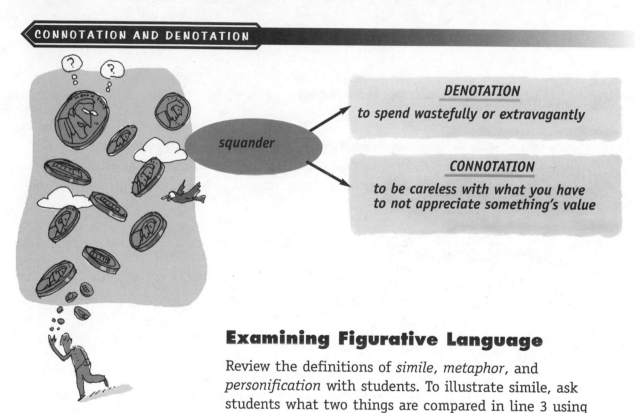

CONNOTATION AND DENOTATION

squander

DENOTATION
to spend wastefully or extravagantly

CONNOTATION
to be careless with what you have to not appreciate something's value

Examining Figurative Language

Review the definitions of *simile*, *metaphor*, and *personification* with students. To illustrate simile, ask students what two things are compared in line 3 using the word *like*. Also highlight the personification in which words are given the human quality of being "shy." Remind students that not all poems have figurative language. Encourage them, however, to get in the habit of looking for examples of figurative language whenever they read poetry.

Noticing a Poem's Images

Review the definition of *imagery*. Remind students that images often appeal to their senses of sight, sound, smell, touch, and taste. Read with students the example and encourage them to talk about how the words help them "see" what the poet is describing. Use the example of "thunderous words of heartbreak" to discuss imagery, since most students will have heard thunder. Ask the students to respond to the sketch on page 428 and what they might have drawn.

After Reading

After reading, have students pause and ask themselves what they learned about the language of poetry. Underscore the importance of asking the two questions on page 428. Encourage students to reread the poem, particularly if they are still puzzled. Do they think the poet wishes people didn't "hoard" words of love and heartbreak? Can they explain "comradely" words and "shy" words? Here are two ways for students to probe the language of the poems they read.

1. Work with a Partner

Suggest that students choose partners with whom to discuss the language of a poem. Suggestions for working with a partner can be found on pages 428–429.

2. Respond and React: Use the Poem as a Model

Have students use "Words" as a model to write a poem of their own. Ask students to change the idea of the poem, but to use approximately the same number of words and lines.

Summing Up

To wrap up the lesson, point out the Summing Up section on page 429. Go back over all that students have learned about the language of poetry: finding key words, connotations, figurative language, and imagery. Then ask students to tell what they learned in their own words.

Assessment and Application

Use the Quick Assess checklist to evaluate students' abilities to read and understand the language in poetry. Give students the opportunity to apply what they have learned through one of the two activities below. For students who are able to work independently, use one of the poems suggested below or another one in your curriculum. For guided help with the strategy, use a *Student Applications Book*.

Quick Assess

Can students

- ☑ explain connotations and denotations?
- ☑ give an example of figurative language?
- ☑ recognize striking imagery?
- ☑ name and explain one strategy?

1. Independent Practice

Ask students to apply the reading strategy and tools they just learned to the special language of poetry in one of the following poems.

- ■ "Martin Luther King, Jr." by Gwendolyn Brooks (found in *I, Too, Sing America: Three Centuries of African American Poetry*)
- ■ "Taught Me Purple" by Evelyn Tooley Hunt
- ■ "Identity" by Julio Noboa

2. Student Applications Books

Grade 6

"Annabel Lee"
by
Edgar Allan Poe

pages 165-166

Grade 7

"Jabberwocky"
by Lewis Carroll

pages 164-165

Grade 8

"The Eagle"
by Alfred, Lord Tennyson

pages 162-163

Focus on Meaning

Goals

Here students focus on the meaning of poetry by reading "Those Winter Sundays" by Robert Hayden. In this lesson, students will learn to:

☑ use the strategy of close reading

☑ recognize clues to a poem's meaning

☑ see the difference between a poem's subject and its meaning

Background

Readers sometimes need to search for the meaning of a poem just as they search for the main idea of an article or the theme of a novel. Help students see how poets communicate meaning. Connect this lesson with students' existing knowledge by asking them to:

■ suggest why they think poems are harder to figure out than novels or magazine articles

■ discuss basic clues to the meaning of a poem, such as the title, any repeated words, and the first and the last several lines

Overview

	Content	Teacher's Guide page	Reader's Handbook page
Selection	"Those Winter Sundays" by Robert Hayden		431
Reading Strategy	Close Reading	282	432, 642
Tool	Two Per Line	283	435, 682
	Paraphrase Chart	284	438, 676

Ancillaries

	Grade	Content	Page
Lesson Plan Book	8	Focus on Meaning, Sound, and Structure	145
Student Applications Book	6	"I'm Nobody" by Emily Dickinson	167–169
	7	"Remember" by Christina Rossetti	166–168
	8	"Sonnet" by Elizabeth Barrett Browning	164–165
Website		www.greatsource.com/rehand/	

Before Reading

Encourage students to preview using the list under Clues to Meaning on page 431 as a guide. Remind them to read the poem for fun the first time, before focusing on its meaning.

Pay special attention to these parts:

■ the title

■ any words that are repeated or stand out

■ the first and last several lines

First Thoughts about Meaning

Ask students to summarize the results of their first reading of the poem. Do they agree or disagree with the notes on the reading on page 431? Encourage students to point out anything else that they noticed.

Students need a plan for studying a poem's meaning. Suggest the strategy of close reading.

Reading Strategy: Close Reading

With **close reading**, students examine a poem word by word. Then they note their own responses to and interpretations of the text. This strategy can be a great help for finding meaning.

Read the five ways to focus on a poem's meaning on page 432. Emphasize the importance of using this approach to find the meaning of "Those Winter Sundays" and other poems that students read.

1. *Look closely at the denotations and connotations of the words.*

2. *Think about what's unusual and important.*

3. *Explore your feelings about the poem.*

4. *Ask yourself what the poet is saying.*

5. *Paraphrase that idea. Put it in your own words.*

During Reading

As they read the poem more carefully, students go through the five ways to focus on a poem's meaning that they have just discussed.

1. Look at Denotations and Connotations

Point out the passage and notes on page 433. Read through the example with students. Focus on the highlighted words and their denotations, or dictionary definitions. Now suggest that students reread the poem, this time with a focus on words, such as *spendthrift* and *squander*, that may mean more than simply their dictionary definitions. Give students a tip: Words that appeal to the emotions are likely to have strong connotations. Model the use of a Double-entry Journal like the one on page 434. Encourage students to copy several words from the poem and to record their thoughts.

2. Think about What's Unusual and Important

Review what students have learned about the special language of poetry—figures of speech, rhythm, rhyme, and so on. Reread the poem with students. Ask them to highlight what they feel are the two most unusual or important words in each line, following the Two Per Line example on page 435. Ask students to write the text they've chosen and their responses to it in a Double-entry Journal like the one on page 435.

TWO PER LINE

WORDS	MY IDEAS
Sundays, father	about his father & Sundays
blueblack, cold	sounds cold and hard
hands, ached	pain in hands—why?
labor, weather	labor = work, weather = cold outside?
No one, thanked	not noticed or thanked
cold, splintering	sounds harsh, like firewood
rooms, warm	sounds cozy—a big change from the cold

3. Explore Your Feelings about the Poem

Remind students that, even as they focus on meaning, they should take stock of how the poem makes them feel and the mood it creates. Have them reread the poem as shown on page 436, noting the responses in the notes. Ask them to talk about their own responses to the same passages or to others in the poem.

After Reading

After reading, ask students to summarize what they've learned about the poem's meaning so far. Underscore the importance of rereading the poem a number of times.

4. Decide What the Poet Is Saying

Remind students that poets sometimes use their work to convey a message or express an idea or feeling. Emphasize the difference between the subject, or topic, of a poem and the meaning of a poem, as discussed on page 437. Relate the confusion of topic and meaning in a poem to the confusion of topic and theme in a novel.

5. Try Paraphrasing

Paraphrasing is a valuable strategy for getting the meaning of a poem. Explain that when students paraphrase, they're expressing the poem's meaning in their own words. Model the use of a Paraphrase Chart, as shown on page 438.

PARAPHRASE CHART

QUOTE	MY PARAPHRASE
"What did I know, what did I know of love's austere and lonely offices?"	When I was younger, I didn't realize that loving and taking care of someone can be so hard.

Here are two additional ways for students to express the meaning of poems:

Suggest that students write a short paragraph summarizing what they think the poem means and their responses to that meaning. Students can then share their reactions with their classmates.

Invite students to choose a poem they like and determine its meaning following the guidelines in this lesson. Then ask them to find a song, book, TV show, or other work that expresses a similar view or topic.

Summing Up

To wrap up the lesson, point out the Summing Up section on page 438. Go back over all that students have learned about finding the meaning of poetry, using the five ways to focus on a poem's meaning discussed in the lesson. Then ask students to tell what they learned in their own words.

Assessment and Application

Use the Quick Assess checklist to evaluate students' abilities to read and understand the meaning in poetry. Give students the opportunity to apply what they have learned through one of the two activities below. For students who are able to work independently, use one of the poems suggested below or another one in your curriculum. For guided help with the strategy, use a *Student Applications Book*.

1. Independent Practice

Ask students to apply the reading strategy and tools they just learned to understand the meaning of one of the poems below or another of your choice.

- ■ "Still I Rise" by Maya Angelou
- ■ "Oranges" by Gary Soto
- ■ "The Rum Tum Tugger" by T. S. Eliot
- ■ "Dust of Snow" by Robert Frost

2. Student Applications Books

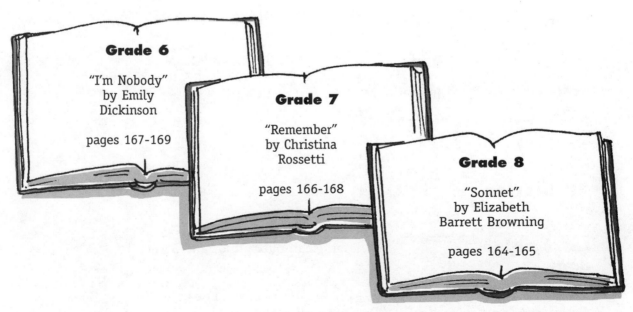

Grade 6

"I'm Nobody"
by Emily
Dickinson

pages 167-169

Grade 7

"Remember"
by Christina
Rossetti

pages 166-168

Grade 8

"Sonnet"
by Elizabeth
Barrett Browning

pages 164-165

Focus on Sound and Structure

Goals

Here students focus on the sound and structure of poetry by reading "The Sloth" by Theodore Roethke. In this lesson, students will learn to:

☑ notice rhyme patterns and the use of sound devices

☑ understand a poem's rhythm

☑ recognize a poem's structure

Background

Though sound and structure are more important in some poems than in others, students should pay attention to the way a poem sounds and the way it is organized. The more details they can see and hear in a poem, the more enjoyable and understandable it will be. Connect this lesson with students' existing knowledge by asking them to:

■ discuss what they already know about the sound and structure of poetry

■ explain how poetry is different from prose in terms of sound and structure

■ explore some of their favorite poems that are good examples of sound and structure

■ discuss why they think a poet would use rhyme and why it might be important

Overview

	Content	Teacher's Guide page	Reader's Handbook page
Selection	"The Sloth" by Theodore Roethke		440
Reading Strategy	Close Reading	287	440, 642

Ancillaries

	Grade	Content	Page
Lesson Plan Book	8	Focus on Meaning, Sound, and Structure	145
Student Applications Book	6	"The Jumblies" by Edward Lear	170–171
	7	"Break, Break, Break" by Alfred, Lord Tennyson	169–170
	8	"Swing Low, Sweet Chariot"	166–167
Website		www.greatsource.com/rehand/	

Before Reading

Help students discover how much they can learn by previewing a poem. Read with them the list of things to notice on page 439. As they read, students should watch for key words, the way the lines are grouped, repeated sounds, rhyming words, and the beat or rhythm.

Guide students in summarizing their findings about sound and structure from the preview. Then remind them that they need a plan for considering the poem more carefully. Suggest the strategy of close reading.

Reading Strategy: Close Reading

Close reading is a strategy that helps students to look very carefully at individual words and phrases in a work. This strategy will be very useful as they read for sound and structure.

During Reading

Tell students that, as they read, they should look for the four things listed and discussed on page 441.

1. Organization of Lines

Point out that "The Sloth" has four stanzas of three lines each. (Remind students that a stanza is in some ways like a paragraph.) Note that most of the lines in each stanza are the same length. Discuss the four different images, one in each stanza. Use the discussion on page 441 as your guide. Talk about use of capital letters, such as to emphasize the rhyme at the ends of lines, and the way the word *Ex-as-per-at-ing* is written.

2. Repeated Sounds

Emphasize that the way a poem sounds can be as important as the way it looks. Encourage students to read the poem aloud and listen to the "music." Do they notice that certain sounds are repeated? Introduce *alliteration,* or review the term. See page 447 in "Elements of Poetry" for an example, description, and definition of alliteration. Ask students to find other examples of alliteration in the poem. Encourage students to think about ways in which the poem would be different without alliteration.

▷ EXAMPLE OF ALLITERATION ▷ ──────────────────

| "s" sound | *"Then off again to <u>S</u>leep he goes,
Still <u>s</u>waying gently by his Toes,"* |

During Reading

3. Rhyme

Use the first stanza as found on page 443 to show students how to mark the rhyme scheme of a poem. Follow the method explained on the page. Suggest that students figure out the rhyme scheme for the other stanzas in the poem. Point out that the rhyme scheme is the same for all three stanzas. See pages 461–462 in "Elements of Poetry."

Have students talk about how the rhyme makes them feel and what effect it has on the poem. Possible answers may include that the rhyme adds a light, humorous tone to the poem.

> **RHYME SCHEME**
>
> In moving-slow he has no Peer.   *a*
> You ask him something in his ear;   *a*
> He thinks about it for a Year;   *a*
>
> And, then, before he says a Word   *b*
> There, upside down (unlike a Bird)   *b*
> He will assume that you have Heard—   *b*

4. Rhythm or Meter

Walk students through the information about rhythm or meter, as explained on page 443. Model the way to mark stressed and unstressed syllables in a poem, as shown in the example on the page. Work with students to be sure that they understand this key aspect of a poem's sound. See page 463 in "Elements of Poetry." Consider writing another line or two from the poem on the board or a transparency and having students help mark the pattern of stressed and unstressed beats.

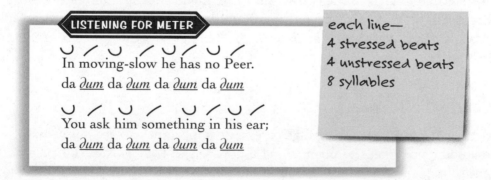

> **LISTENING FOR METER**
>
> ◡ / ◡ / ◡ / ◡ /
> In moving-slow he has no Peer.
> da *dum* da *dum* da *dum* da *dum*
>
> ◡ / ◡ / ◡ / ◡ /
> You ask him something in his ear;
> da *dum* da *dum* da *dum* da *dum*

each line—
4 stressed beats
4 unstressed beats
8 syllables

After Reading

After reading, pause and ask students to review what they know and don't know about the poem's sound and structure. Underscore the importance of rereading the poem a number of times.

1. Connect to the Poem

With students, note the reaction of one reader to the stanza from "The Sloth" on page 444. Ask students if they agree with the comment. What would they write on a sticky note?

2. Reread the Poem

Ask students to reread "The Sloth" on page 440 and then discuss the reader's journal response on page 445. Do they agree the poem is funny? Can they add anything of their own to this reader's reaction?

Here's another way for students to learn more about the sound and structure of poetry.

Write Your Own Poem

Ask students to write a poem of their own. They can model their poems after "The Sloth" or create something very different. The only requirements are that the poem rhyme and have a basic meter. Ask students to share their poems with the class.

Summing Up

To wrap up the lesson, point out the Summing Up section. Go back over all that students have learned about the sound and structure of poetry. Then ask students to tell what they learned in their own words.

Assessment and Application

Use the Quick Assess checklist to evaluate students' abilities to read and understand the sound and structure in poetry. Give students the opportunity to apply what they have learned through one of the two activities below. For students who are able to work independently, use the poem suggested below or another one in your curriculum. For guided help with the strategy, use a *Student Applications Book*.

Quick Assess

Can students

- ☑ explain how sound and structure relate to meaning?

- ☑ give an example of alliteration?

- ☑ mark rhyme scheme?

- ☑ mark rhythm?

1. Independent Practice

Ask students to read "The Dance of the Thirteen Skeletons" by Jack Prelutsky. Have them apply the strategy of close reading, going over the poem several times. Encourage them to mark both the rhyme scheme and the meter. Ask them to identify examples of alliteration. Encourage them to talk about how the sound and structure work to make the poem so haunting.

2. Student Applications Books

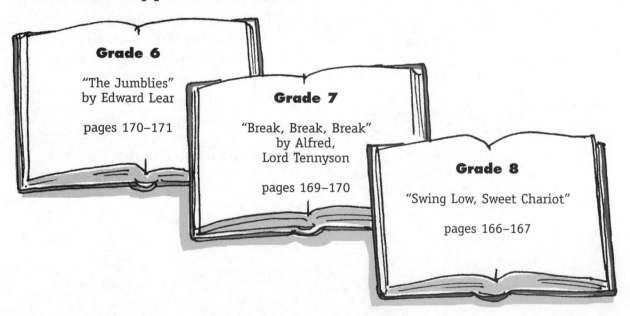

Grade 6

"The Jumblies"
by Edward Lear

pages 170–171

Grade 7

"Break, Break, Break"
by Alfred,
Lord Tennyson

pages 169–170

Grade 8

"Swing Low, Sweet Chariot"

pages 166–167

Elements of Poetry

The terms or elements in this section are commonly used in poetry. In the text, each of these terms is shown in an example, described, and defined.

Use this section to introduce these terms to students so that they will learn what they mean, how to recognize them, and what their overall purposes are in poetry.

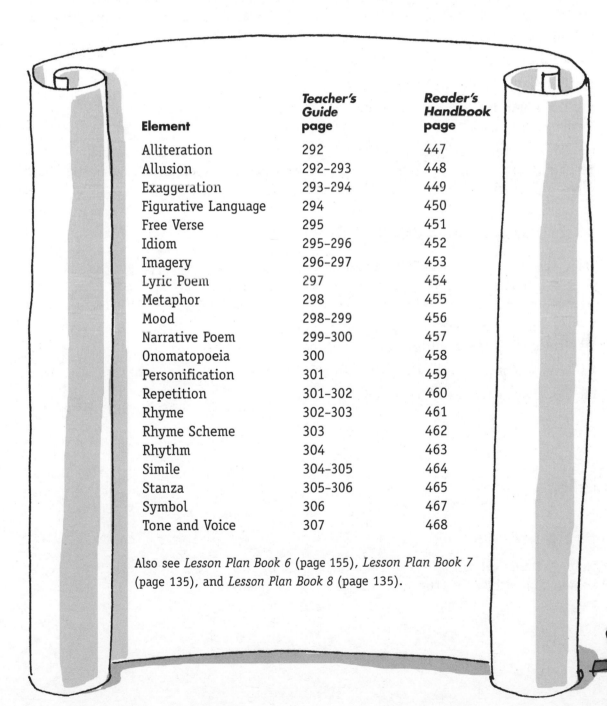

Element	Teacher's Guide page	Reader's Handbook page
Alliteration	292	447
Allusion	292–293	448
Exaggeration	293–294	449
Figurative Language	294	450
Free Verse	295	451
Idiom	295–296	452
Imagery	296–297	453
Lyric Poem	297	454
Metaphor	298	455
Mood	298–299	456
Narrative Poem	299–300	457
Onomatopoeia	300	458
Personification	301	459
Repetition	301–302	460
Rhyme	302–303	461
Rhyme Scheme	303	462
Rhythm	304	463
Simile	304–305	464
Stanza	305–306	465
Symbol	306	467
Tone and Voice	307	468

Also see *Lesson Plan Book 6* (page 155), *Lesson Plan Book 7* (page 135), and *Lesson Plan Book 8* (page 135).

Alliteration

Set Goal

Help students to understand that alliteration is repetition of the same consonant sound and to recognize it in poetry.

Teach and Discuss

Explain that the **Example** on page 447 of the handbook shows how alliteration creates a musical effect. Ask students what they notice about the example. Students probably will say the following:

■ The sound of *s* is repeated often.

■ The words and sounds flow smoothly.

■ The effect is relaxing and beautiful.

Now go through the **Description** with students. **Emphasize that alliteration is a powerful tool used by poets to create an emotional effect.** In this case, the poet repeats the *s* sound in a way that can sound like a soft rainfall.

Check Understanding

Have students review the **Definition** on page 447. To demonstrate understanding, they can read another sample of poetry with alliteration, such as "Sarah Cynthia Sylvia Stout Would Not Take the Garbage Out" by Shel Silverstein. Have them address questions such as these:

■ Where do you see alliteration in this poem?

■ What do you think is the intended effect of the repeated consonants?

■ How does this poem make you feel?

Allusion

Set Goal

Help students recognize an allusion and understand that it is a reference to something with which the reader is likely to be familiar.

Teach and Discuss

Read the **Example** on page 448 with students. Tell them that this poem has an example of allusion—that is, a reference to a person, place, or event outside the poem. Ask students what they notice about the example. Students probably will observe the following:

■ Some words are in capital letters.

■ The poet says the girl tried things and changed while others didn't.

Now go through the **Description** with students. Point out that the poet is alluding to the character Alice in *Alice's Adventures in Wonderland* and that they won't understand the poet's full meaning unless they are familiar with that story. **Emphasize that poets can allude to almost anything—history, fiction, politics, and so on—and that the allusion adds another layer of meaning to the work.**

Check Understanding

Have students review the **Definition** on page 448. Check their comprehension by asking them to read a poem and discuss its use of allusion. Have them address questions such as these:

■ To what is the poet alluding?

■ How is the allusion woven into the original poetry?

■ What is the effect of using the allusion?

Exaggeration

Set Goal

Help students to recognize exaggeration and understand that it is a means of "stretching the truth."

Teach and Discuss

Read the **Example** on page 449 with students. Point out the annotation and highlighted bits of text. Explain that exaggeration is a stretching of the truth. Ask students what they notice about the example. Students probably will report the following:

■ The parts that show exaggeration are "Small as a peanut," "Big as a giant," "Rich as a sultan," and "Poor as a mite."

■ This poem makes the point that everyone is the same when the lights are off.

Now go through the **Description** with students. **Emphasize that the purpose of exaggeration might be to lighten the mood, make the reader laugh, or make a point.**

Check Understanding

Have students review the **Definition** on page 449. Check their comprehension by asking them to read a sample poem with exaggeration and pose questions such as these:

■ Where does the poet use exaggeration?

■ What point is the poet trying to make?

■ How do you react to this poem?

Figurative Language

Set Goal

Help students to recognize figurative language and to understand that it is more about showing than telling.

Teach and Discuss

After reading the **Example** on page 450 with students, explain that it shows Emily Dickinson's use of figurative language. Ask students what they notice about the example. Students probably will report the following:

■ The poem is about hope.

■ The poem gives hope the traits of a bird.

■ The poet suggests that hope is singing in the soul and "never stops."

Now go through the **Description** with students. Focus their attention on Dickinson's use of metaphor to create a beautiful sense of imagery. **Emphasize that poets use figurative language to spark the imagination and create special effects or feelings.**

Check Understanding

Have students review the **Definition** on page 450. To gauge their understanding, have students use a piece of poetry with figurative language, such as "The Eagle" (Alfred, Lord Tennyson), to address questions such as these:

■ How does the poet use figurative language in this poem?

■ What effect does the poet achieve?

■ How would you describe what was communicated?

Free Verse

Set Goal

Help students to recognize free verse and to understand that free verse is poetry without a definite pattern of rhythm or stressed syllables.

Teach and Discuss

Read the **Example** on page 451 with students. Ask students what they notice about the poem. Students probably will report the following:

▪ The poet repeats "the rain" often.

▪ The poem doesn't really rhyme or have any obvious poetic structure.

▪ The poem has a lot of beautiful imagery.

As you go through the **Description** with students, stress that free verse is just free of any set poetic pattern. **Emphasize that in free verse the poet can break with the traditional forms of rhyme pattern and stanzas.**

Check Understanding

Have students review the **Definition** on page 451. To demonstrate their understanding, have them read a poem with free verse and address questions such as these:

▪ Why do you think the poet chose to write in free verse?

▪ How natural does the verse sound?

▪ How did the poem make you feel?

Idiom

Set Goal

Help students recognize an idiom as a phrase with a meaning different from the literal meanings of the words.

Teach and Discuss

Read the **Example** with students and note that it shows an idiom in a song. Ask students what they notice about the example. Students probably will say the following:

■ The song asks someone to come to the singer for help.

■ The song includes expressions heard in conversation.

■ The writer is speaking to a friend.

Now go through the **Description** with students. **Emphasize the idea that idioms are commonly used expressions with nonliteral meanings.** *To swallow pride*, for example, means "to avoid being proud" and has nothing to do with literally swallowing. Read examples of other idioms with students, and ask them to offer their own examples.

Check Understanding

Have students review the **Definition** on page 452. Expand on the definition by asking them to read a piece of poetry with idiom. Have them address questions like these:

■ What expressions are used in the poem?

■ What do those expressions really mean?

■ What effect do these expressions have on the overall poem?

Imagery

Set Goal

Help students recognize imagery and understand that it usually appeals to the five senses and creates pictures in the reader's imagination.

Teach and Discuss

Ask students what they notice about the **Example** on page 453. They probably will observe the following:

■ The poem's words are in a strange shape.

■ The poet describes things in an imaginative way.

■ The poem feels as if it's moving fast, like an automobile.

Now go through the **Description** with students. **Stress that poets use imagery to present a variety of things in a way that appeals to the five senses.** The effect is that the reader will imagine and feel things in new ways.

Check Understanding

Have students review the **Definition** on page 453. To demonstrate their understanding, you might ask them to read a poem with imagery such as "April Rain Song" (Langston Hughes) or "One Blue Door" (Pat Mora). Have them address questions like these:

■ What objects, ideas, feelings, or scenes are presented?

■ How are they presented?

■ To what senses do these images appeal?

Lyric Poem

Set Goal

Help students recognize a lyric poem and understand that it is a short poem, almost like a song, that expresses the poet's thoughts and emotions.

Teach and Discuss

Go over the **Example** on page 454 with students. Explain that this poem is an example of lyric poetry. Ask students what they notice about the poem. Students probably will report the following:

■ The poet uses unusual words, spellings, and expressions.

■ He's professing his love for a woman.

■ He compares his love to a lot of things.

Now go through the **Description** with students. Point out that the poet, Robert Burns, uses a songlike structure to send a personal message. **Stress that lyric poetry is short and expresses a poet's emotions.**

Check Understanding

Have students review the **Definition** on page 454. Check their comprehension by asking them to read a piece of lyric poetry, such as "The Tiger" (William Blake) or "Winter Poem" (Nikki Giovanni). Have them address questions like these:

■ What tells you that this is a lyric poem?

■ How does the style resemble Burns's poem?

■ How does the author use images and rhyme?

■ How does the poem make you feel?

Metaphor

Set Goal

Help students to recognize metaphor and understand that a metaphor compares two unlike things.

Teach and Discuss

Read the **Example** on page 455 with students and explain that it shows a metaphor. Ask students what they notice about the example. Students probably will observe the following:

■ The poem compares the fog to a cat.

■ The fog is said to come in "on little cat feet" and to look over the city on "silent haunches."

■ The fog moves on, as a cat might.

Now go through the **Description** with students. **Emphasize that a metaphor is a comparison in which one thing is said to be something else.** Here, the poet is using metaphor to compare the fog to a cat. The effect of describing one thing as something else is that the reader will see the original subject in a new light. Differentiate a metaphor from a simile, which uses the word *like* or *as* to compare two things.

Check Understanding

Have students review the **Definition** on page 455. To gauge their understanding, have them read another poem that uses metaphor, such as "Broken Sky" (Carl Sandburg). Have them address questions like these:

■ What two things are compared in the metaphor?

■ What effect does the metaphor create?

Mood

Set Goal

Help students to recognize mood and to understand that it is the feeling created in the reader by a poem or story.

Teach and Discuss

Read the **Example** on page 456 with students. Explain that it shows a strong overall mood. Ask students what they notice about the example. Students probably will say the following:

- The narrator seems tired and unhappy.
- The poem seems dark and frightening.
- There's something knocking on the door late at night.

Now go through the **Description** with students. Underscore that certain words create mood because they carry emotional feelings. **Stress that moods of poems vary, depending on the writer's choice of words.** In this poem, Poe uses words such as *weary* and *dreary* as well as a frightening situation to create a dark and scary mood.

Check Understanding

Ask students to show their understanding of the **Definition** on page 456 by reading another poem that creates a strong mood. Poems by Janet S. Wong, such as "Campfire," are often strong in mood. Have students address questions like these:

- How would you describe your overall feelings while reading the piece?
- What words or situations did the poet use to create that mood?
- How did the mood contribute to the overall meaning?

Narrative Poem

Set Goal

Help students recognize a narrative poem and understand that it tells a story in poem format.

Teach and Discuss

Read the **Example** on page 457 with students and explain that it is part of a narrative poem. Ask students what they notice about the example. Students probably will report the following:

- The poem tells a story about a woman's life.
- The poem has a lot of personal information, perspectives, and feelings.
- It's surprising that the poem can sum up this woman's whole life in so few lines.

Now go through the **Description** with students. **Emphasize that a narrative poem has all of the elements of a short story (character, setting, conflict, and plot).**

Check Understanding

Have students review the **Definition** on page 457. To demonstrate their understanding, ask students to read another piece of narrative poetry. Many poems by Henry Wadsworth Longfellow are good examples of narrative poetry. Have students address questions such as these:

■ What short story elements can you point out?

■ What elements make this narrative a poem?

■ What did you learn and how did it make you feel?

Onomatopoeia

Set Goal

Help students to recognize onomatopoeia and to understand that with this element words sound like the thing they name.

Teach and Discuss

Explain that the **Example** on page 458 shows onomatopoeia and ask students what they notice about it. Students probably will say the following:

■ The poem describes a girl walking in the slush.

■ The words used to describe the sounds are unusual.

■ The words sound like what they mean.

Now go through the **Description** with students. **Stress that in onomatopoeia words sound like the thing they name.** For examples, have students read the words listed. Point out that they may have trouble reading them without mimicking the sound they describe. Tell them that onomatopoeia makes poetry more fun.

Check Understanding

Have students review the **Definition** on page 458. To show their understanding, ask students to read a piece of poetry that has onomatopoeia, such as "Our Mr. Toad" (David McCord) or "Cynthia in the Snow" (Gwendolyn Brooks). Have them address questions like these:

■ Which words are examples of onomatopoeia?

■ What effect does onomatopoeia have on the overall poem?

■ How did the words make you feel?

Personification

Set Goal

Help students to recognize personification and to understand that it is a figure of speech in which inanimate things are given human qualities.

Teach and Discuss

Read the **Example** on page 459 with students. Explain that it shows personification and ask students what they notice about the example. Students probably will say the following:

■ The grass and rain are described as if they have thoughts and feelings.

■ The poem is very emotional and imaginative.

■ The rain answers the need of the summer grass for water.

Now go through the **Description** with students. **Underscore the idea that personification means giving human traits to nonhuman objects**. Poets use personification to make ideas stand out in an interesting, more personal way.

Check Understanding

Have students review the **Definition** on page 459. Illustrate the concept by asking them to read a piece of poetry that has personification, such as Emily Dickinson's "The Morns are Meeker." Have them address questions like these:

■ What nonhuman objects are given human traits?

■ What is the poet trying to do by using personification?

■ What is your reaction to the personification?

Repetition

Set Goal

Help students recognize repetition and understand that poets use it to add a sense of rhythm, emphasize an important idea, or set a mood.

Teach and Discuss

Read the **Example** on page 460 with students and explain that it shows how repetition is used in a poem. Ask students what they notice about the example. Students probably will say the following:

■ There are a lot of repeated words and sounds.

■ The sounds create a natural rhythm.

■ The words seem to lull the reader into a sleepy state.

Now go through the **Description** with students. **Stress that repetition in poetry can emphasize important ideas and create rhythm and mood.**

Check Understanding

Have students review the **Definition** on page 460. To show their understanding, have them read a piece of poetry that uses repetition. Have them address questions like these:

■ What is repeated?

■ What effect does the use of repetition have on the poem overall?

■ How would the poem be different without repetition?

Rhyme

Set Goal

Help students to recognize rhyme and to understand that poets use it to emphasize a particular word or sound.

Teach and Discuss

Read the **Example** on page 461 with students. Ask students what they notice about rhyme in this example. Students probably will say the following:

■ The poet uses strange word forms that have the same sounds.

■ The sounds tend to be at the ends of the phrases.

■ The sounds mimic the owl that's being described.

In discussing the **Description** with students, point out the distinction between end rhyme (at the end of a line) and internal rhyme (within a line). **Emphasize that rhyme is the repetition of similar sounds.** Rhyme helps emphasize certain words. In addition, rhyme creates a pleasing musical effect.

Check Understanding

Have students review the **Definition** on page 461. To gauge their understanding, ask them to read a piece of poetry that has both end rhyme and internal rhyme, such as Jack Prelutsky's "Toucans Two." Have them address questions like these:

■ Where do the rhymes occur?

■ What do the rhymes do to put forward the poet's ideas or expressions?

■ How does the poem sound aloud?

Rhyme Scheme

Set Goal

Help students to recognize and mark rhyme schemes and to understand that poets use them to add beauty and a sense of order.

Teach and Discuss

Ask students to read aloud the **Example** on page 462. Explain that the example shows how to identify a rhyme scheme in a poem. Ask students what they notice about the example. Students probably will observe the following:

■ The poem is about Isabel and a bear.

■ Each pair of two lines has the same end rhyme.

■ The rhyme gives the poem a strong structure.

Now go through the **Description** with students. **Stress that poets use rhyming words to express feelings, ideas, and sounds.** Focus on the example's rhyming pattern as you read it aloud with the class. Explain that the sounds at the ends of paired lines create a pattern, which can be charted as *aa, bb, cc* and would continue on as *dd, ee, ff*, and so on. Emphasize that the effect of the rhyming pattern is that it creates a sense of order.

Check Understanding

Have students review the **Definition** on page 462. Ask them to search for a new rhyme scheme by asking them to read a piece of poetry with a different rhyme scheme, such as "Almost Perfect" (Shel Silverstein) or "Abraham Lincoln" (Rosemary Carr and Stephen Vincent Benét). Have them address questions like these:

■ How would you describe this new rhyme scheme?

■ How would it differ from the example in both pattern and effect?

■ What other sorts of rhyme schemes can you imagine?

Rhythm

Set Goal

Help students to recognize rhythm and understand how its musical quality can add to a poem.

Teach and Discuss

Read the **Example** on page 463 with students. Explain that it shows rhythm and ask students what they notice about the poem. Students probably will report the following:

■ The poem is simple and short.

■ The poem seems to have an easy flow.

■ The second word or syllable in each line is emphasized. After that alternative syllables are stressed.

Now go through the **Description** with students. **Emphasize that rhythm adds a lively, musical quality to poems by alternating stressed and unstressed syllables.** Lead students through the poem while clapping out the rhythm to illustrate the point. Connect the rhythm found in poems with the beat students are familiar with in music.

Check Understanding

Have students review the **Definition** on page 463. To show their understanding, ask them to read another poem with strong rhythm. Have them address questions like these:

■ Where are the stressed and unstressed syllables in this poem?

■ Why does the author use this rhythm?

■ How does the rhythm contribute to the overall effect of the poem?

Simile

Set Goal

Help students to recognize simile and to understand that it is a figure of speech in which two things are compared by using the word *like* or *as*.

Teach and Discuss

Read the **Example** on page 464 with students. Ask students what they notice about it. Students probably will report the following:

■ The poem is about two types of trees, a willow and a ginkgo.

■ The poem compares things using the word *like*.

■ The comparisons create mental pictures of the trees for the reader.

Now go through the **Description** with students. **Emphasize that a simile uses *like* or *as* to compare two unlike things to create an effect or image.** By doing this, the poem shows similarities that readers may not have thought about.

Check Understanding

Have students review the **Definition** on page 464. Ask them to create a simile of their own. Check their comprehension by asking them to read a piece of poetry that uses similes, such as "U is for Umbrellas" (Phyllis McGinley) or "Father" (Frances Frost). Have them address questions like these:

■ Where are the similes in this poem? How do you know?

■ How are the compared things similar?

Stanza

Set Goal

Help students recognize stanzas in poetry and understand that stanzas are a basic unit of poetic structure.

Teach and Discuss

Read the **Example** on page 465 with students and explain that it shows a poem ordered in stanzas. Ask students what they notice about the example. Students probably will report the following:

■ The whole poem is made up of six groups of four lines each.

■ Each four-line group tells about some new part of the journey.

Now go through the key points in the **Description** with students. **Underscore the idea that stanzas are like paragraphs in prose because they create a shape or structure and generally focus on one thought or idea.** In the example, there are six stanzas that focus on six different things.

Check Understanding

Have students review the **Definition** on page 466. To demonstrate understanding, students can read another poem with stanzas, such as "Simile: Willow and Ginkgo" on page 464. Ask them questions such as these:

■ How would you describe this poem's stanzas?

■ Is each stanza different from the others in any way?

■ Why do you think the poet chose to organize the poem in stanzas?

Symbol

Set Goal

Help students recognize the use of symbols in poetry and understand that symbols are objects that also are used to stand for something else.

Teach and Discuss

Read the **Example** on page 467 with students and ask them what they notice about the poem. Students probably will say the following:

■ The poet mentions a rock often and also talks about the sun and evening.

■ The poet talks about stealing the secret of the sun.

■ The rock probably is the symbol.

Now go through the **Description** with students. **Emphasize that symbols are things that stand for something else.** Illustrate the concept by offering examples, such as a blue ribbon, a gold medal, and the Statue of Liberty. Each of these objects acts as a symbol because it represents something else. The rock in the poem can be something "solid, safe, and strong." The evening might stand for "darkness" or "tears."

Check Understanding

Have students review the **Definition** on page 467. To show their understanding, have them read another poem with symbols, such as "Street Window" (Carl Sandburg) or "Isn't My Name Magical" (James Berry). Ask them questions such as these:

■ What symbol or symbols are being used in the poem?

■ What do you think the symbol represents to the poet?

■ What do you think the poet is trying to communicate?

Tone and Voice

Set Goal

Help students to recognize tone and voice in a poem and to understand the meanings of the two terms.

Teach and Discuss

Read the **Example** on page 468 with students, and point out that it shows how tone (a certain attitude) and voice (the person speaking) can be used in a poem. Ask students what they notice about the example. Students probably will report the following:

■ The narrator is a hockey fan.

■ The narrator recognizes the violence of the game.

■ The narrator seems to think a hockey fight is part of the game and maybe even fun.

Now go through the key points in the **Description** with students. Tell them that a writer's attitude toward a subject is called the tone. Compare tone and voice in poetry to the way a speaker uses tone and voice to communicate attitude and feeling. Ask students to offer ideas on the narrator's attitude toward hockey. Now point out that students can use clues to determine the voice, or the person speaking. Guide students in reading the bulleted points that analyze the voice in this poem. Be sure students understand that the speaker in a poem may—or may not—be the poet. **Emphasize that tone and voice can make the message of a poem both personal and powerful.**

Check Understanding

Have students review the **Definition** on page 469. To gauge their understanding, have them read another poem with a distinctive tone and voice. Many poems by Richard Armour and John Ciardi are rich in tone and voice. Have students address questions like these:

■ How would you describe the tone?

■ What clues would you use to determine the voice?

■ How do tone and voice contribute to the overall meaning in the poem?

Reading a Play

Ways of Reading Drama

Focus on Theme
Focus on Language

Elements of Drama

Reading a Play

Getting Ready

Goals

Here students read a selection from the Pulitzer Prize-winning play *The Diary of Anne Frank*. This lesson will help them learn to:

☑ understand and appreciate the genre of drama

☑ use the reading strategy of summarizing

☑ understand how plays are organized into scenes and acts

Background

Connect the lesson with students' existing knowledge by asking them to:

■ define or describe the terms *drama* and *play*

■ name the titles and/or authors of any plays that they have seen, read, or performed in

■ discuss reasons that people like to read or watch plays

■ compare reading plays with reading other kinds of literature

Opening Activity

Explain to students that a play tells a story through dialogue, or what is said on stage between characters. A play also has stage directions that describe the setting, actions, and other elements that help the play progress. Ask them to watch for these features as they read.

Overview

	Content	Teacher's Guide page	Reader's Handbook page
Selection	*The Diary of Anne Frank*		474–475, 478–480
Reading Strategy	Summarizing	310	476, 658
Rereading Strategy	Visualizing and Thinking Aloud	318	487, 664
Tool	Magnet Summary	312, 313	476, 481, 674
	Summary Notes	314	482, 680
	Character Map	315	483, 668
	Plot Diagram	316	484, 676
	Storyboard	319	487, 678

Ancillaries

	Grade	Content	Page
Overhead Transparency	6, 7, 8	Previewing a Play	Numbers 29 and 30
Lesson Plan Book	6	Reading a Play	164
	7	Reading a Play	154
	8	Reading a Play	154
Student Applications Book	6	adapted from *A Christmas Carol* by Charles Dickens	172–180
	7	adapted from *Pyramus and Thisbe* by Thomas Bulfinch	171–180
	8	*Trifles* by Susan Glaspell	168–178
Website		www.greatsource.com/rehand/	

Before Reading

A Set a Purpose

Before beginning, ask students to set a purpose for reading *The Diary of Anne Frank*. Focus students on the Setting a Purpose questions on page 473 in the *Reader's Handbook*, and discuss why these are good questions to guide their reading.

Setting a Purpose

■ **What are the main characters like, and what's the relationship among them?**

■ **What is the central conflict, and how is it resolved?**

■ **What is the theme of the play?**

B Preview

Encourage students to preview the selection to get a general idea of what they'll be reading. Use the Preview Checklist on page 473 in the handbook with students. Then walk through what to preview using the Overhead Transparencies.

Point out each item in the Preview Checklist. Suggest that students trace a finger down the page looking for characters' names and the general setting.

Preview Checklist

✔ *the title page, including the title and playwright (author)*

✔ *the cast of characters*

✔ *the general setting*

✔ *the number of pages, acts, and scenes*

✔ *any background information, photographs, or illustrations*

Overhead Transparencies

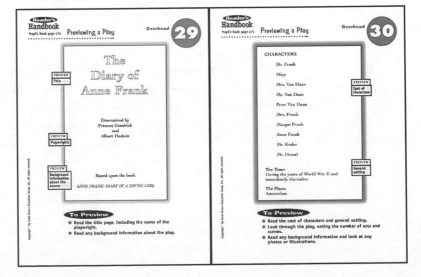

Before Reading

C Plan

Ask students to summarize what they learned in their preview. Then have them make a plan for getting information about *The Diary of Anne Frank*. Suggest using the strategy of **summarizing**. Talk about the reasons this might be the best strategy to use. (One reason is that summarizing puts the story, which is told through dialogue, into a brief, simple form, making it easier to remember.)

Reading Strategy: Summarizing

Summarizing gives students a simple way to pull together information about characters, dialogue, settings, and actions. As students read, suggest that they use graphic organizers that will help them get information from the play. Students need to be familiar with several kinds of graphic organizers.

For example, a Magnet Summary can be helpful because it places a key word at the center of a web that connects to other words. This type of tool can be used to summarize a moment, a scene, or the entire play.

MAGNET SUMMARY

MAGNET WORD

SUMMARY:

_____

_____

_____

_____

During Reading

D Read with a Purpose

While they read *The Diary of Anne Frank*, students note their ideas on graphic organizers.

1. Magnet Summary

A Magnet Summary uses a "magnet word" (key word) in the center that "attracts" (holds together) important ideas from the play. This organizer can help students get a better understanding of the play and pull together ideas about a possible theme.

MAGNET SUMMARY

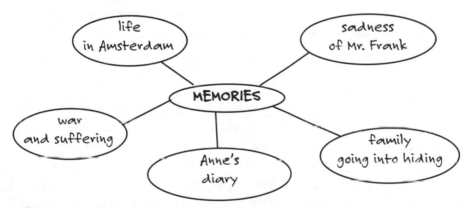

life in Amsterdam

sadness of Mr. Frank

MEMORIES

war and suffering

Anne's diary

family going into hiding

SUMMARY

People's memories may be an important part of this play. Mr. Frank is "a bitter old man" after the war. He has suffered a lot and no longer likes Amsterdam. It has too many painful memories for him. But when a girl named Miep gives him Anne's diary, he seems interested in it. Anne wrote about the war and about when the family went into hiding. Reading it must really stir up her father's memories.

 **During Reading**

 D **Read with a Purpose** continued

2. Summary Notes

A scene-by-scene summary is a more detailed means of tracking a play's setting and key events. With this organizer, students can summarize an entire play in a one-page overview. Point out to students how a few simple notes can clarify the entire play and make it more understandable.

SUMMARY NOTES

PART OF PLAY	SETTING	KEY EVENTS
Act One Scene I	Place is Franks' hideout in the play. Time is November 1945, after the end of World War II.	Mr. Frank tells Miep he is leaving Amsterdam, and she gives him Anne's diary.
Scene II	back in time to early morning, July 1942	Mr. Kraler helps the Franks and Van Daans get settled in their hideout. Mr. Frank gives Anne a diary.
Scene III	after 6:00 P.M., two months later	The Van Daans argue with Anne. Mr. Kraler brings Mr. Dussel to live in the hideout because the Nazis are rounding up more and more Jews.
Scene IV	middle of the night, several months later	Anne has a nightmare about the Nazis and rejects her mother's offer to stay with her.
Scene V	first night of Hanukkah, December 1942	Anne gives everyone gifts for Hanukkah. A thief breaks into the warehouse and hears a noise upstairs.
Act Two Scene I	January 1, 1944, late afternoon	A worker who may be the thief blackmails Mr. Kraler. Anne and Peter have become friends. Food rations are cut.
Scene II	evening, April 1944	Anne visits Peter in his room, and he kisses her.
Scene III	night, June 1944	Mrs. Frank catches Mr. Van Daan stealing food and wants him to leave. Miep brings news of the Allied invasion of Europe.

During Reading

D **Read with a Purpose** continued

3. Character Map

A Character Map gives students a tool for getting to know characters in the play. On it, you can record what the character says, how he or she acts, and how you and other characters feel about the character.

> **CHARACTER MAP**

WHAT THE CHARACTER SAYS
- feels that no one understands her
- loves her father but can't stand her mother
- wants to have fun
- fears the Germans
- believes that people are really good at heart

HOW SHE ACTS
- playful, talks a lot
- speaks her mind
- does what she wants despite what others say
- makes gifts for everyone for Hanukkah

> ANNE

HOW OTHERS FEEL ABOUT HER
- Van Daans and Dussel scold her for being too loud.
- Mrs. Frank tells her to be quieter and feels hurt by the way Anne acts.
- Peter hates her at first, but then comes to like her.
- Margot and Mr. Frank love her.

MY REACTION TO HER
- likable, good person who deals well with a horrible situation
- always looks on the good side of things
- good at showing or telling how she feels

Other Useful Tools

Point out to students the large number of graphic organizer tools in this lesson. Be sure students know that they do not have to use all of them, but it's good to know about them. As with any type of tool, students need to be able to pull out the right one when they need it.

- ■ **Character Development Chart**
- ■ **Paraphrase or Retelling Chart**
- ■ **Plot Diagram**
- ■ **Setting Chart**
- ■ **Storyboard**
- ■ **Topic and Theme Organizer**

How Plays Are Organized

While just about all plays have acts, scenes, and stage directions, the overall organization is up to the playwright. Explain to students that *The Diary of Anne Frank* is told in flashback.

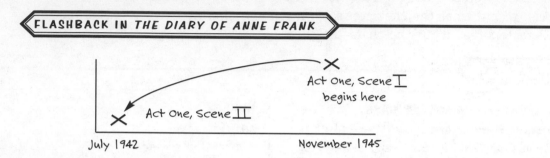

FLASHBACK IN *THE DIARY OF ANNE FRANK*

Help students to find the main stages of the plot, which include:

1. the opening exposition (what happens first)

2. the rising action (building tension)

3. the climax (where the tension or suspense comes to a deciding point)

4. the falling action and resolution (where the problem or conflict is solved)

Then walk them through the completed Plot Diagram shown on page 484 in the *Reader's Handbook*.

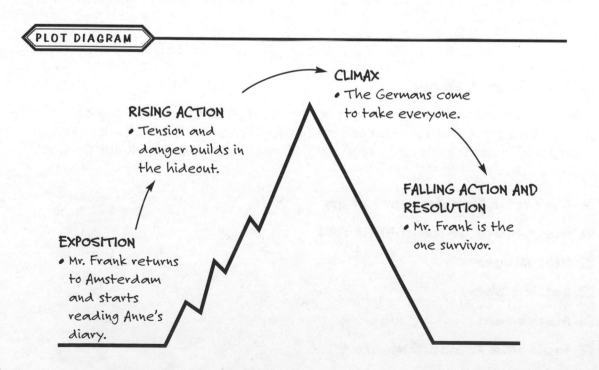

PLOT DIAGRAM

CLIMAX
• The Germans come to take everyone.

RISING ACTION
• Tension and danger builds in the hideout.

FALLING ACTION AND RESOLUTION
• Mr. Frank is the one survivor.

EXPOSITION
• Mr. Frank returns to Amsterdam and starts reading Anne's diary.

During Reading

E Connect

Explain to students that, while reading, it's important to interact and make personal connections with the play. Relating a story to their own lives and experiences will help them to remember it better and get more from it. *The Diary of Anne Frank* is a play that can touch students emotionally. Encourage them to take notes on their reactions to certain parts of the play as the reader below did.

---

from *The Diary of Anne Frank*

(The lights dim out. The curtain falls on the scene. We hear a mighty crash as the door is shattered. After a second Anne's voice is heard.)

Anne's Voice. And so it seems our stay here is over. They are waiting for us now. They've allowed us five minutes to get our things. We can each take a bag and whatever it will hold of clothing. Nothing else. So, dear Diary, that means I must leave you behind. Good-bye for a while. P.S. Please, please, Miep, or Mr. Kraler, or anyone else. If you should find this diary, will you please keep it safe for me, because some day I hope . . .

Just hearing her voice— not seeing her—makes this powerful.

I wonder what Anne thought would happen next.

Interesting last words —I admire her optimism.

You can also help students connect by telling them to:

■ ask themselves questions
  (How would I feel if I were in Anne's situation?)

■ think about the meaning of what they learn
  (Why do these things happen in the world?)

■ think about someone who would share their interest
  (Who would understand how this play makes me feel?)

■ compare what they learn to their own experience
  (How might the Frank family's suffering change my view on life?)

After Reading

F Pause and Reflect

After reading, ask students to stop and consider whether or not they understand the play's meaning. Help students to review their original purposes in reading the play.

Looking Back

■ **Can I describe the main characters?**

■ **Can I explain the central conflict in the play and summarize the plot?**

■ **What is the main message, or theme, of the play?**

■ **Do parts of the play confuse or puzzle me?**

If students can't answer all of these questions or if they have new questions, encourage them to read parts of *The Diary of Anne Frank* a second time. Remind them that rereading is an important part of the reading process.

G Reread

At this point students need a fresh way to go back into the reading. Have them review the play, looking for answers to their questions but using a new strategy.

Rereading Strategy: Visualizing and Thinking Aloud

Encourage students to use this strategy when they return to reread the material. Visualizing and thinking aloud can help them to imagine a play's performance and discuss it with others.

Visualizing can help students "see" the play more clearly, while **thinking aloud** can help them work out what they think is really happening between the characters. A Storyboard like the one that follows is a great way for students to document what they've read with sketches and notes.

 After Reading

 STORYBOARD

Act
One

Scene I: November 1945
Mr. Frank is back at the hideaway after the war, and Miep gives him Anne's diary.

Scene II: July 1942
The action shifts back in time. The Franks and Van Daans settle into their cramped hiding space.

Scene III: Two Months Later
The Franks and Van Daans are getting on one another's nerves, and Mr. Kraler brings Mr. Dussel to hide out with them too.

Scene IV: Several Months Later
Anne has a nightmare and rejects Mrs. Frank's offer of comfort. Anne doesn't get along with Mr. Dussel either.

Scene V: Hanukkah A thief breaks into the warehouse and hears a noise upstairs when Peter knocks over a lamp. The thief may realize Jews are hiding there.

H Remember

At this point, students need an activity that helps them to make what they've read a part of their own life and experience. Encourage them to try the activities listed in the *Reader's Handbook* on page 488 or the creative assignment below.

Creative Assignment: Tell the class that they are going to "interview" Anne Frank and her family. Ask for volunteers who would like to represent these people and allow other students to ask them questions. The class can judge whether the answers are consistent with what they learned by reading the play.

Summing Up

Finally, review the lesson with students. Focus on everything they have learned about strategies and tools for reading a play. Read with students the Summing Up (on page 488 in the handbook). Go over with students the three goals for this lesson. Discuss which ones they feel that they achieved and which ones they feel they need more work on:

1. understanding and appreciating the genre of drama

2. using the reading strategy of summarizing

3. understanding how plays are organized into scenes and acts

Assessment and Application

Use the Quick Assess checklist to evaluate students' abilities to read and understand plays. Give students the opportunity to apply what they have learned through one of the two activities below. For students who are comfortable with the reading process and strategy, use one of the plays suggested below or another one in your curriculum. For guided help with the strategy, use a *Student Applications Book*.

1. Independent Practice

To show that students understand the lesson, ask them to apply the reading strategy of **summarizing** to one of the following selections:

■ *Escape to Freedom: A Play about Young Frederick Douglass* by Ossie Davis

■ *Peter Pan* by J. M. Barrie

■ *The Dancers* by Horton Foote

Ask students to:

1. Create a Storyboard for the play.

2. Create a Magnet Summary for the play.

3. Write a paragraph summarizing the main elements of the play.

Quick Assess

Can students

☑ explain the purpose of stage directions?

☑ name three things to look for when they preview?

☑ name and explain one strategy?

☑ create and use at least one reading tool?

☑ describe how plays are often organized?

2. Student Applications Books

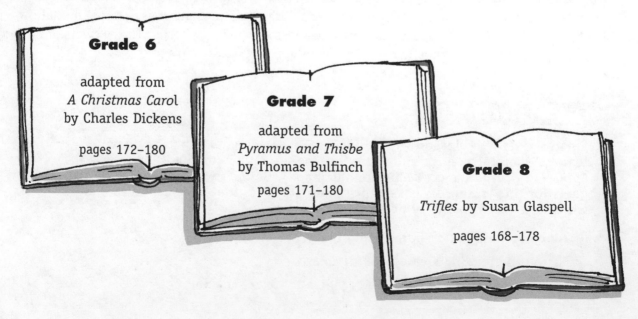

Grade 6

adapted from
A Christmas Carol
by Charles Dickens

pages 172–180

Grade 7

adapted from
Pyramus and Thisbe
by Thomas Bulfinch

pages 171–180

Grade 8

Trifles by Susan Glaspell

pages 168–178

Focus on Theme

Goals

Here students focus on dramatic theme—a writer's statement about life—by reading an excerpt from *The Diary of Anne Frank*. This lesson will help students learn to:

- ☑ look for clues about a play's themes
- ☑ use a three-step plan for understanding the theme in a play
- ☑ understand how plot and characters offer clues about theme

Background

Themes in literature can seem elusive to many students, partly because theme is a message or idea that often isn't directly expressed by the characters. Help students to understand that finding the play's theme—or the message the playwright would like them to understand—can be the key to appreciating what they've read. Connect this lesson with students' existing knowledge by asking them to:

- ▓ describe what they think is meant by *theme*
- ▓ give examples of theme statements that authors might make
- ▓ discuss why theme is important to understanding a play
- ▓ explain the steps they follow or would follow when looking for a theme in a play

Overview

	Content	Teacher's Guide page	Reader's Handbook page
Selection	*The Diary of Anne Frank* by Goodrich and Hackett		491
Tool	Double-entry Journal	323	492, 671
	Topic and Theme Organizer	323	492, 681

Ancillaries

	Grade	Content	Page
Lesson Plan Book	8	Focus on Theme and Language	155
Student Applications Book	6	*A Christmas Carol* by Charles Dickens	181–182
	7	*Pyramus and Thisbe*	181–182
	8	*Trifles* by Susan Glaspell	179–181
Website		www.greatsource.com/rehand/	

Before Reading

Explain that most authors write because they feel they have something important to tell an audience—a message that is worth the effort of "reading between the lines." Assure students that a simple three-step plan can help them find the theme. Read through the steps on page 489 with students.

PLAN FOR UNDERSTANDING THEME

Step 1 *Find the "big ideas" or general topics.*

Step 2 *Find out what the characters do and say that relates to the general topics.*

Step 3 *Come up with a statement of the author's point or message about the topic.*

Step 1: Find the "big ideas" or general topics.

Help students begin by focusing on finding the general topics. Tell students that they can find clues to a play's general topics by previewing the play before they actually read it. Tell them that they should look for these items when previewing any play:

- the title page, including the title and playwright
- the beginning of the play and first scene
- the general setting
- any background information, summaries, or illustrations

Spend time reading and discussing common topics for themes, as listed on page 490. Ask students to name fictional works that they know, including plays, that were about some of these topics.

COMMON TOPICS FOR THEMES

childhood	*growing up*	*loyalty*	*self-reliance*
courage	*hate*	*nature*	*success*
death	*hope*	*patience*	*trust*
faith	*identity*	*patriotism*	*truth*
family	*independence*	*prejudice*	*unhappiness*
freedom	*justice*	*race relations*	*violence*
friendship	*love*	*self-improvement*	*war*

During Reading

As students read a play, they should look for the playwright's "big ideas" that might indicate theme.

Step 2: Find out what the characters do and say that relates to the general topics.

Point out the four clues that might help students find the theme. Read through them with students. Tell students that graphic organizers offer a great way to keep track of their ideas about a play's theme or themes.

Double-entry Journal

Explain to students that a Double-entry Journal can help them infer the meaning of important passages in a play and record their thoughts about them. Read through the excerpt from *The Diary of Anne Frank* on page 491 and discuss the highlighted sentence. Then direct students' attention to the Double-entry Journal on page 492. Ask them what they think about the reader's choice of quotations and what else they might add.

DOUBLE-ENTRY JOURNAL

QUOTE	MY THOUGHTS
"There are no walls, there are no bolts, no locks that anyone can put on your mind."	Mr. Frank's talking about freedom. Even though they're hiding from the Nazis, their minds can be free. He seems like a wise man.

Tell students that once they've found a possible topic, they should watch for references to it elsewhere in a play.

Topic and Theme Organizer

Model the use of a Topic and Theme Organizer as another great way to keep track of theme-related ideas. Read the organizer on page 492 and walk students through the process of making one by writing down topics and examples of what characters do and say that relates to those topics. Remind students that their ideas about the themes probably will change as they continue reading.

After Reading

After reading, help students to pause and pull together their information about the play's theme. Remind them that they should use their notes and their knowledge of the main action and characters to determine the theme or themes. Suggest that they ask themselves what lessons they have learned from the play and compare their ideas with the ideas of classmates.

Students are finally ready to move on to the last step to help them determine the play's theme.

Step 3: Come up with a statement of the author's point or message about the topic.

Now students should review their notes. What clues seem to lead to the theme? Make the distinction between a topic (hope) and a theme (the playwright's message about hope) by having students read one reader's journal entry on page 493.

Reassure students that they may not all agree about the theme of a play. Tell them that the crucial thing is that they have details to support their ideas about what the theme is. Explain that, in most cases, three good examples will be needed to support their ideas about theme.

Summing Up

To wrap up, point out the Summing Up section. Go back over all that students have learned about what theme is and the three-step plan for finding theme in a play. Then ask students to tell what they learned in their own words.

Assessment and Application

Use the Quick Assess checklist to evaluate students' abilities to read and understand dramatic themes. Give students the opportunity to apply what they have learned through one of the two activities below. For students who are able to work independently, use the play suggested below or another one in your curriculum. For guided help use a *Student Applications Book*.

1. Independent Practice

Ask students to apply the three-step plan and tools they just learned to finding theme in *The Monsters Are Due on Maple Street* by Rod Serling or another play for young people.

2. Student Applications Books

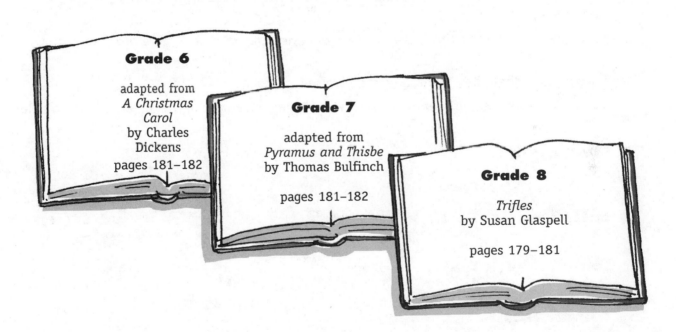

Grade 6

adapted from
A Christmas Carol
by Charles
Dickens

pages 181–182

Grade 7

adapted from
Pyramus and Thisbe
by Thomas Bulfinch

pages 181–182

Grade 8

Trifles
by Susan Glaspell

pages 179–181

Focus on Language

Goals

Here students study language in drama—key lines and speeches, stage directions, and dialogue—by reading excerpts from *The Diary of Anne Frank*. This lesson will help students learn to:

- ☑ study the key lines and speeches in a play
- ☑ consider how the stage directions contribute to a play
- ☑ examine the dialogue to see the way it affects characters, plot, and theme

Background

Point out to students that, unlike prose, a play moves its story forward through the use of dialogue. Tell students that enjoying a live play is not only in hearing what's said but also how it's said. Language is an essential dramatic element that communicates what the playwright would like the audience to feel or to understand. Connect this lesson with students' existing knowledge by asking them to:

- ■ explain what they think is meant by *key lines and speeches, stage directions,* and *dialogue*
- ■ list ways that they think language is used in plays
- ■ name plays they've seen or read in which they thought the dialogue was memorable

Overview

	Content	Teacher's Guide page	Reader's Handbook page
Selection	*The Diary of Anne Frank* by Goodrich and Hackett		496, 497, 498 499, 500, 501
Tool	Double-entry Journal	328	499, 671

Ancillaries

	Grade	Content	Page
Lesson Plan Book	6	Focus on Language	165
	8	Focus on Theme and Language	155
Student Applications Book	6	adapted from *A Christmas Carol* by Charles Dickens	183–184
	7	*Pyramus and Thisbe*	183–185
	8	*Trifles* by Susan Glaspell	182–184
Website		www.greatsource.com/rehand/	

Before Reading

Point out to students that, in a play, language can communicate volumes of information about the characters, action, setting, and theme. It also can create poignant moments that people remember for a lifetime. Reading a play with friends can increase appreciation and understanding.

Point out the three elements that constitute language in a play, as listed on page 495. Tell students that they will focus on each of these in detail.

During Reading

As students read the excerpts from *The Diary of Anne Frank*, urge them to read actively and to write down their comments, ideas, and questions about language.

1. Key Lines and Speeches

Read this section with students, focusing on its major points. Point out that they can find key passages by their placement in the play or by the meaning of the words. Key lines often appear at critical moments or toward the end of the play.

Read with students the first excerpt from *The Diary of Anne Frank* on page 496. Can students explain why this is a possible statement of theme? Then read with students the second excerpt on page 496. Ask them what key idea they get from this passage.

2. Stage Directions

While reading plays, students need to pay particular attention to stage directions. Make sure they understand that stage directions are the playwright's instructions for producing and acting in the play. Remind students that stage directions can include notes about setting, facial expressions, emotions, costumes, and other important elements.

Read with students the first passage from *The Diary of Anne Frank* on page 497. Ask them to point out the stage directions in this excerpt. Discuss how the stage directions are critical because they introduce the most important element of all: Anne's diary. Then look at the next excerpt on page 497 and note that this is the last glimpse the audience has of Anne Frank. The playwright stresses Anne's strong, womanlike courage in rising to meet the terrifying situation, communicating that Anne's ordeal has changed her.

3. Dialogue

Explain to students that, even though stage directions can provide powerful descriptions, most of what they learn from plays will come from dialogue.

Dialogue and Character

Point out to students that learning about a character's personality, values, and viewpoint are essential to interpreting what is going on in a play. That's why students should read actively.

Read with students the excerpt on page 498. Ask students what they've learned from the passage. How would they compare Mr. Van Daan and Anne? Encourage students to draw inferences from this exchange and to defend their viewpoints.

Also model the use of a Double-entry Journal as a way for students to record their reactions to important bits of dialogue. Read with them the Double-entry Journal on page 499 and ask them for their interpretations of this passage.

> **DOUBLE-ENTRY JOURNAL**

QUOTE	MY THOUGHTS
"Mrs. Frank.... Think how lucky we are! Think of the thousands dying in the war, every day ... Anne (Interrupting). What's the good of that? ... That's stupid!"	Anne always says what she thinks. She's got a quick temper. She seems like a typical teenager.

Dialogue and Plot

After you read with students the excerpt, ask them to explain ways in which the conversation might relate to the plot.

Dialogue and Theme

Explain to students that dialogue also can indicate the theme or themes of a play. Tell them to watch for general statements about society or people, like the one Mr. Frank makes in the excerpt on page 500.

Advise students to pay particular attention to the "good" characters, as many writers include a good character to act as a "moral voice." A good character, such as Mr. Frank in *The Diary of Anne Frank*, often conveys the work's main messages.

After Reading

Ask students to think about what they've learned about language in drama. Advise them to reread their favorite passages and to copy them or make notes on what they'd like to remember about characters, plot, and theme.

Walk students through the final excerpt from *The Diary of Anne Frank* on page 501. Read with them the student's journal response to that excerpt, and ask them to discuss their own reactions to this passage or any of the others included in this lesson.

Then suggest two ways for students to remember what they've learned about language in drama. They can make a Double-entry Journal of key passages from a favorite play, with their reactions to what those passages show about character, plot, and theme.

Students can record the functions of the stage directions found in the first few pages of a play. They can share and discuss their finished lists with the class.

Summing Up

Wrap up the lesson by pointing out the Summing Up section. Go back over all that students have learned about language in drama. Then ask students to tell in their own words what they learned.

Assessment and Application

Use the Quick Assess checklist to evaluate students' abilities to read and understand language in drama. Give students the opportunity to apply what they have learned through one of the two activities below. For students who are able to work independently, use one of the plays suggested or another one in your curriculum. For guided help with the strategy, use a *Student Applications Book.*

Quick Assess

Can students

- ☑ explain how to recognize key lines and speeches?
- ☑ give examples of information that could be in stage directions?
- ☑ explain how dialogue relates to characters, plot, and theme?
- ☑ create and use at least one reading tool?

1. Independent Practice

Ask students to apply the Double-entry Journal tool they just learned to the use of language in one of the following plays:

- ■ *Novio Boy* by Gary Soto
- ■ *The Monsters Are Due on Maple Street* by Rod Serling
- ■ *Let Me Hear You Whisper* by Paul Zindel

2. Student Applications Books

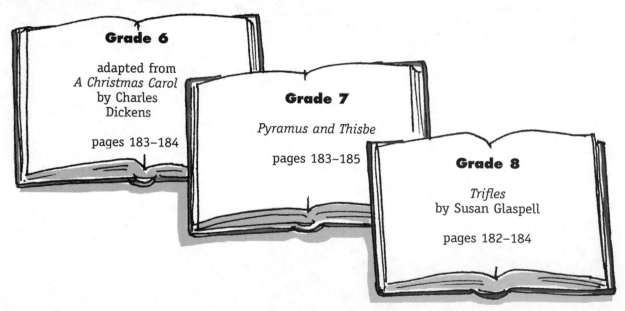

Grade 6

adapted from
A Christmas Carol
by Charles
Dickens

pages 183–184

Grade 7

Pyramus and Thisbe

pages 183–185

Grade 8

Trifles
by Susan Glaspell

pages 182–184

Elements of Drama

The terms or elements in this section are key parts of a drama. In the text, each of these terms is shown in an example, described, and defined.

Use this section to introduce these terms to students so that they will learn what they are, how to find them, and how they function within a drama.

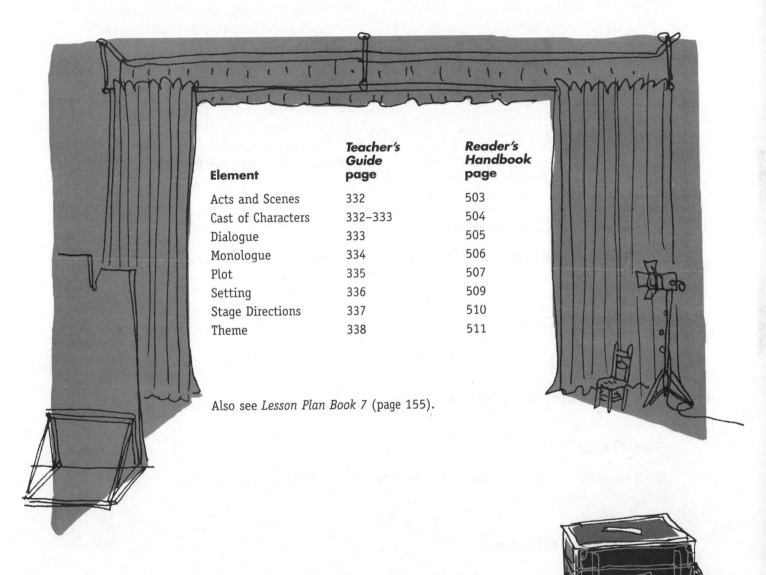

Element	Teacher's Guide page	Reader's Handbook page
Acts and Scenes	332	503
Cast of Characters	332–333	504
Dialogue	333	505
Monologue	334	506
Plot	335	507
Setting	336	509
Stage Directions	337	510
Theme	338	511

Also see *Lesson Plan Book 7* (page 155).

Acts and Scenes

Set Goal

Help students understand and recognize the two main divisions of plays: acts and scenes.

Teach and Discuss

Read with students the **Example** on page 503. Explain that the highlighted text shows the act, the scene, and the time when the scene takes place. Ask students what they notice about the example. Students probably will report the following:

■ It's the first act and the second scene.

■ Apparently the time has changed to "the next evening."

■ The stage directions tell what Helen is doing.

Now walk students through the information about acts and scenes in the **Description. Emphasize that a change of scene normally signals a change of time and place.**

Check Understanding

After reviewing the **Definition** on page 503, ask students to demonstrate understanding by skimming a sample play for answers to these questions:

■ How many acts and scenes are in this play?

■ Why do you think the playwright separated the action into these divisions?

Cast of Characters

Set Goal

Help students recognize a cast of characters and understand why this is a helpful resource.

Teach and Discuss

Explain that the **Example** on page 504 shows the cast of characters as it often is shown at the beginning of a play. Ask students what they notice about the example. Students probably will report that:

■ It's a list from *The Million-Pound Bank Note* by Mark Twain.

■ The characters seem to have English names.

■ Some characters are listed by their profession (for example, Butler).

Now walk students through the main points made in the **Description. Emphasize that characters may be listed in order of importance or in the order they appear in the play and that a cast list can be a handy reference as one reads a play.**

Check Understanding

Ask students to show their understanding of the **Definition** on page 504 by finding the cast of characters in a sample play. Ask them questions such as these:

■ How are these characters listed?

■ What does the character list tell you about them?

■ Why might the character list be an important aid when you read a play?

Dialogue

Set Goal

Guide students in learning to recognize dialogue and in understanding that dialogue is a crucial part of any play.

Teach and Discuss

Explain that the **Example** on page 505 shows an exchange of dialogue between two characters. Point out the speech tags and stage directions that interrupt the dialogue. Ask students what they notice about the example. Students probably will report these observations:

■ The characters seem to be a dolphin and a human named Helen.

■ The dolphin is asking for help.

■ Helen doesn't help the dolphin but says she'll tell "them" that the dolphin said "Help."

Go over the important points in the **Description** with students. Students can keep track of the dialogue by noticing the speech tags. Point out that quotation marks aren't used but that character names appear before each character's words. **Emphasize that playwrights use dialogue to reveal characters, plot, and theme.**

Check Understanding

Ask students to review the **Definition** on page 505 and to examine a sample play. Pick out examples of dialogue and ask these questions:

■ In addition to the obvious meaning of the words, what did you learn from the dialogue?

■ In what ways did the dialogue give you information about characters, plot, or theme?

Monologue

Set Goal

Help students to recognize a monologue or soliloquy in a play and to understand that a monologue is a speech by a character who is alone on the stage.

Teach and Discuss

Read the **Example** on page 506 with students. Ask students what they notice about the monologue. Students probably will report the following:

■ It's from *The Diary of Anne Frank*.

■ The "Anne's Voice" tag shows that Anne is speaking offstage.

■ Anne's speech is from her diary, and it indicates that the Frank family and their friends have been found and are being forced to pack and leave. She leaves the diary behind in hopes that someone will find it and keep it until she returns.

Spend time discussing the major points in the **Description**. Explain that a monologue can have a powerful effect on the audience because it puts a focus on one character's thoughts. Note that a monologue is different from an *aside*, which is something said to the audience that the other characters are not to hear. **Stress that a monologue is often an important dramatic point in the play because it reveals a character's thoughts.**

Check Understanding

To show their comprehension of the **Definition** on page 506, students can look at a sample play with a monologue, such as *The Diary of Anne Frank*, and answer these questions:

■ Under what circumstances is the monologue presented?

■ In what fashion is the monologue delivered?

■ What is the intended effect of the monologue?

Plot

Set Goal

Help students understand that plot is a series of events in a work and recognize the traditional parts into which a plot is organized.

Teach and Discuss

Walk through the Plot Diagram on page 507 with students. First, go over the definitions of the five parts; then show how the plot of *Let Me Hear You Whisper* by Paul Zindel fits that pattern. Ask students what they notice about the diagram and **Example**. Students probably will report the following:

■ The Plot Diagram describes the main elements of exposition, rising action, climax, falling action, and resolution.

■ The plot of *Let Me Hear You Whisper* follows a woman's discovery and rescue of a speaking dolphin that's supposed to be killed.

■ The playwright's plot intentionally builds suspense and concludes in the resolution.

Spend time discussing each of the five main types of conflict in the **Description** on page 508. Ask students whether they can think of examples of these types of conflict, either in a play, another piece of fiction, or real life. **Emphasize that the plot, or action, of a play usually centers around a struggle between opposing forces that builds into the crisis, called the climax.**

Check Understanding

To demonstrate their understanding of the **Definition** on page 508, students can examine a familiar play and prepare a sample Plot Diagram for it. Ask them questions like these:

■ What is the main conflict in this sample play?

■ What event would seem to be the climax?

Setting

Set Goal

Help students to understand that *setting* means "place and time" and to recognize the importance of setting in a play.

Teach and Discuss

Explain that the **Example** on page 509 shows the setting. Ask students what they notice about where and when the action takes place. Students probably will report the following:

■ *Let Me Hear You Whisper* is set in the hallway, laboratory, and specimen room of a Manhattan biology experimentation association.

■ The action begins on a Monday night shift and ends on the following Friday.

■ The place and time are very specific and clearly indicated.

Take time to discuss the **Description** with students. Point out to students that general setting information normally follows the cast of characters in a script. Make sure that students understand the important distinction between a general setting (one main location and time period for the whole play) and immediate settings (specific places and times within the general setting). **Emphasize that a new scene usually signals a change of setting.**

Check Understanding

Ask students to review the **Definition** on page 509. To show their understanding, students can examine a sample play, looking for answers to questions like these:

■ Where is a good place to look for the description of setting?

■ What is the general setting of the play?

■ What are the immediate settings?

■ In what ways might the setting affect the play overall (characters, plot, theme)?

Stage Directions

Set Goal

Help students to recognize stage directions in a play and to understand that stage directions can help a reader imagine how a play might be presented on stage.

Teach and Discuss

Read the **Example** on page 510 with students. Explain that the example shows the stage directions in a play. Point out that the highlighted text and annotations show the kinds of information students can find in stage directions. Ask students what they notice about the example. Students probably will say this:

■ It describes a scene from *Let Me Hear You Whisper* in which Helen is led into a specimen room.

■ The stage directions are in italics, and they describe how Helen looks and feels as well as what she sees in the room.

Direct students to read the **Description**. Discuss its major points. **Emphasize that stage directions are printed in italics and parentheses and that they often tell an actress or actor what to do and how to do it. Stage directions can also give the director instructions on how to present the play and readers a means for imagining the setting, characters, and action.**

Check Understanding

Ask students to review the **Definition** on page 510 and find the stage directions in a sample play, such as *Let Me Hear You Whisper*. Then ask them questions such as these:

■ How often does the playwright use stage directions?

■ What stage directions are typically given? (actor movements, moods, director's instructions, scene descriptions)

■ How do the stage directions help you as a reader imagine or feel something more fully?

■ Can you draw a picture of a scene based on information in the stage directions?

Theme

Set Goal

Help students to recognize a play's theme and to understand theme as an important message from the playwright.

Teach and Discuss

Read the **Example** on page 511 with students. Point out the highlighted text with the theme statement. Ask students what they notice about the speech. Students probably will notice the following:

■ Helen is feeling very emotional and refuses to go along with the cruelty she's witnessed.

■ Helen is supporting her point of view by asking the "butchers" to imagine themselves in the dolphin's place.

■ Helen's theme statement is a general comment about how one should behave in life.

After students read the **Description,** discuss its major points, such as that a theme can be stated directly in a character's speech or reflected in what characters say or do throughout the play. Students can determine the theme by figuring out the playwright's point or message on the topic. **Emphasize that a theme is something said or done that makes a statement about a "big idea," or general life topic.**

Check Understanding

Ask students to review the **Definition** on page 511. To show their understanding, they can reexamine a familiar play, looking for answers to questions like these:

■ What topics are presented in the sample?

■ How does the playwright "comment" on the topic? (character actions, statements, and so on)

■ What themes can you identify?

Reading on the Internet

Reading a Website

Elements of the Internet

Reading a Website

Getting Ready

Goals

Here students read the website for the International Dyslexia Association. This lesson will help them learn to:

☑ use the reading process for websites and a plan for evaluating them

☑ use the strategy of reading critically to examine a website

☑ understand the organization of websites

Background

Connect the lesson with students' existing knowledge by asking them to:

■ define or describe the term *website*

■ describe characteristics and elements of websites

■ compare reading websites to other kinds of reading

■ list their favorite websites and explain why

■ discuss why and how they use the Web

Opening Activity

Explain to students that websites are not designed for page-by-page reading as books are. Instead, they are designed to allow users to move around freely, following their personal interests. Invite students to share what they know about using the Web.

Overview

	Content	Teacher's Guide page	Reader's Handbook page
Internet	The International Dyslexia Association website		517, 521
Reading Strategy	Reading Critically	343	518, 654
Rereading Strategy	Skimming	348	525, 656
Tool	Website Profiler	343, 347	519, 523, 684
	Study Cards	344	520-521, 679
	Summary Notes	345	526, 680
	Critical Reading Chart	345	670

Ancillaries

	Grade	Content	Page
Overhead Transparency	6, 7, 8	Previewing a Website	Number 31
Lesson Plan Book	6	Reading a Website	174
	7	Reading a Website	164
	8	Reading a Website	164
Student Applications Book	6	The Common Cold website	185–193
	7	The International Asthma Association website	186–193
	8	American History from A-Z website	185–192
Website		www.greatsource.com/rehand/	

Before Reading

A Set a Purpose

Before reading, ask students to set a purpose for reading the International Dyslexia Association website. Focus students on the Setting a Purpose questions on page 515 in the *Reader's Handbook,* and discuss why these are good questions to guide their reading.

Setting a Purpose

■ What is dyslexia, and how many people get it?

■ What causes dyslexia?

■ How can dyslexia be treated or cured?

B Preview

Encourage students to preview the website to get a general idea of what it has to offer. Use the Preview Checklist on page 516 in the handbook with students. Then walk through what to preview using the Overhead Transparency.

Point out each item in the Preview Checklist during the class's preview.

Preview Checklist

✓ the name and overall look of site

✓ the main menu or table of contents

✓ the first few lines describing the site

✓ any images or graphics that create a feeling for the site

✓ the source or sponsor of website

Overhead Transparency

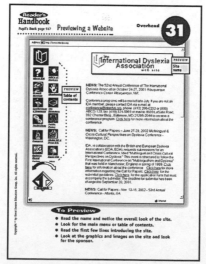

Before Reading

C Plan

Have students summarize what they learned during their preview. Then students should make a plan for getting information they want from the website. Suggest using the strategy of **reading critically**. Talk about the reasons this might be the best strategy to use. (If students are looking for information, it is very important to know whether the source of the information is respected and reliable.)

Reading Strategy: Reading Critically

Tell students that reading critically is essential on the Web since some sites include inaccurate or outdated information. As students read, suggest that they use a variety of graphic organizers to help them get the information they need from the website. Students need to be familiar with several different kinds of graphic organizers.

Website Profiler

After walking students through the steps listed in "How to Read a Website Critically" on page 519 in the handbook, introduce the Website Profiler. Note that this organizer gives them a format for recording information about the reliability of a website.

◀ WEBSITE PROFILER ▶

NAME URL	
SPONSOR	DATE
POINT OF VIEW	EXPERTISE
REACTION	

During Reading

D Read with a Purpose

While reading the International Dyslexia Association website, students record their information on graphic organizers.

Study Cards

Taking notes is a helpful way for students to record what they learn as they navigate a website. They can make notes on file cards or in a notebook.

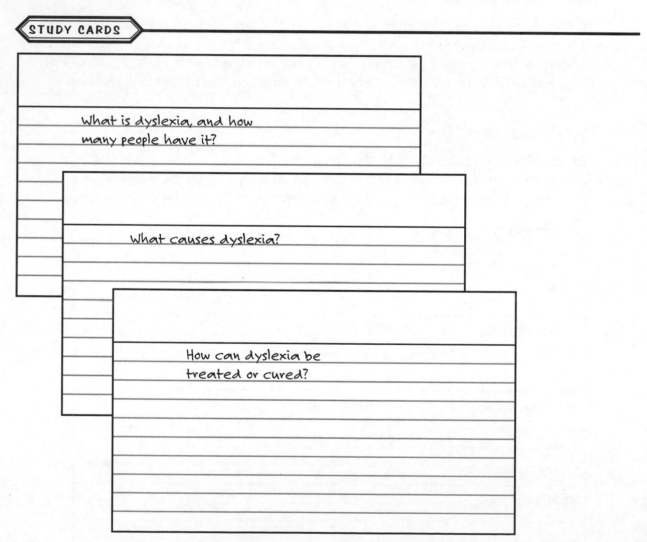

STUDY CARDS

What is dyslexia, and how many people have it?

What causes dyslexia?

How can dyslexia be treated or cured?

During Reading

D **Read with a Purpose** continued

Other Useful Tools

Point out to students that there are many tools they can use to read a website. The more tools they are familiar with, the more likely they are to pull out the right one when they need it.

■ **Summary Notes**

■ **Critical Reading Chart**

> SUMMARY NOTES

(www.interdys.org)

Four things I learned from the IDA website:
1. The cause is not known, but the brain of a person with dyslexia develops and works differently.
2. Dyslexia runs in families.
3. Dyslexia has nothing to do with intelligence. Anyone can have it.
4. Treating dyslexia early can prevent a dyslexic adult from having reading problems.

> CRITICAL READING CHART

1. Is the main idea or viewpoint clear?	
2. What evidence is presented?	
3. Are the sources authoritative and reliable?	
4. Is the evidence convincing?	
5. Is there another side of the story?	

During Reading

How Websites Are Organized

Tell students that websites aren't organized like single pages in a book. Instead, websites are organized in a way that allows visitors to read what they want, in any order, and ignore the rest. Show them the diagram on page 522 in the *Reader's Handbook* to illustrate how web pages are linked for easy access. Discuss how the organizations are different.

ORGANIZATION OF A WEBSITE VS. A BOOK

Students should notice that a website could have as many topic pages, subtopic pages, and links as it requires. Unlike a book, a good website is structured like a web. A book is structured in a sequence—1, 2, 3, 4, 5, and so on. Books move in a straight line, from page to page, whereas websites allow the user to jump around.

Point out that, with a website, students create the order in which they read the material. With a book, an author has already thought through what the best order is and presented the pages in a logical sequence. Help students see that when reading a website they need to be responsible for creating the order.

During Reading

E Connect

Remind students that real learning includes making a personal connection with a reading. They should take time to consider who they are, what they know, and how they feel when they view a website. A Website Profiler can help them record how well they connect, or don't connect, with a particular website.

◀ WEBSITE PROFILER ▶

NAME: International Dyslexia Association
URL: www.interdys.org

SPONSOR: itself	**DATE:** lists events in 2001 and 2002
POINT OF VIEW: The organization helps people with dyslexia.	**EXPERTISE:** It seems to be a good source of information.

REACTION: Site was good but could have been more appealing, such as brighter colors and addition of pictures.

You can help students connect by telling them to:

■ ask themselves questions
(How do I feel about what this site is saying?)

■ think about the meaning of what they learn
(Is this website stretching the facts?)

■ think about someone who would share their interest
(Who else might be interested in this website?)

■ compare what they learn with their own experience
(How does this information compare to what I learned in class?)

After Reading

F Pause and Reflect

After reading, have students stop to think about whether they got the information they wanted. Help students go back and review their purposes for reading the International Dyslexia Association website. (What is dyslexia? How many people get it? What causes it? How can it be treated or cured?)

Looking Back

■ **Can I summarize the most important information?**

■ **Was I confused or puzzled by anything I read?**

■ **What else would I like to know?**

After reading the website, students probably are able to answer most of their original questions. But they may have new questions. If they aren't sure of what they've read, encourage them to return to the IDA site a second time. Remind them that rereading is an important part of the reading process. With websites, it can also provide an opportunity to assess whether a site's information is biased or inaccurate.

G Reread

At this point, students need a fresh approach to rereading the website.

Rereading Strategy: Skimming

Skimming is a great tool when returning to reread. When skimming, readers search for specific information, ignoring any information that they don't need. Help students understand that they can glance quickly at the website, letting their eyes focus first on the table of contents and then on links that are likely to have the information they want to find.

After Reading

Skimming helps students to focus only on the passages or ideas they'd like to clarify. Encourage them to ask themselves questions about what they really know, so that they can skim for what they don't know.

Walk students through the steps for evaluating Internet sources on page 525 in the handbook.

HOW TO EVALUATE INTERNET SOURCES

1. Check the source of the site.
The source or sponsor is often named at the top or bottom of the home page.

2. Check the site's credentials.
Credentials are educational degrees, job titles, or other training or experience that makes a person an authority on a subject. To trust the information on a site, you need to know that the people behind it are knowledgeable.

3. Identify its purpose.
Figure out why the site was created. Is its purpose to sell a product and make money, to promote a cause, or to educate people? Its purpose will help you see its point of view.

4. Check the date the site was last updated.
Recent updates suggest the site will probably have up-to-date and accurate information.

5. Question the accuracy if:
❑ *the source of the website is not identified*
❑ *the source is not well known*
❑ *the purpose of the site is to sell a product or promote a cause or political party*
❑ *the information is dated*
❑ *the text contains obvious errors, grammatical or spelling mistakes, or typos*

After Reading

H Remember

At this point in their reading, students need to make the information they have learned their own. Encourage them to try the activities suggested on page 526 in the *Reader's Handbook* or the creative assignment below.

Creative Assignment: Have the class create a TV advertisement for this website. Lead them in brainstorming answers to important questions. What do they think the site's goals and audiences are? What are the site's main selling points? What kinds of visuals or dramatic situations would "sell" the site best to TV audiences? What music would work best? When the class has made final decisions, create a brief, cartoon-like Storyboard that shows what the TV ad would look like.

Summing Up

Finally, review the lesson with students. Focus on everything they've learned about strategies and tools for reading a website. Read with students the Summing Up (on page 526 in the handbook). Go over with students the three goals for this lesson. Discuss which ones they feel that they achieved and which ones they feel they need more work on:

1. using the reading process for websites and a plan for evaluating them

2. using the strategy of reading critically to examine a website

3. understanding the organization of websites

Assessment and Application

Use the Quick Assess checklist to evaluate students' abilities to read and understand a website. Give students the opportunity to apply what they have learned through one of the two activities below. For students who are comfortable with the reading process and strategy, use one of the websites suggested below for independent practice. For guided help with the strategy, use a *Student Applications Book*.

Quick Assess

Can students

- ☑ name three things to look for when they preview?
- ☑ name and explain one strategy?
- ☑ create and use at least one reading tool?
- ☑ compare the organization of a website to that of a book?
- ☑ explain how to evaluate a site's reliability?

1. Independent Practice

To show that students understand the lesson, ask them to apply the reading strategy of **reading critically** to one of the following websites.

- ■ The Metropolitan Museum of Art, New York (www.metmuseum.org)

- ■ Smithsonian National Air and Space Museum (www.nasm.edu)

- ■ Librarians' Index to the Internet (www.lii.org)

Ask students to:

1. Use Study Cards to take notes on the website.

2. Create a Website Profiler for the website.

3. Write a paragraph evaluating the reliability of this website's information.

2. Student Applications Books

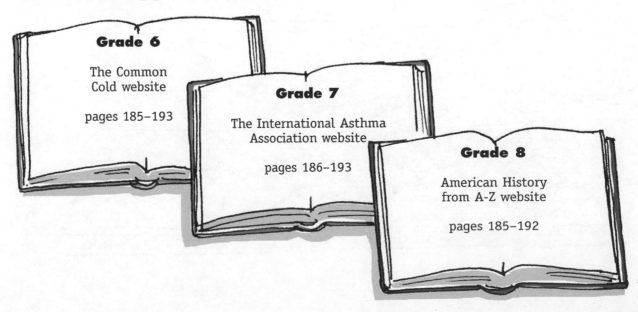

Grade 6

The Common Cold website

pages 185–193

Grade 7

The International Asthma Association website

pages 186–193

Grade 8

American History from A-Z website

pages 185–192

Elements of the Internet

The terms in this section are key parts of the Internet and the World Wide Web. Each of these terms is shown in an example, described, and defined.

Use this section to introduce these terms to students so that they will learn what they are, how to find them, and how they function.

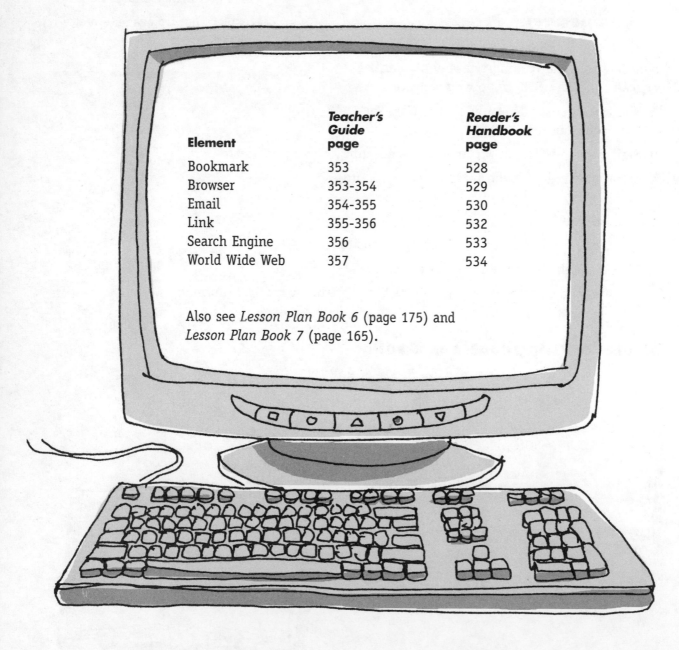

Element	Teacher's Guide page	Reader's Handbook page
Bookmark	353	528
Browser	353-354	529
Email	354-355	530
Link	355-356	532
Search Engine	356	533
World Wide Web	357	534

Also see *Lesson Plan Book 6* (page 175) and *Lesson Plan Book 7* (page 165).

Bookmark

Set Goal

Help students to understand and recognize bookmarks, which are used to return to saved web addresses.

Teach and Discuss

Explain that the **Example** on page 528 shows sample web addresses that a user has saved. Ask students what they notice about the example. Students probably will report the following:

■ Several of the addresses are listed under the names of sites rather than as web addresses.

■ The way these addresses are listed varies from browser to browser.

Now walk students through the main points made in the **Description**. Discuss the purposes and benefits of bookmarks, as well as how they're saved and reused. Instead of remembering and typing in an address, students can simply click on their bookmark list to return to that site. **Stress to students that a bookmark is an easy way to store the web address of a site they would like to revisit.**

Check Understanding

Ask students to review the **Definition** on page 528. To demonstrate their understanding, they can use a browser to find a site, set a bookmark, leave the site, and use the bookmark to return to it. Ask them to answer questions like these:

■ What process did you follow to set the bookmark?

■ Where did you access the saved bookmark, and what process did you use to return to the bookmarked site?

■ For what reasons would you use a bookmark?

Browser

Set Goal

Guide students in understanding that a browser is a tool for viewing a website.

Teach and Discuss

Direct students' attention to the **Example** on page 529. Examine it together. Explain that this sample shows a website that is displayed by a browser. Ask students what they notice about the example. Students probably will report the following:

■ The browser part of the display is at the top and bottom.

■ The browser has space to type an address.

Ask students to read the **Description**. Discuss its major points. **Emphasize that a browser is a software tool that allows people to visit websites, store bookmarks, display images, and play music.**

Check Understanding

Ask students to read the **Definition** on page 529. To show their understanding, students can examine and compare various browsers, such as Internet Explorer, AOL's browser (also a version of Internet Explorer), and Netscape. As they examine each browser, ask them questions like these:

■ How is this browser organized?

■ What features does this browser have?

■ How is it the same as or different from the other browsers?

Email

Set Goal

Help students to recognize email and to understand its basic parts and uses.

Teach and Discuss

Explain that the **Example** on page 530 shows a typical email, as displayed by one email program. Ask students what they notice about the example. Students probably will observe the following:

■ The top information (header) lists who sent the email, to whom it is addressed, the date, and the subject of the email.

■ The middle of the message is like the body of a letter. It contains the sender's message.

■ Emails can include links to a site or email address.

Now take students through the main points made in the **Description**. Point out and explain the parts of an email, as shown in the example. Discuss the issues and safety concerns raised by "chat rooms." Stress that students don't know exactly who is on the other end of their communication. They should never give out their personal information or agree to meet anyone. **Overall, emphasize that email is a widely used service that allows users to send and receive messages all over the world.**

Check Understanding

Ask students to read the **Definition** on page 531. To show their understanding, they can look at or compose and send a sample email. Ask them questions like these:

■ With whom do you regularly exchange emails?

■ How can email help make your life better?

■ Why should you protect your identity in a chat room?

Link

Set Goal

Help students to recognize links on the Internet and to understand that they are used to reach other websites.

Teach and Discuss

Read the **Example** on page 532 with students and explain that it includes a couple of links. Ask students what they notice about the example. Students probably will report as follows:

■ These links are described as good sites for literature.

■ They would click on these links to visit the sites mentioned.

Now go over the main points in the **Description**. Note that website home pages often offer many links to follow. Remind students to skim a page before they select the most promising link. This will save them time. Also point out that links are usually underlined, but some links are in images instead of text. To find those links, they should pass the mouse over the image. If the pointer turns to a hand, they have found a link. **Emphasize that a link is the address for another website or another page and links two pages together through hypertext.**

Check Understanding

To demonstrate their understanding of the **Definition** on page 532, students might examine a sample web page, looking for answers to these questions:

■ Where are the links on this page (underlined and in images)?

■ How are links used?

■ Which links would you follow and which would you ignore? Why?

Search Engine

Set Goal

Help students understand that a search engine is a tool for finding information on the World Wide Web.

Teach and Discuss

Look over the **Example** on page 533 with students. Explain that the notes show the main parts of a search engine. Ask students what they notice about the example. Students probably will report the following:

■ The web address for this search engine (Google) is at the top, and this engine can search over a billion web pages.

■ Users enter key words into an input area and click on a search button to begin the search.

■ The search engine shows the links at the bottom.

Now read through the **Description** with students, discussing its main points. Explain to students that there are hundreds of search engines with various ways of searching, different audiences, and diverse results. Tell them that they may want to try several search engines before choosing favorites for regular use. When looking at search engine results, they should spend time selecting the most promising links. **Emphasize that typing key words into a search engine can help them find what they're looking for on the Web.**

Check Understanding

Invite students to demonstrate their understanding of the **Definition** on page 533 by finding and examining several search engines. They can look for answers to these questions:

■ What kinds of features do you want a search engine to have?

■ Which search engines do you like best and why?

■ Why, after a search, should you be careful to choose the most promising links?

World Wide Web

Set Goal

Help students to understand the World Wide Web and how it allows people around the world to share information.

Teach and Discuss

Look at the **Example** on page 534 with students. Explain that it shows a sample home page with typical World Wide Web elements. Point out each of these elements as you name them: a URL, home page, table of contents with hypertext links, and copyright notice. Ask students what they notice about the example. Students probably will report as follows:

■ The site is about major league baseball.

■ It offers many related things, such as a free subscription to a newsletter, visitor information for the Hall of Fame, and a shop.

■ The copyright is included at the bottom of the page.

Walk students through the main points of the **Description**. Discuss the home page, the links and other features of a website, and website addresses. The home page is like a directory, and clicking on a link opens another web page. Links can be blue underlined text, images, and audio and video files. They are often found at the left side or bottom of the page. Sometimes they appear within text, where they are underlined or highlighted in a different color. **Stress that the World Wide Web offers students many resources from locations around the world.** Remind students that a Website Profiler is a useful reading tool for evaluating and recording information about a site.

Check Understanding

Ask students to read the **Definition** on page 535. To demonstrate comprehension, they can find a website and look for the answers to these questions:

■ What is the site's URL?

■ Who publishes the site?

■ What information does the site contain?

■ How does the site organize its information?

Reading
Graphics

Reading a Graphic

Elements of Graphics

Reading a Graphic

Getting Ready

Goals

Here students learn how to read graphics with a visual of a Gallup poll on crime issues. This lesson will help students learn to:

- recognize different parts of graphics
- use the strategy of paraphrasing
- pay attention to how a graphic is organized

Background

Connect the lesson with students' previous knowledge by asking them to:

- list as many different types of graphics as they can
- name different types of media in which graphics are likely to accompany text
- list as many possible purposes for graphics as they can
- discuss ways in which graphics can be useful as part of a reading

Opening Activity

Talk about the common features of graphics. For example, they might include captions or background, labels and headings, keys and legends, scales or units of measurement, and information about the source. Tell students to watch for these features as they read.

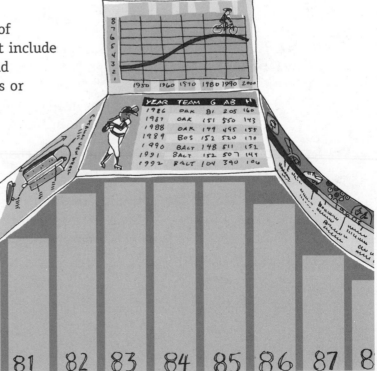

Lesson Resources

Overview

	Content	Teacher's Guide page	Reader's Handbook page
Graphic	"Crime Issues" by the Gallup Organization		539, 542
Reading Strategy	Paraphrasing	362	540, 650
Rereading Strategy	Reading Critically	366	545, 654
Tool	Paraphrase Chart	362, 363, 365	540, 541, 544, 676
	5 W's Organizer	363	672

Ancillaries

	Grade	Content	Page
Overhead Transparency	6, 7, 8	Previewing a Graphic Reading a Graph Reading a Chart or Table	Number 32 Number 33 Number 34
Lesson Plan Book	6 7 8	Reading a Graphic Reading a Graphic Reading a Graphic	184 174 165
Student Applications Book	6 7 8	"U.S. Gas Guzzlers" "Leading Scorers in the NBA 2000-01 Finals" "Changes in Acreage Used for Farming in U.S."	194–199 194–199 193–200
Website		www.greatsource.com/rehand/	
Content Area Guide		This lesson appears in the *Content Area Guide: Math,* the *Content Area Guide: Science,* and the *Content Area Guide: Social Studies.*	

Before Reading

A Set a Purpose

Before students read the "Crime Issues" graphic, ask them to set a purpose for reading. Focus students' attention on the Setting a Purpose questions on page 538 in the handbook and discuss reasons for using these purposes to guide their reading.

Setting a Purpose

■ **What is it about?**

■ **What does it say?**

B Preview

Ask students to preview the graphic before they read it closely. Point out to students the Preview Checklist on page 539. Then walk them through what to preview using the Overhead Transparency.

Direct students' attention to the Gallup "Crime Issues" graphic on page 539. Ask students to look for the relevant items on the Preview Checklist, one at a time. Suggest that students find each feature.

Point out to students that the annotations in the margin are color-coded, so students can match each annotation with the appropriate bit of highlighted text.

Preview Checklist

✔ the title
✔ any captions or background
✔ any labels
✔ the column and row headings
✔ the key or legend
✔ the scale or unit of measurement
✔ the source

Overhead Transparency

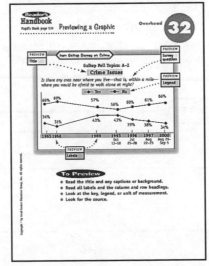

Before Reading

C Plan

Ask students to summarize what they found in their preview. Then explain that they should make a plan for getting information about the graphic. Go over each of the five steps of the Plan for Reading a Graphic on page 540.

> ### PLAN FOR READING A GRAPHIC
>
> **1.** Look at the graphic to gain an overall impression.
>
> **2.** Next, read all of the text.
>
> **3.** Paraphrase, or put in your own words, what the graphic shows.
>
> **4.** Think about the information. Ask yourself if the source is unbiased and if the information seems reliable.
>
> **5.** Make a connection with the graphic. Does this information relate to your life? What do you think of it?

Remember
elbow pads
Knee pads
helmet

At this point, introduce the reading strategy of paraphrasing. Go over some of the reasons this is a good strategy to use. (One reason is that it allows students to put the information presented in the graphic into their own words, making it their own.)

Reading Strategy: Paraphrasing

Tell students that **paraphrasing** means rephrasing and restating the meaning of what they read, see, or hear. Paraphrasing helps to unlock the meaning of a reading or graphic. Discuss each part of the Paraphrase Chart on page 540. Caution students not to quote words and phrases. They may want to use a dictionary.

PARAPHRASE CHART

TITLE	
MY PARAPHRASE	
CONNECTION	

During Reading

D ## Read with a Purpose

While reading the "Crime Issues" graphic, students write down their ideas using any number of different reading tools.

Students can point to various parts of the graphic as they paraphrase the information. Be sure students understand that the copy below is only the middle part of the chart shown on page 541.

◄ PARAPHRASE CHART ►───────────────────────────────

MY PARAPHRASE

1. In 1965 and 1968, just under 70% of the people felt safe walking alone at night in their neighborhoods.
2. In 1989 and 1993, a little more than half the people felt this way.
3. Then, in 2000, about 66% of the people thought their neighborhoods were safe at night.

Other Useful Tools

Explain to students that a number of different reading tools can be used for reading and interpreting graphics. It's a good idea for students to be familiar with these tools so they can pull out the right one when they need it. Other tools that might work well when reading graphics are the following.

■ **5 W's Organizer**
■ **Webs**
■ **Summary Notes**

◄ 5 W'S ORGANIZER ►───────────────────────────────

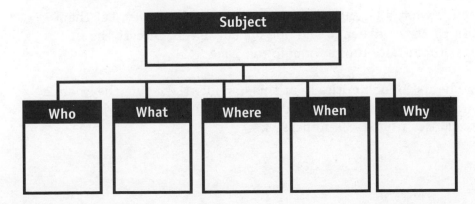

During Reading

How Graphics Are Organized

Explain to students that graphics are organized in a variety of ways, depending on the format chosen and the unique information they present. For students, the "key" to understanding and unlocking the meaning is to focus on the graphic's parts, as noted on page 542.

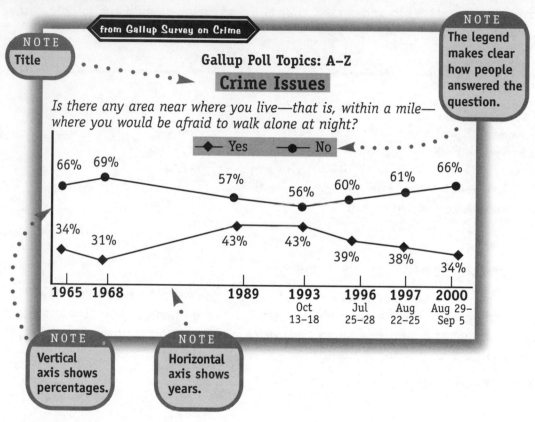

Finding the Axes

Explain what vertical and horizontal axes are and the roles these features play in the Gallup poll graphic. Emphasize how these lines and units of measurement are the keys to understanding how information is organized.

Finding the Legend

Ask students to describe what a legend is and identify it on the survey. Let them point out and explain what the diamond and dot symbols mean. Discuss the information shown in "Organization of a Graphic" on page 543.

It is important for students to look critically at this graphic. Make sure they notice that the diamonds with the 34% are at two different heights and that there is 1% difference in "no" responses from 1989 until 1993.

During Reading

E Connect

Explain to students the importance of reacting to graphics that they read. Their personal connections with the information help them to remember what they're learning. Help students by telling them to:

■ ask themselves questions
(Why did the Gallup organization decide to make a survey like this one?)

■ think about the meaning of the graphic's information
(What is significant about these Gallup poll results?)

■ make judgments about the results of the graphic
(Do people feel safer in 2000 than they did in 1989?)

■ evaluate the results by comparing them to students' prior knowledge
(How does this change the way I see or feel about crime and safety?)

Discuss the completed Paraphrase Chart on page 544 with students. Ask whether they agree with these thoughts and if they would add other reactions to the chart, such as "I wonder why people felt safer in 1993 than in 1968?"

PARAPHRASE CHART

TITLE	CRIME ISSUES
MY PARAPHRASE	1. In 1965 and 1968, just under 70% of the people felt safe walking alone at night in their neighborhoods. 2. In 1989 and 1993, a little more than half the people felt this way. 3. Then, in 2000, about 66% of the people thought their neighborhoods were safe at night.
MY THOUGHTS	The source is the Gallup Organization, a well-known survey company. The information should be reliable.
CONNECTION	I wonder why people are saying they feel more safe in recent years. Is the crime rate dropping? I feel safe walking where I live.

After Reading

F Pause and Reflect

After reading, students pause to reflect on what they've learned from the graphic. Guide them in looking back at their original reading purposes.

Looking Back

■ **Do I understand what the graphic is about?**
■ **Can I explain in my own words what I learned?**
■ **Does anything about the graphic puzzle me?**
■ **Does the information seem fair and unbiased?**

Because the "Crime Issues" graphic is complicated, students probably won't be able to fully answer these questions after one brief reading. If students do not notice the variation in height of some of the same numbers on the graph, point out the differences. Also point out that each set of numbers equals 100%, or close to it. Emphasize that a second, critical reading is important.

G Reread

Reinforce the need for students to be able to make sense of, or draw conclusions about, the data addressed in the graphic. A good way to refocus students' attention to this final effort is to introduce a new reading strategy.

Rereading Strategy: Reading Critically

Have students use the strategy **reading critically** when rereading. This strategy enables them to go beyond the facts and details of the graphic to evaluate the overall changes, patterns, and results the graphic presents.

Reading critically involves looking for and evaluating the main results of a reading. It encourages readers to think about what the facts really mean, to separate fact from opinion, and to assess the quality of evidence in the graphic. Graphics can be slanted in particular ways by the choice of information listed or the way a survey question is worded.

Drawing Conclusions

The chart on page 546 provides a format for evaluating the evidence in this graphic. Read and explain the four steps in the chart and the accompanying notes.

 Reread continued

◇ DRAWING CONCLUSIONS ◇

Questions to Ask

CRIME ISSUES GRAPHIC

1. What is being compared or classified?

It compares how safe people feel walking alone at night in their neighborhoods in different years.

2. What similarities and differences in the data do you see?

In 1989 and 1993, fewer people felt safe walking in their neighborhoods than in the other years.

3. Is there anything unusual about the way the data is presented? Is anything left out?

There is a big gap between 1968 and 1989 when no survey was conducted. There's no data at all for the 1970s, so you can't compare by decades. Were different people asked each time—or the same people in the same neighborhoods?

4. What trends or other relationships do you see?

The percentage of Americans who feel safe in their neighborhoods gradually increased between 1993 and 2000.

H Remember

Point out that sometimes students need to remember the information in a graphic because they are going to use it in some way. Encourage them to try the assignments on page 547 in the *Reader's Handbook* or the creative assignment below.

Creative Assignment: Take a survey of the class by asking them the same question that the Gallup poll asked. Ask them how they felt about this three years ago, two years ago, one year ago, and today. Work with the class to determine the percentages and then create a "Class Crime Issues" chart like the one in the lesson.

After Reading

Summing Up

As a final step, review the lesson with students. Focus on everything they've learned about strategies and a tool for reading a graphic. Discuss with students the Summing Up on page 547. Review each of the three goals for this lesson. Ask students which of these they feel that they achieved and which they feel they need more work on:

1. recognizing different parts of graphics

2. using the strategy of paraphrasing

3. paying attention to how a graphic is organized

Assessment and Application

Use the Quick Assess checklist to evaluate students' abilities to read and understand graphics. Give students the opportunity to apply what they have learned through one of the two activities below. For students who are able to work on their own, use one of the suggestions for independent practice. For guided help with the strategy, use a *Student Applications Book*.

1. Independent Practice

To show that students understand the lesson, ask them to apply the reading strategy of **paraphrasing** to a selected graphic from:

■ a social studies textbook

■ a newspaper or magazine

■ a research site on the Internet

Ask students to:

1. Create a completed reading tool such as a Paraphrase Chart for the graphic.

2. Create Summary Notes for the graphic.

3. Write a list of conclusions drawn about the data, its limitations, the quality of the source, and the applications of the information.

2. Student Applications Books

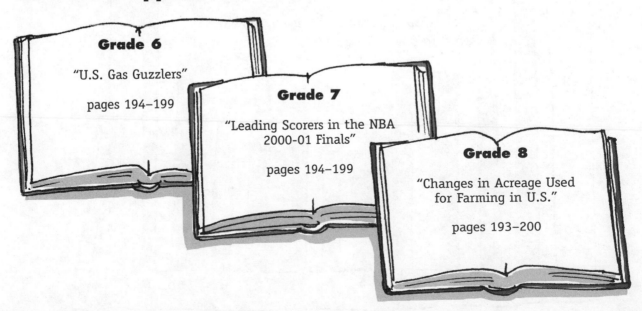

Grade 6

"U.S. Gas Guzzlers"

pages 194–199

Grade 7

"Leading Scorers in the NBA 2000-01 Finals"

pages 194–199

Grade 8

"Changes in Acreage Used for Farming in U.S."

pages 193–200

Quick Assess

Can students

☑ summarize the five-step plan for reading a graphic?

☑ name three things to look for when they preview?

☑ name and explain one strategy?

☑ create and use at least one reading tool?

☑ find and understand a graphic's legend, axes, and labels?

Elements of Graphics

The elements in this section are commonly used with all types of written works and need to be read as carefully as the text that they visually support. For each of these elements, you'll find a teaching goal, an example, a description, and a definition.

Use this section to introduce these different kinds of graphics to students so that they will learn to recognize them and apply the reading process whenever graphics appear.

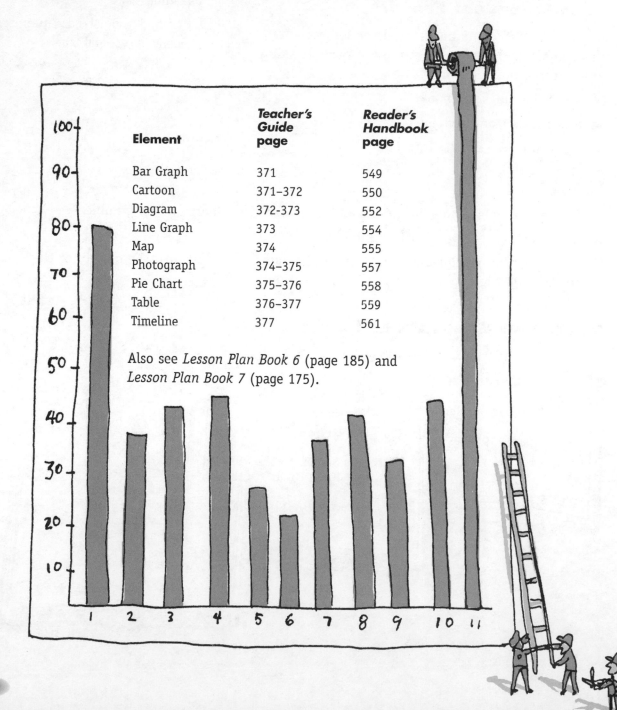

Element	Teacher's Guide page	Reader's Handbook page
Bar Graph	371	549
Cartoon	371–372	550
Diagram	372-373	552
Line Graph	373	554
Map	374	555
Photograph	374–375	557
Pie Chart	375–376	558
Table	376–377	559
Timeline	377	561

Also see *Lesson Plan Book 6* (page 185) and *Lesson Plan Book 7* (page 175).

Bar Graph

Set Goal

Help students learn to identify bar graphs and interpret the data they present.

Teach and Discuss

Read with students the **Example** on page 549. Explain that it is important to learn to identify the key parts of a bar graph as shown by the annotations (title, vertical axis, horizontal axis, and units of measure) and to understand what the bar graph is about (a comparison of the U.S. bald eagle population 1963–1998). Have students discuss what they notice about the example. Students probably will respond with the following:

■ The vertical axis measures population, and the horizontal axis measures years.

■ Vertical bars are used to measure the specific yearly amounts.

■ The population of bald eagle pairs has increased steadily over the years.

Now discuss the major points and bulleted items in the **Description**. Point out that following the steps outlined will make reading bar graphs easier and more fun. **Stress that bar graphs show quantities or compare amounts of something.**

Check Understanding

Ask students to review the **Definition** on page 549. Then have them find and look over other bar graphs in their textbooks, in newspapers, or in magazines. Ask them to point out the main parts of each bar graph and to answer comprehension questions like these:

■ What is the purpose of this bar graph?

■ What is being compared?

Cartoon

Set Goal

Help students understand that cartoons often are used to illustrate a point of view and make it more persuasive.

Teach and Discuss

Look with students at the **Example** on page 550. Point out how this example uses humor and irony to capture and illustrate a specific point of view. Ask students what they notice about the example. They are likely to mention the following:

■ Though one man is laughing, both men are stuck in bottles.

■ The man who is pointing at the other appears to be (ironically) a bigger fool.

■ Cartoons like these would make reading more fun and interesting.

Now read the major points in the **Description** with students, noting that following the key tips will help them get the humor in cartoons. Also examine the "Career Opportunities" cartoon on page 551. Point out the need to pay attention to details in the cartoon, such as the gender symbols on the elevator buttons. **Emphasize the importance of identifying the subject and other key details in order to grasp the main point of view being expressed.**

Check Understanding

Review with students the **Definition** on page 551. Have them find and examine some cartoons from recent newspapers or magazines. To demonstrate understanding, students can answer questions such as these:

■ What is the subject of this cartoon? Does it have a caption?

■ What is the particular point of view, and how is humor used to express it?

Diagram

Set Goal

Help students to identify and interpret diagrams, which are drawings with labels that show the parts of something or explain how something works.

Teach and Discuss

Explain that the **Example** on page 552 uses labels to identify specific layers and structures of the human skin. Ask students what they notice about the diagram. Responses may include:

■ This diagram shows what makes up human skin.

■ The labels and line arrows seem to be very exact.

■ It's important to read the title of a diagram.

Now discuss the key points about how to read diagrams in the **Description** section, using the tooth diagrams on page 553 as a reference. Walk students through the steps in the process of reading diagrams. Try out the process on the example. **Stress that students should focus on what diagrams are intended to show or explain. Explain, too, that diagrams relate to the text.**

Check Understanding

Have students review the **Definition** on page 553. To gauge their comprehension, have students examine one or more additional diagrams from a textbook or from a real-world reading, such as a computer manual or instructions on assembling something. Have students answer questions like these:

■ What are the key parts of this diagram? Is there a caption?

■ What is this diagram trying to show or explain?

Line Graph

Set Goal

Help students understand that line graphs use data points and a line to show the relationship between two things or how something has changed over time.

Teach and Discuss

Look over the **Example** on page 554 with students. Point out that it shows the growth in world population from 1950 to 2050. Have students comment on what they notice. Responses will probably include these ideas:

■ The population is expected to increase dramatically by 2050.

■ The title and both axes should be read to interpret the line graph accurately.

Now discuss what line graphs show and how to read them, as explained in the **Description. Emphasize that after reading a graph students should assess the slant and direction of the line itself. The steeper the line is, the faster the rate of change.**

Check Understanding

Review with students the **Definition** on page 554. To demonstrate understanding, students can find line graphs in their textbooks and in other nonfiction. Have them answer questions like these:

■ What is the subject of the line graph?

■ What does the line itself indicate?

Map

Set Goal

Guide students in identifying different types of maps and their parts—lines, colors, shapes, and symbols—as well as understanding that maps are drawings that show information about places.

Teach and Discuss

Examine with students the **Example** on page 555. Explain that this map has a title, lines, color, shapes, and a scale to present information about the boundaries, shapes, and topographies of the countries on the African continent. Have students tell what they notice about the map. Students will probably say the following:

■ The title says this is a physical map of Africa.

■ The scale measures distances in miles.

■ African countries vary a lot in size.

As you walk students through the major points in the **Description,** take time to discuss the Kinds of Maps graphic on page 556. Also explain how to read a map. Have students try this method of map study on the sample map. **Emphasize that students need to be able to identify the subjects and purposes of the maps they study.**

Check Understanding

Have students review the **Definition** on page 556. To demonstrate understanding, students can use maps from their social studies textbook to answer questions like these:

■ What is the title and subject of the map?

■ Where are the legend and scale on this particular map?

■ What type of map is this?

■ What kind of information is the map showing?

Photograph

Set Goal

Help students to see photographs as images of real life that can carry strong, carefully crafted messages of their own and emphasize points made in a reading.

Teach and Discuss

Examine with students the **Example** on page 557. Explain that this Dorothea Lange photo was taken during the Depression era. Ask students what they notice about the photo. Students probably will observe these things:

■ Life must have been very difficult for the unemployed people in the food lines.

■ This photo conveys strong emotions.

Now cover with students the major points in the **Description,** identifying the subject and reading any caption or text. Walk them through the "Elements of Photographs" section on page 557. Apply this information to Lange's photo. **Stress that students should study details of a photograph to discover how the details work together to convey a message or produce a specific effect.**

Check Understanding

After students review the **Definition** on page 557, they can demonstrate understanding by examining photographs by famed photographers, such as Lange, Mathew Brady, Ansel Adams, Walker Evans, or Alfred Stieglitz. Alternatively, they can examine photos from a high-quality magazine or from their social studies textbook. Ask them to answer questions such as these:

■ What is the purpose of this photograph?

■ What effect do you think the photographer tried to achieve?

■ What is your reaction to the photo?

Pie Chart

Set Goal

Help students to recognize pie charts and understand that they show parts of a whole and the relative size or importance of the pieces.

Teach and Discuss

Look over and discuss the **Example** on page 558. Emphasize that this particular chart breaks down the diet of nesting bald eagles as percentages of a whole. Ask students what they notice about the sample. Responses may include these ideas:

■ It's surprising that bald eagles eat so much fish.

■ It's also surprising that 28% of what they eat is other birds.

■ Bald eagles eat more fish (56%) than the other food sources combined (44%).

Now go over the key points in the **Description** with students, including what to look for when reading pie charts. **Emphasize that the entire circle of a pie chart equals 100% and that pie charts measure and compare the different parts of the whole in percentage terms.**

Check Understanding

Have students review the **Definition** on page 558. Gauge their comprehension by having students find, identify, and examine pie charts in their textbooks, magazines, or newspapers. Have them answer questions like these:

■ What are the key parts of this pie chart?

■ What is this pie chart about?

■ What do these comparisons suggest?

Table

Set Goal

Help students to recognize tables and to understand that they are the most common type of graphic. They present all kinds of data. For these reasons, learning effective ways to read tables is critical.

Teach and Discuss

Look over and discuss with students the **Example** on page 559. Emphasize that this "Mark McGwire Statistics" table presents his career batting statistics from 1986 to 1998, when he broke the home run record, hitting 70 home runs in one year. Have students comment on what they notice about the table. They will probably respond with the following:

■ For non-baseball fans, it takes time to figure out the abbreviations along the top.

■ McGwire played with the Oakland A's for most of his career.

■ His best batting average was in 1993 (.333).

Now go over the major points in the **Description** with students. Walk them through the steps involved in reading tables and apply them to the McGwire example. Use the "U.S. Population Data" table on page 560 as another reference. **Stress that the column and row headings of a table are used to find specific data and that the key is to read down and across.**

Check Understanding

Review with students the **Definition** on page 560. Check their understanding of the material by suggesting that they find, identify, and study tables in textbooks, magazines, and newspapers. Have them answer questions like these:

■ What is the purpose of this table?

■ What specific statistics or details are most significant?

Timeline

Set Goal

Guide students in recognizing timelines and in understanding that they summarize the key events of a period and are intended to give readers a visual picture of the order in which those events occurred.

Teach and Discuss

Look over and discuss with students the **Example** on page 561. Point out that this example spans the years of the colonial rebellion and documents the significant events that occurred, organized by the time when they happened. Walk students through reading the timeline to make sure they understand its layout. Have students mention what they notice about the timeline. Responses may include these ideas:

■ The colonial rebellion seems to have begun with the Boston Massacre in 1770.

■ The rebellion seems to have ended in 1776 when the Declaration of Independence was adopted.

■ The timeline lets you see the key events that happened over time all at once.

Now discuss the key points in the **Description** with students. Spend time discussing the directions for reading timelines, applying each step to the example. **Make it clear that students should begin by identifying titles, labels, and the beginning and end dates of a timeline.**

Check Understanding

Review with students the **Definition** on page 561. Check their understanding by having them find, identify, and examine other timelines from their social studies textbook or an illustrated history book. Have students answer questions like these:

■ What topic or span of time is represented?

■ Why is this timeline a useful tool for study?

Reading
for Tests

Reading a Test and Test Questions

Focus on Kinds of Tests

Focus on Essay Tests
Focus on Vocabulary Tests
Focus on Social Studies Tests
Focus on Math Tests
Focus on Science Tests

Reading a Test and Test Questions

Goals

Here students read a sample test and test questions. This lesson will help them learn to:

- ☑ prepare for different kinds of tests
- ☑ use the strategy of skimming
- ☑ understand the organization of tests and test questions

Background

Connect the lesson with students' previous knowledge by asking them to:

- ▪ describe different kinds of test questions and tests they've taken
- ▪ talk about important tests, both in school and out, that they will take in the future
- ▪ talk about ways that tests and test questions are organized
- ▪ list any problems they have in reading or taking tests
- ▪ discuss reasons that tests can be helpful or hurtful

Opening Activity

Talk about the common elements of tests and test questions, such as time limits, instructions, information on scoring, readings, and different types of questions. Tell students to watch for these elements as they read.

Lesson Resources

Overview

	Content	Teacher's Guide page	Reader's Handbook page
Selection	*Geronimo: His Own Story*		567–570
Reading Strategy	Skimming	382	571, 656
Rereading Strategy	Visualizing and Thinking Aloud	386	577–578, 664

Ancillaries

	Grade	Content	Page
Overhead Transparency	6, 7, 8	Previewing a Test Reading Fact or Recall Questions Reading Inference Questions	Number 35 Number 36 Number 37
Lesson Plan Book	6 7 8	Reading a Test and Test Questions Reading a Test and Test Questions Reading a Test and Test Questions	194–195 184 174
Student Applications Book	6 7 8	"Me and My Parents" from *A Girl Named Zippy* by Haven Kimmel "America's Ballerina: Maria Tallchief" "Captain Hardcastle" from *Boy: Tales of Childhood* by Roald Dahl	200–207 200–206 201–207
Website		www.greatsource.com/rehand/	

Before Reading

A Set a Purpose

Before reading, ask students to set a purpose for reading a test. Focus students on the Setting a Purpose questions on page 565 in the handbook and discuss why these are good questions to guide their reading.

Setting a Purpose

■ **What is the test question asking?**
■ **What information is needed for the answer?**

B Preview

Ask students to preview the test as a way of learning what to expect. Review the Preview Checklist on page 566 with students. Then walk them through what to preview using the Overhead Transparency.

Point out each item in the Preview Checklist. As they preview the sample test, suggest that students point to the test elements that they find.

Point out to students that the annotations in the margin are color-coded to help them match each annotation to the appropriate bit of high-lighted text. On this page, the first notes are for previewing the test and the notes at the bottom are helps in reading the content.

Preview Checklist

✔ the amount of time you have
✔ the instructions about how to mark answers
✔ whether you're better off making a guess than leaving an answer blank
✔ what kinds of readings are on the test
✔ what kinds of questions are on the test

Overhead Transparency

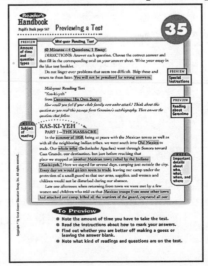

Before Reading

C Plan

Remind students that this sample is based on a test for a reading passage. True-false tests or math tests would be approached differently. Ask students to summarize what they learned during their preview. Then tell them to make a plan for getting the information they need while working on the test. Suggest using the reading strategy of skimming. Explain some of the reasons that this is a good strategy to use. (One reason is that skimming helps students quickly scan and re-scan a passage for specific answers to test questions. This is a basic skill needed to do well on tests because students won't remember everything after one reading of a test passage.)

Reading Strategy: Skimming

Skimming involves scanning or glancing quickly at a reading to find specific information. With skimming, students can pass over unnecessary details to zero in on answers that they need. Caution students that they should not skim all of the test. The questions, for example, need to be read carefully and slowly.

During Reading

D Read with a Purpose

As students read the test passage, remind them to read slowly and carefully. Also point out the importance of the first and last sentences in a paragraph.

Understanding the Question

Discuss with students the information on page 572 about reading questions. Point out the differences between fact or recall questions and inference or conclusion questions.

Fact or Recall Questions

With fact or recall questions, students can find answers "right there" in the test passage and should use key words as a guide during skimming. Tell students that these questions will ask for very specific information. They will need to go back into the passage and skim it to find the answer. Go through the sample on page 573.

During Reading

D   Read with a Purpose continued

Inference or Conclusion Questions

With inference or conclusion questions, students will need to put what they read with what they already know. The way to answer these kinds of questions is to skim until they find the key part of the passage and then read a few sentences before and after that. Point out the example shown on page 575.

INFERENCE OR CONCLUSION QUESTIONS

First, *go to the part of the passage mentioned.*

Next, *find the words mentioned in the test question.*

Then, *read at least* three *sentences. Read the sentence that has the quote, the* sentence *before it, and one or two sentences after it.*

By following this plan and reading sentences around the key words in the question, students will get the additional information they need to answer inference questions correctly. Explain to students the process of skimming for specific details, as described in the *Reader's Handbook* on page 571 and in the Almanac on pages 656–657.

During Reading

D Read with a Purpose continued

Other Useful Tools

A number of reading tools could be helpful with the Mid-year Reading Test. If students aren't permitted to write notes on the test itself, encourage them to create organizers mentally before rushing to start answering the questions. Students should be familiar with a number of tools so that they can pull out a useful one when they need it.

- **Timeline or Sequence Notes**
- **5 W's Organizer**
- **Story String**
- **Outline**

How Tests Are Organized

Explain to students that test questions follow the order of the reading. Remind students to look near the beginning of the reading for the first questions.

Walk students through the general Order of Questions chart for the Mid-year Reading Test.

ORDER OF QUESTIONS

paragraph 1	*key information for question 1*
paragraphs 1–3	*key information for question 2*
paragraph 4	*key information for question 3*
paragraph 6	*key information for question 4*

E Connect

Tell students that connecting what they read on tests to their previous knowledge can be very important. Opening up their thinking in this way can improve their answers to essay and critical thinking questions. Help students connect better by telling them to:

■ ask themselves questions
(What do I think about Geronimo's attitude and character?)

■ think about the effect the events described in the reading had on Geronimo's life
(How did the murders of his family change him?)

■ evaluate the passage by comparing it to what they already know
(How does Geronimo's story compare to what I've already learned about his legacy?)

■ evaluate the quality of the reading
(What do I think of the reading?)

Writing an opinion statement and supporting details can help students to quickly form and outline answers for essay questions. Point out the example of one reader's opinion statement and list of supporting details.

◀ OPINION STATEMENT ▶

OPINION STATEMENT
I think it's terrible what happened to Geronimo and his people.
SUPPORTING DETAILS
#1 They came to Mexico as friends, not enemies.
#2 Their women and children were slaughtered.
#3 They were surrounded and forced to leave Mexico and the bodies of their loved ones behind.

After Reading

F   Pause and Reflect

After reading, students need to stop to consider what they have learned from the passage, what questions remain unanswered, and how much time they have left. Students need to keep in mind their original purpose in taking the Mid-year Reading Test.

Looking Back

■ **Have I answered all of the questions?**

■ **Are there answers I should check?**

■ **What do I need to spend more time on?**

These Looking Back questions serve as a very important guide for students as they finish taking the test. Remind them of the need to reread the passage, review their answers, and spend their remaining time wisely. Now is not the time to give up or rush to finish, but rather to make a final push to answer the remaining (and hardest) questions.

G   Reread

At this point, students need an effective strategy to use with the difficult test questions they haven't answered. A new reading strategy will be helpful.

Rereading Strategy: Visualizing and Thinking Aloud

Encourage students to use this new strategy when rereading. **Visualizing and thinking aloud** is a useful reading strategy that involves making a mental picture of the words in a passage and talking through the ideas about what is being read. (Sometimes people need to "see" something in their minds or say it out loud in order to understand it.) This strategy works with both fiction and nonfiction and is, therefore, an effective reading approach to use on reading tests.

Use the examples on pages 577–578 to show students how to use this strategy. In discussing the Think Aloud, explain that different people would have different approaches, depending ion their prior knowledge and experience.

H Remember

After students have finished the test, they can make the new knowledge they gained from it their own by using the information or recording it some way in writing. Suggest that students try the two activities suggested on page 579 in the *Reader's Handbook* or the creative assignment below.

Creative Assignment: Divide students into small groups and have them draw pictures that show specific scenes from Geronimo's life. Share the results and discuss why students chose those scenes. Which picture best captures the heart of the passage? Which best captures Geronimo's character? Why?

Summing Up

Finally, review the lesson with students. Focus on everything they've learned about strategies and tools for reading a test and test questions. Read with students the Summing Up on page 579. Go over with students the three goals for this lesson. Discuss which ones they feel that they achieved and which ones they feel they need more work on:

1. preparing for different kinds of tests

2. using the strategy of skimming

3. understanding the organization of tests and test questions

Assessment and Application

Use the Quick Assess checklist to evaluate students' abilities to read and understand tests and test questions. Give students the opportunity to apply what they have learned through one of the two activities below. For students who are able to work independently, use one of the suggestions below. For guided help with the strategy, use a *Student Applications Book*.

1. Independent Practice

To show that students understand the lesson, ask them to apply the reading strategy of **skimming** to past reading tests or other sample tests that you have available. An alternative is to create a simple test modeled after the passage and questions in the lesson.

Ask students to:

1. Do a Think Aloud for a passage from a reading test.

2. Create an outline for the passage.

3. Write a paragraph explaining the most important things they learned about reading a test and test questions.

Quick Assess

Can students

- ☑ identify the two main types of test questions?
- ☑ name three things to look for when they preview?
- ☑ explain when it would make sense to skim?
- ☑ explain when it would make sense to visualize and think aloud?
- ☑ describe how test questions are often organized?

2. Student Applications Books

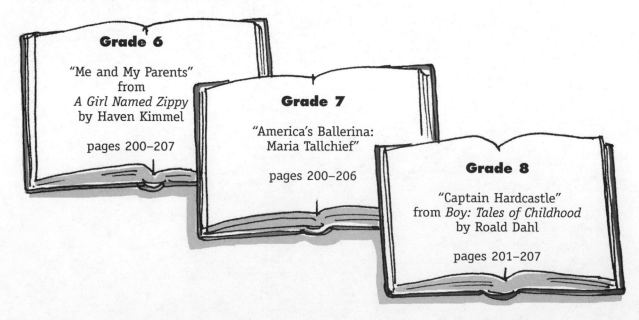

Grade 6

"Me and My Parents"
from
A Girl Named Zippy
by Haven Kimmel

pages 200–207

Grade 7

"America's Ballerina:
Maria Tallchief"

pages 200–206

Grade 8

"Captain Hardcastle"
from *Boy: Tales of Childhood*
by Roald Dahl

pages 201–207

Focus on Essay Tests

Goals

Here students focus on taking essay tests. On quite a few tests, students have to write an answer several paragraphs long to a question at the end of a test. This lesson will help students learn to:

☑ read an essay question and get ready for an essay test

☑ use graphic organizers to help them get ready to write

Background

Students often see essay questions as the hardest part of a test. Essay questions usually come at the end and require students to distill key information in written form in a limited time. Tell students that they need not dread essay questions. A few helpful suggestions can quiet the anxieties about this part of tests. Continue to connect the lesson with students' existing knowledge of essay tests by asking them to:

■ describe an essay question and explain what is involved in writing one

■ discuss their personal feelings and experiences in writing answers to essay questions

■ examine reasons why essay questions are given and why they are important

Overview

	Content	Teacher's Guide page	Reader's Handbook page
Selection	Essay Test Directions	390	581
Tool	Main Idea Organizer	391	582, 674

Ancillaries

	Grade	Content	Page
Lesson Plan Book	7	Focus on Essay Tests	185
	8	Focus on Essay Tests	175
Student Applications Book	6	Mall Rule	208–209
	7	School Board Proposal	207–209
	8	Curriculum Change Proposal	208–209
Website		www.greatsource.com/rehand/	

Before Reading

Help students see how much they can learn by previewing the essay question as soon as the test is handed to them. By reading over the question ahead of time, students will have time to think about and prepare an answer before they reach the end of the test.

Have students skim the "Directions" on page 581, looking for key information. Remind them that it is a good idea to start thinking about the essay part of the test even as they preview.

During Reading

As students read the essay directions again, they can see how an initial preview helped them to get a head start on the essay question. Stress that reading the directions carefully for a second time will help to focus their attention on this part of the test.

Reading Directions

Emphasize the point that many students perform poorly on essay questions because they do not take the time to read the directions carefully.

Read through the "Directions" and "Prompt" on page 581 with students. Ask them for their interpretations of what is being asked. Point out any differences in their interpretations.

Then go over the five key things to look for in directions, as shown on page 581. The annotations and highlighted text are intended to help students find key words.

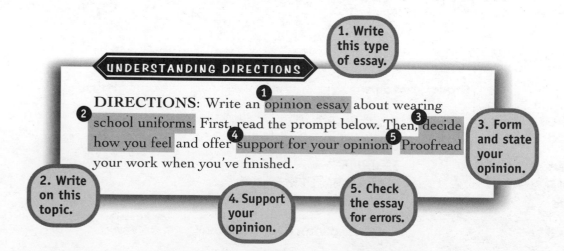

During Reading

During the test, students will need to plan for and write the essay.

Planning the Essay

Help students realize that having a general plan to answer an essay question will improve their score. It prevents them from rushing to throw together an answer. Suggest that students organize essay responses on a Main Idea Organizer like the one shown below.

Show students how using this tool can help them think through and clearly organize their response.

Read with students the filled-in sample of a Main Idea Organizer. Point out that all good arguments need a clear statement, at least three supporting details, and a concluding sentence that reinforces the writer's main opinion. Show students that filling the slots of this organizer is equivalent to writing an essay. All students have to do is piece the ideas and sentences together in paragraph form to produce a completed essay.

◄ MAIN IDEA ORGANIZER ►──────────────

MY IDEA I think school uniforms should be a choice, rather than something students have to do.		
DETAIL 1 Being a kid is all about expressing yourself. The clothes you choose can tell others a lot about you.	**DETAIL 2** School uniforms are expensive. It would be better for us to use the money for books or software.	**DETAIL 3** Uniforms can make our school-to-school rivalries worse. This might lead to more fights in public places.
CONCLUDING SENTENCE School uniforms might make sense for some schools, but they won't work here at Eleanor Roosevelt Middle School.		

Talk with students about how to use the time during a test. If they have ten minutes to write an essay test answer, tell them to spend two minutes planning. Be sure students don't neglect this all-important planning step.

After Reading

Remind students that it is important for them to go back and reread the essay directions as well as their response after completing an essay. Reiterate the need for a final check of the "little things," such as correct grammar and spelling, that can affect students' scores. Explain that following this process can make them more effective writers in the long run.

Help students to remember what they've learned. Present them with written directions for a general essay question. Allow students to use this lesson in their *Reader's Handbook* as they follow the process just described. Make sure that they fill out a Main Idea Organizer before they write. Walking students through the planning process will help them when they have to write under the pressure of time.

Ask students to choose partners and to exchange their Main Idea Organizers and essay question answers. Have them compare and discuss their results with each other. Later lead a general class discussion to find out difficulties and successes that students may have had. Helping students see what they are doing wrong and what they're doing right in a non-threatening environment will help them become more thoughtful about how they approach essay tests.

Summing Up

To conclude the lesson, discuss each of the points in the Summing Up section. Go back over all that students have learned about previewing directions and planning essay questions with graphic organizers. Go on to have students tell what they learned from the lesson in their own words.

Assessment and Application

Use the Quick Assess checklist to evaluate students' abilities to read and understand essay tests. Give students the opportunity to apply what they have learned through one of the two activities below. For students who are able to work on their own, use the suggestion for independent practice. For guided help with the strategy, use a *Student Applications Book*.

Quick Assess

Can students

☑ name two things to look for when they preview?

☑ identify key information in a question?

☑ use a graphic organizer to plan an essay?

1. Independent Practice

Ask students to apply the Main Idea Organizer to an essay test. Look for possible essay questions in the teacher's manuals of students' texts. Ask students to create a list of what each essay question is asking them to do.

2. Student Applications Books

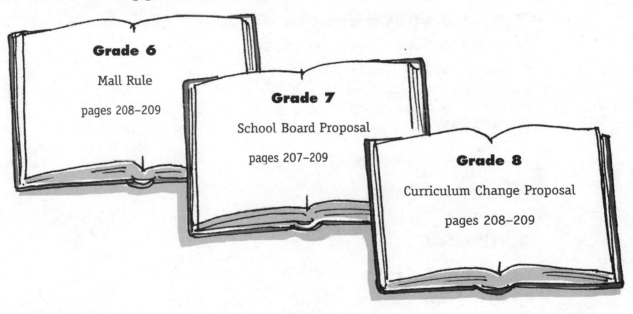

Grade 6

Mall Rule

pages 208–209

Grade 7

School Board Proposal

pages 207–209

Grade 8

Curriculum Change Proposal

pages 208–209

Focus on Vocabulary Tests

Goals

Here students focus on vocabulary tests, which are used to check their knowledge of words, word parts, and analogies (the relationships between word pairs). This lesson will help students learn to:

☑ improve their knowledge of words and vocabulary tests

☑ build their vocabularies

☑ understand word analogies and use context clues

Background

Students often feel uneasy when they confront vocabulary tests. Their command of words may be weak, and they may not know how to figure out the meanings of words that they don't recognize. Connect this lesson with students' existing knowledge by asking them to:

■ talk about the types of questions they usually find on vocabulary tests

■ share their feelings about and reactions to these tests

■ summarize how they study for a vocabulary test

Overview

	Content	Teacher's Guide page	Reader's Handbook page
Selection	Vocabulary Test Questions		586, 587

Ancillaries

	Grade	Content	Page
Lesson Plan Book	8	Focus on Vocabulary Tests	184
Student Applications Book	6	Synonyms	210–211
	7	Synonyms and Analogies	210–211
	8	Synonyms, Antonyms, and Analogies	210–211
Website		www.greatsource.com/rehand/	

Before Reading

Walk students through the main points in the Before Reading section on page 584. Note the two usual parts of vocabulary tests, the general strategies recommended for improving vocabulary, and the need to prepare properly for a vocabulary test. Explain that students should use the tips on page 585 in this lesson for preparing for vocabulary tests.

Tip #1: Use Flash Cards or a Vocabulary Notebook

Point out to students the value of using flash cards or a vocabulary notebook to help them remember words and their meanings. Walk them through the process of preparing and studying with flash cards or a notebook. Model the process on the board, or refer them to the models on pages 609 and 610.

Tip #2: Learn Prefixes, Suffixes, and Roots

Remind students of what prefixes, suffixes, and roots are, as explained in the chapter called Improving Vocabulary, pages 621-625. Show them the list in the Almanac on pages 685–692. Encourage them to read through this list, putting the most commonly used word parts on their flash cards. Go over the list of words beginning with *auto-*. To gauge students' understanding, ask them to think of other words that contain *auto-*.

WORDS WITH AUTO-

automatic	*autograph*	*autobiography*
automobile	*autocrat*	*automaton*
automate	*automotive*	*autonomous*

During Reading

Tell students that after previewing a vocabulary test, they can start working through the test. Carefully work through the During Reading section with students, making sure that they understand its tips and major points.

Tip #3: Use Context Clues

Tell students that drawing on their memory is useful when they are completely stumped by a word. Then examine the sample test question on page 586, asking students to use context clues to find a solution. After students work out the answers on their own, compare their reasoning with the reader's comments on the sticky note. For more work on context clues, refer to Improving Vocabulary, pages 615–620.

Tip #4: Understand Analogies

Make sure that students understand what analogies are. Since these types of questions are particularly hard for many students, walk through the main points made about them. Refer to information on analogies in the chapter on Improving Vocabulary (pages 636–639), if necessary.

Then examine the Common Kinds of Word Analogies listed on page 586. Make sure that students understand each analogy type and the example given. Add examples of your own, and test students' understanding by asking them to name examples as well.

Read with students the sample test question on page 587. Ask them to figure out how the first pair of words is related and then to choose another pair that shows the same relationship. Take your time on this question, explaining why each of the answer choices is correct or incorrect.

After Reading

After students finish a vocabulary test, urge them to reread the test directions and to double-check their answers.

Suggest that students write down the four tips in this lesson to use when they study for their next vocabulary test.

Ask students to write ten vocabulary words from their textbook glossaries on flash cards or in a vocabulary notebook, with their sources and definitions.

Summing Up

To wrap up the lesson, point out the Summing Up section. Go back over all that students have learned about how to improve knowledge of vocabulary and study for a vocabulary test. Then ask students to tell what they learned in their own words.

Assessment and Application

Assess students' abilities to read and understand vocabulary tests. Give students the opportunity to apply what they have learned through one of the two activities below. For students who are able to work on their own, use the suggestion for independent practice. For guided help with the strategy, use a *Student Applications Book*.

1. Independent Practice

Ask students to apply the reading tips they just learned to sample vocabulary tests. To find appropriate tests, ask students to write them. Give students lists of appropriate words and model questions. Then ask groups of students to write tests and exchange them with other groups.

2. Student Applications Books

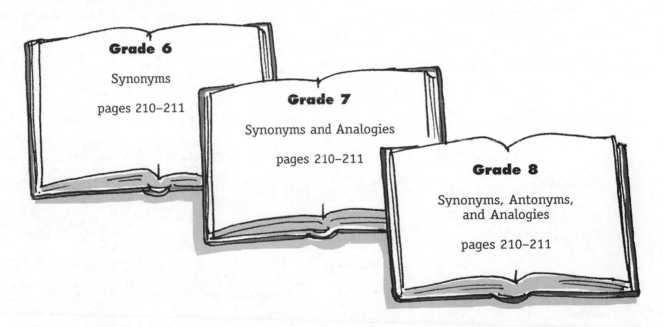

Grade 6

Synonyms

pages 210–211

Grade 7

Synonyms and Analogies

pages 210–211

Grade 8

Synonyms, Antonyms, and Analogies

pages 210–211

Focus on Social Studies Tests

Goals

Here students focus on social studies tests and learn more effective ways to take them. Typically these tests require knowledge of important names, places, dates, events, and ideas. This lesson will help students learn to:

- ☑ get ready for social studies tests
- ☑ preview common elements on social studies tests, including maps and other graphics
- ☑ use their time well and think through possible answers

Background

Many students see social studies as involving extensive memorization of names and dates. Social studies tests can be difficult because of the breadth of the material. Connect this lesson with students' existing knowledge by asking them to:

■ list the types of questions and resources that they usually find on social studies tests

■ explain what they find easy and difficult on social studies tests

■ explain how they usually study for social studies tests

Overview

	Content	Teacher's Guide page	Reader's Handbook page
Selection	Social Studies Test Questions	400, 401	590, 591

Ancillaries

	Grade	Content	Page
Lesson Plan Book	8	Focus on Social Studies Tests	185
Student Applications Book	6	Venezuelan Independence	212–213
	7	Industrial Revolution	212–213
	8	Spanish American War of 1898	212–213
Website		www.greatsource.com/rehand/	
Content Area Guide		This lesson appears in the *Content Area Guide: Social Studies*.	

Before Reading

Help students see that *preparation* is the key to doing well on any social studies test. By reading through the chapters in their textbook well before a test, they will be prepared to answer questions. Make a comparison of getting ready for a race to getting ready for a test. With both, preparation is critical.

Items to Study Prior to Taking Social Studies Tests

∎ **Names, dates, people, and places**
∎ **Key terms and concepts**
∎ **Class notes**
∎ **End-of-chapter questions**
∎ **Maps, timelines, graphs, primary sources, and political cartoons**

Make a distinction with students about the eight tips offered in this lesson. The first three are effective study aids to be done in preparing for the test, while the last five should be done during the test.

Tip #1: Create a Top Ten List

Read this tip carefully with students, explaining that it isn't necessary to study everything for a test. Point out the sample Top Ten List on page 589. Emphasize the importance of having a convenient study list prior to a test. It can be fun to create and will help students feel they are in better control of a broad subject.

Tip #2: Learn How to Read Graphics

Refer to the "Reading Graphics" section in the *Reader's Handbook* (pages 537–561) or to the students' history textbook. Provide sample social studies maps, charts, or other graphics, and have students practice reading titles, labels, and legends.

Tip #3: Use Graphic Organizers

Read this section carefully with students and reiterate the need for and usefulness of graphic organizers. Ask what kinds of organizers would be useful for a social studies test.

Tip #4: Preview the Test

As noted at the bottom of page 589, it is very important to *preview* a social studies test when it is first handed out on test day. Tell students that they should preview to gauge what kind of questions they will be asked to answer. Students need only to read three to five questions in all, but encourage them to read one question at the beginning, one or two in the middle, and one or two at the end.

During Reading

Explain to students that when taking a social studies test, they should answer the easiest questions first. Point out that the sample question is the kind that probably should be answered later, because it is more complex and requires careful thought.

Read this question with students. Use it as a basis for discussing the remaining tips students can use to answer difficult questions as they take the test.

> **SAMPLE QUESTION**
>
> 17. Lincoln's main goal throughout the Civil War was to:
>   A. abolish slavery throughout the nation
>   B. preserve the Union
>   C. break the South's dependence on cotton
>   D. end British control of the western territories

Tip #5: Rule Out Wrong Answers

Point out that students often can find the right answer after they eliminate the wrong ones. Remind them to read through all the possible answers before crossing any out.

Tip #6: Think Through the Answer

Read and discuss this section and one reader's notes on page 590. Emphasize that thinking through the choices that are ruled out will better students' chances of finding the right answer.

Tip #7: Read the Question for Clues

Discuss how clues in the questions themselves can often guide students to the right answer. Point out the words *main goal* in the sample question and show students another sample question that offers the same kind of "hidden" clues.

Tip #8: Read the Graphics

Emphasize the importance of reading visuals carefully by going over each part of the Sample Question and Timeline on page 591. Help students find the beginning and end dates on the timeline. Ask them to put their fingers on these dates.

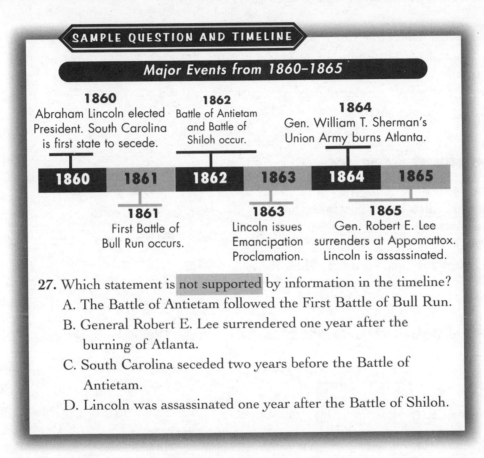

SAMPLE QUESTION AND TIMELINE

Major Events from 1860–1865

1860 Abraham Lincoln elected President. South Carolina is first state to secede.

1862 Battle of Antietam and Battle of Shiloh occur.

1864 Gen. William T. Sherman's Union Army burns Atlanta.

| 1860 | 1861 | 1862 | 1863 | 1864 | 1865 |

1861 First Battle of Bull Run occurs.

1863 Lincoln issues Emancipation Proclamation.

1865 Gen. Robert E. Lee surrenders at Appomattox. Lincoln is assassinated.

27. Which statement is not supported by information in the timeline?
   A. The Battle of Antietam followed the First Battle of Bull Run.
   B. General Robert E. Lee surrendered one year after the burning of Atlanta.
   C. South Carolina seceded two years before the Battle of Antietam.
   D. Lincoln was assassinated one year after the Battle of Shiloh.

Carefully go over the Think Aloud on page 592 in the handbook, which describes working through this timeline question. Reiterate the logic behind this step-by-step approach in which students narrow down the possibilities.

Remind students that questions involving visuals are often used to test their problem-solving abilities.

After Reading

Help students see the need to reread questions and check their answers before their test time is up. They may turn a wrong answer into a right one.

umming Up

As a final step, go over the Summing Up section. Review the importance of early preparation and following the suggested tips. Encourage students to tell what they learned in their own words.

Assessment and Application

Use the Quick Assess checklist to evaluate students' abilities to read and understand social studies tests. Give students the opportunity to apply what they have learned through one of the two activities below. For students who are able to work on their own, use the suggestion for independent practice. For guided help with the strategy, use a *Student Applications Book*.

1. Independent Practice

Ask students to apply the tips they just learned to sample social studies test questions that students themselves create. Put students in groups. Ask them to create a historical timeline and write two questions based on it. Then have the groups exchange and answer the questions.

Quick Assess

Can students

- ☑ name two things to look for when they preview?
- ☑ rule out wrong answers?
- ☑ draw conclusions from graphics?

2. Student Applications Books

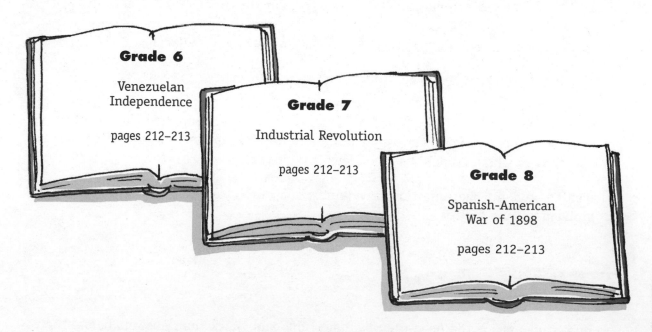

Grade 6

Venezuelan
Independence

pages 212–213

Grade 7

Industrial Revolution

pages 212–213

Grade 8

Spanish-American
War of 1898

pages 212–213

Focus on Math Tests

Goals

Here students focus on taking math tests, which involves learning terms, memorizing formulas, and practicing their problem-solving skills. This lesson will help students learn to:

☑ prepare for a math test

☑ use their time well during a math test

☑ understand word problems, equations, and graphics

Background

Whether or not a student is good at math, math tests are always challenging and require good concentration. The more complicated the mathematics, the greater the challenge. Help to relate this lesson to students' existing knowledge by asking them to:

■ discuss different kinds of math problems and their feelings about math and math tests

■ discuss their past math quiz and test experiences, both good and bad

■ explain how they currently prepare for math quizzes and tests

Overview

	Content	Teacher's Guide page	Reader's Handbook page
Selection	Math Test Questions	404, 405 406	594, 595, 596, 597

Ancillaries

	Grade	Content	Page
Lesson Plan Book	7	Focus on Math Tests	194
	8	Focus on Math Tests	194
Student Applications Book	6	Calculating Averages	214–215
	7	Calculating Costs	214–215
	8	Writing Numeric Equations	214–215
Website		www.greatsource.com/rehand/	
Content Area Guide		This lesson appears in the *Content Area Guide: Math*.	

Before Reading

Help students to understand that considerable preparation and problem-solving practice is necessary to do well on a math test. Orient students to the two general areas that can help them prior to a test—getting ready through sound study practices and previewing the test itself when it is handed out.

Getting Ready

Read this section closely with students, emphasizing each of the study practices highlighted. Distinguish between what students should study days before a test and the review and memorization recommended on *the day before* the test. Explain to students the reason for memorizing formulas right before a test: it's one way to ensure they'll remember them.

Previewing

Point out that a brief preview of the test can help students separate the "easy" from the "hard" questions. Stress the importance of managing their time during the test, which begins by answering all of the easy questions first.

During Reading

Stress the usefulness of making notes beside difficult problems on a math test. This practice can save time by allowing students to resume the problem-solving process where they left off.

Eliminating Wrong Answers

Remind students that they can use logic and common sense to eliminate wrong answers in math problems. Work through the sample question on page 594 for reinforcement. Ask them if they agree with the assumption that the answer would have a decimal.

SAMPLE QUESTION

57. $69.3 + (27.4 \times 3) =$
A. 151.5
B. 109.2
C. ~~139~~
D. ~~225~~

Because two of the numbers in this equation involve decimals, I can assume that the answer will involve a decimal as well. I can eliminate C+D right off the bat.

(Correct answer is A.)

During Reading

Estimating the Answer

Read and discuss with students the first sample question on page 595. Show students how they can eliminate wrong answers by estimating the right answer.

> **SAMPLE QUESTION**
>
> 10. 457 x 6 =
> A. 2732
> B. 1742 (too low)
> C. 2366 (too low)
> D. 2742
>
> 6 x 4 = 24, so 6 x 400 = 2400. That means that the answer of 457 x 6 will be higher than 2400. I can cross out any answers that seem too high or too low.
>
> (Correct answer is D.)

Visualizing the Answer

Students need to be aware that their ability to visualize a situation is a very useful test-taking tool, particularly with word problems. Walk students through the second sample question on page 595. Encourage students to visualize the problem.

> **SAMPLE QUESTION**
>
> 1. Near Chicago, planes take off from two major airfields. One of the fields is capable of sending up a plane every 3 minutes. The other field is capable of sending up 2 planes every 3 minutes. At these rates, what is the total number of planes the two airfields could send up in 90 minutes?
>
> A. 20   B. 90   C. 130   D. 82
>
> I need to figure out how many planes take off from each field and then add those totals.
>
> 1 plane every 3 minutes = 30 planes every 90 minutes.
>
> 2 planes every 3 minutes = 60 planes every 90 minutes.
>
> (Correct answer is B.)

Trying Easier Choices First

After students eliminate obvious wrong answers to a problem, they can pick an answer that looks correct. This is a good approach to problem-solving and can save students considerable time. Use the sample question on page 596 as a model.

After Reading

Go over this section carefully with students. Ask students whether they consider questions that include graphics to be the harder questions of a test. Which questions do they tend to leave until last? Talk about problems that require formulas and ask students how they handle them. Stress that they should study formulas the day before the test to answer these questions well.

Go over the sample question on page 597. Point out how prior knowledge of graphics and formulas can dramatically affect students' scores.

SAMPLE QUESTION

1. Triangle ABC is an **equilateral triangle.**

   What is the **perimeter?**
   A. 600
   B. 750
   C. 800
   D. 300

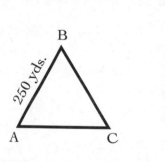

First, look at the graphic. I know that this is an equilateral triangle. That means the sides are equal. I need to find the perimeter.

Second, use the rule for finding the perimeter. To find the perimeter of any triangle, add the lengths of the sides (side + side + side = perimeter). I'm glad I memorized this formula.

Third, write an equation.
250 + 250 + 250 = perimeter

Last, solve the equation.
750 yds. = perimeter

Tell students that in the final minutes of a test, they should wrap up their work by trying to check at least one-third of their answers.

Summing Up

To conclude the lesson, point out the Summing Up section. Review all that students have learned about taking math tests, such as good preparation, separating easy from hard questions, and using effective test-taking techniques. Then have students tell what they learned from the lesson in their own words.

Assessment and Application

Use the Quick Assess checklist to evaluate students' abilities to read and understand math tests. Give students the opportunity to apply what they have learned through one of the two activities below. For students who are able to work on their own, use one of the suggestions for independent practice. For guided help with the strategy, use a *Student Applications Book*.

1. Independent Practice

Ask students to apply the reading strategies and techniques they just learned to a number of math problems taken from quizzes and tests. Allow students to practice taking math tests. You might give them one or two practice tests that accompany their math texts, or create practice problems for students to work through each day for five to ten minutes either at the beginning or end of class.

2. Student Applications Books

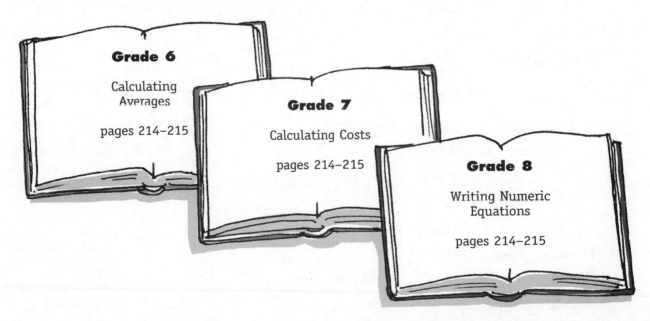

Grade 6

Calculating Averages

pages 214–215

Grade 7

Calculating Costs

pages 214–215

Grade 8

Writing Numeric Equations

pages 214–215

Focus on Science Tests

Goals

Here students focus on science tests, which require them to learn the thought processes and "language of science." This lesson will help students learn to:

☑ prepare for science tests

☑ preview and work through test questions

☑ read science charts, tables, diagrams, and graphs

Background

Some students regard science as a fascinating world; others see it as an extremely complicated area of study. However, all students need to be able to perform well on science quizzes and tests. Connect this lesson with their existing knowledge by asking them to:

▇ list the types of questions they find on science tests

▇ explain the process they now use to study for and take science tests

▇ discuss their feelings about preparing for and taking science tests

Overview

	Content	Teacher's Guide page	Reader's Handbook page
Selection	Science Test Questions	410, 411	601, 602, 603, 604

Ancillaries

	Grade	Content	Page
Lesson Plan Book	7	Focus on Science Tests	195
	8	Focus on Science Tests	195
Student Applications Book	6	Animal Facts	216–217
	7	Planet Earth	216–217
	8	Hurricanes	216–217
Website		www.greatsource.com/rehand/	
Content Area Guide		This lesson appears in the *Content Area Guide: Science*.	

Before Reading

Help students see that the best way to study for a science test is to study their textbook and scientific terms *on an ongoing basis*, as opposed to cramming a day or two before the test. Explain to students that learning to take careful, well-organized notes is a key to good study preparation. Then read with students the following tips on taking science tests. Be sure students understand that nothing will make up for consistent study and preparation throughout the year, but these tips are nonetheless good advice.

Tip #1: Make Visuals

Explain to students the value of drawing visuals to illustrate steps in science processes. Remind them that using graphics makes it easier to remember science concepts. Look through students' science textbook for processes that they can draw. Model how to do this with one process. Then encourage students to make visual notes of the various science processes they encounter in their study. Ask volunteers to put their sketches on the board.

Tip #2: Skim for Science Terms

Emphasize the importance of terms in science. Make sure students understand the purpose and technique of skimming. Help students to see that reviewing key terms by reading and repeating them out loud, along with their definitions, will give students a better command of the material and improve their chances of scoring well on science tests.

Tip #3: Learn How to Read Graphics

Ask students to identify basic types of graphics used in science. Examples are pie charts, tables, diagrams, line graphs, and bar graphs. Because these graphics are frequently found on tests, it's important that students master reading them before a test. Further information about reading graphics is found later in this lesson.

Tip #4: Preview the Questions

Walk students through previewing a science test. Go over each of the points mentioned. If possible, model the process using a sample science test. Explain that students ought to skim a few questions at the beginning, middle, and end of the test. Make sure students know they do *not* have to read all the questions, only gain a general sense of what kinds of questions are on the test.

During Reading

While taking a science test, students need to use their time wisely. Discuss with students the value of following the tips suggested on page 599. (Note with students that some of the same tips appeared in the lesson on taking social studies tests.)

To emphasize the important role graphics play in science tests, first show students the sample chart, table, diagram, and graphs. Make sure they can identify each one and have a general understanding of the differences before going on.

How to Read a Chart or Table

Read with students the steps involved in reading charts and tables, as listed on page 600. Ask students to identify the headings, columns, and rows of the chart and table on page 601. Go over the sample questions to test their ability to find the correct answers.

SAMPLE QUESTIONS AND CHART

Planet	Made of	Atmosphere	Weight (of object that is 100 pounds on earth)	Gravity (compared to earth)
Jupiter	liquid and gas	helium, hydrogen	234 pounds	greater
Uranus	rock	helium, hydrogen, methane	91 pounds	less
Neptune	frozen gas	helium, methane, hydrogen	118 pounds	greater

1. Which planet has no methane in its atmosphere?
2. If you weighed 200 pounds on earth, how much would you weigh on Neptune?

To answer, find the "Atmosphere" heading of the chart and then sort through the facts. (The answer is Jupiter.)

To answer, find the section for Neptune under the "Weight" column. Double the Neptune weight. (The answer is 236 pounds.)

How to Read a Diagram

Make sure students understand what a diagram is and what it shows. Point out the importance of reading labels and captions. Walk students through the sample questions about the rock cycle diagram on page 602. Ask the sample questions and others you make up to further students' comprehension.

During Reading

How to Read a Graph

Go over the steps in reading a graph. Show students the line and bar graphs on pages 603 and 604 and explain the differences between the two. Model the graph-reading steps by applying them to both the line graph and the bar graph. Read over the sample questions and ask partners or small groups to test each other's comprehension.

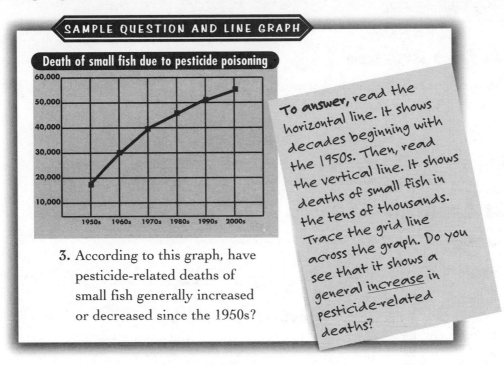

SAMPLE QUESTION AND LINE GRAPH

Death of small fish due to pesticide poisoning

3. According to this graph, have pesticide-related deaths of small fish generally increased or decreased since the 1950s?

To answer, read the horizontal line. It shows decades beginning with the 1950s. Then, read the vertical line. It shows deaths of small fish in the tens of thousands. Trace the grid line across the graph. Do you see that it shows a general <u>increase</u> in pesticide-related deaths?

Walk through the steps of reading a graph, diagram, chart, and table. Be sure students remember the general point that they need to read all of the text with visuals to understand a graphic.

After Reading

Discuss situations in which guessing an answer is appropriate. Reinforce the need to reread questions and recheck answers if time is left at the end of the test.

Summing Up

To complete the lesson, have students read over the Summing Up points. Review all that students have learned about taking science tests in terms of preparation, previewing, and rechecking their answers. Then encourage students to tell what they learned from the lesson in their own words.

Assessment and Application

Use the Quick Assess checklist to evaluate students' abilities to read and understand science tests. Give students the opportunity to apply what they have learned through one of the two activities below. For students who are able to work independently, use the suggestion below. For guided help with the strategy, use a *Student Applications Book*.

1. Independent Practice

Ask students to apply the tips they just learned to sample science tests that they create in small groups. Give each small group two to three visuals and ask them to write at least three questions from them. Then ask groups to exchange test questions and try to answer them.

2. Student Applications Books

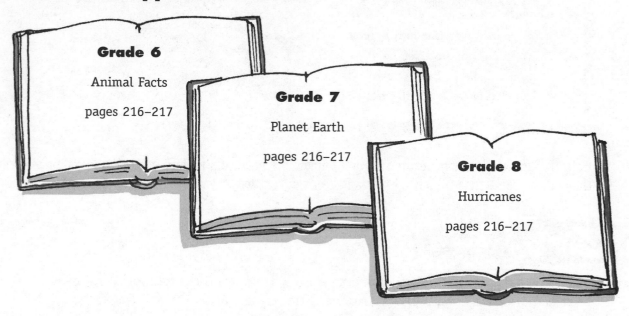

Grade 6

Animal Facts

pages 216–217

Grade 7

Planet Earth

pages 216–217

Grade 8

Hurricanes

pages 216–217

Improving
Vocabulary

- **Learning New Words**
- **Building Vocabulary Skills**
- **Understanding Specialized Terms and Vocabulary Tests**

new words

new words

Thesaurus

new words

new words

Improving Vocabulary

Here students will learn new words, build vocabulary skills, and understand specialized terms and vocabulary tests.

Learning New Words

Discuss with students the importance of words, explaining the value of becoming "word collectors." You might compare the many benefits of "collecting" words to collecting CDs or DVDs, which helps contribute so much to students' enjoyment of life.

Building Vocabulary Strength

Build on the "word collector" concept by comparing vocabulary building to pumping iron or training for competitive swimming. Ask students to list ways in which they benefit from practice in sports and in vocabulary building.

Being a Word Collector

Tell students to open their journals or notebooks and set aside sections for word collecting, as shown on page 609. Model the word collecting process shown in the vocabulary journal graphic.

VOCABULARY JOURNAL

Sept. 12

History

reincarnation, p. 23
dynasty, p. 26
abundant, p. 26
covenant, p. 30

Sept. 21

English

To Kill a Mockingbird by Harper Lee

apothecary, p. 2
piety, p. 3
imprudent, p. 4

Science

1. Ready, Set, Record!

Here students learn a process for collecting words and building vocabulary.

A. RECORD UNFAMILIAR WORDS

Emphasize the importance as well as ease of jotting down words. Explain that noting the source of a word will help students remember the word's context. Discuss the vocabulary journal example on page 609.

B. LOOK THEM UP

Ask students how many of them regularly look up words in their textbook glossaries or a dictionary. If few are familiar with these resources, take time to show them how to use these valuable tools. Then read the dictionary entry on page 610 and highlight the usefulness of sample sentences. Students should see the dictionary as one of the most important, handy reference books available to them. The more they use the dictionary, the more they will build vocabulary.

C. WRITE THE DEFINITIONS

Show students that they are building vocabulary simply by jotting down a word's definition. Explain the value of using index cards as shown on page 610. The benefit of index cards is that students can study them anywhere and anytime. The drawback to them is that students might lose them or drop them.

D. SAY THE WORDS

Discuss the importance of saying and repeating new words. Explain to students that this will help them move words into their active vocabularies and recognize the words when others use them. Show students how to "break up" a word into syllables and explain some of the special markings.

With students, examine the tips for learning definitions and the vocabulary journal graphic on page 611. To be sure that students understand this, ask them to try the process for themselves and discuss the results.

2. Move Words into Long-Term Memory

Explain that to remember new words, students have to get into the habit of using them. Read each item in the memorizing words graphic with students so they understand the process of committing new words to their long-term memory. Explain that these vocabulary-building sessions are like doing sit-ups or going for a quick morning jog.

3. Start Owning Words

Explain that after students collect words and memorize them, they are ready to begin using them frequently. Go over each of the tips on page 613.

> ◄ TIPS FOR USING NEW WORDS ·
>
> **1.** *Try to use the new word when you answer in class and when you speak to friends and family.*
>
> **2.** *Include the new word when you write answers to questions at school and when you plan and write paragraphs, letters, and essays.*
>
> **3.** *Think about the word's meaning when you meet it again in your reading. Ask yourself, "Did I learn something new about this word's meaning?"*

Boosting Your Vocabulary

Help students see that learning new words can be easy and done in many ways.

1. Read for Fun

Discuss how jotting down and looking up unfamiliar words in magazines they like will help students build vocabulary while they're having fun.

2. Listen and Ask

Read this part with students. Stress that making a habit of asking family and friends what an unfamiliar word they use means will really boost students' vocabularies. People also will be flattered that students are listening carefully to what they're saying.

3. Play Word Games

Encourage a discussion of these vocabulary-building suggestions. Let students know they can come up with their own word games in addition to the ones described.

4. Go on a Scavenger Hunt

Read over the directions for the game with students, emphasizing the fun of searching for a set of words and actively hearing and learning a lot of new words along the way. Ask students to come up with their own versions of this or another vocabulary game.

Building Vocabulary Skills

Introduce this section to students by reviewing that the context of a word is the other words and sentences near it. Stress that they can learn meanings of words by actively using a dictionary and thesaurus and by figuring out meaning through context clues.

Becoming a Context Clue Expert

Discuss the concept of context clues. Explain that students often will be able to derive the meaning of a word from clues in the surrounding words and sentences.

Spotting Context Clues

Discuss what is involved in spotting context clues in a reading. Take time to read over the two examples from *Lyddie* on pages 615–616. Make sure that students are able to identify the hidden clues in each example. Ask them to explain their thought processes. Then talk about kinds of clues.

Kinds of Context Clues

Read this section carefully with students, going over the eight types of context clues listed. Write examples on the board as you discuss them. Suggest to students that they take notes on the eight kinds of context clues along with examples for later reference.

1. DEFINITIONS OR SYNONYMS

Point out that writers sometimes offer definitions of or synonyms for difficult words. Remind students that a synonym is a word with the same or nearly the same meaning as another word. Tell students to make a note of clue words that signal definitions or synonyms, as listed on page 616.

> **from *Experiencing World History***
>
> Most castles had high walls and were surrounded by
> a water-filled ditch called a moat.

2. CONCRETE EXAMPLES

Discuss ways in which examples often help to illustrate the meaning of a difficult word. Provide other sentences with examples using the signal words presented on page 617.

3. CONTRAST CLUES

Make sure students understand what *contrast* means. Discuss the example on page 617. Ask students questions to gauge their understanding of the way the meanings of *nippers* and *spraggers* can be figured out from the passage.

> **from *Growing Up in Coal Country* by Susan Campbell Bartoletti**
>
> Nippers, spraggers, and mule drivers envied the miners and laborers, whose strength was measured in coal.

4. DESCRIPTION CLUES

Explain how authors sometimes provide a description or example of a difficult word to elaborate or promote understanding. Discuss the excerpts on page 618, noting that descriptions can appear well after the word.

5. WORDS OR PHRASES THAT MODIFY

Read closely with students, making sure they understand what modifiers—such as adjectives, adverbs, phrases, and clauses—mean and do. Use the example on page 618 to explain how the meaning of *rumor* is derived from the context.

6. CONJUNCTIONS SHOWING RELATIONSHIPS AND CONNECTING IDEAS

Context clues sometimes show up in phrases and clauses linked by conjunctions. Review the lists of coordinating and subordinating conjunctions on page 619. Point out that the way conjunctions are used can at times be keys to sentence structure, as well as to figuring out the meaning of a challenging word.

7. REPEATING WORDS

Use the example on page 619 to help students to see that a word's meaning sometimes becomes clearer when the author repeats the word.

8. UNSTATED OR IMPLIED MEANINGS

Explain to students that the situation often can suggest a word's meaning, as in the example on page 620. Students' knowledge and previous experience are the key tools for finding implied meanings.

After discussing these eight types of context clues, review the list with students. Ask them to look through their textbooks or other readings for examples of each type of context clue.

Beyond Context Clues

Where context clues don't exist, students should simply jot down the word and look it up in a dictionary, as noted earlier.

Understanding Roots, Prefixes, and Suffixes

Explain to students that they now will learn about three types of word parts—roots, prefixes, and suffixes. Students should understand that a root word is the basic part of the word that carries the meaning, a prefix is added to the beginning of a word to change meaning, and a suffix is added to the end of a word to change the way it is used.

Word Roots

Explain that many English words are built from Greek and Latin root words. Once students know the meaning of a common root word, they can decode similar words. Walk through the examples of word roots on pages 621–622, asking students to explain what each of these words means. Ask students to turn to the word parts in the Almanac for further examples. Challenge students to brainstorm lists of other words based on the roots you discuss.

WORDS WITH *LUC* AND *LUM*

luminous	*lucent*	*illumine*	*illuminate*	*illuminator*
lucid	*lucidity*	*translucent*	*translucence*	*illuminative*
luminescent	*luminosity*	*lumen*	*luminary*	*luminaria*
luminousness	*lucidly*	*illumination*		

Prefixes

Read this section carefully with students. Make sure that they understand what prefixes are and how they can change a word's meaning, as shown with *antisocial*. (Point out that the prefix of *prefix* itself is *pre-*, which means "before, in front of.") Direct students again to the Almanac pages 685–687 and go over other examples. Encourage students to come up with new examples of words that use common prefixes.

Suffixes

A suffix comes at the end of a word and can change a word's part of speech as well as its meaning. Go over the examples shown on page 622 with students and refer to the Almanac pages 687–688 to discuss other examples of suffixes. Ask students to suggest examples of their own.

SUFFIXES AND PARTS OF SPEECH

Word	Part of Speech	Meaning
clamant	*adjective*	*noisy*
clamorer	*noun*	*one who makes noise*
clamor	*verb*	*to make loud sounds*
claimant	*noun*	*a person who makes a claim*
exclaimed	*verb*	*shouted suddenly*
exclamation	*noun*	*noisy talk; outcry*
exclamatively	*adverb*	*in a noisy manner*
exclamatory	*adjective*	*expressing emotion*

Putting Word Parts Together

Walk students through the four tips about roots, prefixes, and suffixes shown on the chart on page 623. Read and elaborate on each tip, and have students come up with their own examples when appropriate. Encourage them to use their Almanacs during this exercise.

Learning Word Parts

Now that students know the basics about word parts, explain that they will learn different ways to use them in order to remember them and boost their vocabularies.

Tip #1: Collect Roots and Related Words

Discuss each point of this helpful plan for collecting and learning word parts. Explain to students that they can conveniently collect roots in their vocabulary notebooks alongside the vocabulary words they collect. Read over and discuss the root *cert* example on page 624, citing it as a model they can use when collecting roots.

◄ ROOT LIST ▶─────────────────────────────

Word Root <u>cert</u>

from Latin meaning "sure"	Prefixes	Suffixes
certain		<u>-ain</u>, adjective
certify		<u>-ify</u>, verb
recertify	<u>re-</u>, again	
certification		<u>-cation</u>, noun
certainly		<u>-ly</u>, adverb
uncertain	<u>un-</u>, no, not	
certifier		<u>-er</u>, noun
certifiable		<u>-able</u>, adjective

Tip #2: Play Word Games

Help students to see that they can learn word roots through a variety of games such as Concentration, as explained on page 625. Divide students into small groups to play the game. Ask students to share their ideas about other games that could help them learn and remember word parts.

Tip #3: Use the Words

Discuss with students how easy and useful it is to learn a new word part each week. Read carefully over the one-word-part-a-week plan on page 625. Explain that in a year they would learn 52 word parts. With six related words for each part, they could boost their vocabularies by at least 312 words.

Dictionary Dipping

Spend time making sure that students are familiar with the dictionary. Stress that all readers need to develop the habit of consulting their dictionaries. Explain that trying to read without a dictionary is like playing baseball without a glove or tennis without a racket.

The Right Tool for the Job

Read over and discuss with students the differences among different kinds of dictionaries. You might even have a number of kinds available to discuss. Encourage students to have a larger "junior" dictionary at home for homework and a smaller, portable one to use in classes at school, if at all possible.

What's in Dictionaries?

Students need to know the differences among dictionaries, as noted on page 627. Discuss the basic questions that can be answered by all dictionaries and refer to the examples of *immune*.

If possible, use a large and a small dictionary to highlight other unique features and differences. Point out that the paperback dictionary shows the spelling, pronunciation, and part of speech. It also gives very brief definitions.

The student dictionary shows the spelling, pronunciation, and part of speech. In addition, it gives more definitions and more complete definitions. It provides sentence examples. The word history has more information than the histories in the paperback and collegiate dictionaries.

The collegiate dictionary, like the other two, gives the spelling, pronunciation, and part of speech. The definitions are more difficult to read and the examples are not complete sentences.

Learning to Use a Dictionary

In order to use a dictionary effectively, students need to be aware of its key parts. As you read these key parts, refer to the dictionary page graphic on page 628.

from American Heritage Student Dictionary

(1) **olive /omission**

(2) **ol•ive** (ol´ iv) *n.* **1.a.** The small, oval, greenish or blackish fruit of the Mediterranean region, having a single hard seed. Olives are eaten as a relish or pressed to extract olive oil. **b.** The tree bearing such fruit. **2.** A dull yellowish green. **(3)** [First written down before 1200 in Middle English, from Greek *elaia.*]

olive branch *n.* **1.** A branch of an olive tree, regarded as a symbol of peace. **2.** An offer of peace.

olive oil *n.* Oil pressed from olives, used in salad dressings, for cooking, as an ingredient of soaps, and as an emollient.

O•lym•pi•a (ŏ lĭm´ pē ə *or* ə lĭm´ pē ə) *n.* A plain of southern Greece in the northwest Peloponnesus. It was the site of the ancient Olympic games. The statue of the Olympian Zeus was one of the Seven Wonders of the World.

om•e•let (om´ ə lit *or* om´ lit) *n.* A dish of beaten eggs, cooked and often folded around a filling, as of cheese. **(4)** [First written down in 1611 in Modern English, from Old French *amlette.*]

(5) **o•men** (o´m ən) *n.* A thing or an event regarded as a sign of future good or bad luck. [First written down in 1582 in Modern English, from Latin *ōmen.*]

om•i•nous (om´ ə nə s) *adj.* **(6)** Being a sign of trouble, danger, or disaster. **(7)** —**om´i•nous•ly** *adv.* — **om´i•nous•ness** *n.*

o•mis•sion (o mish´ ən) *n.* **1.** The act of omitting something or the state of having been omitted: *the omission of several* **(8)** *letters from a word.* **2.** Something that has been omitted: *several omissions from the guest list.*

1. Guide Words

Point out the guide words on a dictionary page. Ask students to find the two guide words among the entries on the page. Stress that the purpose of guide words is to help people find words quickly and easily by showing the first and last words on the page. Ask students to suggest words and use the guide words to locate them.

2. Entry Word
Take time to point out the features of an entry word, as explained on page 629 in the *Reader's Handbook*.

3. Definitions
Since a word can have many definitions, stress the importance of reading all the definitions to find the one that is most appropriate for the context of the word students are looking up. Offer examples to make sure that students understand this important point.

4. Word History
Point out how a word origin is shown in a dictionary entry. Explain that using word histories will help students with their ongoing study of Latin and Greek word roots, as well as broaden their awareness of modern English language and all the places from which it comes.

5. Pronunciation
With students, examine the way that entry words are respelled in parentheses to show how they are pronounced. Write the dictionary pronunciations for a number of simple, everyday words on the board to highlight how to read the symbols for sounds and the accented syllables. Try writing the pronunciation of a word students know on the board and asking them to identify the word by pronouncing it.

6. Part of Speech
Use the example dictionary page to point out how parts of speech are identified in a dictionary. Note for students that some words can be used as more than one part of speech.

7. Inflected Forms
Use the example dictionary page to show how inflected forms are shown in a dictionary. Help students see how useful this feature can be to the correct spelling of the various forms of words.

8. Illustrative Example
Encourage students to read any short examples that come along with a word, since examples will help them understand the word's usage and meaning. Reinforce this idea with the word *omission* and other examples.

Reading a Thesaurus

To introduce this important kind of reference book, pull out a thesaurus and ask students if they know what it is. With students, read page 630 in the *Reader's Handbook* carefully. Refer to the example entry for *pretty,* stressing the key features and usefulness of learning the synonyms and antonyms of the word. As an additional exercise, give students practice in using a thesaurus by letting them suggest words to look up and discussing what they find.

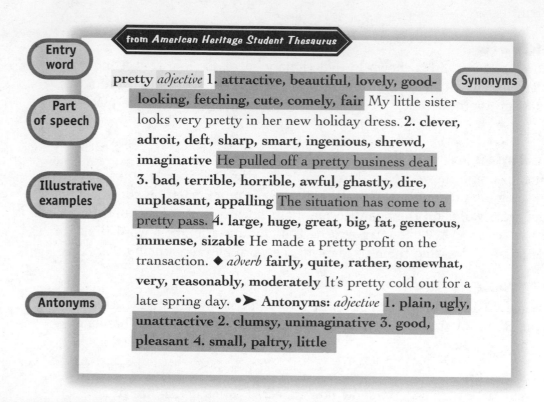

from *American Heritage Student Thesaurus*

Entry word

Part of speech

Illustrative examples

Synonyms

Antonyms

pretty *adjective* **1.** attractive, beautiful, lovely, good-looking, fetching, cute, comely, fair My little sister looks very pretty in her new holiday dress. **2.** clever, adroit, deft, sharp, smart, ingenious, shrewd, imaginative He pulled off a pretty business deal. **3.** bad, terrible, horrible, awful, ghastly, dire, unpleasant, appalling The situation has come to a pretty pass. **4.** large, huge, great, big, fat, generous, immense, sizable He made a pretty profit on the transaction. ◆ *adverb* fairly, quite, rather, somewhat, very, reasonably, moderately It's pretty cold out for a late spring day. •➤ Antonyms: *adjective* **1.** plain, ugly, unattractive **2.** clumsy, unimaginative **3.** good, pleasant **4.** small, paltry, little

Understanding Specialized Terms and Vocabulary Tests

Help students see the benefit of having a strong vocabulary, not only in school or on tests, but in most aspects of their everyday lives.

School Terms

Emphasize to students that nearly every area of life has a specialized language, from sports talk to refrigerator repair to the study of algebra. Ask students to name some of their classes, such as science or English or computer lab, and suggest examples of specialized terms they've encountered in these classes.

1. Record Key Terms

Read and discuss this section with students. Highlight the fact that it is critical to learn the specialized words in math and science in order to do well in these classes. Encourage them to apply the word-collecting strategies they have learned to record important terms in their vocabulary notebooks. Refer to the examples on page 631.

2. Get Savvy about Textbooks

Explain that people who write textbooks usually try to highlight and define special terms. Use a textbook as an example. Show students the bold or italicized terms at the beginning or within chapters, as well as the glossary in back. Read and discuss the tips on page 632 to explain how to use these tools effectively.

TIPS FOR LEARNING SCHOOL TERMS

1. *Read the list of new words in a chapter.*

2. *Find each word in the chapter as you read and see how it is used.*

3. *Then, at the end of the chapter, reread the list. How many words do you know?*

4. *Write any words you don't know in your vocabulary notebook or create index cards for the words you don't recall.*

5. *Use the glossary of your textbook to find definitions for the words.*

3. Use Webs and Concept Maps

Emphasize that whenever terms are complicated, students can make better sense of the material by pulling it together in their notes using Webs or Concept Maps. Explain that Concept Maps can help them keep track of related terms or ideas, as shown in the example for *digestion* on page 633. Take a moment to explain how Concept Maps are structured and what the benefits are of organizing complicated study terms in this way.

CONCEPT MAP

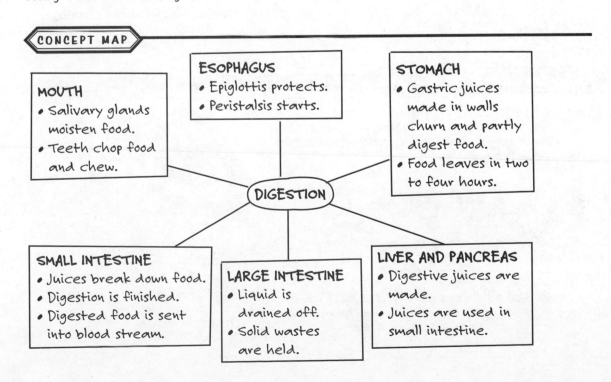

MOUTH
• Salivary glands moisten food.
• Teeth chop food and chew.

ESOPHAGUS
• Epiglottis protects.
• Peristalsis starts.

STOMACH
• Gastric juices made in walls churn and partly digest food.
• Food leaves in two to four hours.

DIGESTION

SMALL INTESTINE
• Juices break down food.
• Digestion is finished.
• Digested food is sent into blood stream.

LARGE INTESTINE
• Liquid is drained off.
• Solid wastes are held.

LIVER AND PANCREAS
• Digestive juices are made.
• Juices are used in small intestine.

4. Learn Specialized Terms

Ask students when they study specialized terms. Most will answer, "Just before a test." Point out the value of learning specialized terms as a daily routine, and remind students that learning new words takes time, practice, and commitment.

Vocabulary Questions

Bring to students' attention the need to study the different kinds of vocabulary questions they will run into on tests, as noted on page 634. Explain that some inside knowledge of how these tests work can help them to succeed.

Synonyms and Antonyms

Before reading, ask students if they can recall what these terms mean. Ask them to offer several examples of each. After reading, have students point out ways in which learning the synonyms and antonyms of words can boost their vocabularies and help them perform better on standardized tests.

Standardized Vocabulary Tests

Students need to be aware that they will face vocabulary questions on standardized tests in the future, and that these tests are not easy. To perform well, they have to not only know what the challenging words mean but also be familiar with the style of questions. Go over the examples on page 635, discussing the answer-elimination logic of "How to Choose the Best Answer." Test students' comprehension by writing other examples on the board.

Preparing for Vocabulary Tests

Help students see that the habits of reading and collecting difficult words in their vocabulary notebooks or journals are the most practical and effective ways to prepare for tests and build their vocabularies over the long term. Read and discuss the tips on page 636, emphasizing how following each one increases their chances of doing well on tests.

VOCABULARY TEST-TAKING TIPS

1. Read the directions carefully. Know whether you are looking for synonyms or antonyms.

2. Read the word and ask yourself if you've seen it in your reading or heard others use it. Perhaps you know the meaning of the word parts.

3. Cross out the answer choices you know won't work. You can usually immediately cross out one or two choices.

4. Use your knowledge of the word's part of speech and choose the answer that is the same part of speech.

Analogies

Since analogy questions are used often on vocabulary tests, students need to know what they are and how to answer them. Explain how analogy questions test their knowledge of the similarity or relationship between words or things.

How to Read Analogy Questions

Explain how to read analogy questions and ask students to practice reading them aloud. Then ask students to answer the sample questions on page 636.

SAMPLE ANALOGY QUESTIONS

1. *pencil : pen :: shirt :* _____
   a. striped   b. pants   c. cotton   d. buttons
2. *panic : terror :: reveal :* _____
   a. mask   b. artistic   c. disclose   d. cover

Types of Analogies

Students need to be aware that there are many different types of analogy relationships on tests. Stress the importance of being able to identify exactly what is being compared in each question. Take time to go over the examples with students.

1. ANALOGIES IN WHICH WORD ORDER IS NOT IMPORTANT

Work through each of the sample questions. Help students to identify the comparison in the sample pair. Then ask them to offer answers and to explain the logic or strategies they used to figure out each item.

2. ANALOGIES IN WHICH WORD ORDER IS IMPORTANT

Explain the difference between this type of analogy question and the previous type. Emphasize that in certain analogy questions, word order is critical. Stress that students need to be able to identify these types of analogy questions to answer them correctly. Take time to discuss each of the analogy categories and ask students to discuss the logic they used for each.

Summing Up

To conclude the lesson, discuss and reinforce the points made in the Summing Up section. Review all that students have learned about building their vocabularies and preparing for tests, such as keeping vocabulary notebooks, using dictionaries and thesauruses on a regular basis, focusing on specialized school terms, and so on. Then have students tell what they learned from the lesson in their own words.

Assessment and Application

Use the Quick Assess checklist to evaluate students' understanding of ways to improve their vocabulary. Give students the opportunity to apply what they have learned through one of the two activities below. For students who are able to work independently, use one of the suggestions listed. For guided help with the strategy, use a *Student Applications Book*.

1. Independent Practice

To show that they understand the chapter, students can do one of the following:

■ Read a magazine article or novel to find examples of words that can be figured out using context clues. They can list the words with the clues on Study Cards or in a notebook.

■ Skim a newspaper for unfamiliar words and look the words up in a dictionary. Students can record words and definitions in a notebook or vocabulary journal.

■ With a partner, create examples of analogies in which word order is not important. Students can identify the relationship for each analogy.

■ With a partner, create examples of analogies in which word order is important. Students can identify the relationship for each analogy.

Quick Assess

Can students

■ explain three ways to learn and remember new words?

■ recognize and use several kinds of context clues?

■ give an example of a prefix, suffix, and a word root?

■ identify four key parts of a dictionary?

■ talk through synonym, antonym, and analogy questions?

2. Student Applications Books

Grade 6
"Learning New Words"
pages 218–219
"Building Vocabulary"
pages 220–221
"Dictionary Dipping"
page 222
"Reading a Thesaurus"
page 223

Grade 7
"Learning New Words"
pages 218–219
"Building Vocabulary"
pages 220–221
"Dictionary Dipping"
page 222
"Reading a Thesaurus"
page 223

Grade 8
"Learning New Words"
pages 218–219
"Building Vocabulary"
pages 220–221
"Dictionary Dipping"
page 222
"Reading a Thesaurus"
page 223

Strategy Handbook

Explain to students that the Strategy Handbook provides them with a collection of key reading strategies they can use to read more effectively and gather information from a variety of types of reading.

Introduce each of these strategies to students to make sure that they understand what the strategy means, its purpose, how it is used, and when to use it.

For each strategy, this *Teacher's Guide* includes a goal, teaching and discussion tips on how to introduce the strategy and model its use, and ideas for checking understanding by having students apply the strategy.

Key Strategies	Teacher's Guide page	Reader's Handbook page
Close Reading	430	642–643
Looking for Cause and Effect	431	644–645
Note-taking	432	646–647
Outlining	433	648–649
Paraphrasing	434	650–651
Questioning the Author	435	652–653
Reading Critically	436	654–655
Skimming	437	656–657
Summarizing	438	658–659
Synthesizing	439	660–661
Using Graphic Organizers	440	662–663
Visualizing and Thinking Aloud	441	664–665

Close Reading

Set Goal

Introduce and model the strategy of **close reading** and give students practice in using it.

Teach and Discuss

Read and discuss with students the **Description** on page 642. Discuss the **Definition** of close reading on page 643 and the types of readings for which it is used. Ask students to tell in their own words what the strategy means to them. Explore their answers and make sure they see the benefits of using the strategy.

Choose a selection that contains some difficult passages for which close reading would be useful, such as a poem, a short speech, an essay, or a biography. Distribute this reading to the class.

Using this reading, walk the class step by step through the **Using the Strategy** process described on pages 642–643. Draw a Double-entry Journal on the board. Fill it out during class discussion.

Check Understanding

Divide students into three or four groups.

■ Ask higher-level students to apply the strategy with independent reading.

■ Assign the average students practice in a *Student Applications Book*:

Grade 6, pages 154–164

Grade 7, pages 154–163

Grade 8, pages 154–161

■ Help the lower-level readers through guided practice and paired practice.

Looking for Cause and Effect

Set Goal

Introduce the strategy of **looking for cause and effect**, and give students a model for using it. Give students practice in using this strategy.

Teach and Discuss

Read over the **Description** on page 644 with students. Make certain that students understand the definitions of *cause* and *effect*. To test their understanding, ask students to give examples of cause and effect in everyday life. Have students explain in their own words what the strategy means to them. Build upon their answers, as necessary, making sure that they see the benefits of using the strategy.

Select a reading for which a Cause-Effect Organizer would be useful, such as a passage in a textbook, a biography, or other nonfiction. Distribute this reading sample to the class.

Using this reading, discuss with students the steps in the **Using the Strategy** process described on pages 644–645. After explaining the sample graphics, draw one type of Cause-Effect Organizer on the board. Point out how it can help readers understand the relationships of ideas and events. Discuss the sample reading, and have students help fill out the organizer, using a format that's appropriate to the reading.

Check Understanding

Divide students into three or four groups.

■ Ask higher-level students to use the strategy on a biography or another nonfiction selection of their choice. Let students choose the reading as a group, analyze it independently, and discuss their results.

■ Assign the average students practice in a *Student Applications Book*:

Grade 6, pages 72–79

Grade 7, pages 71–79

Grade 8, pages 68–77

■ Help the lower-level readers use the strategy under guidance and in paired practice.

Note-taking

Set Goal

Introduce students to the strategy of **note-taking**, provide a model, and give students practice in using it.

Teach and Discuss

Students may be familiar with the practice of jotting notes in their notebooks to help them remember important material. They also need to be aware that there are numerous more effective organizational approaches to note-taking.

Read and discuss with students the **Description** on page 646. Reinforce this by reading and discussing the **Definition** of note-taking on page 647. Talk about the many types of readings for which it is useful.

Distribute a sample reading for which the note-taking strategy would be effective, such as a section from the students' history or science textbook.

Discuss the four different note-taking techniques and organizers under **Using the Strategy** on pages 646–647. Encourage students to explain why they would choose a certain approach and to highlight its particular benefits. Also point out the tools in the Almanac for Classification Notes and Process Notes. Have students decide on a useful organizer for the sample reading, draw the selected organizer on the board, and have students direct you in filling it out.

Check Understanding

Divide students into three or four groups.

■ Have higher-level students select a textbook chapter they haven't read yet, discuss and select a note-taking method for this chapter, and take notes on it.

■ Assign the average students practice in a *Student Applications Book*:

Grade 6, pages 39–48

Grade 7, pages 37–47

Grade 8, pages 37–45

■ Help the lower-level readers to create Key Word Notes for a selection from their science books.

Outlining

Set Goal

Introduce and model the strategy of **outlining**, making sure students understand that it is a very effective way of keeping track of key topics and details in a selection. Give students practice in applying this strategy.

Teach and Discuss

Read and discuss with students the **Description** of outlining on page 648 and the **Definition** on page 649. Then describe the types of readings for which outlining is valuable. After taking students through the structure and content of the "Kinds of Waves" sample, have students point out why outlining is particularly useful for nonfiction readings.

Select and distribute a sample reading for which outlining would be useful, such as an essay, a detailed news story, or a section from students' history or science textbook.

First read over and discuss the different types of outline approaches highlighted in **Using the Strategy** on page 649. After reading the sample, have students determine which outline approach would be most useful and explain why. Then ask them to direct you in creating the frame of an outline on the board based on the topics, subtopics, and details of the selection. Have them lead you through filling in the outline. Afterward, have them explain why outlines are useful study tools.

Check Understanding

Divide students into three or four groups.

■ Let higher-level students create outlines of a newspaper article of their choice.

■ Assign the average students practice in a *Student Applications Book*:

Grade 6, pages 62–71

Grade 7, pages 61–70

Grade 8, pages 58–67

■ Guide the lower-level readers in making an outline of a section from a recent lesson in one of their textbooks.

Paraphrasing

Set Goal

Introduce the strategy of **paraphrasing**. Provide a model of this strategy and give students practice in using it.

Teach and Discuss

Take time reading over and discussing with students the **Description** on page 650. Also read the **Definition** of paraphrasing on page 651 to reinforce what students are learning. Make it clear to students that they can paraphrase virtually any kind of reading or graphic. Have students tell in their own words what the strategy means to them. Emphasize that students need to make their paraphase sound like their own writing.

Pass out to the class a short sample selection for which paraphrasing would be helpful—anything from a textbook excerpt, a poem, or an essay to newspaper or magazine charts or maps.

Using this reading, slowly walk the class through the step-by-step paraphrasing process described in **Using the Strategy** on pages 650–651. Once students have a good understanding of the key points, ask each of them to write a short paraphrase of the reading in the sample handout. Caution them not to quote directly. Have several volunteers read their paraphrases aloud for the class. Using the examples, write a model response on the board. Ask students to explain the value of using paraphrasing with this sample.

Check Understanding

Divide students into three or four groups.

■ Ask higher-level students to paraphrase a short fictional text passage, an editorial cartoon, or a science chart.

■ Assign the average students practice in a *Student Applications Book*:

Grade 6, pages 194–199

Grade 7, pages 194–199

Grade 8, pages 193–200

■ Guide the lower-level readers in paraphrasing a section in one of their textbooks.

Questioning the Author

Set Goal

Introduce the reading strategy of **questioning the author**. Provide a model and give students practice using this strategy.

Teach and Discuss

Read through and discuss with students the **Description** on page 652. Follow this by reading the **Definition** of this strategy on the following page. Talk about the different types of readings for which the strategy can be used. Then ask students what the strategy means to them. Build upon their answers by making sure they see the benefits of using this strategy.

Find a model section with some difficult passages for which this strategy would be helpful, such as a poem, essay, or short story. Pass this reading out to the class.

With the reading as a reference, read and reinforce the step-by-step process and list of questions in **Using the Strategy** on pages 652–653. Help students understand the nuances that are involved in inferring an author's intentions in writing something in a particular way. Using the board, have students go through this process with the sample reading. Write students' questions, inferred answers, and conclusions. Make sure that students can defend their interpretations with clues in the text. Discuss their evaluations of the author's overall writing purpose.

Check Understanding

Divide students into three or four groups.

■ Have higher-level students apply the strategy to a poem or essay of their choice.

■ Assign the average students practice in a *Student Applications Book*:

Grade 6, pages 100–108

Grade 7, pages 101–110

Grade 8, pages 97–106

■ Guide the lower-level readers through this process using a short, less challenging reading.

Reading Critically

Set Goal

Introduce and model the strategy of **reading critically**, giving students practice in using it.

Teach and Discuss

Closely read and discuss with students the **Description** on page 654, particularly the types of "deeper" questions that critical readers ask about a reading. Go over the **Definition** of reading critically on page 655, pointing out all the different types of readings for which it can be used. Have students express in their own words the value they see in becoming critical readers.

Find a model selection for which critical reading would be appropriate, such as an editorial, essay, website, or news story. Distribute this reading to the class.

Before examining this selection, carefully read and discuss the step-by-step process in **Using the Strategy** on pages 654–655. Make sure students understand that critically evaluating an author's evidence and sources will help them determine the validity of the argument. Draw a Critical Reading Chart on the board. Read the selection together and take time to fill out this chart, based on the model students have been given. Discuss the main idea or message and the quality of the writing and viewpoint.

Check Understanding

Divide students into three or four groups.

■ Ask higher-level students to apply the strategy to a newspaper editorial or opinion article.

■ Assign the average students practice in a *Student Applications Book*:

Grade 6, pages 90–99

Grade 7, pages 91–100

Grade 8, pages 88–96

■ Guide the lower-level readers through a less challenging selection, using paired practice.

Skimming

Set Goal

Introduce students to the strategy of **skimming**, modeling its use and giving students practice in using it.

Teach and Discuss

Read and discuss with students the **Description** on page 656, citing the **Definition** of skimming on page 657 for additional emphasis. Stress to students that skimming can be used with any type of reading or graphic. Have students explain in their own words what the strategy is and suggest kinds of reading for which they have used skimming.

Select and distribute to students a sample reading for which skimming would be helpful, such as a news story, a train schedule, or a test.

Before skimming the reading, discuss with students the purposes for skimming that are mentioned in **Using the Strategy** on pages 656–657—skimming for general ideas, skimming for specific information, skimming paragraphs, and skimming on tests. Ask students to explain the process of skimming in their own words and have them determine which skimming approach would work best for the reading that has been distributed. Write the process of finding the information on the board, step by step.

Check Understanding

Divide students into three or four groups.

■ Have higher-level students skim a lengthy reading or their thesaurus.

■ Assign the average students practice in a *Student Applications Book*:

Grade 6, pages 200–207

Grade 7, pages 200–206

Grade 8, pages 201–207

■ Encourage the lower-level readers to practice skimming using a table of contents, an index, or a bus schedule.

Summarizing

Set Goal

Introduce the strategy of **summarizing**, modeling its use and giving students practice in using it.

Teach and Discuss

Closely read and discuss the **Description** on page 658 with students. To broaden students' understanding, read the **Definition** on page 659. Explain that summarizing can be used with any type of reading. Have students describe in their own words what the strategy is all about. Caution them that summaries should be brief. They can leave out the details.

Select a reading for which summarizing would be useful, either a fiction or a nonfiction selection. Pass this reading out to the class.

Students need to have a good understanding of how to summarize before they begin, so carefully read and discuss the questions and elements involved in summarizing fiction and nonfiction in **Using the Strategy** on pages 658–659. Have students apply the appropriate guidelines for summarizing the sample reading. Draw either a Fiction Organizer or a Nonfiction Organizer on the board. Fill it out through class discussion.

Check Understanding

Divide students into three or four groups.

■ Call on higher-level students to summarize a short story or article.

■ Assign the average students practice in a *Student Applications Book*:

Grade 6, pages 172–180

Grade 7, pages 171–180

Grade 8, pages 168–178

■ Have the lower-level readers summarize a newspaper article through paired practice.

Synthesizing

Set Goal

Introduce and model the strategy of **synthesizing**, giving students practice in using it.

Teach and Discuss

Read through and discuss with students the **Description** on page 660, citing the **Definition** on page 661 for emphasis. Students need to be aware that synthesizing involves pulling together the different parts or details of a reading in order to make sense of the material as a whole. Explain that synthesizing can be used with all kinds of readings, both fiction and nonfiction. Let students explain in their own words what the strategy means to them and its benefits.

Find a selection for which synthesizing would be useful and distribute it to the class. The reading could be a short story, play, or biography.

First take time to go through the different approaches and Key Topics charts for fiction and nonfiction readings in **Using the Strategy** on pages 660–661. Students need to have a good understanding of the pulling together and evaluation process described in point 3. Have students apply this strategy to the sample reading. Use the board to jot down and discuss the different parts of the reading and students' evaluation of the reading as a whole.

Check Understanding

Divide students into three or four groups.

■ Call on higher-level students to use this strategy on a novel of their choice.

■ Assign the average students practice in a *Student Applications Book*:

Grade 6, pages 129–140

Grade 7, pages 129–140

Grade 8, pages 128–139

■ Guide the lower-level readers through practice using this strategy on a short biography of a famous person.

Using Graphic Organizers

Set Goal

Introduce the strategy of **using graphic organizers,** modeling its use for students and giving them practice in applying it.

Teach and Discuss

Read through and discuss the **Description** on page 662 with students. Also read the **Definition** on page 663 for emphasis. Make sure students understand that graphic organizers can be used with all kinds of readings. Once they have an understanding of this approach to study, have them explain how the strategy could improve their skills in reading. Support their responses by highlighting the benefits of using organizers like these.

Find and distribute a sample reading for which a variety of graphic organizers would be worthwhile, such as a short story, poem, or news article.

Before deciding on a particular tool or tools to use, read and discuss the four common graphic organizers in **Using the Strategy** on pages 662–663. Point out that it's important to become familiar with a number of organizers and practice using them. That way, students can more easily decide which tool works best with a particular purpose in reading. Have students determine the most useful tool or tools for the sample reading. Work through the reading, modeling the use of one or more organizers on the board. Fill the organizer in during class discussion.

Check Understanding

Divide students into three or four groups.

■ Let higher-level students use the strategy on a poem, short story, essay, or biography of their choosing.

■ Assign the average students practice in a *Student Applications Book*:

Grade 6, pages 116–128

Grade 7, pages 118–128

Grade 8, pages 116–127

■ Guide the lower-level readers through using the strategy on a newspaper or magazine article.

Visualizing and Thinking Aloud

Set Goal

Introduce the strategy of **visualizing and thinking aloud**, model its use for students, and give them practice in using it.

Teach and Discuss

Closely read and discuss with students the **Description** on page 664 as well as the **Definition** on the following page. Explain to students that by seeing something in their minds or saying it out loud, they can greatly facilitate their understanding of any kind of reading. Take time to explain the word problem example and how readers visualize and think aloud. Mention that artistic ability isn't a prerequisite for using the strategy of visualizing.

Choose and distribute a reading for which visualizing and thinking aloud would be helpful, such as a math problem or or science process.

Walk students through the visualizing and thinking aloud process in **Using the Strategy** on page 665. Once students have a grasp of the process, have them use the strategy on the sample reading. Jot down their responses on the board and discuss how using this strategy can improve their comprehension of difficult concepts.

Check Understanding

Divide students into three or four groups.

- ▣ Let higher-level students apply the strategy to a process from their math or science textbooks.
- ▣ Assign the average students practice in a *Student Applications Book*:

  Grade 6, pages 48–57

  Grade 7, pages 48–56

  Grade 8, pages 46–53
- ▣ Help the lower-level readers use the approach on a less challenging word problem through guided or paired practice.

Reading Tools

Blackline Masters

Each of the thirty-six reading tools in the Almanac of the *Reader's Handbook* is included in this *Teacher's Guide* in a format suitable for copying. Use the blackline masters that follow to reinforce and supplement the lessons in the handbook.

Argument Chart

Cause-Effect Organizer

Character Development Chart

Character Map

Class and Text Notes

Classification Notes

Concept Map

Critical Reading Chart

Double-entry Journal

Fiction Organizer

5 W's Organizer

Inference Chart

Key Word or Topic Notes

K-W-L Chart

Magnet Summary

Main Idea Organizer

Nonfiction Organizer

Outline

Paraphrase or Retelling Chart

Plot Diagram

Process Notes

Setting Chart

Storyboard

Story Organizer

Story String

Study Cards

Summary Notes

Thinking Tree

Timeline or Sequence Notes

Topic and Theme Organizer

Two Per Line

Two-story Map

Venn Diagram

Viewpoint and Evidence Organizer

Web

Website Profiler

ARGUMENT CHART

An Argument Chart helps you examine and analyze persuasive writing, such as a speech, magazine article, or editorial.

Viewpoint	Support	Opposing Viewpoint

CAUSE-EFFECT ORGANIZER

A Cause-Effect Organizer helps you sort out what are causes and what are the effects coming from them. It shows the relationship between them.

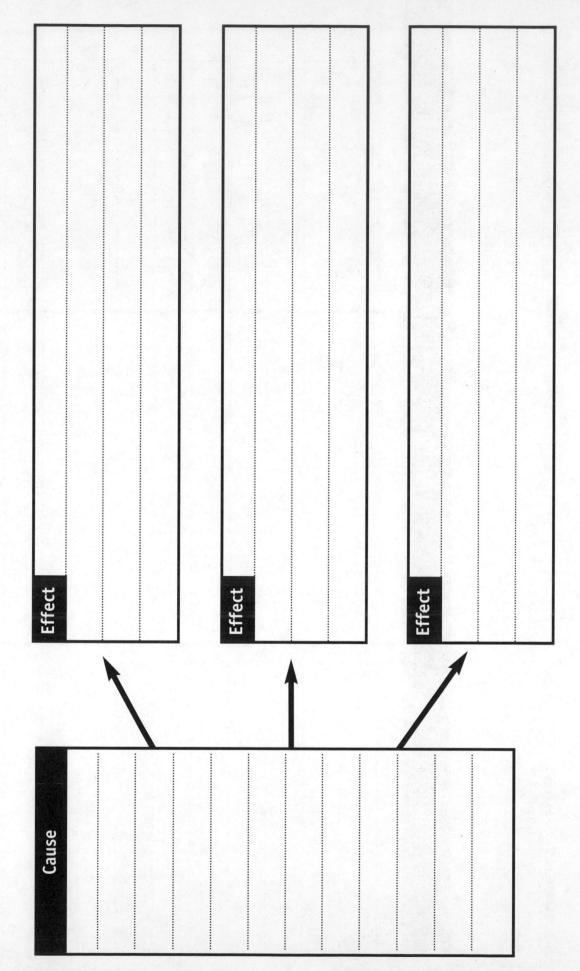

Cause

Effect

Effect

Effect

CHARACTER DEVELOPMENT CHART

A Character Development Chart helps you follow how characters change in a story, play, or novel. The changes in a character help you understand the theme.

Beginning	Middle	End

Possible Themes:

CHARACTER MAP

A Character Map helps you understand and analyze a character in a story, play, or novel. This tool helps you see how you—and other characters—feel about the character.

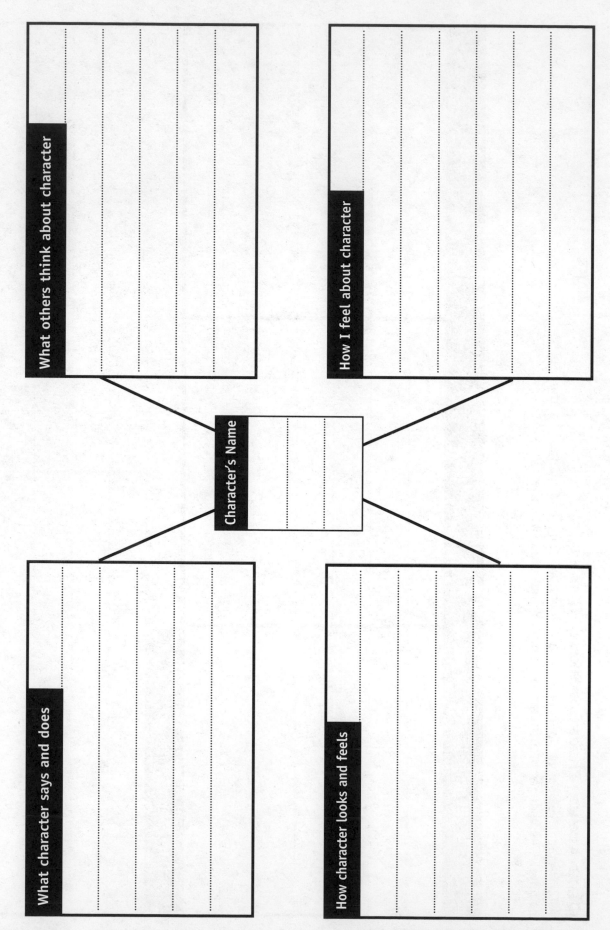

What others think about character

How I feel about character

Character's Name

What character says and does

How character looks and feels

CLASS AND TEXT NOTES

Use Class and Text Notes to connect what your teacher says in class with what you're reading in your textbook. These 2-column notes help you organize your ideas.

Text Notes

Class Notes

Classification Notes

Use Classification Notes to help you organize separate types or groups and sort out characteristics about them.

NAME

CONCEPT MAP

A Concept Map helps you organize everything you know about a concept or idea.

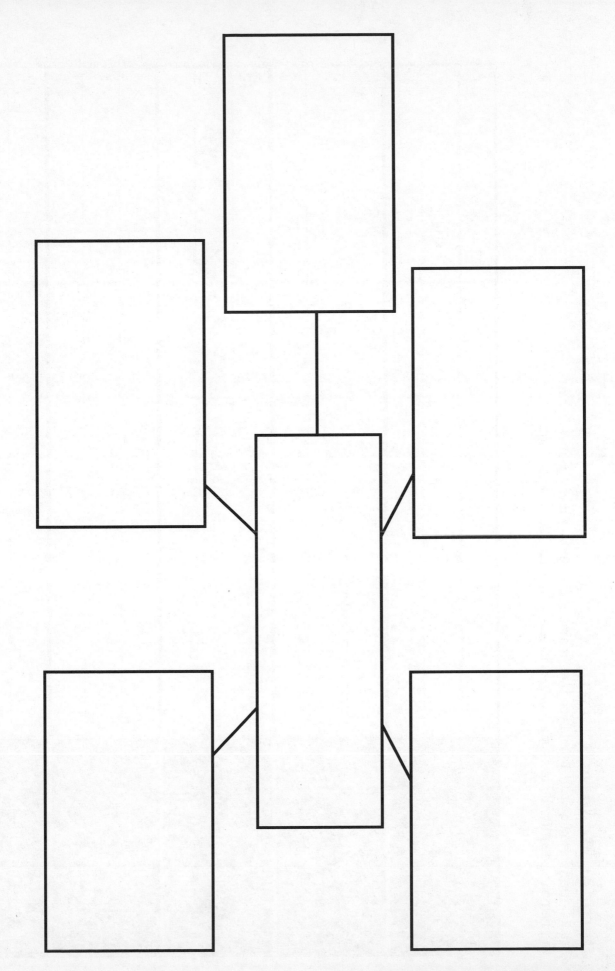

CRITICAL READING CHART

Use a Critical Reading Chart to analyze the information an author gives you. The chart will help you identify the facts, opinions, evidence, and main idea or viewpoint.

1. Is the main idea or viewpoint clear?	2. What evidence is presented?	3. Are the sources authoritative and reliable?	4. Is the evidence convincing?	5. Is there another side of the story?

DOUBLE-ENTRY JOURNAL

A Double-entry Journal helps you interpret a text.

Quote	My Thoughts

FICTION ORGANIZER

Use a Fiction Organizer to collect all of the key information about a story, novel, or play.

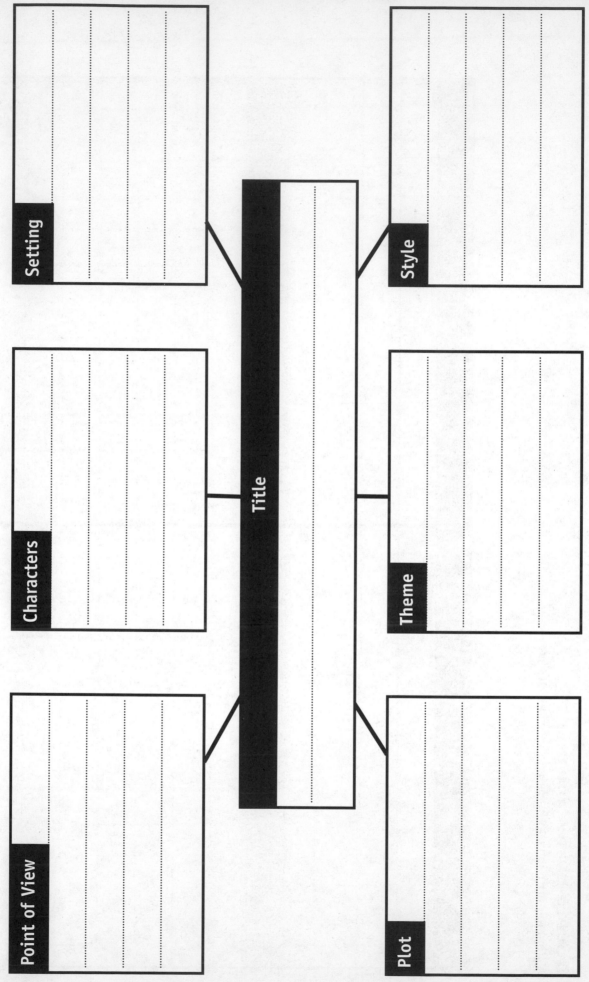

Setting

Style

Characters

Title

Theme

Point of View

Plot

5 W's Organizer

Use a 5 W's Organizer to gather key information about a subject. By asking yourself a reporter's questions (*who, what, where, when,* and *why*), you can learn most of the important information about a subject.

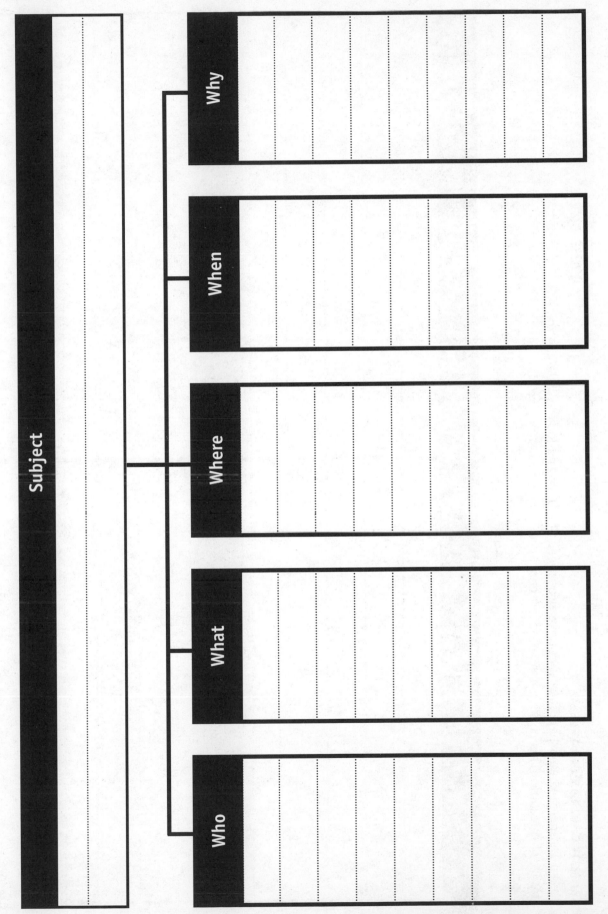

Subject

| Who | What | Where | When | Why |

Inference Chart

Use an Inference Chart when you have to read between the lines and look a little closer at part of a reading. This chart helps you draw conclusions about what you read.

NAME _____

Text	What I Conclude

KEY WORD OR TOPIC NOTES

Use Key Word or Topic Notes to help you stay organized and pull out the main ideas from your reading. Key Word or Topic Notes work well for taking notes on textbooks and other nonfiction.

Key Words or Topics	Notes

K-W-L Chart

Use a K-W-L Chart with nonfiction. This chart helps you draw on what you already
know about a subject, focus on what you want to know, and identify what you learned.

What I Know	What I Want to Know	What I Learned

MAGNET SUMMARY

Use a Magnet Summary to help you organize your thoughts after reading. Choose one word that is important to what you have read. Then, collect all of the other words, ideas, and details you can think of around it and summarize your ideas about the "magnet word."

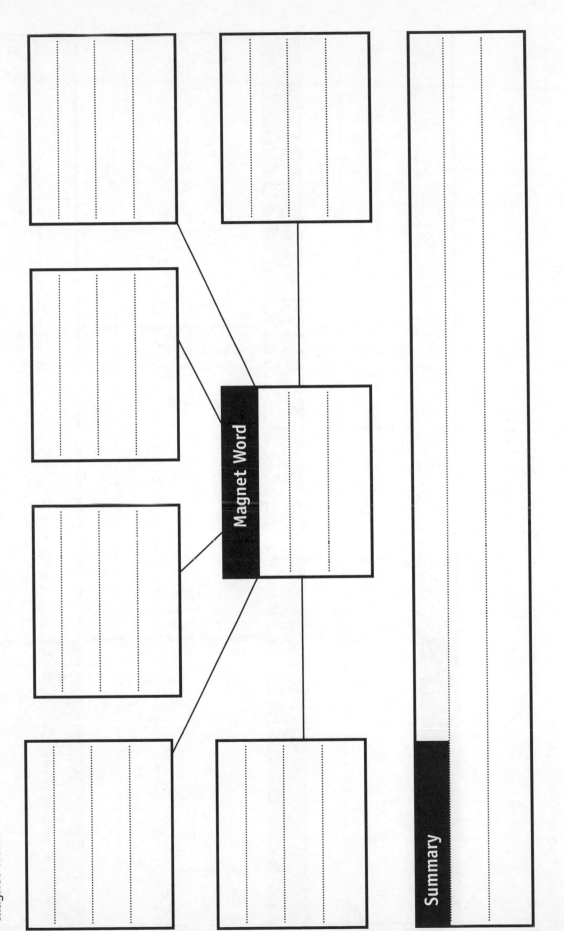

Magnet Word

Summary

MAIN IDEA ORGANIZER

A Main Idea Organizer helps you sort out the big ideas and the smaller details.
This tool works best with nonfiction, such as biography, magazine articles, persuasive writing, and textbooks.

Main Idea

Detail

Detail

Detail

Conclusion

NONFICTION ORGANIZER

A Nonfiction Organizer helps you sort out what you learn in essays, articles, speeches, editorials, and so on. It divides these nonfiction works into three parts: introduction, body, and conclusion.

Subject

Introduction

Body

Conclusion

NAME

OUTLINE

An Outline helps you understand the organization of what you're reading. Use words or phrases (Topic Outline) or full sentences (Sentence Outline) to sort out main ideas, topics, and subtopics.

I. Main Topic 1

A. subtopic ....

B. subtopic ....

C. subtopic ....

II. Main Topic 2

A. subtopic ....

B. subtopic ....

C. subtopic ....

III. Main Topic 3

A. subtopic ....

B. subtopic ....

C. subtopic ....

NAME

PARAPHRASE OR RETELLING CHART

A Paraphrase or Retelling Chart helps you do two things at once. It helps you understand parts of a text or graphic by putting them in your own words and helps you collect your own thoughts about the work.

Lines	My Paraphrase

My Thoughts

PLOT DIAGRAM

A Plot Diagram shows you how a story is organized. It highlights the five main parts of a story.

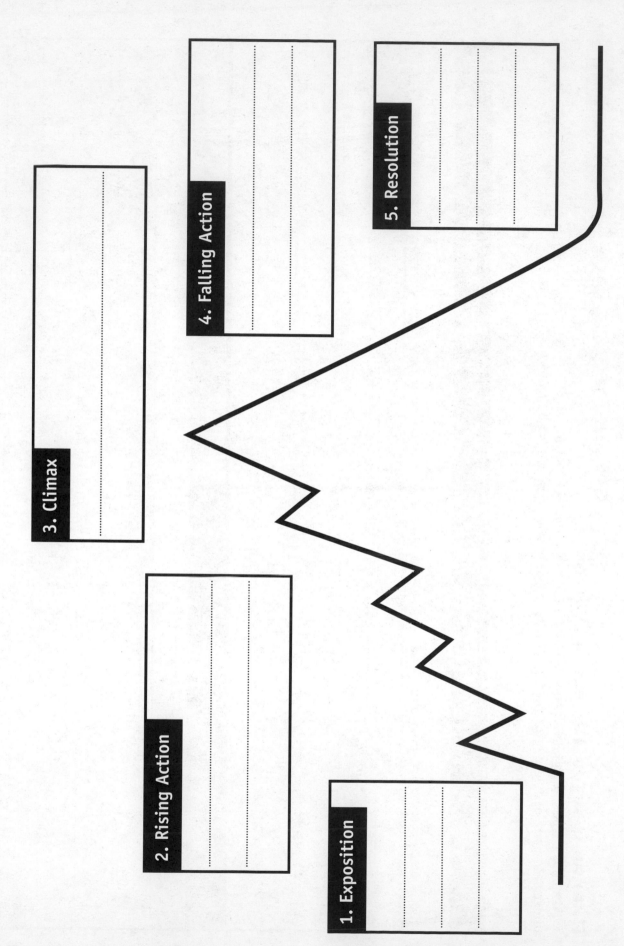

3. Climax

2. Rising Action

4. Falling Action

5. Resolution

1. Exposition

PROCESS NOTES

To keep track of a series of steps, stages, or events, use Process Notes. They work especially well for science and history, which often tell about how things develop or work.

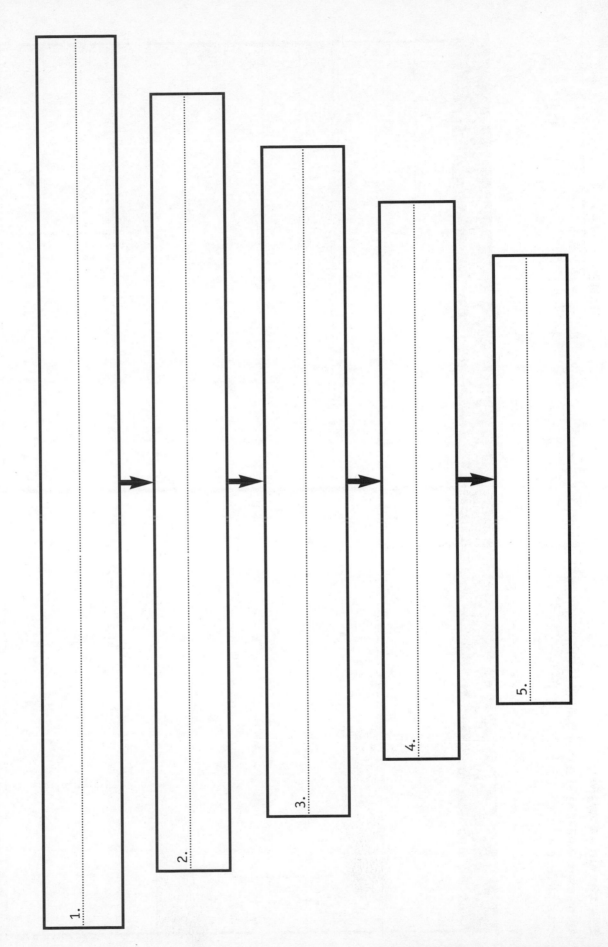

1.

2.

3.

4.

5.

SETTING CHART

To help you understand fiction and keep track of details about when and where a story took place, create a Setting Chart. Make a chart for each major scene or setting.

Clues about place	Clues about time

STORYBOARD

A Storyboard can help you keep track of events in a story, novel, or play. It works best for longer works that have a lot of events. A Storyboard helps you remember what happened and in what order things happened.

STORY ORGANIZER

A Story Organizer is a chart that helps you sort out what happens in a story. It highlights the three main parts of a story.

Beginning	Middle	End

STORY STRING

To keep track of a series of events in a story, novel, or play, use a Story String. It helps you see a chain of events and keep the time order straight, so you can remember what caused what in the story.

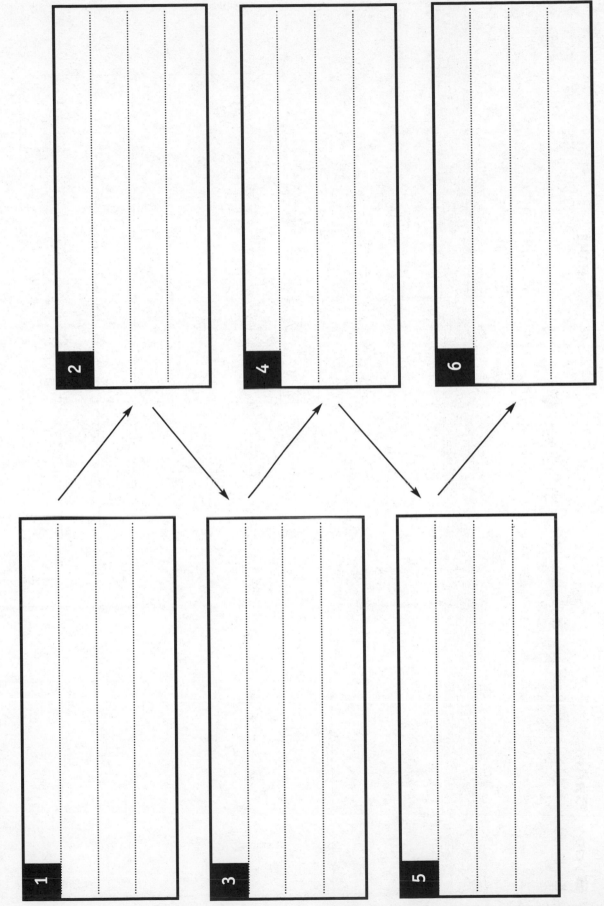

STUDY CARDS

Use Study Cards to help you learn key terms, facts, and ideas from your reading.

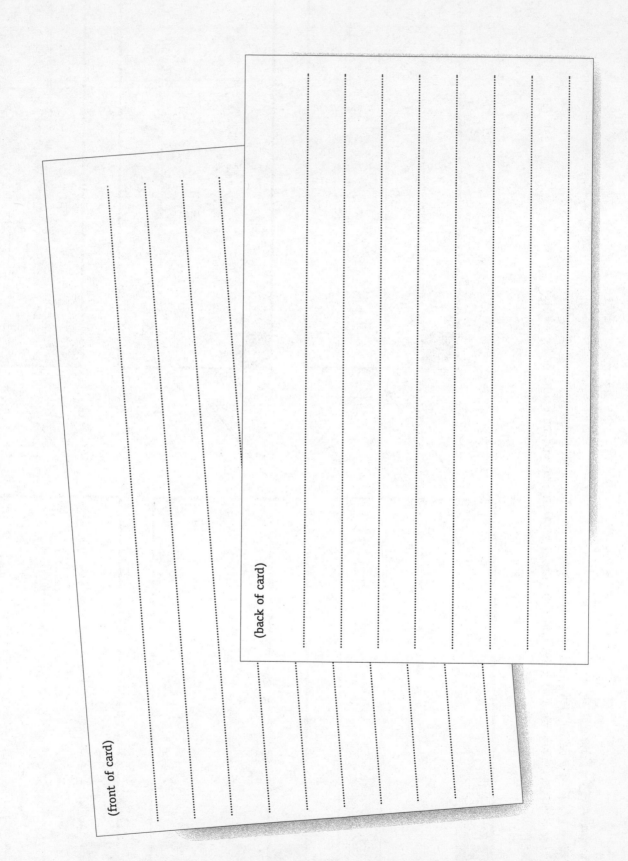

(front of card)

(back of card)

SUMMARY NOTES

Summary Notes help you focus on the most important parts of what you're reading.
You can create a summary for each page in your textbook, each scene in a play, or each chapter in a book.

Title or Topic	**Main Point**	
		1.
		2.
		3.
		4.

THINKING TREE

A Thinking Tree works well when you have little or no idea what a reading will be about. It helps you see connections among different ideas or details. Use a Thinking Tree to list an author's ideas and branch related ideas off one another.

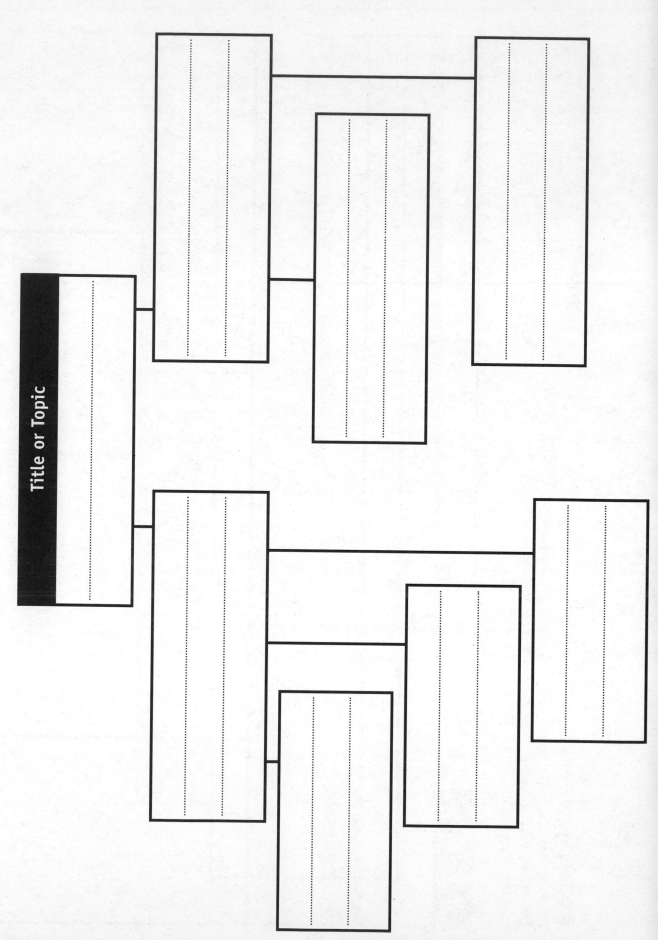

Title or Topic

TIMELINE OR SEQUENCE NOTES

Use a Timeline or Sequence Notes to keep track of a series of dates or events.
They work best when you need to put events in order.

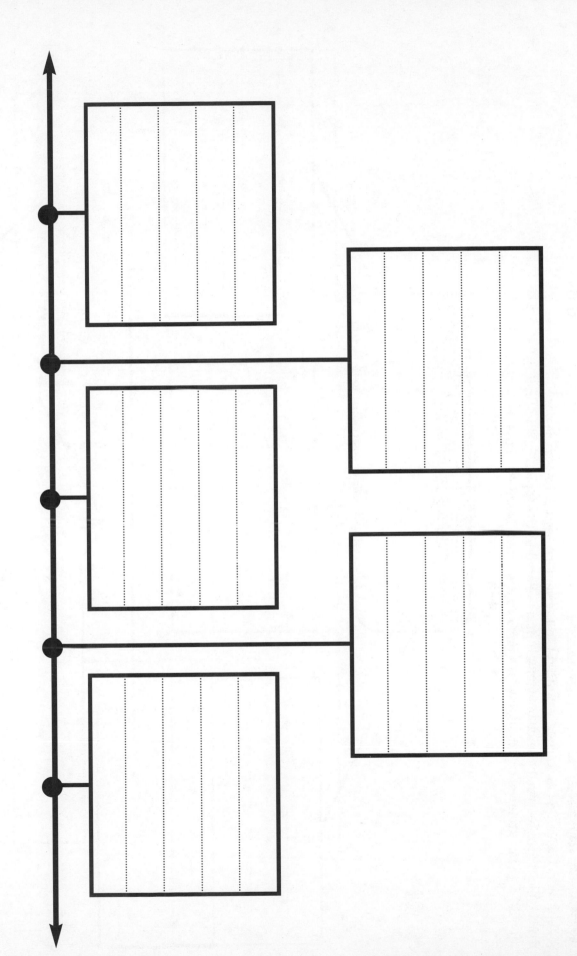

TOPIC AND THEME ORGANIZER

A Topic and Theme Organizer helps you find the theme. First, write the big idea or main topic. Then, tell what the characters say or do related to the topic. Finally, come up with a theme statement that says what's important to learn based on those details.

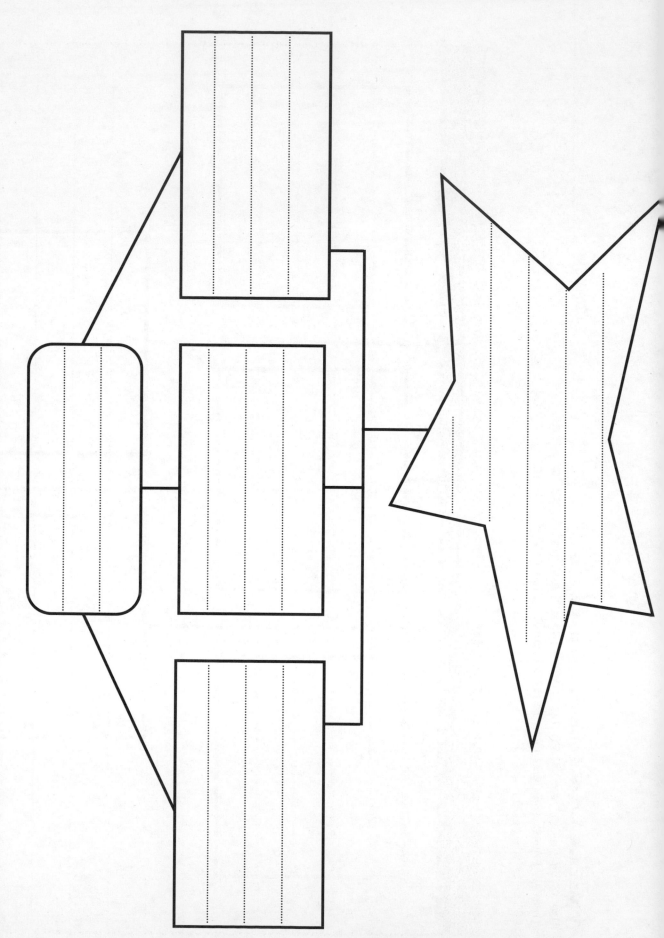

TWO PER LINE

To understand poetry or fiction, do a Two Per Line. Pick a key paragraph or passage. Write it out, mark the two most important words in each line, and then write your ideas about the passage.

My Ideas	Text

Two-story Map

Use a Two-story Map to compare and contrast the major elements of two works.
This reading tool will help you organize your ideas about the works.

Title

Characters

Plot

Theme

Title

Characters

Plot

Theme

Conclusions

VENN DIAGRAM

To compare two characters, stories, poems, settings, essays, and so on, use a Venn Diagram. This tool will help you see what's different and what's the same when you compare two things.

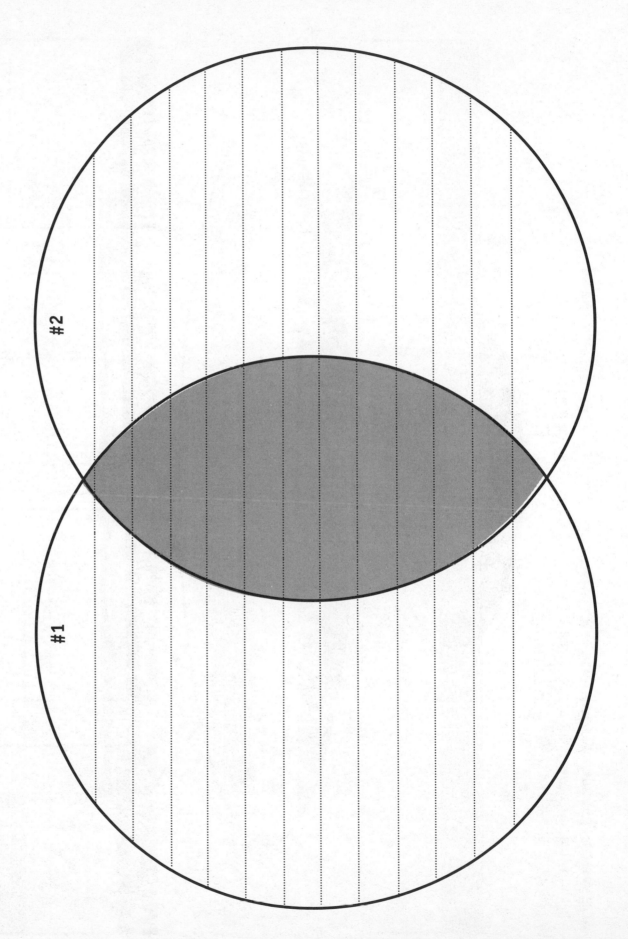

#2

#1

VIEWPOINT AND EVIDENCE ORGANIZER

For nonfiction, use a Viewpoint and Evidence Organizer to help you figure out what an author's opinion is and how well it is supported.

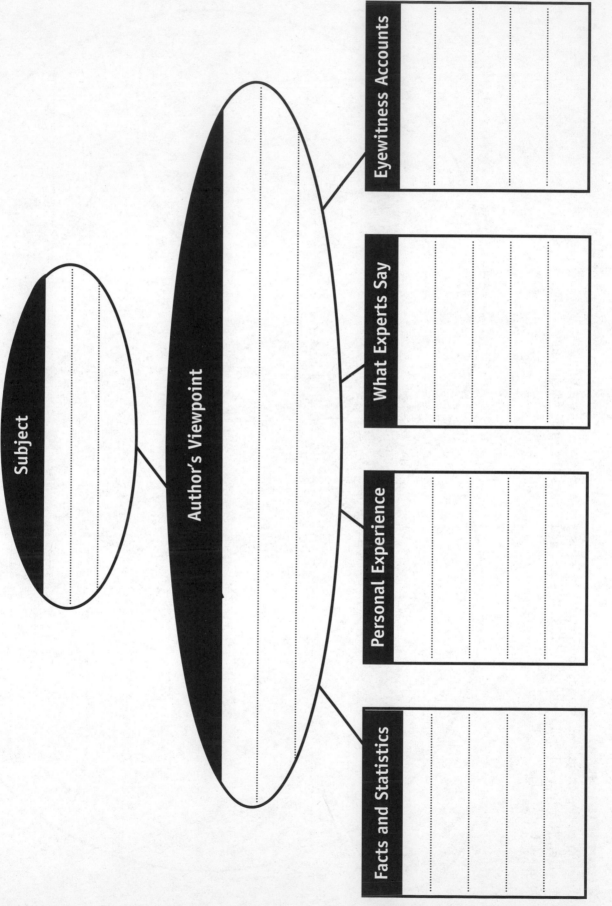

Subject

Author's Viewpoint

Eyewitness Accounts

What Experts Say

Personal Experience

Facts and Statistics

WEB

NAME ....

Webs are great all-purpose organizing tools for taking notes. They work for fiction and nonfiction and link supporting details with main ideas and topics. Use Webs to organize and brainstorm ideas about a character, an event, a word, a viewpoint, and so on.

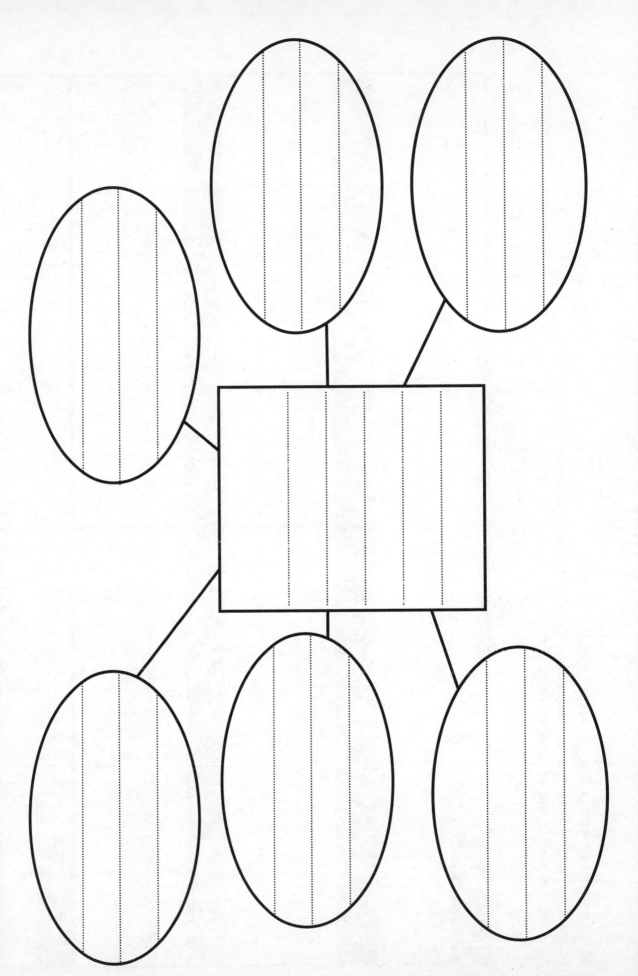

WEBSITE PROFILER

To check out how trustworthy a website is, use a Website Profiler. It looks at who made the site, when it was updated, its point of view, and how good its information is. A Website Profiler helps you judge how reliable a site is.

Name (URL)			Date			Expertise					
Sponsor						Point of View			Reaction		

Acknowledgments

57 (58) From *America's Past and Promise* by Lorna Mason, Jesus Garcia, Frances Powell, and C. Frederick Risinger. Copyright © 1995 by Houghton Mifflin Company. All rights reserved. Reprinted by permission of McDougal Littell Inc.

68 (69) From *Geography: The World and Its People* by the National Geographic Society, David G. Armstrong, Richard G. Boehm, and Francis P. Hunkins. Copyright © 2000 by The McGraw-Hill Companies, Inc.

81 From *Prentice Hall Science Explorer Earth Science* by Michael J. Padilla, Ioannis Miaoulis, Martha Cyr, Joseph D. Exline, Jay M. Pasachoff, Barbara Brooks Simons, Carole Garbuny Voge, and Thomas R. Wellnitz. © 2001 by Prentice Hall, Inc. Used by permission of Pearson Education, Inc.

90 From *Passport to Mathematics: An Integrated Approach, Book 2* by Roland E. Larson, Laurie Boswell, and Lee Stiff. Copyright © 1997 by D.C. Heath and Company. All rights reserved. Reprinted by permission of McDougal Littell Inc.

119 (123) From NOT THAT YOU ASKED by Andrew A. Rooney, copyright © 1989 by Essay Productions, Inc. Used by permission of Random House, Inc.

134 Reprinted by the permission of Russell & Volkening as agents for the author. Copyright © 1955 by Ann Petry, renewed 1983 by Ann Petry.

154 (155) © 2001, *Los Angeles Times*. Reprinted with permission.

165 Copyright 2000 National Wildlife Federation. Reprinted from the August/September issue of *National Wildlife Magazine*

202 "Charles" and excerpt from "Charles" from THE LOTTERY AND OTHER STORIES by Shirley Jackson. Copyright © 1948, 1949 by Shirley Jackson. Copyright renewed 1976, 1977 by Laurence Hyman, Barry Hyman, Mrs. Sarah Webster, and Mrs. Joanne Schnurer. Reprinted by permission of Farrar, Strauss and Giroux, LLC.

214 (234, 235, 244) From ROLL OF THUNDER, HEAR MY CRY by Mildred D. Taylor, copyright © 1976 by Mildred D. Taylor. Used by permission of Dial Books for Young Readers, an imprint of Penguin Putnam Books for Young Readers, a division of Penguin Putnam Inc.

268 (269, 271, 272, 273) © By Permission of Nikki Giovanni.

277 © The Estate of Pauli Murray, Reprinted by Permission of The Charlotte Sheedy Literary Agency.

288 "The Sloth" copyright 1950 by Theodore Roethke, from THE COLLECTED POEMS OF THEODORE ROETHKE by Theodore Roethke. Used by permission of Doubleday, a division of Random House, Inc.

317 (323, 328) From THE DIARY OF ANNE FRANK by Frances Goodrich and Albert Hackett, copyright © 1956 by Albert Hackett, Frances Goodrich Hackett, and Otto Frank. Used by permission of Random House, Inc.

401 From *Creating America: A History of the United States* by Jesus Garcia, Donna M. Ogle, C. Frederick Risinger, Joyce Stevos and Winthrop D. Jordan. Copyright © 2001 by McDougal Littell Inc. All rights reserved. Reprinted by permission of McDougal Littell Inc.

Photo Credits

364 "The Gallup Poll" a registered trademark of The Gallup Organization, Princeton, NJ. All rights reserved. Reprinted with authority. www.gallup.com © 2001 - The Gallup Organization

Lesson Index